Political Psychology:
Neuroscience, Genetics, and Politics

Political Psychology

Neuroscience, Genetics, and Politics

George E. Marcus
Williams College

New York   Oxford
OXFORD UNIVERSITY PRESS

Oxford University Press is a department of the University of Oxford.
It furthers the University's objective of excellence in research,
scholarship, and education by publishing worldwide.

Oxford New York
Auckland Cape Town Dar es Salaam Hong Kong Karachi
Kuala Lumpur Madrid Melbourne Mexico City Nairobi
New Delhi Shanghai Taipei Toronto

With offices in
Argentina Austria Brazil Chile Czech Republic France Greece
Guatemala Hungary Italy Japan Poland Portugal Singapore
South Korea Switzerland Thailand Turkey Ukraine Vietnam

For titles covered by Section 112 of the U.S. Higher Education
Opportunity Act, please visit www.oup.com/us/he for the latest
information about pricing and alternate formats.

Published by Oxford University Press.
198 Madison Avenue, New York, New York 10016
http://www.oup.com

Library of Congress Cataloging-in-Publication Data
Marcus, George E., 1943–
  Political psychology: neuroscience, genetics, and politics/George E.
Marcus.
    p. cm.
  Includes bibliographical references and index.
  ISBN 978-0-19-537064-5
  1. Political psychology.   2. Political psychology—Research.   I. Title.
  JA74.5.M363 2012
  320.01'9—dc23
                                                    2012009282

Printing number: 9 8 7 6 5 4 3 2 1

Printed in the United States of America
on acid-free paper

BRIEF CONTENTS

CONTENTS

TO ONE AND ALL

Most textbooks are written in the voice of impersonal imperial authority. But every book is written by one person, or sometimes, a group of individuals. Each author is writing at a particular point in time and has her or his views shaped by their specific experience. And what each author knows is subject to the various limitations of human fallibility. My goal in writing this book is to help you undertake your own doing of political psychology. If I succeed then each of you will form your own vision of political psychology, what it is, what it should be, and what you want to pursue. There are various ways of doing political psychology and none of us masters them all. Our different personal interests and our ability to master the skills that we find most adapted to our abilities inevitably means that each of us will find our own way.

One consequence of this goal is that each of you *should* find places in this text where you disagree with the views I express. You will find some topics given too little attention and others too much. You may find some methods of research of greater appeal to you than they may be to me, and others less. That is as it should be for it will be a good indication that you have begun doing political psychology on your own and in your own way.

I have had the benefit of some wonderful mentors and colleagues; so many that I cannot mention them all. Four stand out as having been of singular generosity: Psychologist Donald T. Campbell, friend and colleague John L. Sullivan, and neuroscientists Jeffrey A. Gray and John T. Cacioppo, each by example and each by teaching me how to find my own path in doing political psychology. I hope that this volume offers some of what they offered to me, encouragement, insights, and advice. I hope you will come to enjoy your journey as much as I have mine. I would also like to thank the following reviewers for their feedback: C. F. Abel, Stephen F. Austin State University; Ted Brader, University of Michigan; Erik Bucy, Indiana University; Rebecca J. Hannagan, Northern Illinois University; Paul L. Hathaway, Jacksonville State University; Benjamin Knoll, University of Iowa; Michael D. Martinez, University of Florida; Patrick R. Miller, University of Cincinnati; Michael Parkin, Oberlin College; Jerrold M. Post, The George Washington University; Jacquelien van Stekelenburg, VU University.

TO STUDENTS

My intention in this text is to give you the tools you need to function as a political psychologist. That does not mean that I expect that most you you will enter the discipline perhaps as a researcher or a teacher, or both. That may be the case for some of you. Certainly if the discipline of political psychology is going to grow it must have new blood and some of you might well be among the next generation of teachers and schol-ars. I hope so. But all of you, I hope, will be active and engaged citizens. Here, applying your knowledge of political psychology, as a way of asking and answering questions can be a major tool in your citizenship toolkit.

For example, as citizens we often rely on trust to guide our decisions. Trust applies when we rely on our friends, or on our political, religious, leaders, or on some pundits or experts whose ideological values we share. But, as political psychologists, we rarely trust anyone. Rather, in various ways, we try to minimize the authority of those who are presenting some analysis, some argument. Political psychologists are trained to keep who is saying something separate from our consideration of the evidence that sus-tains (or not!) the claim being advanced. Instead, political psychologists ask for empiri-cal evidence to corroborate what is otherwise a hypothesis, a speculative explanation (however seductive).

Often, as citizens, we would do well to set aside our trust in those who guide us, even if our history with them has been quite good. Rather, as political psychologists, we citizens can, at least sometimes, find our political psychology training can serve us bet-ter by directing us to consider the weight of the evidence before we defend, or attack, a policy decision we confront. And, our political psychology training also can be applied to ourselves. Whom do we trust? And why? And, should we trust those we do?

Political psychology brings with it many relevant questions that can help us be better citizens. And, political psychology brings with it a different way of going about answering those questions that what we practice in everyday life.

Along the way you will find discussion of some but hardly all of the topics that make up the discipline. I expect that you will find some of the areas that make up the field are of greater interest, and some of lesser interest. That is normal. Each of us will gravitate to the topics that we find important and interesting. But political psychology is more than a long laundry list of topics. It is a way of creating explana-tions. Different disciplines have different ideas as to what constitutes an adequate explanation.

Here the focus will be on what makes a credible political psychology explanation. Among these are:

Creativity: New explanations have to come from somewhere, why not from you?
Collaboration: Working with other people, especially those who might think about things differently, can greatly enrich the generating and testing of explanations.
Critical thinking: We want our explanations to be more than idle speculations, so how can we know that an explanation actually works?

Finally, the discipline is also a community. It is a community made up of students, practitioners, journalists, and scholars located in various countries around the world. It is also a community that extends back in time many hundreds of years. We have a wide array of ways of communication with colleagues near and far, of reaching out to contact others also working in this field. We can, and should, rely on the earlier con-versations handed down in the surviving literature because the foundational issues that drive the research questions are quite old. What our predecessors asked, and found in their inquiries, continues to shape how we understand human experience and the possibilities of politics. By learning how to reach out and participate you can make your own contributions and also benefit from active engagement with your peers in this wide and open community. Welcome.

You must acquire a complex series of skills to learn how to make explanations. Throughout this text you will find exercises designed to enable you to practice and master these skills. Much as in music or sports, you prove that you know something when you display what you know in action. Hang in there and see how much fun it can be to do something more than listening, reading, and taking exams.

TO FACULTY

As you well know the field of political psychology is enormous. And, the research output is exploding not only in quantity but in theoretical perspectives. And, further still, new disciplines are contributing to political psychology. Even if I were able to discuss each topic in the field and each theory, in the briefest of fashions, the resulting text would require a course of least a year's length (and even then would likely be critiqued for leaving something important out or giving short shrift to too many topics).

This text differs in three ways from conventional textbooks:

First, this text provides an historical account of the guiding ideas, the normative aspirations that undergird the field. Political psychology has an ancient lineage. In that lineage exists deep intellectual roots that begin with the search for how to govern ourselves, individually and collectively. Conventional texts in the field typically ignore this aspect of the field leaving the field denuded of its full vitality and its central importance.

Second, this text is intended to depict where the field is going. The field is changing, as do most living disciplines, thus, where it is today is not what it will look like in five, ten, or twenty years. Although surprises await, some trends are clear. Among these are the explosion of research applying neuroscience, cognitive science, and genetics to politics. Old topics, such as personality, are being re-examined in light of that work. This text, as do I, embraces these changes and puts them to the forefront.

Third, this text is lean, it provides a skeletal design, to allow you to augment the text with added readings to allow adjustment to the subject topics of local interest (though I have selected a variety of suggested readings for various topics).

I kept the topics to a reasonable number all in the service of enabling students to master the skills of doing political psychology. I kept the chapters short. The design of many chapters is such that they do not, intentionally, offer a full treatment of the subject. Rather, I present a framework to introduce students to key ideas and conceptual understandings so that specific readings, and your lectures, can then add the necessary details. For example, on the topic of personality, there are many topics that can readily claim our attention, that fall within that broad span. I make no attempt to offer an encyclopedic coverage. In any case any coverage given the limited pages available to devote to the topic would in due time become dated, and would preclude focused consideration of such topics as most interest you (and thereby the students).

Hence, the usefulness of this book is that it enables, indeed is designed, so that you add topics, add readings, and choose the specific topics that you find most interesting. I hope you will augment the text with topics, theories, discussions, and readings that enable you to convey your excitement in doing political psychology. I offer some suggestions but they are merely that, suggestions.

George E. Marcus
Paris, France, Summer 2011

Political Psychology:
Neuroscience, Genetics, and Politics

SECTION

Introduction

CHAPTER I

The Importance of Political Psychology

This chapter is divided into four sections. Sections 1 and 2 present two different views of political psychology. In the first, "The Field of Political Psychology," I offer a conventional, but not complete, overview of the topics that are explored by political psychologists. This survey is a convenient way of showing the various subjects and theories in political psychology. My guess is that for each of you some topics will be very engaging, while others less so. Given how many topics there are it would be surprising indeed if each and every one of these subjects will be interesting to each and every one of you. I hope you will find if not many, at least some of these subjects fascinating enough to motivate you to engage with political psychology.

Political psychology, as with all scholarly disciplines, is a living organism. It grows, it changes focus, it shifts focus from one topic to another. For example, "authoritarianism" became a dominant topic in the aftermath of World War II when interest focused on what types of people supported fascism and why. Although that topic remains important to many scholars, today interest in "terrorism"—how people respond to terror threats—has sharply increased after the worldwide expansion of terrorist tactics in Northern Ireland, Sri Lanka, Israel, Iraq, Afghanistan, India, Spain, France, England, the United States, among other locales. Hence, focusing on topics, apart from confronting the vast array that makes a complete review tedious, also faces the problem of being time bound.

In the second section, "The Core Concerns of Political Psychology," I turn to another way to consider the field of political psychology. As the section title suggests, although the array of topics explored is sweeping, the fundamental issues have proven remarkably enduring. For millennia humans have been examining their nature to learn how to govern themselves, individually and collectively. It is in this section where I hope you will find that the central importance of political psychology becomes evident. Answering the questions, how to live and how to govern ourselves, are the two preeminent concerns that lie at the core of political psychology.

BOX 1.1   The Science of Human Nature

Political psychologists use empirical data to test a given theory. One test of the validity of a theory is whether it accurately predicts the observed results in the focus variable. But, prediction is not the end of science. The true end of science is understanding.

The better theories offer an account that predicts the pattern of results and identifies precisely the causal links by which the results obtained. When we say, "this causes that" we are saying our theory tells us *why* things happen as they do.

Section 3, "Doing Political Psychology," describes the field in yet another way, as a scientific method of asking and answering questions. The goal is to begin to show how you can act as your own political psychologist, whether as a scholar or citizen. Some of you may go on to further training and pursue careers as political psychologists. All of you, I hope, will be active citizens. Political psychology offers tools to help us interpret our world, to make sense of it, to enable us to challenge pundits and experts, and to enable us to consider evidence in light of rigorous scientific stands. In this section I show how you can you use political psychology to engage your interests, whether those interests are academic or to empower you as a citizen in the domain of politics.

Finally, in section 4, "The Plan of the Book," I give a brief description of the sections and chapters to follow.

Let us begin…

I. THE FIELD OF POLITICAL PSYCHOLOGY

The principal social sciences disciplines—psychology, anthropology, sociology, economics, and political science—have been around for more than a century when they became key segments of university curriculum and faculty organization. While individual scholars have long been engaged in political psychology research, the multidisciplinary field of political psychology appears to be quite young. We can date the formal launch of political psychology as a recognized discipline in its own right with the founding of the International Society of Political Psychology (ISPP) in 1978.[1] In addition, there are political psychology sections in different disciplinary organizations, such as the political psychology sections of the American Political Science Association and the Midwest Political Science Association, training programs, such as the Stanford University Summer Institute of Political Psychology (SIPP), and other settings such as the bi-annual New York Columbia University Political Psychology Colloquium, which just completed its twenty-fifth year of activity.

There are quite a few definitions of political psychology (Kuklinski 2002; Monroe 2002). Here is my definition: Political psychologists examine human nature to better understand the interplay of human nature and politics.

This is a very broad definition. It applies to every facet of politics and has been explored in an extraordinary range of overlapping and often conflicting theories.

---

1. You can join the society. If you do, you will meet the many scholars who are also members. You can check out recent scholarship by examining recent programs of the annual meeting of the society by visiting ispp.org.

Table 1.1 presents a *partial* survey of the work that makes up this field. If I chose a representative selection of articles and books published in political psychology that list would be very confusing and would have to be even longer to represent all the work that has been published in recent years. To give the literature some organization I labeled each example as exemplifying one, or *more*, of the four approaches. I arrayed the four from the most comprehensive (labeled "theory focus") to the least (labeled "solution focus"):

1. **Theory focus:** The goal is to develop a comprehensive theory of human psychology that has wide, even, universal application. Often, these ambitious efforts are the result of importing a theory from some discipline outside of political science to explain politics. Two examples are rational choice theory, which came from economics and psychodynamic theory, which came from Freudian psychology.

2. **Field focus:** The goal is less comprehensive but still broad. The field is narrowed to some bounded topic within psychology or politics. Scholars focus on a political topic that engages a community of scholars. I mentioned earlier one example: The interest in why people supported fascist regimes that focused on authoritarianism as a possible explanation. That is but one example. To take yet another important area, scholars have shown enduring interest in the topic of when and why people engage in various forms collective action.

3. **Problem focus:** This category is even narrower than field focus in that there is a specific property, or variable, that has engaged one of more scholars. There is a specific problem, or *dependent* variable, that researchers are trying to better understand. An example would be to understand when and why people are politically tolerant (and of course, when not). The goal is to take a specific dependent variable (e.g., the level of political tolerance) and through research discover which factors explain the observed variation.

4. **Solution focus:** The interest is developing a new independent variable that can explain a wide range of phenomenon. As with the problem focus, the solution focus is quite narrow as it takes up a specific property, or independent variable, that scholars think may explain a range of political phenomenon. The focus shifts from the end result, the dependent variable, to the explanation, the independent variable. For example, scholars Jim Sidanius and Felicia Pratto investigated a new independent variable, *social dominance orientation* (SDO). Social dominance orientation is defined as a stable individual level preference for ordered stability within hierarchical social settings. As an individual difference trait, some of us are very concerned with sustaining established hierarchies, order, whereas others are much less concerned and find greater importance in sustaining individual autonomy (Pratto et al. 1994).

These four categories are not meant to be exhaustive or definitive. I hope they help make some sense of a very big and often confusing array of topics that political psychologists study. You will quickly see that many of these topics overlap. Scholars have many priorities. Making the field easy to understand is not a high-order priority of most scholars.

Table 1.1. A taxonomy of topics in political psychology

Topic	Focus	Examples
Psychodynamic theory	Theory: holds that subconscious drives largely shaped by early childhood experiences shape politics	Leadership biographies; leader–follower linkages; leader charisma
Economic theory	Theory: holds that costs and benefits guide politic actions, much as it guides economic actions	Rational choice theory—most often applied to decision making
Biology	Theory: holds that as biological creatures, humans are constrained and enabled by their biology	Interest in genetic and physiology as determinants of political belief and action
Neuroscience	Theory: holds that brain functions are best understood by reliance on neuroscientific scholarship (theories and methods), thereby informing politics	How brain functions, including affective processes, shape politics
Cognitive science	Theory: holds that brain functions are best understood by reliance on cognitive science scholarship (theories and methods), thereby informing politics	Mapping cognitive processes to understand how information is stored and linked in the human brain, for example, schema theory, and then applying to politics
Sociology	Theory: holds that social organization shapes individual conception and action as well as collective action	Group dynamics; group identification; ingroup–outgroup dynamics; cultural influences; social organization; role theory applied to politics
Psychology	Theory: holds that the study of individuals by observing their behavior in various natural and experimental settings using measures of subjective reports of their attitudes and behaviors, observed and intended	Both social psychology and personality fields; the need for conformity; the dynamics of obedience; taxonomies of individual difference; each applied to politics
Literature	Theory: holds that metaphors and semantic rules guide conceptions and hence political behavior	Rhetoric in politics; metaphors and traditions that shape understanding and hence applied to politics
Mass media	Field; problem; solution	How the public responds to news and leaders
Political communication	Field; problem; solution	How the public responds to news and leaders
Attitude formation and change	Field; problem; solution	How the public responds to news and leaders; how the public forms attitudes, and when they alter them
Voting behavior	Field; problem	Who votes, for whom, and why
Ideology	Problem; solution	Presumes an enduring organization of political attitudes, beliefs, principles or values and then studies who has an organization (solutions focus); presence or absence of ideology shapes politics (problem focus)
Political socialization	Field	How do people learn and how does that learning shape their political attitudes and actions; applies both to early (i.e., childhood) and late (i.e., adulthood) learning

Table 1.1. (*Continued*)

Topic	Focus	Examples
Political cognition	Field	How do people process information; how do they organize memory and contemporary perceptions, beliefs, and values; then connect attitudes and beliefs; how do those beliefs then shape politics
Affect or emotion	Field; problem; solution	How people do feel and how do feelings shape their political beliefs and actions
Leadership	Field; problem; solution	How do leaders emerge, when do they succeed or fail? How do they mobilize public support?
Political tolerance	Field; problem	How do people acquire civic norms that sustain respect for civil liberty and when do people apply them
Patriotism, nationalism	Problem	The role of patriotism and nationalism in shaping collective identity and group behavior
Terrorism and political violence	Problem	What leads to adoption of terrorism and violence as a political tactic; when is it effective and when is it not; how do the public and leaders respond and deal with terror and violence; how are violent conditions resolved
Gender	Solution	Gender as a potent factor shaping perceptions, action, and group formation
Identity	Solution	Identities incline or inhibit people to group engagement and collective action
Genocide and holocaust studies	Problem	How, when, and why do such extreme conditions of violence lead a dominant group to try to exterminate smaller groups
Mass movement and political protest	Field	How and when do people become engaged in collective action that confronts established authority
Collective action	Field	When do people engage or withdraw from collective action
Foreign policy decision making	Field	How do elites and publics engage in foreign policy; supporting or opposing war or peacemaking; coalition building with supranational organizations
Social justice	Field	Contrasting self-interested and normative and ethical concerns; when do people engage the first or second orientation, and which normative orientations do people adopt as legitimate

A myriad of additional topics could just as well be included in table 1.1. For example, consider the following topics *not* included in the table: ethnocentrism, moral judgment, conflict resolution, deterrence, and racism. That would make table 1.1 even longer. If you search the journals that publish political psychology research, you will find, I am sure, still other topics that could and should be included. Therefore, table 1.1 is incomplete. Any number of alternative "table 1.1s" can be generated and defended as useful overviews. A complete list would be tedious because only some of those topics will interest you, which ones of course will vary from person to person. For now, just consider this listing a rough sampling of the many topics that collectively make up the subjects that fall within political psychology. A menu that I hope will awaken your appetite for more.

Some of these subjects and topics clearly overlap. Terrorism, violence, genocide conflict resolution, ethnic cleansing, are clearly interested in the same domain of issues. In a similar fashion, voting behavior, mass media, political communications, leadership, collective action, attitude change, ideology, among others, also have much that joins them. It is natural that some dominant topic shapes a field. The rise of fascist and totalitarian regimes in the twentieth century, or the increase in terrorism in the late twentieth and early twenty-first century for example, provoked a surprisingly vast array of scholarship. Or, the research on political tolerance in the United States that was a response to the 1950s "Red Scare," which introduced loyalty oaths at some American universities, which in turn found Congress passing a law prohibiting membership in the American Communist Party, as well as many efforts to blackball suspected "fellow travelers" (those thought to favor communism). Once these dramatic issues of great import arise it is natural for people to become engaged in scholarship to better understand. Events shape the academic agenda. The period we live in influences many things, among them topics that engage political psychologists.

It is also typically the case that scholars become devoted to some theoretical focus and methodological tools that allows them to have some purchase on their research. It is not surprising to find that that scholars of personality turn to personality theories to understand why people have stable political beliefs and values. It is not surprising to find scholars trained in the neurosciences turning to functional magnetic resonance imaging and other methods to examine the same phenomenon. And, it is the case that all the various research that falls inside the boundary of political psychology is beyond the capacity of any individual to read let along master. Scholars focus on the scholarship they can read and master. That limitation is overcome by having a community do the work that is beyond the capacity of any one scholar.

All of this leaves us with a sprawling array of topics, methods, and theories, some coming into vogue, such as the increasing impact of the neurosciences, and some retreating, such as psychoanalytic accounts. And, new topics have joined the list of late, a fact that is always going to make life difficult for those seeking to give some coherent and all inclusive account of the field. Historical account of this field can be found in various places, but that's history and not, in point of fact, all that useful to learning how to do political psychology. Perhaps another way of gaining some sense of the field can be found in its organization. Let's see.

The Social Organization of Political Psychology

Political psychology is not just a broad array of topics. Political psychology is a discipline. That means it is a community of practitioners who are organized around various practices. Among these practices are: positive anonymous peer reviews as a standard condition for publication of research reports (in books or journals); frequent conferences where researchers can share and discuss their ongoing work; supported archives (among them the Roper Center at the University of Connecticut and the ICPR at the University of Michigan, both in the United States) where researchers send their data for other scholars to replicate their work or use their data to test other theoretical propositions.

A helpful way to get up to speed on a topic is to start with a good focused literature review. There are handbooks of political psychology published from time to time. Other handbooks in political science and psychology will have chapters that are of interest to political psychologists. Therein senior scholars are asked to provide a critical overview of a particular topic within their area of expertise. There are also foundations, both public and private, that provide research support to scholars, as well as centers where scholars and others can go to focus on their research. Collectively these elements provide public venues in which scholars can present their work, find support to conduct their research, and find the critical audience to assess the value and probe for weaknesses in their work.

Donald T. Campbell's (Campbell, Brewer, and Collins 1981) approach to the social sciences gives special insight into the "best practices" of scholarship. He advised that it was best to think of research from an evolutionary approach. He coined the term evolutionary epistemology. By that he meant that ideas obey the same evolutionary dynamics as do the physical changes in species. Species mutate in various random ways, tossing out variations on all sorts of features. Sexual reproduction in which an offspring shares some of the genetic material of two people ensures that each offspring is somewhat different from the earlier generation, and likely somewhat different from others in their same age cohort. Reality then rewards mutations that give some advantage and punishes those that offer some disadvantage.

Campbell argued that the success or failure of ideas depends on their fit with reality. In Campbell's view, developing ideas, lots of ideas, is the best that we can do. We cannot *intentionally* come up with good ideas or prevent ourselves from thinking up bad ideas.

BOX 1.2 Citizenship and political psychology:

As citizens we develop habits of thought and stable preferences. We often defend them and those who articulate them on our behalf (political leaders, interest group spokespeople, columnists, and pundits). Notice that the discipline of political psychology, as other scientific disciplines, goes to considerable effort to set aside such established patterns of trust. Rather, as political psychologists you are asked to set aside convictions and instead rely on rigorous reliance on evidence.

As citizens, when we confront public policy disputes, we may be best served by applying this alternative orientation to the dispute. That would lead us to press experts and leaders to present *evidence* that their recommendations have merit.

It is safe to predict that political leaders will not offer evidence if their supporters and critics are satisfied by the rhetoric of debate on warring ideological verities.

Whether an idea is good or bad is going to be the *result* of its impact in reality. Reality decides what is a good idea or a bad idea. Hence, he argued, your task is to come up with as many ideas as possible and then let reality determine which work. What you can do is generate research to test your and others' ideas. It will be up to reality, research, to sort out the good from the bad. Our task, in doing political psychology, is to *test* conventional wisdom, to probe whether even the most trusted accounts are valid. We already have a full complement of conventional, familiar, explanations. Which of those novel explanations will be proven remains unknown until research is conducted. Our task is to generate novel explanations that we hope will prove to be superior to existing accounts. And even then, researchers will probe to see that the findings remain robust after further testing against newer alternatives. In sum, we develop theories, test them, and refine our theories in light of what our empirical tests find. We reject those theories that fail.

In sum, the discipline of political psychology is committed to the following equalitarian principles:

- No one has privileged data sources. The evidence, data, must be made available to all.
- No one has privileged status. That some investigators have more prestige or status is undeniable, but it does not credit them with authority over explanations.
- There are no privileged beliefs. Dogma is rejected in favor of "propositions" and "hypotheses."
- There are no privileged findings. If findings cannot be corroborated or replicated they are suspect.
- There is no closure. No findings are ever ineluctably final. All findings, at best, are the best we have for now—until the next explanation tested with data comes along that proves more persuasive.

Having a grasp of the research topics is one thing, mastering the core concerns of political psychology is another. These core concerns are evident in its long tradition, a tradition that began millennia before the field became organized as a social science discipline. The advantage of returning to the tradition is that the tradition offers some clarity and cohesion that currently escapes the current diverse array of scholarship.

II. THE CORE CONCERNS OF POLITICAL PSYCHOLOGY

Humans have been examining themselves, trying to identify human nature, for a very long time. The question they have long sought to answer is: What are the essential qualities of being human? One of the most, perhaps the most, important motivation for this question is because what we think about our human qualities shapes our view of politics, the problem of governance. Humans have lived under various regimes. A regime is some practice that guides our collective actions and ensures compliance with norms of collective action. Among the regimes humans have relied on are:

1. living in a family group (small, or large as in a tribe or clan), where authority often rests with elders;
2. living in kingdoms where authority is given to some king or queen, often aided by some members of the society designated to be "nobles";

3. living in feudal or caste society where authority rests with a sector of the society (a clan that dominates all other clans, or some self-proclaimed elite, an aristocracy, what is often called a "class");

4. living in a religious-based community where authority rests with a priestly class (**e.**g., Vatican City or Shaker communities in the late nineteenth century);

5. living in a democracy where authority rests with the people; or

6. living in a dictatorial regime, of left or right variant, where authority rests with an individual, party, or sect, and is often imposed by the force of police, secret agencies, armed forces used to intimidate and overwhelm any resistance (many examples exist in the world today).

Each of these and others have their evident advantages and disadvantages, though it is also the case that we often find disagreement concerning what these advantages and disadvantages are (both in the abstract and in specific historical cases).

It has been common practice for thinkers to offer their recommendations for how politics should be arranged, who should rule and how, with claims about human nature. Among the most engaging, and of continuing importance, are such famous names as Plato, *The Republic* (1974); Aristotle, *The Politics* (1983); Thomas Hobbes, *The Leviathan* (1968), Niccolò Machiavelli (*The Prince*); Charles de Secondat Montesquieu (*The Spirit of the Laws*); John Locke (*An Essay Concerning Human Understanding* or *Two Treatises of Government*); Jean-Jacques Rousseau (*On the Social Contract*); David Hume (*A Treatise on Human Nature*); Adam Smith (both *The Theory of Moral Sentiments* and *The Wealth of Nations*); James Madison, Alexander Hamilton, and John Jay (*The Federalist Papers*); Alexis de Tocqueville (especially his Introduction to *Democracy in America*); and Karl Marx, *The Communist Manifesto* (Marx and Engels 2002). These are just some of the many important texts that provide the history of how scholars have tried to connect an understanding of what we are to a recommendation of how we can best govern ourselves. Each is a wonderful source of ideas as well as a part of the history of the great debates between them.

I draw on some of these philosophers because they often write more clearly and with a deeper understanding than the often opaque language of the social sciences. Even more important, unless you understand the core issues, issues that are too often taken for granted by many scholars in the political psychology discipline, you will not be able to distinguish the core from the periphery, the primary from the secondary. If you read the classics, you too will find that many modern ideas, current ideas, are actually of ancient heritage. More important, by reading at least some of these classics you will find greater perspective, as I try to demonstrate later, and escape the risk of taking for granted that was current conventional wisdom are what it claims to be wise. I begin with two of the most influential of these classics.

Aristotle (384 BC–322 BC) generated a famous and long enduring taxonomy to identify what he considered to be the basic political regimes types. For thousands of years his taxonomy defined the choices. More important, his taxonomy identified the central challenge of human nature. How do we govern ourselves, individually and collectively? They remain the fundamental issues of political psychology today.

BOX 1.3 **Taxonomy**

Is a system of classification. Generating a taxonomy is one of the first and most basic steps in science. A taxonomy provides the categories into which all relevant observations can be assigned. Some famous examples: flora and fauna. All living things are thereby assigned to either the plant kingdom (flora) or the animal kingdom (fauna). A taxonomy is designed to be comprehensive, that is, to assign any and all instances into one, and only one, of the classes. Taxonomies often turn out to be flawed. Scientists often modify them when flaws become evident.

Aristotle's taxonomy was constructed by taking into account two basic considerations. The first consideration was an *empirical* determination: How many people rule?

His classification identified three possible regime types: 1) rule by one person; 2) rule by a small group of people; or 3) rule by all the citizens of a city, city–states being at that time the dominant social unit in ancient Greece. His second consideration was a *normative* determination: How well do the rulers rule? He identified two possibilities:

1. *virtuously*: by which he meant rule that achieved the enduring well-being of the city–state;
2. *corruption*: by which he meant nonvirtuous rule, whether from malfeasance, misfeasance or any kind of selfish indulgence. Hence, any *action*, or *inaction*, that did not serve the enduring well-being of the city–state was corrupt.

These two considerations generated a 3 × 2 taxonomy: three rows, each of which lists one empirical kind of regime and two columns each of which applies a normative assessment. Table 1.2 shows the resulting taxonomy.

In table 1.2 observe that democracy appears in both columns, the virtuous and the corrupt. In the modern world few argue against democracy even as many observe its many failings. Even rulers in the most despotic regimes often claim they represent the will of the people. For example, the East German state installed by the Soviet Army after World War II labeled itself the German Democratic Republic, the GDR. And, even as despotic regimes kill to preserve their hold on power they often proclaim they are doing so on behalf of the majority (I hope each of you can quickly recall recent examples, from those in the Middle East during spring and summer of 2011, or going back some years to Tiananmen Square or in Tibet, in China).

BOX 1.4 **Empirical**

Is a description of some quality or property of the world; observations about the world by relying on our senses.

Normative

Is a prescriptive evaluation using some norm of behavior.

Table 1-2 Aristotle's taxonomy of regimes

Regime type: Who rules?	How do rulers rule?	
	Virtuous rule	Corrupt rule
Rule by one	Monarchy	Despot
Rule by a few	Aristocracy	Oligarchy
Rule by the many	Democracy	Democracy

Aristotle believed that rule by the many, all citizens coming together to make collective judgments about how to govern, *could* be the best regime. However, Aristotle also recognized that rule by the many often lead to tyranny. The many might use their numbers for corrupt purposes, just as a despot or a powerful wealthy class.

Although democracies of late have grown increasingly prevalent in the world, we often find their failings more evident than their virtue. And, that recognition fuels much of the research that political psychologists conduct. If virtue in government was natural then it would be easy to establish them and we would not need, or likely have, disciplines of political science and political psychology. In this book I discuss the many ways in which political psychologists explore the linkage between psychology and politics and more precisely between our nature in all its variety and the possibility of government, both corrupt and virtuous.

The Usefulness of Taxonomies

Aristotle's taxonomy reveals the principal advantage of having a taxonomy. There are now hundreds of different governments in the world (and even more so if we add the many regional and local governments that exist within nation states). Aristotle's scheme enables us to place every government into one of just six categories. Science and systematic knowledge requires us to set aside the precise uniqueness of every individual, every element in the world, and every circumstance. If we want a "type" (here political regimes), then we must have some criteria that allows us to ignore the unique specificity of each of the hundreds of governments, past and present so that, based on some grouping criteria, we can assign each to one of these six cells. If we sought very precise description of each and every government we would find not similarities but differences. No two governments would be alike. That would be good history, precise description. But, it would be poor science because science is always searching for patterns across different cases.

Aristotle also recognized that his typology was too simple. He considered another type of government, a category that he called mixed because a mixed regime included elements from each row. Nonetheless his six-fold system of classification remains very influential because it highlights the critical question about how we find ourselves governed: virtuously or corruptly. The distinction between virtue and corruption remains the fundamental consideration of how to secure the former and prevent the latter.

With a taxonomy we can study an entire class of regime types, for example rule by the few, and form an empirical generalization about how well or poor this regime type performed. We can make comparisons across categories: How do aristocracies compare to democracies, for example. Are aristocracies more or less likely to engage in war than democracies? This is quite different than approaching the topic from a historical vantage point or as a case study. A case study would tell you a lot about a particular regime, for example, a particular monarch's rule, a specific British or Nepalese king, but such a study would not tell you that much about the entire class of rule by monarchs.

This last point is very important as it goes to the heart of how science generates knowledge. We seek to understand why things happen as they do. Often as we go about our daily lives we have to explain ourselves. For example, we may have to explain to our colleagues, why we are late for a meeting or to a friend, why we voted for this party or that candidate. In these instances we are often seeking to account for a single event: Why we are late for this meeting and why we voted for McCain or Obama for president in 2008. Science, on the other hand, generates explanations that are meant to be applicable to all relevant cases, and therefore to be universally applicable. I have more to say on these points so you can learn to apply scientific explanation.

The practice of science requires that scientists present their theories in universal form so that the empirical claims of the theory can be tested anywhere, anytime, and by anyone. If observations collected by someone, in some locale, in some historical period, undermine the theory then the theory fails. It will either be replaced by a better theory or modified to address its failings.

Let us, briefly, return to Aristotle.

Human Nature and Human Politics

Aristotle argued that we have to rule ourselves. He famously described us as a political species. But, humans often fail to govern themselves, often doing things that prove to be foolish, evil, or ill considered. And, when we gather together, we often make collective decisions without much evidence of "virtue." Instead, political regimes, the system of rule making and rule enforcing, often prove to be corrupt. Monarchs often become despots. Rule by the best, in ancient terms the aristocratic class, in modern terms, experts in matters economic, social, and political, too often becomes rule by those, whether rich or just powerful, rule to secure their privileged positions. And, democracies often fail because the majority too often put their selfish interests before the collective good. James Madison, in Federalist Paper No. 10, put the challenge of creating a virtuous democratic government best:

> …As long as the reason of man continues fallible, and he is at liberty to exercise it, different opinions will be formed. As long as the connection subsists between his reason and his self-love, his opinions and his passions will have a reciprocal influence on each other; and the former will be objects to which the latter will attach themselves.
>
> …No man is allowed to be a judge in his own cause, because his interest would certainly bias his judgment, and, not improbably, corrupt his integrity. With equal, nay with greater reason, a body of men are unfit to be both judges and parties at the same time.

If you read Madison slowly and carefully you will discover the following assertions.

First, humans do rely on reason but the consequence of using reason does not necessarily produce virtue, it often produces corruption because reason is used for selfish

BOX 1.5 Reading

Reading someone of a different period often proves to be a challenge. Moreover, in today's world we scan instead of reading precisely so that we can quickly and efficiently get the gist, the essential meaning. Some scholarship can and should be scanned to get the gist, but some scholarship is worth *close reading*. Having explicit reading strategies you can select and apply will pay you great dividends.

In the example from Madison, note that the first fragment is presented as a certain linkage ("as long as the connection subsists between ... reason and self-love...[then]") while the second fragment includes a *conditional* linkage, "and, not improbably, corrupt his integrity." Is that important?

When you come across a phrase, for example Madison later refers to *enlightened statesman*, you can come to a more insightful understanding by using the following method. For each word, *enlightened* and *statesman*, generate its opposite, what are the antonyms of *enlightened* and *statesman*? For the first, *benighted* (i.e., to be in the dark) and for the second, *politician* (i.e., unlike the statesman whose concern is for the state, the politician represents the polis, the people). Then re-interpret Madison's meaning in light of these oppositions. Try the same with another phrase from Madison, "the permanent and aggregate interests of the community," what are the antonyms here?

Considering an argument in detail offers excellent training for thinking theoretically. And for prompting you to come up with extensions, variations, and alternative accounts.

purposes. When humans reason they produce judgments that are not just flawed but flawed in a biased way: Our errors in reasoning somehow end up favoring ourselves. If our flawed reasons were flawed in a random way half the time we would make errors that hurt our interests and half the time errors that favored our interests.

Second, Madison offered an explanation for this bias. His theory holds that humans attach a positive emotion (love) to their beliefs (which makes opinions "our" opinions) hence we like, no, we love our own opinions (and by extension what do we make of the opinions held by others?).

Third, this attachment is "reciprocal" so that when we find our opinions attacked by others, or by experience as experience often challenges our beliefs, we defend the beliefs, no matter how flawed. Madison expected that our passion will rise to defend our opinions. And, having come to these conclusions, by extension, as Madison said in the second passage, this dynamic applies to "interests" and not just opinions. Even in the absence of opinions and reason, we find ourselves corruptly pursuing what benefits us, what is in our interest, rather than what is in the public interest. Finally, Madison held that people acting collectively also are susceptible to corruption for he said that not only are we unfit to judge as individuals, we are also unfit to act as a "body of men."

However, justice requires even-handed treatment. So, to be just, we have to make decisions with equal regard for everyone. Hence, Madison concluded that our natures make us ill prepared to extend justice and govern in an even-handed manner. This remains a vital and recurring issue—how should and how do we treat strangers, immigrants, those unlike "us"? This question dominates today's politics. Hence, Madison's view of human nature has direct implications for today's politics. If reason is the primary basis for politics, democratic, aristocratic, or monarchial, then reason, Madison argued will produce corrupt, self-serving judgments. If that is the case, and he made a compelling argument, then we have not as yet found the answer to how to govern ourselves.

Let's consider another example of a philosopher linking human nature to politic. There are other choices I could have chosen, among them, John Locke, Jean Jacques Rousseau, or Karl Marx, but because his work remains of particular importance to contemporary politics, I chose Thomas Hobbes (1968). He still offers a sound and parsimonious explanation for the linkage between human nature and politics, for why we need a discipline of political psychology.[2]

Many of you have come to the field of political psychology from one of two disciplines, psychology or political science. Psychology is a very large discipline that touches on many topics and in many of these, politics often rarely intrudes.[3] And, as it seems for many psychologists, politics seems to result from misunderstanding, ignorance of various types, and such factors as prejudice. Politics rests on conflict, and conflict is fueled by misperception and misunderstanding. Hobbes offered a telling corrective. The rest will come from political science, which often focuses, appropriately, on the institutions that deal with conflict—parliaments, constitutions, judicial systems, executive systems, and the like—and the history and traditions of the people who form groups within which and between which conflict often appears. These are the aspects of politics that may seem, if properly understood, to be sufficient to fully understand politics. Here again, Hobbes offered a telling corrective. Hobbes, then, still has much to offer, to educate us, in the fundamental way in which human nature undergirds ourselves and our politics.

Thomas Hobbes published *The Leviathan* in 1651, just at the time the English Civil War was coming to an end. He saw much of the violence in England, as Catholic and Protestant kings each tried to impose their religious convictions in part by destroying those who resisted conversion. He drew his direct observations on that violent world and on his learning. To those who might consider government unnecessary he offered the following portrait of what life would be like without an effective government:

> every man is enemy to every man, the same consequent to the time wherein men live without other security than what their own strength and their own invention shall furnish them withal. In such condition there is no place for industry, because the fruit thereof is uncertain: and consequently no culture of the earth; no navigation, nor use of the commodities that may be imported by sea; no commodious building; no instruments of moving and removing such things as require much force; no knowledge of the face of the earth; no account of time; no arts; no letters; no society; and which is worst of all, continual fear, and danger of violent death; and the life of man, solitary, poor, nasty, brutish, and short. (chapter 8)

---

2. Why bother with a scholar whose thinking did not have the benefit of current scientific thinking? Who did not know about genes (and the later work of Gregor Mendel), or DNA (and the double helix), or evolution (and the work of Charles Darwin) let alone the current work in neuroscience and psychology? Well, largely because his work was carefully attuned to the challenge of creating a liberal and stable political regime, a challenge that remains no less vital now, some 450 plus years after his great work, *The Leviathan*, was first published. In addition, his identification of three fundamental qualities, described later, requires no qualification in light of recent work, even as we elaborate by taking into account insights not available to Hobbes.

3. There are, as I shall point out in later chapters, many very important and influential exceptions.

BOX 1.6 **Suggestion**

An excellent and exciting book to read, *Njal's Saga* (1960) is the story of Iceland's failed effort to preserve freedom from kingly rule. The saga covers the sixty-year period from 960 to 1020 AD. Iceland was then a feudal society. The saga depicts the destruction of the society as a consequence of blood feuds. It is a wonderful companion to Hobbes's *The Leviathan*. In it you will find unforgettable people, some brave, some not, some duplicitous, and some honor bound. Some are high born and some low, you will find them each depicted in ferocious and honest detail.

He offered us a specific political psychology, the results of his inquiry into human nature, to support his conclusion that a monarchy was the sole and best solution. He began by asserting that the human species has three distinguishing qualities. They are: *liberty, imagination, and desire.*[4]

Here's a brief summary of Hobbes's argument. Humans are creatures of liberty if we are brought up in a condition of liberty, in an environment that allows our distinct qualities to be nurtured and thereby to grow their fullest extent, we will be autonomous and able to manifest our qualities. We are born as fragile infants, dependent on nurturance for many years before becoming adults.

Lack of liberty will stunt our development. Maturity requires more than just birth and minimal sustenance. When mature, we likely will be quite different from each other. Some will grow to be tall, some short. Some will become more interested in the arts and others in the selling and buying of goods. In sum, we will differ in many ways depending on our individual natures, but only if we are allowed to express our qualities.

Let me interject here: You can easily observe that Hobbes's vision is, today, violated in many ways in just about every current society. Those who cry for the importance of traditional values, whether secular or religious are decrying against liberal autonomy. Those who say "our traditions demand compliance" are saying, in various formulations, that individuals must express and comply with values and principles set by others no matter how they may feel about the matter. They should subordinate their own values to those of the wider community. And, authoritarian governments, of all sorts, demand fealty and compliance with government rules no matter how onerous. When governments censor and imprison those who dissent they are obviously denying liberal autonomy. How many examples can you find both in your own society and in other parts of the world? However, let's return to the seventeenth century and Hobbes for more.

Hobbes also asserted that humans have the faculty of imagination. We do more than passively experience the world. We also think up new ideas and new possibilities. We can imagine dragons, mermaids, aliens from other planets, and of course imagine

---

4. Further, if you read the quote carefully you will note that Hobbes also grasped an essential point of psychology, that we are all somewhat different along these dimensions, some with greater and some with lesser imagination, some with greater and some with lesser desire, and so on. Hence, although ignorant of genes and DNA, he fully understood that individual differences are an essential aspect of human nature, thus anticipating the field of personality in which scholars seek to determine the fundamental dimensions of these individual differences, a topic we discuss in chapter 7.

BOX 1.7 Comment

It was comforting for many to believe that the human species was the only species that has a nature requiring politics. However, that view has been challenged by scientists who study other species, most notably primates. Read, for but one example, Frans de Waal (2007), *Chimpanzee Politics: Power and Sex among Apes and Good Nature: The Origins of Right and Wrong in Humans and Other Animals.*

---

new landscapes to paint, new ideas on where and how to live. Because we are each liberal creatures, if allowed, we will use the faculty of imagination in different ways and to different purposes and ends. And, unless we want to live alone, we will find ourselves with different imaginings of how to live, and therefore, if we want to live among others, we have to sort through the various imagined ways to live. Conflict is thus inherent in our natures.

Last, having ideas is one thing, putting them into practice is quite another. And, that brings us to Hobbes's last human quality: desire. Ideas linked to desire are what move us to take action. Ideas by themselves are fascinating but merely that. It is only when thoughts are bound to desire that we act. Note that in this last claim, the linkage between passion and action, Hobbes advanced a hypothesis that Madison adopted. We are different, we want different things, and our passions cause us to eagerly pursue what we imagine can be ours.

But without an effective government we find ourselves either living a life of solitude or with others in a Hobbesian state of nature, a condition of war and violence.

What government would work given these fundamental features? For Hobbes only a monarchy would be best able to rule, to effectively deal with the clash of ideas that liberty, imagination, and desire ensures. Only a monarch, he argued, would be able to protect these qualities and rule with virtue. Of course others have offered different recommendations, as you might.

Of course Hobbes's inventory of essential qualities can, and has been, critiqued. What other essential properties would you add? Are there, among Hobbes's threesome one or more that you would move down, or even off, his list?

One core quality that many would argue should be at the very top of any such list is sociability. We are a social species, needing the active involvement of others for our birth, for essential care during infancy, and indeed every stage of life.[5] Emile Durkheim (1951), the French sociologist, and based on his research argued that freedom from the moral and social constraints of custom and tradition did not lead to individual autonomy and freedom. Rather, he argued that it led to the condition he named *anomie*, a despairing sense of isolation so painful that if sustained for very long could lead to suicide. Durkheim is just one alternative to Hobbes. If you read widely you will find other possibilities. We do have imagination and with the invention of writing and publishing, we can capture and retain what imagination has produced.

There are many answers on how to govern. For some the solution lays in faithful adherence to common doctrine (be it a religious faith or an accepted tradition). On

---

5. Two useful readings advance these points: Bowlby (1973) and Cacioppo and Patrick (2008).

the other hand, revolutions such as the American, French, and Russian, all led to new regimes that broke longstanding traditions. Invasion can also lead to changes in regime as in the aftermath of World War II in the cases of Italy, Germany, and Japan. The question of governing applies not just to the issue of what type of regime rules in a nation state. Different families have different regimes, systems of organization and governance as result of culture, traditions, and individual preferences. Some families are large and extended reaching to clans and tribes. Other families are quite bounded, the so-called "nuclear" family. Some families are quite hierarchical with hierarchies that favor male authority over female, older over younger, whereas other families are organized in a more egalitarian fashion, if not fully so. Work places and social environments are also places in which conflict and politics unfolds. In that broader sense, governing is all around us in every instance where more than one person is engaged. Political psychology explores all of these seeking to test which work, which does not, and why.

Political psychology is a discipline devoted to using scientific knowledge to explain who rules, why, and with what consequences. Although the subject matter of political psychology is very old, extending back millennia, the discipline of political psychology is quite young, measuring, at best, some decades. What's the difference? Many individual scholars, such as Harold Lasswell (1948) and Alexander George (1989), have long sought to apply their understanding of the human *psyche* (the Greek word for breathe or the soul from which derives the science of the soul, *psychology*). What does it mean to say there is a discipline of political psychology?

Individual scholars do not make a discipline. A discipline is an organized program of inquiry. It is a coherent means of addressing the issues that engaged Hobbes, Madison, and so many other scholars, ancient and modern. To offer an analogy, an athlete engages in athletic performance, just as a scholar engages in understanding. Each has its particular array of talents and training. But the discipline of athletics involves more than just a large number of athletes, it involves coaches, training manuals, sports medicine, training camps, codes of conduct such as being a good sportsman, a good competitor, antidoping rules and procedures, and much more. Going for a bike ride as casual exercise is one thing, racing in the Tour de France is quite another. The former is the act of an amateur, the latter a professional. As a science, political psychology is a way of generating and scientifically testing explanation. It has rigorous standards that do not apply to amateur scholars. It is an array of activities that must be learned, hopefully with able mentoring, and ever subject to rigorous critique. And, it is institutionalized with a number of organizations, publishing outlets, some national and some international. And although political psychology is unusual in that it regularly draws on many other disciplines, not just psychology and political science, but also philosophy, economics, sociology, anthropology, and others, political psychologists do practice the doing of political psychology.[6]

We turn to detailing those activities next.

---

6. Some describe political psychology as multidisciplinary, which is accurate, or it could be called a metadiscipline. These are useful to point out the broad streams that feed into political psychology, but while relying on many streams political psychology is organized as a discipline, even if multidisciplinary.

BOX 1.8 **Comment**

This gives me the opportunity to introduce the idea of *concept* or *variable*. It is clear that humans engage in conflict, but humans also engage in cooperation. You can observe both all around you. Science has a particular way of understanding this assertion.

The two terms, conflict and cooperation are each understood, in science, as *concepts* and *variables*. That means that each must be defined clearly so that each has a range, from low to high, that each varies (hence a variable). Sometimes we cooperate, sometimes we go it alone. Sometimes we fight and sometimes we don't. Doing so invites two questions: 1) what other property might cause each to vary, that is, can we connect a *cause* to the *effect*? And, 2) how can we test that proposed linkage? Concepts and taxonomies are two of the building blocks of science.

Rather than describing aspects of the world by applying common words, political psychology, as a science, describes by identifying and applying variables. How science differs from normal observation I explain and explore later.

III. DOING POLITICAL PSYCHOLOGY
Political psychology is an activity. It is best learned as an activity.

> I hear and I forget
> I see and I remember;
> I do and I understand.
>
> *—Confucius*

Politics is natural to humans because we have diverse opinions and those opinions when enacted by our passions often leads to conflict.

If we want to understand when and why people sometimes fight, and when they do not, how might we proceed? That, in part, depends on our purpose. If our task is to judge whether we should invade another country or negotiate a joint pact of peace, we might want to know how they would respond before we make such a momentous decision. We could examine the history of that nation, its leaders, and its people. We might examine that history to see if we can discern any clues on the assumption that the past will be a reasonable guide to the present moment. We could inquire into the personality of the leadership group. Maybe there is a pattern of belligerence or a pattern of honest negotiating. Or, we could ask experts who are familiar with that nation. There are many ways we could proceed. I previously identified two features that define science, now I am going to add a third.

The first feature of science is that it poses its questions in the universal language of theoretical statements, not in the particulars of what will this specific nation do at this specific point in time.[7] Scientific claims will take the following form: Nations, when

---

7. Here, it is worth pointing out that "nations" do not do anything. People do. When we speak of, for example, nations going to war, that is a sleight of hand summary of what is going on. In that example, some go to war (soldiers, generals, workers in munitions factories), but some do not (objectors, resisters; for example, the students who made up the White Rose resistance in the Nazi regime). Collective action is a variable (group solidarity is not a constant), so even when we speak of nations or groups as if they had a common and shared mentality we are asserting an empirical condition that has to be shown to be true and most often, it is not (Gould 2003).

challenged to engage in conflict by another country will respond with war; on the other hand, when nations offer negotiation, nations will respond with an affirmative willingness to do likewise. The basic theoretical claim is that of universality. This formulation is independent of historical specificity, it is a statement, which if corroborated by research, would apply to any nation to nation interaction, past, present, or future.

Second, science challenges any theoretical claim with organized doubt. If a specific claim was offered but limited to a time and place then other instances of nations choosing between conflict and negotiation would be of little value in testing that veracity of the proclaimed explanation. Having the theoretical assertion formulated as a universal relationship invites research into the question from anywhere as well as from anyone. If all research, each and every project looking at the different instances of nation to nation negotiating corroborates a particular finding then the collective pattern of results adds to our provisional confidence that the relationship is reliable.

Of course, additional research may produce results that reveal complications. For example, another variable, say the relative strength of the nations in the negotiation, may reveal that the simple theory is too simple. A stronger nation may offer more punitive terms for a settlement, and a weaker nation may be eager to secure some alliance with another neighbor nation to help equalize the strength balance before engaging in negotiations. We may have to restate the theoretical formulation so that these complications are formulated as variables and the theoretical statements enlarged to specify how these new additions modify the theory (e.g., in this instance, when equal strength nations negotiate, then...; when nations of unequal strength confront each other they will negotiate if the weaker obtains an alliance with a third nation to create a condition of more equal strength. ...).

We are likely to begin with a simple theory, valuing parsimony. We would like to have the simplest and most powerful theory. That is to say, we seek a theory with the fewest explanatory variables that will do the job in explaining why the variable of interest takes on high, or low, values. Third, science begins with the simplest of theoretical statements and then, grudgingly accepts more complex theoretical statements as prove necessary.

To better understand scientific knowledge it is useful to return to James Madison. The next quote comes from his Federalist Paper No. 37. In this paper, his task is to explain how and why the 1787 Convention in Philadelphia came to produce a new Constitution that, in his view, recommended the approval of the voters of New York. Adopting the new Constitution required that each of the thirteen states of America, the former colonies, obtain approval from the people. All knew that if New York approved the other states would fall in line.

Madison begins by laying before his readers the general problem facing understanding and explanation. To help you read through this quotation it might help to list the topics as he discusses them. He begins with the challenge of taxonomy. Recall that Aristotle also began with taxonomy so that each unique object can be grouped with others of its kind. Madison then turns to the next challenge. If we have a taxonomy we can use it to put objects into the appropriate class, and requires that we rely on our perceptions. Last, if we accomplish these two tasks, we then have to put our knowledge into language so that we can convey it to others. And, on each of these steps he has some cautions to offer us that remain no less valid today. Let us now turn to Madison (1961):

…The boundaries between the great kingdom of nature, and, still more, between the various provinces, and lesser portions, into which they are subdivided, afford another illustration of the same important truth. The most sagacious and laborious naturalists have never yet succeeded in tracing with certainty the line which separates the district of vegetable life from the neighboring region of unorganized matter, or which marks the ermination of the former and the commencement of the animal empire….

When we pass from the works of nature, in which all the delineations are perfectly accurate, and appear to be otherwise only from the imperfection of the eye which surveys them, to the institutions of man, in which the obscurity arises as well from the object itself as from the organ by which it is contemplated, we must perceive the necessity of moderating still further our expectations and hopes from the efforts of human sagacity. Experience has instructed us that no skill in the science of government has yet been able to discriminate and define, with sufficient certainty, its three great provinces the legislative, executive, and judiciary; or even the privileges and powers of the different legislative branches….

The experience of ages, with the continued and combined labors of the most enlightened legislatures and jurists, has been equally unsuccessful in delineating the several objects and limits of different codes of laws and different tribunals of justice. The precise extent of the common law, and the statute law, the maritime law, the ecclesiastical law, the law of corporations, and other local laws and customs, remains still to be clearly and finally established in Great Britain, where accuracy in such subjects has been more industriously pursued than in any other part of the world. The jurisdiction of her several courts, general and local, of law, of equity, of admiralty, etc., is not less a source of frequent and intricate discussions, sufficiently denoting the indeterminate limits by which they are respectively circumscribed. All new laws, though penned with the greatest technical skill, and passed on the fullest and most mature deliberation, are considered as more or less obscure and equivocal, until their meaning be liquidated and ascertained by a series of particular discussions and adjudications. Besides the obscurity arising from the complexity of objects, and the imperfection of the human faculties, the medium through which the conceptions of men are conveyed to each other adds a fresh embarrassment. The use of words is to express ideas. Perspicuity, therefore, requires not only that the ideas should be distinctly formed, but that they should be expressed by words distinctly and exclusively appropriate to them. But no language is so copious as to supply words and phrases for every complex idea, or so correct as not to include many equivocally denoting different ideas. Hence it must happen that however accurately objects may be discriminated in themselves, and however accurately the discrimination may be considered, the definition of them may be rendered inaccurate by the inaccuracy of the terms in which it is delivered. And this unavoidable inaccuracy must be greater or less, according to the complexity and novelty of the objects defined. When the Almighty himself condescends to address mankind in their own language, his meaning, luminous as it must be, is rendered dim and doubtful by the cloudy medium through which it is communicated.

Here, then, are three sources of vague and incorrect definitions: indistinctness of the object, imperfection of the organ of conception, inadequateness of the vehicle of ideas. Any one of these must produce a certain degree of obscurity. The convention, in delineating the boundary between the federal and State jurisdictions, must have experienced the full effect of them all.

Madison's argument remains as compelling now as it was when he wrote this passage over two-hundred years ago. In sum, taxonomies are often vague, observations are often flawed, and language is often imprecise. How social science, including political psychology attempts to overcome these challenges is the topic that follows.

Explanation in Political Psychology

From "I know" seems to decide a state of affairs which guarantees what is know, guarantees it as a fact. One always forgets the expression "I thought I knew."
—Ludwig Wittgenstein, *On Certainty*
(Wittgenstein, Anscombe, and von Wright 1969, 12)

I begin this section with an epigram because it reminds us of a natural human tendency. We can easily excuse the failures of our beliefs by quickly forgetting that they failed us.[8] Political psychology seeks to test our beliefs by relying formal, public, and accountable practices that uses empirical data to determine which of our explanations warrants provisional acceptance. I begin by reviewing the basics of explanation in its scientific variant. There are other types of explanation, some of them I describe to demonstrate the differences with and similarities to social science as a practice of generating and testing explanations.

I begin with an account given by an astute observer who in the 1850s was perplexed by the then current rage in America for mysticism and spiritualism. The author's account illustrates some enduring issues. In the 1850s, thousands of people were enthused by the prospect of speaking to those who had died.[9] According to the anonymous author (1854, 13), "In the city of New York, to which circle our personal investigation has been confined, there are, at the least calculation, forty thousand sincere believers in Spiritual Rappings." The author – who identifies him (or her) self solely as a searcher after truth – clearly put forth his (or her) intention in the book's dedication, "to The People of the United States This Work…with the ernest hope that it will form a mite towards destroying a delusion which is daily working evil among thousands."

Let's begin with a description of "Spiritual Rapping." The author offered this account (1854, 15–17):

The disciples of the Spiritual Rappings believe that, on the death of the body, the spirit passes into another world, the position of which, in the sphere of worlds, or

8. The beliefs of people, investors, and economists especially, before and after the latest "bubble" has burst offers many examples of this phenomenon. So do wars that fail to unfold as those who advocated them predicted. So also do the recurring predictions that the religiously inspired make that the world will end on a given date. And, so do politicians when they claim that implementing their opponents policies bring doom.
9. A hope that persists among the gullible.

the particular nature of which, they do not pretend to describe. They say it is not Heaven, neither is it Hell; it is not midway between the two, and it is not a place where God can be seen.

...They believe that the inhabitants of the Spirit World are ever wandering about this; and that not only the spirits of a man's dead relatives and friends are around him, or at least ready to answer his call, but that any other spirit is ready to answer him, and communicate with him; nay, even volunteer to do so...The Spiritual Rapping disciples believe that communication with the Spirit World can only be had with through the intervention of what is called a Medium; that is some particular mortal to whom either the spirits take a fancy, or who is spiritual enough for them to hold direct intercourse with.

...The Mediums place their hands on a table, in connection with those who seek communication, and the table tips, or raps are heard on it or under it, and thus the spirits testify their presence and willingness to to be interrogated. Three raps or taps mean "yes;" one "no;" and two, "I don't know," or "doubtful."

The investigator went to various locations in New York State and took part in quite a number of séances. The author reported on each occasion: what took place, how many took part, keeping anonymous the names of the participants though giving detailed reports on the ages, gender, personalities, and other features of each person in each group. The author visited some mediums more than once.

The investigator noted the occurrence of the following: the séance table would "tip and dance about," first rising above the heads of the party and then lowering itself, while all present would hear raps on it; and yet no one could be seen to touch it, "strange spiritual lights" were seen to reflect on the table; several present exclaimed that they were "touched by the spirits"; the medium's hand was made to move "without his own free-will." The author was satisfied that the spiritual lights were simply the reflection of natural or artificial light and discounted the claim that spirits touched people because he [I do not know the gender of the author, it may have been a woman] was not so touched. He nevertheless felt obliged to find a nonspiritual explanation for the movement of the tables and the apparent involuntary hand movements of the mediums. After considering a variety of alternatives, he settled on an explanation that posited the existence of a new form of energy, called the Od, or odyle, force, that could account both for the movements of the table and the involuntary movements of the medium. The author described his theory as follows (1854, 233):

It is to this theory of a resistless current—an invisible, but extraordinary agency, which is not electricity, nor magnetism, but which partakes more of the character of the latter than of the former—that we may assign the origin of the involuntary and "vital" forces which have puzzled more than the "spirit-rappists" themselves.

One puzzle remains. If there is a newly discovered force that can move objects, how are we to explain why some people are, and others not, influenced by this Od force? We need an explanation of *individual differences*; why some people are affected and others are quite insulated from the Od force? The author explained that many people cannot become mediums because (1854, 190):

It is the property of the brain to receive impressions, but it is the prerogative of the self-conscious, self-determining, disciplined mind to reject or to receive their influence.... An undisciplined mind has no control over the brain.... This is why, in order to develop a medium, a suspended state of mind, a passive will, is found necessary.

It is important to note that although all of this seems quite comical over 150 years later, the emotions and convictions were then so high that the author remained anonymous and signed the book "a searcher after truth." Although the particular events may have passed into history and the explanations tested and then offered in that work are no longer given much currency, beliefs we hold as important remain as bound up with emotion and conviction as the belief in talking to the dead was over 150 years ago.

More important, I begin this section on explanations with this story of a "searcher after truth" because it highlights a number of very important lessons about social science as a method for producing accounts of human activity. We can learn from this research into "Spirit Rapping."

- Careful observation is an important skill.
- Although this is not to claim that careful observation is error free.
- More observations are better than fewer observations. Recall that the author had to apologize that due to lack of resources investigations could only be extended throughout New York State. However he, or she, did repeat his investigations of some mediums. Repeating a study to see if the same results obtained is called *replication*.
- Developing explanations to account for phenomena requires effort to find what other, alternative, explanations are available. We must know the research literature to find what facts other studies have reported and what other explanations have been offered.
- Explanations serve not only to satisfy ourselves that we understand something, but also to persuade wider audiences.
- The search for new explanations that confront, and potentially discredit existing accounts and beliefs, can be a dangerous business. Remember that "the searcher after truth" felt it prudent to remain anonymous.
- Finally, and most important, social science, as all other systems for generating explanations, is prone to accepting false explanations. It is the hope of social scientists to produce explanations that are less error prone than other types explanations.

One difference between social science and other methods of producing explanations is that good social scientists are trained to treat all explanations as suspect. It is easier to be dubious about those we disagree with than with our own explanations. But the social science enterprise gives no special favor to an explanation merely because of its source or its endorsements, each explanation must prove its mettle again and again.

In general, social science methods, by drawing attention to the many sources of error in reaching conclusions and generating explanations, force the researcher to grapple explicitly and systematically with each potential threat to credibility.

Description and Explanation in Political Psychology

I already touched on a variety of elements that go into social science explanation, taxonomy, empirical observation, and the universal form that explanations take. Now let's begin with one of the most important differences: description. Our natural way of describing things, events, people, is "thick" description. A good biography or a good memoir is thick description, so too is a well told history of some period or some major event. Herodotus (2005) and Thucydides (1996), the first historians, produced histories that are very thick. In a similar fashion, a novel is a fictive version of thick description. We come to know and understand by getting rich details of most aspect of a life. The layering of details adds to our understanding. If mysteries remain, we ask for more details or look for specific hidden details. Of course some details may be hard to obtain. Governments often keep secrets for a variety of reasons.

Political psychologists rely on "thin" description. What is thin description? Thin description begins with a taxonomy to identify the key properties. These properties include those we wish to explain, dependent variables, and those properties we hope that explain, independent variables. Let's begin with an example. In many democracies, many people are eligible to vote. Of interest is why some who can vote do, while others who can vote do not.

The property, or variable, we identified is voting. Why do people show on election day and cast a ballot, in person, or by absentee ballot or where permitted, by mail? We then go on to theorize why some vote and why some do not. We have a dependent variable and we have variance that some eligible people vote while others do not. *Variance* is just a technical term for a property, voting, that can take on more than one value, in this case two: voting; nonvoting. We seek to explain why this variation?

An explanation consists of demonstrating an empirical linkage between some property, a variable, that we think might explain why some voters vote and others do not vote. Let me suggest three possible explanations by listing possible independent variables: 1) partisanship, 2) distance from work, and 3) the perceived policy differences between the candidates.

The first is suggested by the surmise that those who have identified with a political party are more engaged with politics and, hence, more likely to vote than are nonpartisans. To test this hypothesis we need very little information about the voter. We want to know whether that individual voted. We do not need to know the age, the gender, or the history of the voter, or many other possible details. And, with regard to partisanship,

---

BOX 1.9 Theorizing

Thinking up possible properties, variables, that may be related to the variable you wish to explain and then specifying how those independent variables might be related to the dependent variable. I shall briefly cover some of the ways independent variables can explain dependent variables.

Theorizing is a vital skill to learn. So, practice. Here, the dependent variable is voting (a simple dichotomy, voted or did not vote).

How many factors, can you add? The more the better so come up with as many as you can.

BOX 1.10 Sampling

In most instances we are not likely to be able to study every single case of voting. We cannot study *all* voters in *every* election past and present. And of course, we cannot study voters in elections that have not yet happened. We are really not interested in explaining the voters we study; we are interested in whether those we study confirm the general theory.

There is a science of sampling that explains how to select cases from a population of interest (i.e., how to generate a sample) from which we can then generalize back to the population with a known level of accuracy. This science is the basis of survey research. Public opinion polling is the best known example of sampling.

all we need to know is whether the voter identifies as a member with any political party (and as formulated, here we don't need to know which party).

This is an example of thin description.

The second independent variable I propose is the distance between where the voter is before leaving to vote and where the voter has to travel to vote. Perhaps the voter has to travel to a school or if a mail ballot is involved, to the nearest the mail box. Again, remember this is thin description. As earlier, we do not care about many facets of the voter, not the voter's name, occupation, marital status, family size, or wealth. As to our second independent variable, we have a clear measure: length, measured in miles, kilometers, yards, or some other measure of distance. Here though, you might object that the real variable is not distance but another property: effort, that is, does it take a big effort to vote or little at all. In either formulation the independent variable is not dichotomous; it is a gradient running from zero, no distance or effort, to very high, with many intermediate values of distance, or effort.

This highlights another point about science. There is a difference between the property and the actual measure we use to assign values to each case. Someone who sends in a mail ballot might forget to sign it in the designated way or place thus producing a ballot that might be refused by the electoral commission assigned to count votes. Or, someone might turn up at the ballot location, go in and obtain a ballot but decide to leave it blank, or even to just not turn in the ballot. Are these instances of voting, or of nonvoting? I return to this issue of measurement later.

BOX 1.11 Measurement

The practice of assigning some score to each and every case for each and every variable included in the research. It is good practice to use more than one *measure*, or *indicator,* so that you can check whether, as one might hope, all the variables, indicators, of a single property, vary together. Having multiple indicators allow a researcher to test whether the indicators are reliable and valid.

Reliability is concerned with how much random error is associated as all indicators have some error. Validity is concerned with ascertaining whether an indicator is actually measuring the property. Properties, or factors, are best thought of as *latent*—unobserved. Variable, measures, or indicators, on the other hand, are *manifest*—observed.

Can you think up some latent properties? And can you also think up some plausible indicators?

Having these two variables, distance from balloting and the outcome (voting or not voting) offers a test of the second hypothesis of voting.

Together, these might suggest a theory of voting. A theory includes not only a hypothesis, but a narrative that tells the causal story. In our voting theory, the causal story is that voting takes effort, and if the costs of that effort are raised by external events, such as a long distance between a voter and the voting location, then voting declines. But to that we can add the partisanship hypothesis that asserts that partisans are more willing to make an effort than nonpartisans.

Consider, in addition, the third variable that may matter to voters, the perceived distance between the policy positions of the candidates. The hypothesis here is: The greater the difference between the candidates, the greater the results will have on future government policy, and hence the greater the value to the voter of casting a ballot. This hypothesis might apply more to "top of the ballot" races than to those farther down the ballot (that would form a fourth hypothesis). That is, more to the race for president, or member of parliament, than to local mayor. Indeed, if that were shown to be true, that would also offer the narrative basis of our theory, the more the election matters to the voter, the more likely they are to vote.

There are a number of ways to present a hypothesis, all equivalent. We can use words, we can use a mathematical formula, or we can use a diagram. For now it is only important that at least one of these make sense to you. As you master the methods of political psychology, you will learn why these are all equivalent ways of saying the same thing.

The first hypothesis offered earlier can be stated as follows:

H_1: Partisans have a greater probability of voting than do nonpartisans.

The hypothesis can also be presented as a mathematical formula:

H_1: $V = f(P)$,

where V is voting (yes or no) and P is partisanship (voter identifies as a member of a party or does not). The f signifies some function whereby partisanship impels voting.

Or, in statistical terms, as:

H_1: $Y = a + bX + e$,

where Y is the dependent variable voting, a is some constant (i.e., a baseline level of voting when, here, the voting population is bereft of partisans), X is the independent variable partisanship, b is a coefficient that allows us to calculate how values of X inform values of Y. The letter b is a numerical value and we expect, here, given our hypothesis to take on a positive sign, but can take on negative sign. Finally, e, is an error term (reflecting that we are typically dealing with a sample of voters and hence are getting an approximation of the actual relationship that exists in the population and, as with any sample, the sample statistic might be higher or lower than the population parameter).

The hypothesis can also be presented as a diagram as seen in figure 1.1.

One advantage of this diagram, more precisely described as a *path model*, is that it makes the causal direction visibly explicit. I also added a sign, here a plus sign (+), to indicate that the stronger the partisanship the more likely a higher turnout of voters. If we obtained numerical values for a and b we could predict the voting turnout of a

Figure 1.1 Hypothesis 1-The more partisan the voter (the stronger their identification with their political party), the more likely they are to vote.

district relying on the proportion of the electorate in that district that is partisans. It is easy to modify a path model by including more properties (or variables) and also make explicit what measures we are using. As an exercise redraw the figure as a full path model for voting adding the two additional hypotheses (distance and perceived policy differences between candidates).

One useful way to read a research report, such as an article or book, is to diagram its theory as a path model. Then see if you can identify some plausible ways in which those models might be improved. For example, you might consider adding a new variable that the researcher(s) did not consider, or you might consider changing the *specification* of the model, that is, how the variables are related one to another, as in the following example.

Consider the following explanations, these from Sparky Anderson, the manager of the Detroit Tigers, after they had won the World Series in 1984:

> Sparky Anderson, asked by a sportscaster if it would be harder to win the World Series a second time: "Yes, because everybody is gunning for you."
>
> Sparky Anderson, asked by another sportscaster if would be easier to win the Series a second time: "Yes, because you know how to do it."
>
> —*Sports Illustrated*, March 18, 1985

The two quotes suggest two contradictory hypotheses but in fact they are not contradictory. If we translate these assertions into variables, we get three in all. The dependent variable is the probability of winning the World Series. Sparky Anderson then identifies two independent variables, the effort of competing teams and the knowledge of how to perform at the highest level of athletic competition. We can readily combine them into one path model as seen in figure 1.2.

In the path model in figure 1.2, there are three variables and two hypotheses, derived from Sparky Anderson's proclamations. And as you can see each and both can be true. Whether they help explain whether a team repeats as World Series champions will depend on gathering data on each of the three variables. You would need to have: measures of effort by the competing team; some measure, or measures, of knowledge of competing, for example, the proportion of the team that was on the previous winning team as against new members, whether rookies or members obtained by free agency or trade; and of course, the dependent variable, repeating as champion or not. This is an instance of a *multivariate* model, a model that has more than one independent variable.

We can write this path model as a statistical equation (perhaps getting our data from surveys of players on winning and competing teams from major league baseball):

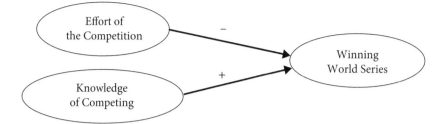

Figure 1.2 Path Model of the likely effect of wining World Series as a consequence of two independent variables

$$Y = a + b_1 X_1 + b_2 X_2 + e,$$

where X_1 is the variable effort of the competition, X_2 is the variable knowledge of how to compete, and b_1 and b_2 are their respective coefficients.

Can you think of other variables that might have an effect on winning? One might be the number of injuries. Can you think of others that might influence the likelihood of winning as repeat champions?

Let's now examine some other hypotheses drawn from common sayings. One familiar saying goes like this: "look before you leap." This suggests that we should consider all the aspects of a situation before we act. On the other hand, there is another familiar saying that goes: "He who hesitates is lost." This saying suggests the hypothesis that we should act instantly to get the best result. These seem to be in contradiction. How can they both be true? Yet we often act as if they are true, generally by raising these explanations in a post hoc, after the fact, fashion. So that we may apply these rationales only to the circumstances in which they seem most suited, thereby avoiding cases in which they seem to offer ill-advised guidance. Actually, even though the two seem to propose two mutually exclusive hypotheses—one or the other is true but not both— there is a multivariate model that can accommodate both: an *interaction* model.

The key to an interaction model is that some variable acts to modify the way in which two other variables relate to each other. Consider the two clichés, taking your time or acting swiftly. Maybe each is an appropriate strategy but only in specific conditions. Treating those conditions as a variable would give us an interaction effect. Athletes diligently train so that in competition they can act swiftly and in such instances, thinking is most likely to distract, slow the performance, in other words, degrade the quality of performance. On the other hand, when something unusual happens, our learned habits, our "gut instincts" may not be the best guide given the novelty of the situation, better to observe, learn, and ponder the alternatives before acting. Therefore, the nature of the circumstances, whether novel or familiar, may condition the relationship between our independent variable, how long to take in preparing to act: acting swiftly or taking a long time to consider all the options. There are a number of ways of diagraming such a model, figure 1.3 is just one variant.

Let's assign each variable to range from 0 to 1 (when the situation is familiar, novelty takes on the value of 0 and when it's unusual, a value of 1; and the same for time and quality of results). So, when the situation is familiar, X_2 (novelty) is 0 and the multiplication of X_1 by X_2 produces a value of 0 (as 0 multiplied by anything is also 0). Hence,

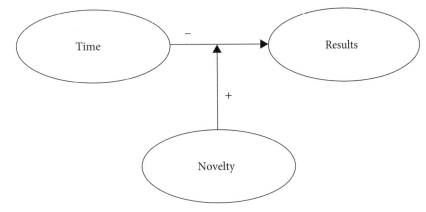

Or, where Y = Quality of Results; X_1 = Time before Acting; and, X_2 = Novelty of Circumstance. Then:

$$Y \text{ (quality of result)} = X_1 + X_1 * X_2$$

Figure 1.3 Interaction Path Model: Time, Quality of Result, and Familiarity

in familiar circumstances, novelty has no effect and the less time we take to make a decision the better will the results be (see the negative value on the causal link from time to results). But when novelty is high, it impacts on that relationship. A positive value for novelty multiplied by a positive value for time produces a positive number, so when we are in familiar situations we should act without thinking, but when we are in a novel situation, the greater the novelty the greater the amount of time we should take to consider our options before deciding. The theory here is that we should act swiftly in familiar situations (when our habits benefit us), but we should take time to think before acting when we are in unfamiliar terrain.

BOX 1.12 **Mediating variables**

This is one more basic relationship that frequently arises in political psychological theories. An independent variable has no *direct* effect on the dependent variable, but it impacts on some intervening variable that in turn does directly affect the dependent variable.

The model of political tolerance developed by Sullivan, Piereson, and Marcus (1982) includes a good example: Education does not have a direct effect on the level of political tolerance, but it does have a direct effect on support for norms of democracy, which in turn has a direct effect

on Political Tolerance. It is the variable, support for norms of democracy that acts as a mediating variable—sitting between education and political tolerance.

Can you diagram these relationships? Try. What such a model says is that education, while not directly encouraging political tolerance, can encourage a better understanding of the norms, that is, the rules, of democracy. But it is understanding and supporting those rules that encourages political tolerance, not education in and of itself.

One of the benefits of science is that scientific scholars are eager to rigorously test explanations because science has an empirical focus. We derive our concepts from some taxonomy that identifies which properties, among the many possible, we should consider to formulate as part of a theory. Now, after we identify a property we also have to decide how to *operationalize* the property or variable. And, a rigorous test of any theory should consider how well our choice of measures work, indeed whether they work at all.

In a research project on political tolerance my colleagues, John Sullivan and Jim Piereson, and I theorized that the variable Threat—it is common practice to capitalize the names of properties to identify them as latent concepts—would have a negative impact on the variable Political Tolerance. The hypothesis is: the *greater* the threat, the *less* politically tolerant, a negative relationship. As an exercise, take a moment and try to convert that semantic formulation of the hypothesis, its statistical form, and its graphic form as a path model.

When we then turned to test that hypothesis with a national survey of American adults, we had to develop measures of Threat. Variables are normally written as lower case to visually identify them as empirical measures. Being tolerant means extending support for political rights to those who we despise. Supporting political rights for ourselves and our friends is natural but not aptly described as tolerance. So, how did we attempt to ascertain whether Threat plays the role our hypothesis anticipates?

Briefly, we asked people to rate the group that they most disliked on several rating scales. Among these were such ratings as how *powerful* they rated that group, how *distrustful* they rated the group, and so on. We had a total of eight questions in all. Each of these ratings was a measure of threat, or so we expected. Our analyses of the data showed us that two of the measures of threat formed one set of measures that assessed how strong people perceived the group. The other six, also grouped together in a different set. These assessed how much people perceived the group as violating societal norms (e.g., as being violent or untrustworthy).

We can also use a path model approach to diagram the relationship between concepts and their measures. Social scientists use ovals to indicate latent concepts and squares to indicate manifest measures (here the eight ratings). Notice that the arrows go from the concept to each measure in as much as we assume changes in the level of the concept, which we cannot directly observe, will be reflected in changes in values of the measure, which we can observe. If we were correct in our expectations we would have found one concept (and oval) fed by eight boxes, our eight ratings. But that's not what we found. Figure 1.4 shows what we found.

The eight measures form two concepts of Threat. Threat A finds that two ratings measures how strong people perceive the group. The set of six measures measure a second concept of Threat B, which measures how much the group is violating accepted norms of behavior. This distinction was unexpected. We had expected the eight indicators to be equally good measures of one concept, Threat. Instead this finding led us to revise our understanding of Threat, rather than a singular concept we now understand it as two different concepts; so different that we found that the two concepts are not correlated at all. People assess whether groups are complying with social norms and people also judge whether groups are powerful but these two assessments are completely unrelated one to the other. And, when we analyzed the data we found that how strongly

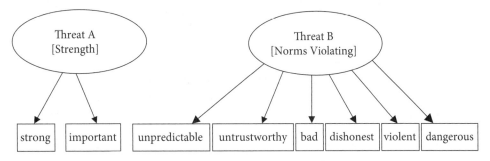

Figure 1.4 Measurement model of Threat

people judged their disliked group had no impact on whether they would support the rights of that group to practice their rights: None at all. For another exercise, can you diagram the path model that depicts that result?

On the other hand, it was the second concept of threat, malevolence, that proved to be the single most important independent variable in explaining when people would be politically tolerant. Our results told us that it is a mistake to formulate a global claim about Threat. Rather, we have to be mindful of the different kinds of perceptions about groups that people can make. We found that people do perceive how much power groups have and they perceive how much malevolence they sense from the groups. But, the former proved to be of no benefit in explaining why people were political tolerant, itself an important finding. It was only the latter, perceptions of malevolence that has a very powerful impact, explaining the variance we observed between those who are more tolerant and those who are less tolerant. You might consider expanding this point to other forms of politics. Where else might how people are acting matter more than how much power they have?

One of the pleasures of doing research is that it can surprise you (and others) by challenging conventional wisdom. If all political psychology did was confirm what we already know then it would not be worth the effort that doing research requires.

IV. PLAN OF THE BOOK

The book has a plan. The two core ideas are as follows.

First, political philosophers have been examining the issues of self- and collective governance, psychology and politics, for thousands of years. At their best, they give clarity to to the many conflicting ideas that are worth exploring with systematic scientific research.

Second, the discipline of political psychology is changing. This text focuses on where the discipline is going more than on where it has been. The neurosciences enable us to re-examine many of the key concepts. The personality of leaders and citizens that previously was guided by psychoanalysis is now being reconsidered by those guided by the new research on DNA, genetics, and the neural structures of the human brain. The same can be said for just about every topic in political psychology.

Third, this book is designed to help you learn by doing. To help you master the analytic skills I have added some exercises so that you can practice doing political psychology. Reading can convey information, but using tools, intellectual as well as physical, requires practice. The exercises are meant to give you some experience in doing so that you learn political psychology as an activity.

Section I, the "Introduction," begins with this chapter. Three more chapters follow. The next chapter is an important one, "A Brief Methodology Primer for Political Psychologists." If you have already had an introduction to the methodologies of the social sciences you might briefly review this chapter. However, if you have not covered the topic before, it is important to get a basic grounding in what it means to have data, to evaluate variables, and to engage in empirical analysis. Chapter 3 offers a history of the long concern with human nature and politics. Political psychology as a discipline is very young only three decades or so as of this writing. But the core concerns dates to the emergence of civilization in the human species. The final chapter of this section, introduces not the old, the long tradition, but the newest, neuroscience. This juxtaposition is intentional. Neuroscience, in my view, offers a new perspective as well as new tools that can reinvigorate old questions and old debates. In this chapter, I attempt to show why.

Section II, "Political Psychology," also offers four chapters. In chapter 5, I use the orientation of chapter 4 to show how new investigations of the brain from neuroscience, have led to new understandings of the brain and consciousness. Chapter 6 takes up the task of how the new and established both work to combine to explain human action. In both of these chapters I also show how our understanding of politics is enhanced by this new array of knowledge, methods, and theories. Chapter 7 continues with the contribution of "personality" or temperament as it has been understood over various permutations, and as its value to explaining politics. Chapter 8 integrates all these various orientations and addresses the particular challenge of understanding democratic politics.

Section III, "Political Social Psychology" has but two chapters. Chapter 9 expands our focus from the purely psychological (how our individual features explain our actions), to add a more expansive focus, that of social psychology (and also of sociology), how the context in which we find ourselves impinges on our actions. This should be understood to mean that context can both limit and empower. Both are considered in this chapter. Finally, in chapter 10, some final summary reflections on political psychology and politics, and then I let you go to do political psychology on your own.

EXERCISES

In this chapter I offer exercises that your instructor might ask you to undertake. In the chapters that follow, the exercises at the end are designed for you.

Exercise 1: Select two or three of the major theorists (e.g., Aristotle, Plato, and Hobbes, or Locke, Rousseau, and Madison's Federalist Paper No. 10), assign segments of their readings, and form the class into groups of two to four students and have each group prepare a summary of the major psychological claims each theorist advances and the political implications that follow from that (this means that each group should speak to how that view of human nature leads to a conclusion about what political regime is best).

Exercise 2: Individually, or in groups of two to three, have students take an article (the journal *Political Psychology* is a good source) and re-present its core theoretical argument with each of the three forms (sentence, formula, graph). If time is available, present in class with queries and critiques.

Exercise 3: (follow up)... Propose an extension of the research explored in exercise 2—add a variable that might add or modify the results, or change the expected relationships (maybe by adding an interaction term), applied to a different cultural setting or a different domain—reformulate the theory consistent with the new changes.

REFERENCES

Anonymous. 1854. *The Rappers, Or, the Mysteries, Fallacies, and Absurdities of Spirit-Rapping, Table-Tipping, and Entrancement.* Translated by W. Rhys Roberts. New York: H. Long & Brother.

Aristotle. 1983. *The Politics.* New York: Penguin Books.

Bowlby, John. 1973. "Affectional Bonds: Their Nature and Origin." In *Loneliness: The Experience of Emotional and Social Isolation,* edited by R. S. Weiss. Cambridge, MA: MIT Press.

Cacioppo, John T., and William Patrick. 2008. *Loneliness. Human Nature and the Need for Social Connection.* New York: Norton.

Campbell, Donald Thomas, Marilynn B. Brewer, and Barry E. Collins. 1981. *Scientific Inquiry and the Social Sciences.* San Francisco: Jossey-Bass.

de Tocqueville, Alexis. 2000. *Democracy in America.* Translated, Edited, and With an Introduction by Harvey C. Mansfield and Delba Winthrop. Chicago: University of Chicago Press.

de Waal, Frans. 1996. *Good Nature: The Origins of Right and Wrong in Humans and Other Animals.* Cambridge, MA: Harvard University Press.

———. 2007. *Chimpanzee Politics: Power and Sex among Apes.* Baltimore, MD: Johns Hopkins University Press.

Durkheim, Emile. 1951. *Suicide, a Study in Sociology.* Glencoe, Ill.: Free Press.

George, Alexander L., and Juliette L. George. 1998. *Presidential Personality and Performance.* Boulder, Colo.: Westview Press.

Gould, Roger V. 2003. *Collision of Wills: How Ambiguity about Social Rank Breeds Conflict.* Chicago: University of Chicago Press.

Herodotus. 2005. *The Histories.* New York, NY: Barnes & Noble Classics.

Hobbes, Thomas. 1968. *Leviathan.* London: Penguin Books.

Hume, David. 1984. *A Treatise of Human Nature.* London: Penguin Books.

Kuklinski, James H. 2002. *Thinking About Political Psychology.* Cambridge: Cambridge University Press.

Lasswell, Harold D. 1948. *Power and Personality.* New York: Norton.

Locke, John. 1975. *An Essay Concerning Human Understanding.* Oxford: Clarendon Press.

———. 1993. *Two Treatises of Government.* London: Everyman.

Machiavelli, Niccolo. 2005. *The Prince.* Translated by Peter Bondanella. New York: Oxford University Press.

Madison, James, Alexander Hamilton, and John Jay. 1961. *The Federalist Papers.* Cleveland, OH: World Publishing.

Marx, Karl, and Friedrich Engels. 2002. *The Communist Manifesto.* New York: Penguin Classics.

Mendel, Gregor, and Ronald Aylmer Fisher. 1965. *Experiments in Plant Hybridisation.* Edinburgh: Oliver & Boyd.

Monroe, Kristen R. 2002. *Political Psychology.* Mahwah, NJ: Erlbaum.

Montesquieu, Charles de Secondat. 1989. *The Spirit of Laws*. Translated by Anne M. Cohler, Basia Carolyn Miller, and Harold Samuel Stone. Cambridge, UK: Cambridge University Press.

Njál's Saga. 1960. Translated by Pálsson Hermann. Baltimore: Penguin Books.

Plato. 1974. *The Republic*. New York: Penguin.

Pratto, Felicia, Jim Sidanius, Lisa M. Stallworth, and Bertram F. Malle. 1994. "Social Dominance Orientation: A Personality Variable Predicting Social and Political Attitudes." *Journal of Personality and Social Psychology* 67:741–63.

Rousseau, Jean-Jacques. 1983. *On the Social Contract*. Translated by Donald A. Cress. Indianapolis: Hackett.

Smith, Adam. 1959. *The Theory of Moral Sentiments*. Indianapolis, Indiana: Liberty Fund.

———. 1986. *The Wealth of Nations*. New York: Viking.

Sullivan, John L., James Piereson, and George E. Marcus. 1982. *Political Tolerance and American Democracy*. Chicago: University of Chicago Press.

Thucydides. 1996. *The Landmark Thucydides: A Comprehensive Guide to the Peloponnesian War*. Tranlated by Robert Crawley. New York: Free Press.

Wittgenstein, Ludwig, G. E. M. Anscombe, and G. H. von Wright. 1969. *On Certainty*. New York: Harper.

CHAPTER 2

A Brief Methodology Primer
for Political Psychologists

If you have already been through a methodology course in psychology, political science, or another social science, the material in this chapter should be familiar. Nonetheless, a brief review might be in order. For those who have not yet been introduced to how social science observes the world, formulates theories, and then generates evidence to assess those theories, this chapter provides a basic foundation. The chapter contains five sections. The first briefly examines explanation as it often is used in daily life and examines how it differs from explanation in science. The second covers the role of imagination in the social sciences. How do political psychologists germinate ideas and translate them into testable theories? The third section covers what it means to test a theory in political psychology. If we are going to test theories, what do "data" and "observations" mean, and how do we obtain them? In the fourth section, I consider a critical topic, often ignored, measurement theory. Names are assigned to observations by researchers. We say we are obtaining measures of, for instance, "authoritarianism," but how secure are we asserting that our variable, authoritarianism, is being measured? That assessment falls within what is called measurement theory. Finally, in section 5, once we have hypotheses to test, data to test them, and have confirmed that our concepts, variables, are both *valid* and *reliable* (more on what those two words mean in section 3)—once we have a theory and some observations, observations that we have confidence measure our key variables—we want to know whether our theory's linkages, the causal connections we hypothesized actually hold. How do political psychologists do that? That is our last topic: data analysis.

I. EXPLANATIONS AS PERSUASION OR JUSTIFICATION AND EXPLANATION AS KNOWLEDGE

We use many explanations in our daily lives. We also rely on others to explain matters to us. Among those we turn to may be political leaders, doctors, religious leaders, and teachers. We also often rely on a family member or a good friend to help us understand. Those we entrust to guide us often draw on traditions, folk sayings, conventional wisdom, their life experience, or some body of knowledge they have mastered. We rely on them for their experience, wisdom, expertise, or just reassurance.

We often rely on *analogy* and *metaphor* to persuade us of the rightness of our beliefs. Analogy is a form of argument. Analogy relies on some asserted equivalence between one thing and another thing. Analogies, when used to explain, work by making the claim that what happened in the past will duplicate in the present (or near future). Analogies assert a prediction about some current or anticipated event based on the presumption that what happened in the past will repeat itself because of proclaimed equivalence.

For example, in the period September 2002 to October 2002 when the Republican administration was preparing the American public for the coming military invasion of Iraq, members of the administration drew an analogy between the past, specifically Hitler's aggressive preparation for war in the mid-1930s and Saddam Hussein's supposed pursuit of nuclear weapons and other weapons of mass destruction to justify their proposed course of action. The full analogy went as such: When an aggressive dictator is bent on expansive war it is better to step in early than await a later and more calamitous situation. This is not to claim that the administration was suggesting that Iraq was bent on starting a world war or that Iraq posed as much of a military threat to the world as did Germany in the late '30s, rather it was a calibrated analogy, Saddam as a "smaller" Hitler as it were.

Of course, this was met by an alternative analogy presented by the opponents of the administration's policy. They drew on the Vietnam War, arguing that Iraq would be a quagmire, that is, a war in Iraq, as with Vietnam as its predecessor, would prove to be a long drawn out war of great cost with little promise of a good outcome. As a result the American public was presented with dueling analogies, Iraq is like Vietnam in the 1960s–1970s, or Iraq is like Hitler's Germany in the 1930s.

Historical analogies are used a lot in politics. You should be able to come up with quite a lot of examples.

There are two major problems with analogies as evidence, as a way of sustaining an explanation. Analogies offer an attractive cause and effect story. But suggesting a causal story is not the same as providing a rigorous basis that sustain the causal claim.

The first problem is that an analogy is useless if the audience is not knowledgeable about either the prior event or the current event. The audience must be more than

---

BOX 2.1   Two examples of analogies

In the United States, politicians often use historical analogies. Those that identify one's partisan opponents with a favored course of action are very popular. Republicans often celebrate the tax cuts introduced by President John F. Kennedy to justify their support for ever more tax cuts. Democrats often celebrate the tax increases supported President Ronald Reagan to argue the necessity of tax increases. In each instance advocates proclaim the certainty of good results. Each believes repetition of the policy they proclaim will "obviously" be just as efficacious as the earlier experience.

familiar with both; they must also accept each event as important and pregnant with meaning. For example, one of the challenges of establishing a new and stable regime is putting into place a system of justice that commands the respect of all segments of a society. There are many historical instances of new regimes, some that have succeeded in creating a new and legitimate regime, for example, Japan after World War II. But there are others that have failed. For example, many of the newly independent African nations at the end of the colonial period, while beginning as democracies they quickly turned into authoritarian dictatorships that exploited the people and the land for the profit of the ruling groups.

It is often the case that many individuals do not have the historical knowledge of the specific example for a reference to that specific instance to be all that useful. The power of an analogy comes from a thick understanding of the established event that is familiar to and widely shared by the intended audience. For example, the power of the Great Depression during the 1930s as an analogy is of less and less usefulness as most of the world's population is now too young to know it from direct experience and few have studied the period.

The same problem exists when using metaphor. Restricting the choice of metaphorical and analogical stories to the familiar is of course a critical requirement if they are going to be successful, which is especially important for politicians and campaign strategists.

The second problem with analogy is which of many instances does one choose? The most likely choice is the one that "proves" the case you already endorsed, as in the prowar argument that invading Iraq will be like the "good" war, World War II, and in the antiwar argument that invading Iraq will be like the "bad" war, Vietnam. This naturally leads to selection bias. That is, we choose the analogy based on whether we think we can persuade the audience of our desired political course of action. This is a normal part of the political process. The task of the politician is not to be fair but to be persuasive. As such, relying on analogy is not a strategy for generating knowledge. The use of analogy and metaphor puts aside the problem of knowledge, how do we know something, for a quite different problem, how can we persuade?

Another option is to turn to an expert, to entrust someone else to make a decision for us, on our behalf. We can turn to a general, hopefully one who is competent (not all have proven to be so), for knowledge about how to win a war. Or, in the case of negotiations, we could turn to a diplomat on how to best to achieve favorable results, or if

---

BOX 2.2 Two examples of analogies

METAPHOR

In the case of an analogy the assertion is that two things are alike (event A = event B). In the case of metaphor, two *different* things are matched to show some shared quality. For example, James Madison often used metaphors, as in this example from Federalist Paper No. 10: "Liberty is to faction what air is to fire, an aliment without which it instantly expires." Here he drew a parallel between natural phenomena, air and fire, and human affairs to persuade you, the reader, that faction, people engaged in collective action, are equally natural phenomenon. So, the metaphor asserts that just as we cannot eliminate fire without eliminating air, we cannot eliminate faction without eliminating liberty.

ill, to a medical expert. But in political psychology we accept two burdens. First, we do the work of generating our own explanations. And, second, we subject explanations to empirical testing for corroboration. Let's begin with the first. I turn to the second in the section that follows.

II. GENERATING EXPLANATIONS: THEORIZING

One way to begin theorizing is by direct observation. You see something, its puzzling. You ask: "why is that?"

The query invites the possibility that things could be otherwise. And, having entertained that possibility, you have made the important initial step in theorizing. You have converted your observation into a *variable*. And, by asking "why is it like this" you are searching for a cause. If there is no conception of change, then things cannot be otherwise, and we have no need for explanation. For things that do not and cannot be changed, we need no explanation. The capacity for puzzlement is the first skill to indulge. It is an example of our capacity for imagination. As Thomas Hobbes (1968) reminded us, it is a faculty we each have in some measure, and a skill you can and should practice.

Different historic periods and different places can make asking such questions more or less likely. For example, in the United States, in the 1960s as the Vietnam War became more visible and more worrisome to the public even as some of the supporters of the war proclaimed seeing "light at the end of the tunnel" the question of when war succeeds or fails became more salient. At that same time, social conventions dealing with gender, race, and sexual practices all became subject to rapid change such that many found it natural to ask what was happening and why. Turbulent times invite inquiry. More complacent times, times of peace and stable economic growth, offer less incentive for inquiry as people experience good circumstances as normal and nonperplexing.

In doing political psychology, having an inquiring mind and taking a somewhat alienated stance when confronting the world you inhabit is an advantage for it invites

BOX 2.4   **Being prepared**

You can never know when you might be reading something or seeing something that perks your interest, that prompts theorizing. I always carry with me some sticky notes so that I have something to write on, so that I

can capture the thought or observation. A smart cellphone adds the ability to take pictures and type notes. Developing this habit of noticing and recording is one means of sharpening your talent for asking *why?*

you to ask: why? And, that query invites a search for possible causes. Seeing a lot, reading a lot, allowing yourself to be puzzled, asking how "this" might be otherwise is a vital skill you need to develop.

Whether the thing that puzzles is something you see before you or perhaps something you have just read or just seen on a news broadcast, if you turn that sense of puzzlement into a general problem, then you have begun to theorize. In general, I mean the following: You notice some phenomenon. You turn it into a variable. By doing so you treat that observation as an instance of a universal phenomenon (i.e., one not tied to a specific historic place or time). This is the key central step in scientific thinking. You will not likely experience all moments in your life as variables. There are many occasions when we experience the world and ourselves in a natural and spontaneous way. But, when you consider events and circumstances as a stranger might, you are taking the opportunity to theorize.

There is another way to go about the task of theorizing. There are two reasons you should become familiar with published and unpublished literature on the topics in political psychology that interest you. I touch on some of the more important topics in the chapters that follow. Readings will be assigned that expand on the range of topics. The first reason to read widely in the political psychology literature is to see where the field has been and where it is going. Has anyone explored a specific concept that has caught your interest? If so, what have they come up with as a theory? Are there competing theories? And, is there a body of published research findings? You might find that your interest has already been thoroughly explored. Even so, you should ask: Was it rigorously tested and to your satisfaction? If not, what problems do you see? If not, then you have identified a gap in the literature and who better to fill that gap than you? You can design a research project that has the promise of rectifying the problems you've identified.

How can you find what others have done? For published research there are a number of sources that are ready at hand and easy to use. First, similar to other social science disciplines, political psychology has a number of publication outlets. Periodically handbooks of political psychology are published. The editors of these handbooks generally invite senior scholars to write chapters that will review many, if not all, of the major domains of research in political psychology. In addition to the most recent handbooks, it is worth reading the earlier volumes. Doing so enables you to track which topics are moving up in importance and which have declined; inviting speculation as to why.

In addition, some journals publish review papers, in which authors are asked to write a summary overview of the theories and research findings on a topic. Another useful strategy is to find the most recent article on a topic that has engaged you and then search the articles cited in that article's bibliography. This strategy helps identify which older articles and books still shape the field and which scholars are the main actors. There are a number of useful Internet sources. Google Scholar[1], particularly if you select advanced scholar search option, offers a powerful tool. It enables you to find articles and authors that are likely to be very helpful in giving you a beginning bibliography.

---

1. Google Scholar can be accessed at http://scholar.google.com.

BOX 2.5   Search strategies

I already mentioned one strategy: Search for the most recent article on a topic and then use that article's bibliography to widen your search and identify what that author thinks are the most important and relevant publications. Another strategy is to try to identify the leading scholars and then find other articles or books they have published. For example, Jim Sidanius on the topic of social dominance orientation or Martha Crenshaw on the topic of terrorism.

Most academic and public libraries have a variety of search engines that enable you to find articles based on either topic or author. Some search engines are offered by a publisher that enable you to search their journals. Other search engines aggregate across a discipline, for example, in political science, JSTOR, and in psychology, PsychArticles and PsychInfo.

However, to get the latest work you should also look for as yet unpublished papers. Political psychologists, as do most scientists, present their work at conferences. These papers will often be work in progress, early results of projects in their infancy. And, many of the conferences run by social science organizations put their conference papers online for anyone to download.

For example, the International Society of Political Psychology (ISSP) hosts an annual scientific meeting. The conference runs for four days and consists of panels, roundtables, plenary sessions, and poster sessions. Participants are graduate students, junior and senior scholars from many nations, as well as nonacademics who hold a variety of positions in foundations, nongovernmental organizations (NGOs), and governments. Presenters come from a number of social science disciplines (mainly social psychology and political science but other fields are also represented). And many, if not all, of the papers and the conference program for prior years are posted on the Society's website where you can search by topic, author, or both: check out ISPP.org (note: there is no www as part of the web address).

All of the social science disciplines have organizations, such as ISPP, that maintain websites giving you access to the latest work in the field. Although most of the conference papers will not be published, those that are published will not appear in print for about one or two years. Conference papers are often revised many times before submission to journals. And, the review process can take up to a year and more to complete. By getting access to conference papers you get access to the most recent work.

When you read, what should you be trying to accomplish?

- Identify the variables (independent and dependent). Then ask: do different scholars use the same concepts? Do they argue about the proper definition of a key concept? Do they use different concepts?
- Identify the theory specification. What are the effects between independent and dependent variables, direct or indirect, linear or nonlinear, or interactive?
- Identify how concepts are operationalized. How are these concepts defined and how are they measured? Do different programs of research use the same measurement or different measurements?

- Identify how the data was collected (e.g., by experimental design, by survey research, by archival sources, etc.). If there were different methods used, did they produce the same or different results?
- And, then having mapped out the theory, the research design, and weighed them against the research findings, see if you can judge where there might be vulnerabilities in the research. Consider whether you can think of new theoretical interpretations of the findings.

There is another source and method for helping you theorize. If you immerse yourself in the classic literature, including some of those listed on page 11 of chapter 1, and practice close reading you will find them replete with ideas that are worth exploring. Let me give you an example, this from the Preamble to the United States Constitution.

> We the People of the United States, in Order to form a more perfect Union, establish Justice, insure domestic Tranquility, provide for the common defence, promote the general Welfare, and secure the Blessings of Liberty to ourselves and our Posterity, do ordain and establish this Constitution for the United States of America.

What would a close reading of this passage suggest? First, and most obvious, that this Constitution is expected to help ensure that the United States will become "a more perfect Union" and that it will "secure the blessing of Liberty to ourselves and our Posterity." But we can see that the quote offers a good deal more. The preamble lists what will be improved, what makes a more perfect union. Following the stated goal, that is, a more perfect union, is a list:

- establish justice,
- ensure domestic tranquility,
- provide for the common defense,
- promote the general welfare.

Whenever you come across a list you should ask yourself what type of list is it. Is it random? Does it have chronological ordering (oldest to youngest, youngest to oldest)? Is it a listing in terms of importance (most to least, or the reverse)? This particular list is none of these. This list is an argument. It is argument of how to achieve "the blessing of Liberty to ourselves and our Posterity."

This list is actually is a *causal* argument about the sequence of what has to be done. First, establish justice, for if you don't, you cannot achieve domestic tranquility. And, if you hope to provide for the common defense against some foreign enemy, you had better have the support of the entire populace, for divided we will fall, and to have that support you had best have a regime that has established justice, for those who might think it does not may be unwilling to fight to protect the regime, indeed they might even be willing to go over to the other side.

Finally, if the regime has established justice, has achieved domestic tranquility, and can protect against foreign invasion, only then can it take effective actions to promote the general welfare (e.g., provide roads, schools, build canals, other actions that will better enable people to achieve their aspirations). The authors of the United States Constitution offer in the preamble a theory, a causal story, a series of causal arguments that can be tested by observing new regimes, see if they followed this recommended

Figure 2.1 Political Development as Envisioned in the Preamble to the US Constitution

course of actions, measure whether the stages were undertaken in the recommended order, and if so, with what success. The theory of development can be diagramed as a causal or path model. Figure 2.1 shows what that might look like. As depicted in figure 2.1 is the specific claim that a more perfect union requires each of these actions to be secured and in this specific order: first establish justice and so on. Failure to execute these steps in the proper sequence and succeed at each step and the nation building effort will stagnate or fail.

In sum, when you come across lists read them as theoretical arguments (often implicit, but nonetheless readily decoded).

Then, turn those arguments into testable theories.

III. GETTING OBSERVATIONS: DATA, SAMPLING, AND GENERALIZATION

Let's consider what happens after we have produced a theory, a *general* assertion that this variable when it varies, *causes* some other variable to vary as well. Let's begin with the simplest form of a theory, a proposed *independent* variable, the cause, and a *dependent* variable, which we believe changes as consequence, an effect. Then what? What does it mean to say we are going to "test" this theory with data?

Let's return to my earlier proposed theory about voting: partisanship, those who are more partisan in their self-identification, which cause people to turn up and vote at polling locations more so that those who are nonpartisan. As formulated, this hypothesis suggests that it should be a general explanation, as should all political psychology theories. If proved to be a valid theory, it should apply to voters in any nation. It should apply to any people, no matter their language or their culture. It should apply to any voting based political system that requires voters go somewhere to vote. The hypothesis should apply when voting systems require only that people vote via the Internet, as some voting systems allow, or to voting systems that rely on the mail to submit a ballot. But, it would not be applicable when a brutal regime uses violence and intimidation to

---

BOX 2.6 Exercise

Take the hypotheses in figure 2.1 and see if they explain when and why nation building programs succeed or fail (e.g., applicable to Spain after the death of Franco, Yugoslavia after the death of Tito, Iraq after the 2002 invasion, or Afghanistan after the fall of the Taliban). Craft the hypotheses and then conduct research on nation building to test them. Can a nation be developed by focusing on providing for the common defense but not establishing justice?

force its subject population to show up and cast a public ballot. Given that important qualification, we have a theory to test, but with what empirical data?

To a candidate running in a particular district for a particular office, or a campaign strategist whose job it is to win in this district, the choice of observations is clear. Voters in elections in that specific district will do just fine; indeed voters elsewhere are of little interest. But for political psychologists who want to test whether this hypothesis is sustained by empirical data, the choice of observations is more problematic. We are not interested in local validity that the pattern holds here and now. We want to know whether it holds here and now, to be sure, but also anywhere else and whether it will hold in the future. We cannot study all voters in every electoral system past, present, and of course, those voting in the future. But to test this hypothesis we do need some data, some observations, and we need to have a sample. And, it would be best if we have a *sample* of voters who are representative of the *population* of all voters.

Surveys—Samples from a Population of Interest

It is useful to point out that sometimes we want to obtain data from everyone. And, with enough resources, we can. A *census* is a complete enumeration of each and every member of a population. For example, to determine how many members of Congress each state shall be allocated, the United States Constitution, article 1, section 1, clause 3 provided for a census:

> Enumeration shall be made within three years after the first meeting of the Congress of the United States, and within every subsequent ten years. …

However, censuses are very expensive and given that we are often interested in diverse populations it is not possible to collect voters in this and that nation, in this and that cultural tradition, and so on. As a result most political psychologists use means other than a census to generate empirical observations. We are far more likely to opt for a survey rather than a census. A survey relies on a *sample*, a selected number of cases from the population of interest. The benefits of using a sample of observations are twofold. First, using a sample helps us reduce costs, and second, using a sample of observations, if done properly, enables us to make an inference that what we observe in the sample is comparable to what we would find if had obtained a full census of the population. We use some observations, the sample, to make an inference about the entire population of observations.

BOX 2.7 Nonrandom samples

ABC's show Nightline introduced call-in polls. The host of the show poises a question on a topic and invites viewers to call a number to express their view with the show updating the tally during the course of the evening. This has proved a popular way of generating "news" but it is a terrible way to "sample" opinions.

Calling in by a phone, the Internet, or text message takes time, effort, interest, and money. These resources are not distributed equally through a population. Those who opt to respond are clearly going to be systematically different from those who do not. Some who do not call in may not have a phone, or may not have a phone handy, or just aren't very interested in the topic. These are just a few of many other differences between those who call in and those who do not.

There are rules that scientists use to select a sample from a population. The rules enable researchers to make rather careful statements about sample data. What we want to know, whether as citizens getting some evidence on a matter of interest, or a scholar reading a published paper, is whether the results obtained from that sample are what we would find if we had gone to the expense and trouble of obtaining a complete census. There are several rules we must follow in compiling samples, but the one that is most commonly applied in what is known as a simple random sample.

A simple random sample must meet two conditions.

First, in a simple random sample, each element in the population of scores has an equal chance of being selected for the sample. This condition is most easily met if there is a list of everyone in the population. We can assign a number to each element, in our example, to each eligible voter, and then select voters to participate in our study, in our sample, by using a random procedure, such as selecting the numbers from a table of random numbers.

A second condition that must also be met is that every possible combination of elements from the population must have an equal chance of selection. One typical procedure in sampling is to interview only one person from any selected address or at a given telephone number if, as often the case with fixed telephone lines, even when a number of people share use of that line. If the rule is that only one individual is selected from a particular household, all other members of the household are eliminated from consideration. The result is not a random sample. This might happen if the researcher is worried that the answers given by one member of the household might somehow influence those given by other members. If three individuals—Mary, Susan, and Thomas—live in a particular apartment, and we call and Mary answers and thus falls into our sample, then Susan and Thomas are eliminated for fear that their answers will not be independent of those given by Mary. Then Mary and Susan, or Mary and Thomas, have a zero probability of being selected together, whereas Mary and any other member of the population have at least some (nonzero) chance of being selected together for the sample. For a sample to be considered a random sample, then, both of these conditions—equal probability of selection and equal probability of all combination of elements being selected—must be met.

A random sample, a sample that meets these two conditions, can be an *un*representative sample. This means that the data we obtain from any particular sample drawn at random from a population can be wildly different from what we would obtain if we collected all the data describing that population. Just by chance, when random selection procedures are being used, a very atypical group of respondents could fall into the sample.[2] This does not happen very often, but it will happen. Random selection produces samples that are unbiased estimates of the population from which they are drawn but being unbiased does not mean that they do not produce error. They do produce error, but the amount of error is predictable and it is also random. The science of statistical inference allows us to calculate precisely how much risk we take in making an inference

---

2. With the growing popularity of public opinion polls there will often be a number of available polls on a policy issue or on an upcoming election. When multiple polls, each independently conducted, are available, they will often produce a range of results. When there are a lot of polls on a common topic, all within a narrow date range, all measuring the public's opinion on an issue or their vote preference, then the average of those polls, if they are properly done, will likely be a better estimate of the population than any one poll.

that what we find in the sample will be close to what we would find if we had obtained data from the full population.

There are two common ways that surveys have been used to good effect. In a *cross-section* survey the attempt is to collect a representative snapshot describing the population on the variables of interest at one time. This is useful when time is not a crucial part of the theory. However, when time is important, for example, if we are interested in how long a relationship lasts, or how much time degrades the effect of some stimulus, then we are likely to use a panel survey. In a panel survey, two or more surveys are conducted, re-interviewing people at some specified interval, perhaps days, weeks, months, or even generations. Panel designs are very useful if we want to learn how people's political beliefs change as they mature (Jennings and Niemi 1981).

If we rely on nonrandom samples we will get unrepresentative samples. The problem here is that there is no way to determine how severe the problem is in any given instance. It may happen every time or it may only happen seldom. The advantage of random sampling is not that it *guarantees* a representative sample or even an accurate estimate of a particular population. Rather, random sampling makes it is possible to determine how often, in the long run, very unrepresentative outcomes will occur. In sum: When we are describing what we find in a universe of scores, as from a census, the term used to describe what we find is parameter. The *parameter* describes the population value, say the average age. When we are describing a sample the term used is *statistic*. The statistic describes the sample, say its average age, but we are really not interested in the sample statistic except as it describes the population from which the sample was drawn. That requires us to take some risk that this sample is but a poor approximation of the population parameters. Sampling theory allows this. If we use random sampling we can state the risk. All samples have some measurable level of risk, called sampling error. But, because getting a complete census is both expensive and very time consuming, we rely on statistics for almost all of our theory testing.

It is beyond the scope of this book to explain how and why random samples work, and how to use them, that is, how to calculate how close they come to approximating the population. There are many fine books that cover the topic. Moreover, surveys are merely one way that political psychologists collect observations. And, as do all means of collecting data, survey data have strengths and weaknesses. On the strength side is the ability to generalize from sample to the population. On the weakness side is the challenge of demonstrating the causal linkage between variables. Because surveys collect all their data at some specific point in time, all that survey data can demonstrate is correlation. Correlation is demonstrated when two variables vary together. It is much harder to demonstrate causation as in when this variable changes, that variable will change as a consequence.[3] We will return to what a correlation is in the final section on data analysis.

---

3. In surveys, data are collected at the same point in time. We may *believe* that this variable is the *dependent* variable (i.e., that the pattern of change *depends* on the influence of other independent variables). But demonstrating causation, independent of our beliefs, is more of a challenge. Two variables may covary not because there is a causal relationship between them but because they each are dependent on some third variable (in which case the relationship between our two relationships may be *spurious*, that is, due to their joint relationship to the third variable, not to a causal link, one to the other). And, if our data does not include that "third" variable, if it is *missing a key variable*, then we may easily misstate what "the" data finds (if we had the key variable our results might look quite different).

Experiments

Experiments are another means of data collection, a methodology increasingly being adopted by political psychologists. This method of data collection has its strengths and weaknesses as well. In surveys, we have an easy time making valid generalizations, what is referred to as *external validity*. That is, we can say something about what is going on in the actual population (by using our sample to generalize to the population). However, surveys have a more difficult time in demonstrating causality because we are collecting data on both the dependent variable and independent variables at the same time. We can test the covariance of the variables, which changes in each variable are co-occurring, but we cannot be certain that a change in the one causes the change in the other.

Experiments offer a strong case for the validity of a causal relationship in the data because we are changing the independent variable and can observe if that change causes the dependent variable to change as well. Most experiments offer a weaker case for the external validity because the people who participate are not selected at random from a population therefore we have no way of knowing how well the results in the experiment might generalize.[4] That is, what we find to be the case in the experiment has no specific means for generalizing to the wider population. Rather than samples (the basic unit of survey methodology), the basic unit of experiments is groups of subjects. In its most basic form, an experiment consists of two groups, a *treatment* group and a *control* group. The treatment is the independent variable of interest. So, let's take the same example, the hypothesis that comfort with social change is going to impact on ideology and we think this is something we could study as an experiment.

Experiments begin with the *null hypothesis*: We begin with a number of people and randomly assign them two groups. Because of random assignment, the two groups will be very much alike. For example, if we had a number of citizens, and then randomly assigned them to one of two groups, the citizens in each group should have on average, the same average and distribution of scores on some ideology measure. Say we had a score for ideology that ranged from 0, very conservative, to 1, very liberal, if we found, after randomly dividing everyone into one of two groups, the first group has a mean value of .57 so should the second group (plus or minus a small amount of variance that would be quite small if we had a large number of cases). We can readily test that assertion by statistical methods. Doing so is called testing the null hypothesis (i.e., that there is no difference, the null, between the two groups). H_o is the symbol for the null hypothesis.

How might we test a more meaningful hypothesis using an experiment? Say our hypothesis, in this example, is that ideology is a dependent variable. Yes, people are often fairly constant in their ideological convictions but that is not always so. We further speculate that events can, if perhaps only briefly, persuade people to move left or right. To test that hypothesis, we might show one of two film segments to the two groups. Those in the first group might be shown a film showing scenes of rapid change in various social settings (perhaps old neighborhoods being torn down, and new construction going up; or a suburb with lots of new people moving in or older residents

---

4. One way to overcome this limitation is to use survey experiments. To build experiments into surveys thus benefitting from the strengths of each method of gathering data.

leaving; or the desegregation of the US military in the mid-twentieth century, and so on). Those in the second group might be shown benign film segments perhaps on various upcoming cultural events.[5]

If we do not show the two groups these film segments, statistical sampling theory tells us that the two groups should be alike as to how liberal or conservative they are (or the null hypothesis that the mean of ideology of the first group should be very close to the mean of ideology of the second group). If we do show the groups these two films, each group getting one of the two films, then any differences between the two groups will be fairly attributed to the seeing of the film segments.

We normally hope to reject the null hypothesis (i.e., we want to establish that our treatment, here the films, matter). Here, we have an alternative hypothesis to the null hypothesis: Our hypothesis is that if we expose people to social change, we will make them more uncomfortable than those who do not see this film segment, and we expect that those in the group shown the discomforting film about social change should move in the direction of more conservative responses. That is, we hope to find a robust relationship such that those who watched one film prove to be ideologically different, here more conservative, than those who watched the second film. Can you think of a film segment that might move people to the left? What sort of events might do that?

Here's a second example. Let's consider an experiment as a way to test one of the hypotheses offered in chapter 1: The hypothesis that the more voters perceive a difference between parties, the more likely they will vote.

We can readily design an experiment to test that hypothesis. We invite a group of citizens eligible to vote to come to our lab to participate in a study. We randomly assign them to one of two groups. We then give two different sets of background material to the participants as we ask them to participate in a mock election. In the first set of materials, the two contending candidates are described as being very similar on policy positions. In the second set of materials, the two candidates are described as taking quite different positions. Our dependent variable then might be asking them a single question: "How likely do you think you would vote in this election?" Our hypothesis is that the first group, with similar policy profiles, would generate a lower percentage of positive replies when compared to the second group.

Any difference we find between these two groups is due to the difference in the two sets of materials. Scientists always have to test against one alternative explanation: random variation, the so-called null hypothesis. Experiments offer a robust way of testing the causal relationship between variables. We can make this experiment more interesting by adding other factors to the experiment, for example, familiarity of the candidates can be manipulated to be high or low. In a similar fashion attractiveness of the candidates can be manipulated to be high or low and so on. These elaborations would allow us to test alternative theories in one or a series of experiments about what would induce those eligible to be more likely to vote.

A relatively recent pattern is to combine experiments and surveys into so-called survey experiments. In survey experiments rather than giving all participants in the

---

5. There is more to executing a good experiment than I am discussing here. For example, is the first film segment really about social change and is the second film segment really benign? How would we establish those two claims? I set that, and other topics, aside.

survey the same questions, some questions of the survey are produced in different versions and participants are randomly assigned to respond to the different versions to see if they respond differently. Other ways survey experiments have varied the order in which questions are presented or with different instructions. This general strategy, which combines the advantage of surveys to generalize the populations from which the sample is drawn, is called *externally validity*. A result is externally valid when the results from the data also apply to the larger population. The advantage of experimentation is that we can be confident that the causal interpretation is sound. When there is an empirical result with a rigorously demonstrated causal linkage, it is called *internally valid*.

Another method for gathering data is the field experiment where real participants in real life participate in experiments. For example, we could try a field experiment with on voting turnout. Perhaps, just a reminder of the upcoming election would suffice to prompt people to vote. And, indeed that has been shown to be the case. Political scientist Harold Gosnell (1927) did just that, sending postcards that addressed the upcoming election to some districts and not to others, thereby using the reported voting turnout by voting district as his dependent variable and the districts that he sent postcards to as the treatment condition, and those districts that he did not send postcards to as the control condition. Pushing this idea further, and using one of the earlier hypotheses I proposed, with respect to the perceptions of difference, we could prepare two sets of postcards to mail, one set that emphasizes how different the two parties, or candidates are, one set that emphasizes the issues, making little mention of the parties' or candidates' differences, and then using turnout to see if the postcards made a difference.

Experiments have raised yet another consideration, ethics. Two famous experiments could probably not be repeated (the technical term is *replicated*) to see if their results remained stable over time. Psychologist Stanley Milgram (1974) did a famous study where subjects were asked to give what they understood to be electrical shocks to supposed participants in a learning study. Unknown to the study subjects, there were no electrical shocks and the people in the learning study were trained to respond as if they were shocked by generating grimaces, groans, and cries as the supposed severity of the shocks increased. Milgram was interested in whether people would stop shocking subjects as the pain they were inflicting became increasingly severe, or so they thought (subjects had both a switch that supposedly inflicted the shock and a dial that read out the supposed level of electricity; the instructions to the subjects was to increase the level of electricity if the learning subject made errors in the learning phases, which they did). Although the dial had its highest level clearly marked in red as very dangerous, many subjects did as they told and increased the severity of the supposed shocks even into the highest danger zone. The second study, the Stanford prison experiment, under the direction of psychologist Philip Zimbardo (Haney, Banks, and Zimbardo 1983), relied on a simulated prison, actually in the basement of a Stanford University building. Subjects were randomly assigned to be either prisoners or guards to see if the institutional setting elicited aggressive and brutalizing behavior by the guards and passive and de-individualized responses by the prisoners (as the latter were given numbers and their names not used within the experiment). Over the course of the days of the experiment the apparent impact on the participants was so severe that Zimbardo prematurely stopped the experiment (Zimbardo 2008). In response to these and other experiments the federal government of the United States mandated that all studies with human subjects be reviewed by independent boards, including lay individuals, to protect subjects from harm (these boards are called institutional review boards or more commonly known by their acronym IRB). US colleges and universities have their IRB review all human subject research, even if not funded by the US government. Some research is rejected as too harmful, some requires positive evidence that no substantial harm will result, or require that studies be modified to protect subjects against harm. And, ethical considerations have extended to all methods of collecting data from human subjects, experimental or not.

Other Data Collections Methodologies

Some data does not require humans to obtain it. These types of data fall under the category unobtrusive measures (Webb 1966). Data collection is unobtrusive when, as in the case of some field experiments, the subjects are not aware they are participating in a scientific study. Another example of unobtrusive data collection is when political psychologists rely on textual records such as those found in in memoirs, autobiographies, news accounts, government records of legislative and executive branch speeches and hearings, diplomatic communications, and, of course, court rulings. And with film and video becoming more widely used, political psychologists can examine these to study the gestures that leaders may make or their facial expressions. Most of the data that political psychologists collect is obtrusive, as in the case of experiments or surveys.

With development of neuroscience a new array of methodologies for data collection have begun to be more evident in political psychology. Among these are: fMRI, PET scans, lesion studies, single cell monitoring, GSR (galvanic skin response), and facial EMG.

Functional magnetic resonance imaging (fMRI), as does PET scan technology, can show in approximate real-time areas of the brain that are active. This has already been used to good effect in revealing some quite interesting findings. Joshua Greene (Greene and Haidt 2002; Greene et al. 2004; Greene et al. 2001) used fMRI in the brain to show that where moral judgment seems to be located that when subjects wrestle with moral dilemmas these regions "light up." Michael Spezio and colleagues (2008) used fMRI brain imaging technologies to determine that the appearance of candidates (how attractive they are) matters more for candidates who lost than for candidates who won. There is one important limitation to brain imaging methods. Neural functions work both by activation and by inhibition. And, most applications of these methodologies are focused primarily on activation, often presuming a one-to-one relationship between an area that is active and some brain function. But as the timing is approximate and areas that have been inhibited are not generally considered, the interpretations of such data are likely to be incomplete. And which you choose for any particular research effort will depend on two factors. First, which of these are best suited to the theoretical issues you wish to explore; and, second, which of these you have mastered sufficiently to be comfortable in executing.

IV. MEASURING CONCEPTS: MEASUREMENT THEORY

The earlier section was primarily concerned with the risk of taking a limited number of observations: We have *some* empirical data, and inferring that the results we have provides a sound basis for generalizing to *all* pertinent empirical situations. Measurement theory is concerned with a second problem of inference. The problem for measurement theory is that we would like to treat our empirical observations as valid measures of the theoretical concepts that comprise the theory. When justified we can we treat our measures (empirical observations) as equivalent to our concepts (theoretical terms). Central to measurement theory is the distinction between *observations*, (i.e., empirical data) and *concepts* (i.e., names, ideas).

There are some basic strategies available for determining whether our concepts are well measured by assigned scores that constitute our empirical observations. First and foremost is the strategy of using *multiple indicators* for each theoretical concept. We often in daily life have concepts in mind, and we often think that measuring them is straightforward. If we have just a single indicator we have only two ways of determining whether it truly measures the concept good or bad. One way is what is called *face validity*. Face validity is the *seemingly* obvious linkage between the concept and our chosen measure that is it seems on its face to be a good measure. Mindful of how fallible human judgment is this is not a very stringent test. The second option is *predictive* or *criterion* validity. If we have a known relationship between our concept and another, and the other has a good measure, then we establish a degree of predictive validity if the measure we have chosen for our concept has the anticipated relationship to the measure of the criterion measure. This is helpful but limited for it is not likely that we will have a precise standard for how strong the covariation must be between our concept's measure and the criterion measure for it to validate the former.

Figure 2.2 shows the challenges a single measure, here a_1, has in winning confidence that it measures what it purports to measure. The figure uses some standard conventions: Concepts are capitalized, measures are lower case. We do not have a direct measure of our criterion concept, we have a measure, b_1, which we presume is a valid and reliable measure of our criterion concept. That presumption might be true, but it might not. In effect we are put in the position of trusting that the variation we observe in b_1 is due solely to the causal impact of the criterion concept. We think we know the

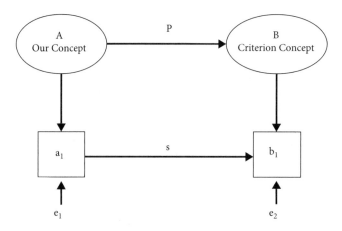

Figure 2.2 Measurement Model for Predictive Validity

value of P, the parameter that shows the relationship between our concept and the criterion concept, but typically it is at best a crude assertion. We might know from other studies that that relationship, P, should be positive. From that we can advance as an expectation that s, the statistic, should be positive but how positive? Then, if our concept is the sole factor influencing our measure, a_1, then the relationship, which we do have, between a_1 and b_1, will confirm that measure a_1 is a valid measure of our concept. But empirical measures always contain some measurement error. We do not know how much error we have in each of our measures, which is indicated by the causal arrow from e, error, to the measure. So, the observed variation in each measure is driven by error and by the presumed causal force of its latent concept. Well there are a lot of "ifs" in all of that.

A measure is often a question. It also can be an action, such as casting a ballot (or not). Adding even just one more plausible measure of a concept can provide considerable purchase on establishing the validity of a measure. In the example that follows, the measures discussed are questions that people in the study were asked to rate a group they find objectionable on various perceptions they might have of that group. Recall in chapter 1, I described how we asked people to rate the group on eight perceptions. Chapter 1 presented one advantage of including more than one measure. In that instance the concept of Threat was shown to be too broad. In that case we had eight measures available of how people might judge a group they find objectionable. Analysis of the eight measures, the empirical data, showed that people made a distinction between how strong a group is and bad they are. Two of the indicators grouped together as measures of how strong or weak people judged a group. Six of the measures grouped together as measures of how much people perceived the group as violating established norms of society. This suggested that instead of a single threat measure we discovered two different concepts, only one of which acted how a threat measure is expected to act (i.e., predicting how people would change their behavior as threat varied from low to high). The correlations suggested two concepts of threat: Perceptions of Strength and Perceptions of Normative Violation. Had my colleagues and I grouped all eight items into one summary measure, called threat, we would have created a *confounded* measure. A measure is confounded when it measures not one property but two, hence confounding, creating confusion as to what was being measured. Scientific concepts should measure one and only one attribute.

Another advantage of having multiple measures is that we can assess the *reliability* of our measures. Perhaps some of the subjects do not have the same vocabulary as others, hence finding some words confusing or lacking clear meaning; perhaps some subjects were distracted when they answered or perhaps they were just sloppy with their answers. For these and other reasons, their actual answers might be close to what they would have given if they gave their carefully considered assessment or maybe not. The basic model of reliability is the following:

Actual score (i.e., answer) = true score + random error.

Having multiple questions allows us to estimate how serious (how large) the problem of random error is, and even, how we can correct for the problem. Going into details on how this is accomplished is beyond the scope of this brief introduction. However, one more caution, reliability is a different consideration than validity. Consider, for example, asking people their attitudes about other racial or ethnic groups. In the United States, some sixty years ago or earlier, it was not uncommon for people to be quite comfortable in expressing disparaging remarks about groups they perceived as being lazy, dirty, stupid, or otherwise negatively. Few people are willing to give such responses in a discussion with a stranger who is interviewing them, or even in seemingly anonymous settings such as an online survey. Asking people if they agree with blatantly negative stereotypes about social groups, even when they might privately hold such attitudes, is likely to generate *biased* responses that systematically veer toward socially acceptable. That is their actual response, scores, are systematically, not randomly, different from their true scores. For those of you interested in this problem, and how political psychologists have tried to overcome it, you might find the following readings a good place to begin (Kinder and Sears 1981; Sears and Henry 2003; Sniderman et al. 1991).

Here is another example of how having multiple indicators can challenge and inform. A concept that plays a central role in the study of peace and war is severity of conflict, a continuous concept because the idea of severity can range in smooth increments from no conflict to all consuming, from peace to global war. We might use such a concept to explore how the public perceives an ongoing or an anticipated war, or how leaders do. Robert C. Butterworth (1978) assembled data on the 310 interstate conflicts from the period 1945 to 1974. Two indicators, empirical variables, are available in the data he collected: fatalities, the number of deaths directly related to each international conflict, and duration, the number of years between the first emergence of serious contention and the settlement or disappearance of each conflict. The plausible measurement model is that severity of conflict can be measured by the number of fatalities (as the deaths increase the conflict is more severe) and by duration (as the conflict lasts longer it is more severe).

Butterworth's data showed that the correlation between the variables, fatalities and duration, showed them to be completely independent. That is conflicts high in fatalities are neither especially long nor are they especially short. Conflicts low in fatalities are neither especially long nor are they especially short. Because the measurement model proposed assumes that fatalities increase and conflicts last longer as conflicts become more severe, and both indicators vary in response to changes in the level of severity, this finding violates the claim of equivalence between the two indicators, each to the other, and to the concept.

In this way, having an explicit measurement model can tell us when our conceptions are poor representations of the world. If this happens, the appropriate response is to modify your *taxonomies* and the *concepts*. The advantage is that having multiple indicators can reveal that our concepts may be too broad or too narrow. Reality, via empirical analysis, can tell us that our beliefs about how to group and label the world

---

BOX 2.8 **Measurement models**

See if you can diagram the measurement model for severity of conflict. You will need one oval to represent the *latent* concept, two rectangles for the two empirical measures, and four causal arrows.

should be revised. Let's consider one of the most popular concepts in political psychology, political science, and increasingly in social psychology as well, conservatism. Here, as with many other concepts, social scientists begin with every day terms, terms such as patriotism, nationalism, and, in this case conservatism. These terms serve us well in our daily lives. The terms "conservative" and "liberal" are widely and commonly used in everyday discussions and in coverage of politics.

A common definition would suggest that many people differ on how conservative or how liberal they are, how they experience the world, with conservatives generally being more risk averse and more valuing of tradition and stability while liberals are generally less risk averse and more willing to value change and novelty.[6] What measures could we come up with; quite a large number actually. We could ask people to identify themselves by asking them whether they think of themselves as a conservative or liberal, perhaps adding gradations such as "extremely liberal" and or "somewhat conservative." We might also try other ways of coming up with measures of conservatism-liberalism. We might choose an array of policies that conservatives and liberals, at least those in the United States, disagree on. In the American political scene, abortion, gun control, raising the minimum wage, mandating English language in all dealings with the government, regulating corporations to achieve policy goals, and tax policy. If we did a multi-indicator analysis we would find that the correlations among the social issues (abortion, English as the official language, gun control, and so forth) would be highly correlated, as would the correlations between the economic issues (raising the minimum wage, tax policy, government using regulations to achieve desired results). But, the correlations between the two sets are lower, much lower. This result indicates that people in the United States are economic conservatives or social conservatives, and the same for liberals, either social liberal or economic liberal. There are some who are liberal on all issues. There are some who are conservative on all issues. But, for the most part, people are either social liberals or social conservatives, and that is unrelated to whether they are economic liberals or economic conservatives.

Another line of work on ideology (Alford, Funk, and Hibbing 2005) has suggested that ideological inclination may well have a genetic basis, much as our height or our skin color has a genetic component. If we follow that route, then we want to collect not only what people say about the label they adopt to define their ideology, and in addition collect what issue positions they support, we also want to collect DNA samples to identify the appropriate genetic markers. But even if we collect all of these indicators we have not exhausted the possible measures. We might rely on more general attitudes than the focus on political policy issues, on such attitudes as punishment versus nurturance as the best route to good behavior, on the best methods of child rearing, strict or loving, among others. Still other possible indicators might emerge with some more reliance on our imaginations. And, if we collaborate with others, by asking others to lend their imaginations, we could well come up with yet more possible measures. And, we might find that in having multiple measures we can then see whether our general conception of ideology remains coherent after analyzing all these indicators or whether our conception is too broad and requires refinement.

---

6. If you are interested in a deeper discussion I recommend the following to get you started: Amodio et al. (2007); Carney et al. (2008); Feldman, 2003; Jost et al. (2003); and Jost, Federico, and Napier (2009).

Quantitative and Qualitative Approaches

There has been a long-enduring conflict between scholars who espouse one or the other approach as the best. Indeed each side will often go so far as to proclaim their view as the only legitimate approach. This is often argued as a matter of deep epistemology. Epistemology is the theory of knowledge, what is true and what is false.

In my view, there are four considerations that should be foremost as you consider each approach. First, there is less difference between the two approaches then either side is likely to concede. Whether we assign a number to an observation, whether we rely on the apparent precision of statistical analysis, we still have the same general challenges.

Second, do our specific observations fairly represent what we would find if we studied the entire population and are our empirical observations reliable and valid? This has to do with wishing to use our results to make valid generalizations to the larger world, past, present, and future.

Third, we may have to settle for data we can collect rather than the data we would like to have. Our results may have to be quite provisional, rather than providing a final and unquestionable basis for determining the truth of a theoretical assertion.

Fourth, some scholars and some students are more comfortable and adept at numbers and therefore find statistical analysis easy to learn and apply. Others are less comfortable. The level of comfort you experience in mastering statistics is likely to influence the execution of your research.

In any case, whether using qualitative or quantitative data, it is a common result that when we begin with everyday concepts and try to craft a scientific concept, one that defines one and only one property, we have to narrow the concept. Many common everyday concepts, such as democracy, justice, patriotism, threat, and war, are too broad and too all encompassing for scientific use. These words, although useful in our everyday discussions in which we readily adapt different meanings, do not serve well in scientific searches for explanation because such words are too often confounded. They have multiple meanings and when scientific concepts have multiple meanings, we cannot conduct careful empirical research.

It is also commonly presumed that the concept we have in mind and the data we have to measure that concept are one and the same. Examining the purported equivalence that the indicators are in fact measuring the concepts we have in mind will expand the opportunity for data to inform us, to confirm or to surprise us, to confirm our ideas or to challenge them. And that is as it should be.

In many cases you will use items and scales generated by other political psychologists. Some, perhaps most, have been widely used, so their reliability and validity most likely has been previously reported. Therefore using published items and scales for your research is a good strategy. That said you should show in your data and in your project that items you used are reliable and valid. For more on measurement, I recommend the following readings: Campbell (1988); Carmines and Zeller (1979); Sullivan and Feldman (1979); Robinson, Shaver, and Wrightsman (1999); and Robinson et al. (1991).

V. WHAT CAN OBSERVATIONS TELL US? HOW CAN WE FIND OUT?

All forms of explanation rely on the idea of covariation. Some examples of *covariation* are:

1. People become authoritarian because they were raised by authoritarian parents. The level of authoritarianism in people is much the same as the level of authoritarianism in their parents; measures of each will covary.
2. Wars occur because of miscalculation by political leaders. Wars covary with miscalculations by political leaders; when political leaders do not miscalculate there is less occurrence of war (wars and miscalculations covary).
3. International crises create public support for the political leader of nations involved in the crisis. When international crises occur, the political leaders standing in their public rises compared to the absence of crises. Standing, high or low, and crises, present or not, covary.

We form an explanation by linking *cause* and *effect*. The principal elements are twofold. First we need a concept that we identify as a *cause*. In the above examples the possible causes might be: the level of authoritarianism in some families but not in others, the misunderstanding or miscalculation of political leaders, and international crises. Second, we need a concept we identify as an *effect*. In the above examples the effect concepts are, respectively: the degree of authoritarianism of an individual, the occurrence of war and of peace, and the degree of support for the president.

However, we generally cannot observe concepts (which are names and ideas). Rather, we observe specific instances, cases or examples, which we take to be equivalent to and typical of what we would learn if we could observe the concepts. To be more precise, concepts are general names given to a class defined by a theoretical taxonomy. Concepts are *latent* or unobservable. What is *manifest*, what is observable, are the answers to questions, or the actions that can be observed, produced by the specific measures we use to exemplify that concept:

1. Concepts are *infinite* and as such can be applied to any appropriate setting, now, in the past, or in the future. Concepts are ideas. Concepts are theoretical.
2. Observations are *finite* and as such have specific temporal and spatial qualities. Observations are empirical.

Keeping these two points in mind, you should choose observations for your research that meet two criteria. First, observations should be appropriate for your research hypotheses, that is, theories that attempt to explain how individuals feel, think, or act requires observations on individuals whereas theories that attempt to explain how groups interact with each other requires observations on groups. Second, as observations are always finite, you should choose observations that are likely to be widely accepted as confirming the general claim.

If we have concepts that we linked to have a theory, a cause and effect story, and further, if we have a good case that the measures we developed or borrowed from others are reliable and valid proxies for each of our concepts, we can proceed to analyze the data we obtained. Data can be collected in surveys, experiments, content analysis of textual material, or measures of electrical signals from specific brain regions. Once collected, data can tell us how much variance we observed in each of our measures. And further, using approaches such as statistical measures, we can even quantify how much covariation we observed.

BOX 2.9 **Property space**

For the most part we rely on computers to calcu-late our statistics, such as correlations. Computers can also generate property spaces, most often called "scatter plots" or "scattergrams" when the data are continuous. When the data are not continuous but just differences, such as religious affiliation, property spaces will be called "cross-tabulations."

What constitutes data analysis? We can observe and record quite a number of details about the world and its creatures. Each observation records a value on an attribute. The spread of observations and the location of observations, on the attribute of interest are called *variations*. It is also very important that the range of possible scores be broad enough that the observations can be located at accurate locations on the dimension. We are better served if we can assign numbers rather than rely on words. "Lots" or "some" or "no" influence is less precise than having both numbers and semantic labels as in the following example: "agree very strongly, 5"; "agree somewhat, 4"; "neither agree nor disagree, 3": "disagree somewhat, 2"; and, "disagree very strongly, 1." We expect to find observations dispersed along the range of the dimension. When observations are dispersed observing that dispersion should prod us to wonder why. The discovery of dispersion or variation is an incentive to ask the question: why are not all these obser-vations at the same point? Why are they different? How can we explain why some are above average and others below average on that dimension?

The place to begin to look for an answer is in a property space.

A property space is formed when two or more measures, each unidimensional, are then arranged perpendicular to each other. When two dimensions are so arranged they form a square (or when there are three indicators, a cube). In the simple case, a property space is a Cartesian plane with an x-axis that defines the horizontal dimension and a y-axis that describes the vertical dimension. A property space requires that any observation must locate within the endpoints of each dimension. That is, each observa-tion must fall within the edges defined by the two dimensions of the plain, the, x- and the y-axis. A property space will look like figure 2.3.

Inside this space will fall all of our observations, our data. Where they fall tells us what the relationship is between the two properties, here X and Y. If Y changes as a function of X, then we should see observations falling into a small range of *cojoint* loca-tions. To plot the data requires that each observation, each data point, has two values, one on property Y and one on property X. Here, if the data is high on X that tells us that Y will also be high and when X is low, then Y should also be low. We expect our data observations, when plotted into this space, will fall along a rising line, low values of X and Y in the lower left, middle values of X and Y in the center, and high values of X and Y falling into the top quadrant.

In figure 2.4, four observations (the small circles) are displayed to demonstrate such a result. This is what a positive relationship, though here with just four observations, looks like. To the right of each data point is a label for that value (x_1, x_2, etc.). And, to the right of the identifying label for each observation is a parenthetical item that indicates the cojoint values that places that observation at specific location in the property space.

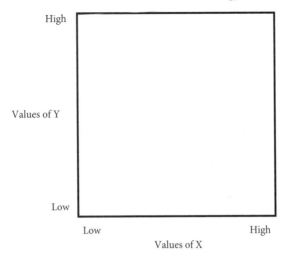

Figure 2.3 Property Space for Two Attributes, X and Y.

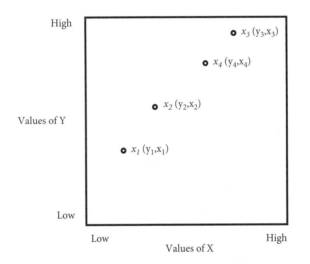

Figure 2.4 Property Space with four observations

The first, the value of that observation on Y indicates how high or low on the vertical axis. The second, the value of that observation on X, indicates how much to the left or right on horizontal axis. By convention, we put the independent variable (the X variable) on the horizontal axis and the dependent variable (the Y variable) on the vertical axis.

Of course, two other patterns could show up in this same property space. There may be no relationship between A and B. What would we see in this case? Our cojoint observations would be randomly distributed around the property space. And, there may be a negative relationship such that high values of X are associated with low values of Y, and the converse. Our theory tells us what to expect and the observations will tell us whether the empirical observations confirm our theory.

Correlation

Here again, a vital topic and not the space to fully cover the topic. But, I can provide a summary overview for you to grasp the basics. The key to any theoretical assertion is that one thing causes another. To be more precise, some of interest varies, that is it is a variable. Some people are more liberal, others more conservative. Some conflicts last a long time, some end very quickly. Hence, ideology varies. And, so do do conflicts (here, to be more specific is how long they last). Correlation is the most basic measure of how two different measures or variables move or covary. Let's consider one specific hypothesis, the ideology of a person is related, covaries, with how comfortable they are with social change (to be more precise: the more comfortable a person is with social change the more likely they are to be liberal, the less comfortable the more conservative).

So, how would we obtain a measure to test whether that hypothesis is correct? Let's see how that works.

Let us say we have a number of people in the next room (our sample perhaps, a randomly selected number of voters). And, let's say that our sample is the people in the next room and that we have one-hundred participants. We prepare a questionnaire that asks the participants a question about how comfortable they are with social change. They record how comfortable (or uncomfortable they feel). On the questionnaire we also ask them to describe whether they consider themselves very conservative, very liberal, or somewhere in the middle. To each of these questions, we assign a numerical score. The actual numerical values do not much matter except with the following requirement. The numerical values must range from the highest possible score to the lowest possible score (therefore, in this example, we could equally assign the most liberal to be 100 or 1,000; and the least liberal, or most conservative, –100, or –1,000). The purpose of the scores is to ensure that people who gave the same response to a question are given the same numerical score, and further, that the numerical values align with the verbal labels (here, the level of comfort and the level of liberal conviction).[7]

In the next room are one-hundred participants: we have their responses. If a single person came out and into our room, and we do not know their actual answers, what should we guess as to their ideological convictions? Statistics gives us a "best" strategy. If we take the one-hundred responses, add up the total, and divide by the number of responses, here one hundred, we would get the average answer (called in statistics the *mean* response). If we had to make a guess about the ideological label that they had self-assigned, our best guess would be the average, or mean, response. And that would be true if after that first person, came a second, a third, and so on to the last, or one-hundredth participant. Guess the mean. Of course, some people are more liberal than the average and others less. We can use the following formula to measure that difference:

Mean response – actual response (of that person).

Example: $.57 - .67_i$,

---

7. The assignment is equally valid to reverse to the numerical assignments in this example. We could assign numbers to measure how *uncomfortable* people feel about social change, higher scores now mean more *uncomfortable*. And, we could do the same with ideology (so that the higher score means more conservative).

where .57 is the average ideological value of the one-hundred participants and .67 is the actual response of the ith participant, so that for that ith person, the average was .10 too low.

If we followed this same procedure we would get the error value for each of the one-hundred participants in our sample. The statistical calculation of the mean – actual score is the basic element of almost all statistical analysis. Before we expand on the use of that let's point out some obvious points.

Errors of estimation (the actual response is different than the mean) will have either positive or negative values (i.e., sometime the mean will be too low for that participant, while too high for another). Overall, we will find less overall error by calculating the mean value than if we were to use any other value. That means that the mean is a very efficient estimate to use (it is also an unbiased estimate).[8]

If we square this term [(mean – actual score) × (mean – actual score)] we get an overall measure that tells us how much the actual scores differ from the mean. And, if we divide that squared term by the number in our sample, N, we get a statistic called *variance*.[9] Therefore, we get the following equation:

variance = (mean – actual score)^2/N.

A small number means that most of the scores are quite close to the mean, that is, there is very little variance. A higher number means that the mean is in the center of a range of scores but the scores vary a lot. And a lot of variance is exciting to scientists. Why? Because when variables vary a lot that is when science is relevant. If things do not vary they do not need an explanation. Things that do not vary are always the same. They are constants. Science is interested in variables. If we have lots of variance in the variable of interest, our dependent variable, and some plausible explanatory variables, independent variables, then we have possible explanations that we can test (or to put that matter another way, no variance in the independent variables, then no explanation).

In our example, we next add all our comfort questions into an index. After doing so we can convert that index so that its numerical scores also range from 0 (very uncomfortable with social change) to 1 (very comfortable with social change). Each participant in our sample then has two scores, the comfort index and the ideological identification as very liberal, some intermediate score, or very conservative. And, we hope, lots of variation in each variable!

The correlation then is a ratio of covariance (the variance of our dependent variable here, ideology multiplied by the variance in our independent variable, here, comfort with social change), divided by the total variance of both variables.

Or, correlation between comfort with social change and ideology, here the Pearson correlation coefficient (r):

---

8. An efficient estimator is one that guarantees we will have less error than a less efficient estimator. An unbiased estimator means that our errors will not favor one side or the other, neither the high side nor the low side of the scores. It will be fairly in the exact middle.

9. For samples, rather than dividing by N, the number of participants in our sample, we would actually divide by N – 1, here 99. The reasons have to do with our using a sample, rather than a census of the entire population. A basic text in statistics will cover the whys and wherefores.

$$r = \frac{\text{Variance of X} \times \text{Variance of Y}}{(\text{Variance of X})^2 + (\text{Variance of Y})^2}.$$

This ratio has a very simple and straightforward interpretation. The ratio, the correlation, has a maximum upper bound, or value. That upper bound is 1.00. And that means that in every case the two variables move in lockstep, and therefore a higher score on one variable is always a high score on the other variable. The ratio, the correlation, has a maximum lower bound, or value. That lower bound is –1.00. And that means that in every case the two variables move in opposite directions, and therefore a higher score on one variable is always is matches up with the low score on the other variable. Finally, if the correlation is 0 then that means that the variance in one variable is completely unrelated to the variance in the other variable. If you examine the equation, earlier, you will see why those statements are always going to be the case whether there are one-hundred participants in a sample, or one thousand, or 723, or any number larger or smaller. The correlation coefficient thus ignores the actual scores, the number of participants, but nonetheless has the same meaning for every set of data:

1. a positive value for the correlation between two variables means that high positive scores means that high values of one variable are consistently found with high values of the other variable (i.e., the more this is true, the higher that positive score will be with a maximum value of +1);
2. a negative value for the correlation between two variables means that high values of one of the variables are consistently found with low values of the other variable (i.e., the more this is true, the higher the negative score will be with a maximum value of –1); and when high and low scores of one variable are unrelated to the high and low scores of the other variable, then the correlation takes on the value of 0.

There are two other basic statistical analyses, ordinary linear regression (OLS) and its expansion, multiple regression, and analysis of variance (ANOVA). A basic text in statistics will introduce these methods. They, as correlation, are based on the core foundations of variance and covariance. If you understand the basics of the term for variance (the distance of the mean to the observation): When that value is large and when small, when positive and when negative, you will have mastered the core of most forms of statistical analysis.

Forms of Relationships
The description just explained presumes that the relationship in this general example is linear, best summarized by a straight line that passes through the observations in the property space. But there are other kinds of relationships, nonlinear, such as step functions and when there is more than one independent variable there can be interactions where the impact of a third, or fourth, variable alters the relationship between one independent variable and a dependent variable.

Having more than one independent variable in a theory leads to many possible models. Even with just two independent variables there are four different models possible. Consider the role of education and belief in civil rights and their respective relationships to political tolerance. Figure 2.5 shows the four alternative ways that just

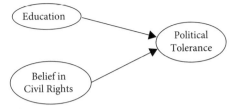

Model I: Two Uncorrelated Independent Variables

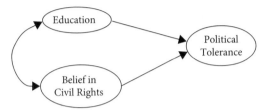

Model II: Two Correlated Independent Variables

Model III: One Independent Variable and One Intervening Variable

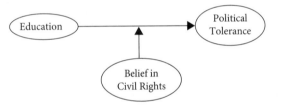

Model IV: One Independent Variable and One Mediating Variable

Figure 2.5 Four Possible Models with Two Independent Variables

two independent variables might be related to a dependent variable, here political tolerance.

The first model shows each independent variable unrelated to the other, those who are educated are no more, no less, likely to belief in civil rights, but each of these explains who is more and who is less, political tolerant. Model II shows, contrary to model I, that those who are educated are no more likely to believe in civil rights and as in model I, both explain political tolerance.[10] Model III, however, shows that education has no direct effect on political tolerance, but it does increase support for civil liberties, those who are more educated are more likely than those not educated to believe in civil rights, and that belief in turn does increase political tolerance. Model IV modifies that:

10. In the interest of simplicity, I did not include the signs, in this case, positive or negative, to indicate the direction of the relationships. However, in the case of political tolerance, the expected results are positive relationships (Sullivan, Piereson, and Marcus 1982).

Model IV shows that education does have a direct effect, but that effect is mediated by the strength of the belief in civil rights. When there are more than two independent variables, the possible relationships grow increasingly complex. The discipline of generating path models is useful to require theoretical clarity as to exactly what one's theory expects. Hayes (2009) offered a useful primer on distinguishing between direct effects (as in model I), indirect effects (and in model III), and mediating effects (as in model IV). A very useful extension, structural equation modeling, combines requiring theoretical clarity among concepts with clarity as to how those concepts are operationalized (i.e., measured; Bollen 1989).

Finding interactions, as in model IV, requires a powerful theory that, in advance, identifies which independent variables will interact, and where such dynamic interrelationships will be found. A course in statistical analysis will train you on how to choose the best statistical method and analyze the data you have collected.

In sum, empirical observations can be used to bolster or challenge a hypothesis if: First, the observations are selected by the proper sampling procedures. We seldom study every element in a population. We need enough observations to be confident that the patterns we find are typical. We want to make an inference that what is found in the sample is applicable to the population. To accomplish this we need to know how to select a sample of cases from the population so that what we find can be generalized. When we use samples to make inferences, we are making use of inferential statistics.

Second, we assign words or numbers to ascribe values that can be distributed in a property space. We require numbers to determine the precise location of observations distributed in a property space. When we use numbers to describe objects in a property space or when we use words to locate approximate locations, as in cross tabulations, we rely on descriptive statistics to determine the relationships.

Finally, we need to evaluate the reliability and the validity of the words and numbers obtained. When we use numbers to measure our values we can assess the success of our measurements. Such assessments rely on the tools of measurement theory.

Political psychologists, as all scientists, accept that our theoretical expectations can be proven false; indeed more often than not they are. Subjecting our expectations to the rigor of empirical testing is one important way in which science differs from other systems of knowledge.

VI. CONCLUSIONS

Most of the data we collect comes from or is about humans. Some of that data will come "second-hand" from archives such as the Roper Center, the Inter-University Consortium for Political and Social Research at the University of Michigan, or other archives. To generate data, in almost every instance, at least some financial support is necessary. Foundations, public and private, support research as do colleges and universities. A very positive development for political psychology is the development of Time-Sharing Experiments for the Social Sciences (TESS[11]). TESS offers scholars the opportunity to propose studies for a collective survey experiment that recurs at frequent intervals with fast reviews and open competition.

---

11. You can find more information about TESS at http://www.experimentcentral.org/.

However, working with human subjects has one more aspect to consider: The ethical obligation not to do harm to those who participate as research subjects. The Nuremberg trials of the Nazi doctors revealed how evil scientists can be.[12] As discussed earlier in this chapter, in the United States it now common for project that propose research with human subjects to go before formal review boards to consider and limit what scientists can and cannot do in the way of research. Beyond that, the possible danger to subjects is another ethical concern. Governments and private organizations often use social science research for their own purposes. Sometimes the intentions are beneficial. For example, how could you design a policy to reduce violence, improve health outcomes, diminish the damaging psychological effects of poverty, or diminish poverty itself? However, sometimes what is requested of social scientists is quite horrific. The Nuremberg trials of Nazi doctors are sadly not the final instances of evil reliant on government direction and the willing compliance of experts putting their trade to malevolent purposes. Democratic governments are not immune from temptation sad to say. In the aftermath of 9/11 the United States government for a period relied on psychologists to make their regimes of torture more "effective". Other governments have used torture as well even though international and national laws prohibit its use. Governments need just a few willing partners to help advance their efforts, and sadly, they do find willing partners.

You may be required to have your research plans reviewed and authorized by some group whose task it is to consider the ethical aspects of political psychology research. Whether your research is required to be reviewed, you should give careful consideration to the experience of the subjects you plan to study and whether your project will in some fashion damage them and then modify your program of research to eliminate any damage that may be anticipated. You should also think about how your work might be misused and ponder carefully if asked to use your expertise on behalf of some authority, public or private. It is likely that had such a review process been in place, some of the earlier classic research that we discuss later in this book would not have been permitted.

EXERCISES

Exercise (Theorizing) 1: Some new regimes create a legitimate and trusted system of justice, others fail. We have a variable: success or failure of a system of justice. How many variables can you propose that might explain why regimes succeed or fail? That is devise as many independent variables as you can. Then, formulate the causal relationships (i.e., how changes in the independent variable impacts on the dependent variable, the legitimacy of the justice system of a nation).

Exercise (Theorizing) 2: Read Richard Hofstadter's (1965) famous essay, "The Paranoid Style in American Politics." Convert it from a historical narrative to scientific theoretical propositions. That is, who is likely to be more (and who less), paranoid? Why? What factors does Hofstadter identify that can be treated as independent variables?

Exercise (Changing Methods) 3: Either with a new article, or continue with the article you previously used, modify your article by:

---

12. More basic introductory materials can be found at http://www.ushmm.org/research/doctors/index.html.

First, change the measurement (i.e., different measures—find in literature if there are different ways of measuring the same concepts).

Second, change the data collection methodology (e.g., if a survey study, redesign as an experiment; if a focus group or individual interview, as often is the case with studies of leaders, change to survey; or consider neuroscience as an approach). See if you can test the same hypothesis but with a different research methodology.

Exercise (Theorizing) 4: Find a natural setting where people are active and to some degree public. Identify two or more features of the people in that setting that intrigue you. Convert those features into variables. Then, generate hypotheses that link the variables (which means you must theorize which is the cause, the independent variable, and which is the effect, the dependent variable).

REFERENCES

Alford, John R., Carolyn L. Funk, and John R. Hibbing. 2005. "Are Political Orientations Genetically Transmitted?" *American Political Science Review* 99:153–67.

Amodio, David M., John T. Jost, Sarah L. Master, and Cindy M. Yee. 2007. "Neurocognitive Correlates of Liberalism and Conservatism." *Nature Neuroscience* 4:1246–47.

Bollen, Kenneth A. 1989. *Structural Equations with Latent Variables*. New York: Wiley.

Butterworth, Robert L. 1978. "Do Conflict Managers Matter?: An Empirical Assessment of Interstate Security Disputes and Resolution Efforts, 1945–1974". *International Studies Quarterly* 22:195–214.

Campbell, Donald T. 1988. *Methodology and Epistemology for Social Science*. Chicago: University of Chicago Press.

Carmines, Edward G., and Richard A. Zeller. 1979. *Reliability and Validity Assessment*. Beverly Hills, CA: Sage.

Carney, Dana R., John T. Jost, Samuel D. Gosling, and Jeff Potter. 2008. "The Secret Lives of Liberals and Conservatives: Personality Profiles, Interaction Styles, and the Things They Leave Behind." *Political Psychology* 29:807–40.

Feldman, Stanley. 2003. "Enforcing Social Conformity: A Theory of Authoritarianism." *Political Psychology* 24:41–74.

Gosnell, Harold F. 1927. *Getting Out the Vote: An Experiment in the Stimulation of Voting*. Chicago: University of Chicago Press.

Greene, Joshua D., and Jonathan Haidt. 2002. "How (and Where) Does Moral Judgment Work?" *Trends in Cognitive Sciences* 6:517–23.

Greene, Joshua D., Leigh E. Nystrom, Andrew D. Engell, John M. Darley, and Jonathan D. Cohen. 2004. "The Neural Bases of Cognitive Conflict and Control in Moral Judgment." *Neuron* 44:389–400.

Greene, Joshua D., R. Brian Sommerville, Leigh E. Nystrom, John M. Darley, and Jonathan D. Cohen. 2001. "An fMRI Investigation of Emotional Engagement in Moral Judgment." *Science* 293:2105–8.

Haney, Craig, Curtis Banks, and Philip Zimbardo. 1983. "Interpersonal Dynamics in a Simulated Prison." *International Journal of Criminology and Penology* 1:69–97.

Hayes, Andrew F. 2009. "Beyond Baron and Kenny: Statistical Mediation Analysis in the New Millennium." *Communication Monographs* 76:408–20.

Hofstadter, Richard. 1965. *The Paranoid Style in American Politics, and Other Essays*. New York: Knopf.

Jennings, M. Kent, and Richard G. Niemi. 1981. *Generations and Politics: A Panel Study of Young Adults and Their Parents*. Princeton, NJ: Princeton University Press.

Jost, John T., Christopher M. Federico, and Jaime L. Napier. 2009. "Political Ideology: Its Structure, Functions, and Elective Affinities." *Annual Review of Psychology* 60:307–37.

Jost, John T., Jack Glaser, Arie W. Kruglanski, and Frank J. Sulloway. 2003. "Political Conservatism as Motivated Social Cognition." *Psychological Bulletin* 129:339–75.

Kinder, Donald R., and David O. Sears. 1981. "Prejudice and Politics: Symbolic Racism versus Racial Threat to the Good Life." *Journal of Personality and Social Psychology* 40:414–31.

Hobbes, Thomas. 1968. *Leviathan*. London: Penguin Books.

Milgram, Stanley. 1974. *Obedience to Authority*. New York: Harper and Row.

Robinson, John P., Phillip R. Shaver, and Lawrence S. Wrightsman. 1999. *Measures of Political Attitudes*. San Diego, CA: Academic.

Robinson, John P., Phillip R. Shaver, Lawrence S. Wrightsman, and Frank M. Andrews. 1991. *Measures of Personality and Social Psychological Attitudes*. San Diego, CA: Academic.

Sears, David O., and P. J. Henry. 2003. "The Origins of Symbolic Racism." *Journal of Personality and Social Psychology* 85:259–75.

Sherif, Muzafer. 1966. *Group Conflict and Competition*. London: Routledge & Kegan Paul.

Sniderman, Paul M., Thomas Piazza, Philip Tetlock, and Ann Kendrick. 1991. "The New Racism." *American Journal of Political Science* 35:423–47.

Spezio, Michael L., Antonio Rangel, Ramon Michael Alvarez, John P. O'Doherty, Kyle Mattes, Alexander Todorov, Hackjin Kim, and Ralph Adolphs. 2008. "A Neural Basis for the Effect of Candidate Appearance on Election Outcomes." *Social and Cognitive Affective Neuroscience* 3:344–52.

Sullivan, John L., and Stanley Feldman. 1979. *Multiple Indicators*. Berkeley, CA: Sage.

Sullivan, John L., James Piereson, and George E. Marcus. 1982. *Political Tolerance and American Democracy*. Chicago: University of Chicago Press.

U.S. Const. art. I, § 1, cl. 3.

Webb, Eugene J. 1966. *Unobtrusive Measures: Nonreactive Research in the Social Sciences*. Chicago: Rand McNally.

Zimbardo, Philip G. 2008. *The Lucifer Effect: Understanding How Good People Turn Evil*. New York: Random House Trade Paperbacks.

CHAPTER 3

A Short History of a Long Tradition

My primary purpose in this chapter is to acquaint you with the longstanding, but often hidden, agenda of the social sciences and more specifically, political psychology. Science is normally associated with an unfettered and, therefore open, search for truth. Political psychologists, as all scientists, develop theories to provide possible explanations for phenomenon that interests them. Empirical research then allows them to develop data-based conclusions, conclusions that either confirm or disconfirm the explanations advanced. This very broad summary suggests a very open process, one designed to weed out theories that work from theories that do not work. It also suggests, and most political psychologists affirm, that as a scientific endeavor, unlike an ideological account, the theories we advance we hold subject to empirical verification. Moreover, as new empirical tests are always welcome, theories are never certain but at best provisionally accepted.[1]

This rather reassuring account is satisfying as it seems to proclaim science as a fully open process. Scientists seek to test theories, rejecting those theories that fail to explain the empirical patterns observed. And, for those theories that empirical data confirm, the response is still more testing and a welcome consideration of alternative theories. Theoretical imagination is disciplined by empirical data and human proclivity to find comfort in one's own beliefs is limited by the various norms of science, such as anonymous consideration of manuscripts by anonymous referees.

Although accurate as far as it goes, this account in many important ways is incomplete. The social sciences do bring a substantive agenda. This agenda has shaped much of social science for quite some time. Though scholars study different topics and make use of different methods, many also share some common understandings. And it

---

1. Ideologies are typically conveyed as certainties. Their normative assertions are primary, and as such, they serve to direct human affairs and justify specific courses of action. Insofar as empirical evidence is engaged, it is largely the case that the ideological seek to ignore or discredit evidence that is contrary and embrace with glee even the smallest and flawed tidbits that are confirming.

these understandings that shape their research agendas in important ways. An agenda identifies what is important and what we expect to find. The agenda that shapes the social sciences, in general, and political psychology, in particular, comes to us from the intellectual ferment of the seventeenth and eighteenth centuries in Europe and in the United States (then, for much of that period, colonies of the British crown). We call that ferment and the ideas that evolved therefrom, the enlightenment. Those ideas, and the agenda that they defined, have become so widely shared and deeply embedded that they have become largely invisible with so few to challenge its presumptions. And, as Plato (1974) argued, shared beliefs are not only likely to become invisible, when the rare iconoclast raises a challenge to accepted wisdoms, the response is hardly a welcome one.

Why does this matter, and why should it matter to you? As we shall see in chapter 4, our brains do a lot of work to provide a coherent integrated view of the world we inhabit. Much of that work is hidden. Among what is hidden are the implicit meanings that give shape and form to the world. Thus although we are free to imagine and explore widely we will often not see what we most need to explain because we cannot see it. Our brains not only hide much of what gives unity to our world of sensation they protect that unity. Many of the classic studies in psychology and political psychology demonstrate the vigor of that protection. Leon Festinger's work (1956, 1957), especially vividly told in *When Prophecy Fails*; and even more vividly in Milton Rokeach's (1964) study, which brought together three men who each believed themselves to be Jesus Christ returned to earth, humans powerfully defending their convictions. As we shall see Plato anticipated this research by more than two millennia. But though Festinger's work was on a doomsday cult, and Rokeach's on individuals being restrained in mental institutions, their work should not be taken as applying solely to aberrant groups at the fringe of our social order. Rather we all evince this same protective shield. The goal of the sections that follow is to make the invisible visible. This chapter is intended to ruffle some feathers: yours in particular.

To that end, I am going to examine two different components of the enlightenment perspective and contrast them to the pre-enlightenment alternatives. In both cases the components, first, how we understand time, and second, how we understand reason and emotion. Though "time" has the same name, before and after the enlightenment, what we mean by "time" has taken on a new understanding and that matters mightily in what we expect of politics. In a similar way, what we mean by the terms "reason" and "emotion" also has changed and that also affects politics and psychology.

Contrasting a word that had one meaning but now has acquired a quite different meaning is a useful way of making the invisible visible. It is by comparing different conceptions that we can make presumptions, definitions, and derivative implications clear (Burke and Hyman 1964). There are other comparisons, premodern and modern, that one could make, but these two will serve quite well because they are so foundational to how we, as citizens, go about our daily business, and how we as political psychologists identify what is variable, what is problematic, and what is worth researching.

This chapter has three sections. In the first, I examine time because it is one of the two foundational aspects of reality (space being the other). Time seems rather benign. What does time have to do with psychology or politics? After all, we all know what time is yet, as I shall explore later, we moderns accept both the old (premodern) notion of time as well as the new, enlightenment, conception of time. These two contrary conceptions argue for quite different agendas for political psychology. Because time is fundamental, foundational, what conception of time, political psychology presumes, will impact on all other conceptions that radiate outward including, most obviously, what we can expect from the future?

In the second section, the familiar notions of reason and emotion are explored. Emotion and reason, what they are, how they are related to each other, and how they influence what we are and what we do infuses premodern and modern thinking about politics. And, they remain consequential because both those conceptions are very engaged in almost every corner of political psychology.

Finally, in section three, I touch on the unexpected consequences of conceiving of time as progress. The expectations of a smooth transition as progress unfolds have not proven to be as anticipated.

I. TIME

It is a common modern notion that the latest is the greatest. Progress is the expected result in all matters related to human affairs. This expectation comes from the enlightenment thinkers; it was not much in evidence before that time. But, time has not been overly kind to that expectation. That leaves us with a conundrum: The modern cliché that democracy and the spread of and reliance on reason are joined together so that democracy and reason will replace reliance on faith and autocratic rule seems no longer certain. And, that our new faiths, science, reason, and progress, have been shaken are in part due to our failure to rigorously examine especially what we could not see. Let's turn to the hidden.

Understanding Premodern Conceptions of Time

Time would seem to be easy to grasp. There is yesterday, today, and tomorrow. Nonetheless, that simple array of past, present, and future, hides two quite different understandings of time. And, those two different understandings shape the premodern and modern sensibilities. It would be a mistake to assert that the premoderns had one conception and the moderns a different conception. Life is not so easily categorized into errorless taxonomies (as I hope you will recall from Madison's argument in Federalist Paper No. 37). It is more accurate to say that in the modern era some hew, by and large, to the premodern conception, some hew to the modern conception, and most of us adhere, haphazardly to one or the other as circumstances warrant. But that is getting ahead of ourselves. So, what is the premodern conception of time?

Philosopher Hannah Arendt (1968) advanced the critical insight that the distinction between the premodern and the modern was at its core a radical change in the conception of time. She used the concept of revolution to illustrate the difference between the premodern and the modern. This example is quite useful as it explicitly focuses on the political. For, as I noted in chapter 1, one of the core issues of political psychology is to help ascertain the type of political regime that is best suited to the vagaries of human nature. And, revolutions mark change from one type of regime to another.

Why apply the word "revolution" to a change of regime type? For the word *revolution*, literally, means to revolve around something. Hence, it should not seem to be apt to describe how one type of regime (say a monarchy) is overthrown and a republic established in its place as "revolving." In the modern era we associate political revolutions, such as the American, French, and Russian, with the introduction of something new, a new regime. So, how can a word that expresses a revolving be applicable? Well, that depends on our conception of time.

As Arendt (1968) noted, in the premodern world the predominant notion of time was time as repeating cycles. Look around and we observe natural cycles, repetitions, all around. Time's passage is readily understood as recurring repetition, both in its daily course, morning, noon, afternoon, and night, and its yearly transit through the seasons, spring, summer, fall, and winter. These cycles mirror those of our natural lives, spring = birth, summer = growth into adulthood, fall = passage to old age, winter = death. And, we see the same cycles in agriculture, planting in the spring, crops growing in the summer, crops being harvested in late summer, in the fall plowing the fields to prepare the soil for the dormant period of winter. The life cycle is replicated throughout the plant and animal kingdoms.

The planets and stars in the sky also seem to move in recurring cycles, as do the oceans tides. Human activities have long been linked to these cycles, for example, when to plant, when to harvest, when to expect the birth of animals. It is not then surprising to find that the development of calendars in all societies marks the important connections between natural cycles, lunar and annual transit of the sun, and recurring human events.

Cycles are revealed throughout human affairs, as in the "natural" growth of empire: its vigorous youth, its mature phase, followed by aging into decrepitude through indulgence and torpor, and finally its death. Historians tell such stories well. And, we often claim to see cycles in human affairs. Economists speak of the business cycle. Political scientists describe election cycles. So do those who believe in astrology. We search for recurring patterns that provide us with confidence that our past foretells the future. Libraries are full of tales of repetition, and time is the passage through repeating cycles (Gibbon 1900).

If time recurs in cycles, then it makes sense to speak of violent and sudden change from an "old" regime to the "birth" of a new regime as a revolution. Thus, we apply the analogy to human births, which also are marked by blood and pain, and sadly, the occasional death of the birth mother, much as many revolutionaries are consumed in the turmoil and fight for power of the events they help initiate (see the French and Russian revolutions for many examples). After their victory, French revolutionaries celebrated their overthrow of the monarchy by dressing in Roman togas. They understood what they had done as toppling a decaying corrupt dying regime so that a new republic could be born to take its place. They took as their aspirational model the Roman Senate, hoping that something young and vigorous would arise to replace the monarchy they toppled.

A revolution describes the destruction of the monarchy, much as in agriculture the prior season's crop's detritus must be plowed under to make way so that the new crop can be planted. They understood what they had accomplished as a revolution, using

BOX 3.1   Ancient Greek myths

In ancient Greek mythology three goddesses were charged with presiding over the birth and life of humans. Each person's life course was presented as a thread that was spun, measured, and cut by the three fates, Clotho, Lachesis, and Atropos.

Or, consider the myth of Icarus while flying, with fabricated and hence unnatural, wings who flies too close to the sun, which melts the wax that binds the feathers to his arms, causing him to fall to his death in the sea.

violence to push the *wheel* of history a bit faster. This conception of time enables an empirical connection to become a normative framework. If spring is when life begins anew then that is when it is best to plant and begin.[2] As all living things age and die, so it will be political regimes and empires. All come to a natural end.

The revolving cycle of life is also apparent in the notion of *fate*, that is, that life has a natural order. Though often hidden from view, our fate controls our destinies.

Our lives, thus, express the natural order. To rebel against our fate is at best futile, and at worse risks destruction. It is best to "accept one's fate." If we would but accept the natural order has often become both a religious and secular admonition that remains influential even in the modern era. Hence, this conception of time is much infused with political significance. Those who defend the *natural* order of things are doing so because to do otherwise is to challenge nature, whether we conceive of nature as secular or as divinely infused. Those who would wish others ruled, or that other social and political practices be installed, are risking destruction. Time as cyclical, especially when married to the idea of fate and destiny, is inherently conservative, protective of the established social order, established political authority, and dominant traditions.

In addition, with time as cyclical, the debate between advocates of democracy, such as Aristotle (1983), and those who advocated aristocratic rule, such as Plato (1974), is stable. Nothing new will alter that debate for human nature is fixed and our natures either suit us for democracy, as some have it, or for aristocracy, as others have it. With time expressed as recurring cycles there is no escape, we are destined by our nature to live within the constants of time's passage.

Within the premodern perspective of time as cyclical, we have a use for political psychology, but it would have a very limited agenda: How do we find the individuals who have the talent to rule, and how do we train them to obtain the clarity and knowledge suited to challenges of ruling? A political psychology that works within the premodern conception of time will focus on the pattern of recurring cycles. How fast do regimes retain their vigor? What options are there for when a regime's natural life saps and declines? Can a younger generation produce new leaders able to take power? And, is that natural transition helped or hindered by the array of traditions and institutions in place? Moreover, the power and aspirations of ruler would be tempered by the natural limits of cyclical time. Because life and death are natural, the most governments

---

2. Deans and presidents of universities often hold to this conception of rotating wheels of history. They expect that after the dormant winter, students will awake in the spring and, hence, spring student riots are to be expected, as proved to be the case in France in May 1968.

and politics can do is to ease the passage for many. It would be folly to challenge the natural limits of time. Youth can replace the old and infirm, but our natures are, apart from its passage through the stages of life, fixed. Our agenda would turn to such topics as political socialization and of course its partner, the study of personality. We would want, then as now, to focus on what produces virtue and what corrupts. A particular concern would be how to master passages as when those who rule become, as time's passage ensures that they will, decadent and lethargic.

There is one further insight that I want to call to your attention. If natural and human affairs are repetitive, then knowledge has a particular focus. Those who know are those who have been in a position to observe the recurring patterns of life. Close observation, apart from the mysteries of luck, gives clarity as to the future; if human affairs are cyclical in their evolution then knowledge of cycles, whether astronomical, natural events on earth, or human, should be the basis of authority. We can observe that in many communities newer residents are expected to be quiet and rely on the local wisdom of the longtime residents. Elders, who have the wisdom gained by long life and long observation, are best able to guide the young. Traditions should be respected as they have proven their worth through the repetitive patterns of many seasons. Here an epistemology has a clear impact on politics and more precisely the issue of who should rule. Those who can best read the past and present are better able to guide the city or nation. A theory of time becomes a normative theory of rulership.[3]

Time as recurring cycles, resplendent with analogies drawn from nature, the seasons, and so on, leads to a political psychology bound within the restraints of time so conceived. Free those restrictions, find a new and different conception, and new possibilities become evident. And, with the enlightenment, came a new conception of time. Rather than time as a wheel that rotates from beginning to recurring end and return again in endless repetition, the enlightenment thinkers reconceived time as an engine that, as a train on tracks, drives along a line from past to future. Time as progress replaced time as cyclical repetition.

Understanding Modern Time

The social sciences emerged in the modern era largely shaped by the enlightenment. And, political psychology, in particular, has its foundational beliefs closely tied to the foundational beliefs of the enlightenment. There are many fine books (Frazer 2010; Hirschman 1977; Porter 2001) that cover this development but I will keep the presentation short.

The enlightenment was an expression of a profound change in how humans placed themselves in history. The modern conception of time understands time as a linear progression from an older and archaic way of life to a new, younger, and more progressive way of life. Life progresses through stages, and further, the earlier stages are simpler and less adept than the newer stages that better enable us to meet life's challenges. Karl Marx and Hegel (Hegel and Baillie 2003; Hegel and Dyde 2005), exemplified this view of time, as do most democracy theorists. Marx (Marx and Engels 2002) described

---

3. The recurring interest in the stars, astrology, is premised on the linkage of human cycles with astrological. And, belief in time as a wheel encourages reliance on enduring dynasties on the belief that the qualities of rulership will pass from older to younger. It is easy to observe the continuing seductive attraction of astrology and of dynastic reliance to some among us in the modern world.

a system of class organization tied to a functional view of conflict that would drive change, inevitably, from older to newer forms of organization, from feudal to mercantilist, then to capitalist, to socialist, and finally, when time would stop, to communism.

Time becomes an arrow, a linear movement that always leaves the past behind to enter into an always new future. For different thinkers, different arrows, different engines of history, caused the change of past to future. For Marx, the engine was class struggle; for Immanuel Kant it was war (Kant 1970b). But let us look to another argument, one that speaks directly to a debate between Plato and Aristotle that we shall take up in the next section.

Alexis de Tocqueville visited the United States supported by a grant from the French revolutionary government to prepare a report on the new penitentiary system for dealing with criminals then underway in the United States.[4] Although that was the rationale that provided the funding, that was not the real purpose that led de Tocqueville to come to America. The real reason was to study democracy. So, in 1831, at the age of 25 years, Alexis de Tocqueville came to study America. There he found more than democracy; he found a democracy that was going to inevitably spread well beyond its current borders. In his introduction to *Democracy in America* (two volumes the first published in 1835 and the second in 1840), he explained why hierarchical systems of authority would be replaced by more democratic systems (de Tocqueville 2000):

> Once works of the intellect had become sources of force and wealth, each development of science, each new piece of knowledge, each new idea had to be considered as a seed of power put within the reach of the people Poetry, eloquence. memory. the graces of the mind, the fires of the imagination, depth of thought. all the gifts that Heaven distributed haphazardly, profited democracy, and even if they were found in the possession of its adversaries, they still served its cause by putting into relief the natural greatness of man; its conquests therefore spread with those of civilization and enlightenment, and literature was an arsenal open to all, from which the weak and the poor came each day to seek arms.

> When one runs through the pages of our history, one finds so to speak no great events in seven hundred years that have not turned to the profit of equality.

> If you examine what is happening in France every fifty years from the eleventh century on, at the end of each of these periods you cannot fail to perceive that a double revolution has operated on the state of society. The noble has fallen on the social ladder, and the commoner has risen; the one descends, the other climbs. Each half century brings them nearer, and soon they are going to touch.

> And this is not peculiar to France. In whichever direction we cast a glance we perceive the same revolution continuing in all the Christian universe.

---

4. At that time jails and prisons held people who had committed crimes, or who had debts they were unwilling or, more commonly unable, to pay. There was no expectation that punishment of imprisonment would do other than keep these malefactors off the streets during their term of imprisonment.

The penitentiary movement intended to replace prisons with penitentiaries. Therein rules of isolation and silence were intended to make those held engage in penance. By reflection on their actions it was expected that the penitents would feel sorrow and remorse. And, if repentant, would be changed to a person morally reconstituted thus more safely able to participate in civil society.

Everywhere the various incidents in the lives of peoples are seen to turn to the profit of democracy; all men have aided it by their efforts. those who had in view cooperating for its success and those who did not dream of serving it; those who fought for it and even those who declared themselves its enemies; all have been driven pell-mell on the same track, and all have worked in common, some despite themselves, others without knowing it, as blind instruments in the hands of God.

The gradual development of equality of conditions is therefore a providential fact, and it has the principal characteristics of one: it is universal, it is enduring, each day it escapes human power; all events, like all men, serve its development.

If de Tocqueville was right, then human imagination is the engine of history, would drive us to ever greater conditions of equality. As more people are given the minimal means to participate in the generation and distribution of ideas, then the dynamic that de Tocqueville identified will become even stronger. Hence, democracy becomes the institutional regime most likely to accelerate progress because a democratic regime enables more people to engage in private and public deliberation on the means by which their sundry preferences can be justified and realized. The development of institutions such as a free press and an expansive public education also will contribute to the speed of this unfolding of progress.

We also can point to some recent examples to illustrate de Tocqueville's interpretation. The availability of consumer video cameras, and their ready adoption, enabled a bystander to capture the beating of Rodney King. This instance and many more have the predictable result of undermining the police's general authority to have exclusive authorship to depict what happened and who was to blame.[5] In a similar way, the wide spread and inexpensive availability of digital cameras and cell phones equipped with cameras enabled the mistreatment and even murder of prisoners under US administration within the prison Abu Ghraib to be distributed throughout the world. Absent publicly available technology such as smart phones, digital cameras, flip cameras, and the like, soldiers observing the brutal treatment of prisoners and wishing to make public what they had observed would have been left pitting their words against the authority of the US military and the US government. Though not developed for that purpose, cheap and highly compact digital cameras *leveled*. The pictures they provided destroyed the initial claims offered by authorities that nothing serious happened. The pictures sent throughout the world, degraded the authority of the United States throughout the world and prevented the traditional ability that the militaries have full control over information. The invention of the Internet also makes control of information far more

---

5. A not surprising result has been, in the United States and in some states, the passage of laws prohibiting the filming of police officers as they do their work. This is hardly unique to the United States. During World War II, the German military, the Wehrmacht, forbade its soldiers from sending photos from the front with particular concern for images that depicted the army's role in the killing of Jews. The prohibition was generally effective, though some violated this rule sending images back to their families. Had cameras been as ubiquitous as now no doubt there would have been more images sent.

It has long been common practice of militaries to practice censorship of communications from the front to secure military advantage and to prevent embarrassing information from leaking out and undermining support on the "home front."

difficult for governments. The Internet levels, as do the technologies of instant messaging, e-mail, and the like that enable people to bypass governments' control of postal systems. In addition, Google enables swift discovery of information. Cheap, even free, software enables anyone who can learn to use it to create webpages or to blog. Each of these further enhances the equality of condition that de Tocqueville observed during his visit to America.

If de Tocqueville was correct about the role of imagination then democracy in its various guises will spread replacing monarchial and aristocratic regimes. And, this shift will go only in one direction, from a past in which hierarchies predominate, to a certain future, in which hierarchies will give way to democratic forms of authority.

The expansion of equality would also fuel yet more enlightenment: The spread of education would weaken established traditions and hierarchical authorities because wider education would enable more to make fuller use of reason rather than relying on traditions and deference to their "betters." Hence, the capacity of a public to engage in collective judgment would be an *emergent* property revealed as progress proceeds.

Because imagination is a condition of our nature, then the trajectory of change carries with it the presumption of certainty. The trajectory cannot be stopped; it can be slowed, and perhaps momentarily deflected, but its fundamental trajectory cannot be altered.

The modern science of human nature rejects the view that our fates unfold. Charles Darwin (1966) exemplified this new way of understanding our place in time. Rather than a pattern of recurring cycles, he found that evolution, not revolution, driven by an ever changing and harsh reality, rewarded species if they could respond to an every changing environment. Species prosper if they evolve, or they decline and even disappear if they remain stagnant in the face of serious environmental challenges. Rather than life being a recurring and ever repeating passage from birth and vigor to torpor and death, modern time shows patterns of mutation, evolution, and extinction. Psychologist Donald T. Campbell (1960; 1988) extended this argument to the evolution of ideas. Ideas that succeed are those that "fit" the needs of the moment as tested by their ability to help us survive the challenges we confront much as do some physical mutations.

In sum, modern time affords new possibilities. Whichever formulation of the engine of history we might adopt, de Tocqueville's, Karl Marx's, or some other, is less important than the broad underlying presumption. If the past is something we leave for good at each and every moment of the present, then the past is no longer the sole and certain foundation for knowledge. No longer is knowledge of the past a stable guide to what will happen. And, therefore, those who hold ancient wisdom will have less authority to make decisions that will govern the future than those who generate a new kind of knowledge, the knowledge of progress. As the future is a departure from past and present, then knowledge has a difference character than in the premodern era. And, those who can obtain and make good use of this new knowledge shape those who can and should govern. As the conception of time changes so does the conception of knowledge, and so does what we think knowledge can accomplish and what it cannot. More important for political psychologists, changing conceptions of time and knowledge also change our understanding of politics, and specifically, who should govern, why, and to what ends.

II. EMOTION AND REASON SHAPING POLITICAL PSYCHOLOGY

A second difference between the premodern and the modern turns on the conceptions of reason, of passion, and of their relationship one to the other. These terms, then as now, turn on a crucial normative depiction of humans. The fact that humans can reason, subject to what we mean by that claim, is less significant than the normative assertion that because we exhibit reason we can be self- and collectively governing. On the other hand, emotion was then and since understood, by many but not all, as disruptive of cerebral reason.

The interest in reason and emotion arose because it addressed the foremost question that has long engaged us: Where can we find the knowledge so that whichever regime we adopt it will be virtuous? The ancients formulated the enduring debate between those who argued that only the few have knowledge sufficient to rule as against those who argued that the many can and should rule because they indeed have sufficient knowledge to contribute to collective decisions. And, deeply implicated in what they and we believe about knowledge, what knowledge is and who can obtain it, are the twin ideas of reason and emotion. The debate over who can know, how, and why has extended for millennia, but few, if any, have done it better than Plato and Aristotle.[6]

Plato (1974), in *The Republic*, set forth the basic aristocratic argument for who should rule in the section, "The Simile of the Cave." Speaking in the voice of Socrates, his teacher, to one of his students, Glaucon, Plato set forth,

> And now, I said, let me show in a figure how far our nature is enlightened or unenlightened:—Behold! human beings living in a underground den, which has a mouth open towards the light and reaching all along the den; here they have been from their childhood, and have their legs and necks chained so that they cannot move, and can only see before them, being prevented by the chains from turning round their heads. Above and behind them a fire is blazing at a distance, and between the fire and the prisoners there is a raised way; and you will see, if you look, a low wall built along the way, like the screen which marionette players have in front of them, over which they show the puppets.
>
> GLAUCON: I see.
>
> And do you see, I said, men passing along the wall carrying all sorts of vessels, and statues and figures of animals made of wood and stone and various materials, which appear over the wall? Some of them are talking, others silent.
>
> GLAUCON: You have shown me a strange image, and they are strange prisoners.
>
> Like ourselves, I replied; and they see only their own shadows, or the shadows of one another, which the fire throws on the opposite wall of the cave?

---

6. The debate was not just an intellectual matter. The city state of Athens formed the first democracy and had its celebrators, notably but not just Pericles. Sparta, among other Greek city–states had both the most powerful land army and was ruled by a stable monarchy–aristocracy. Plato and Aristotle made arguments, of course, but they also had the animosity of the two aspirant city–states in mind, with the former idealizing Sparta and the latter staying loyal to the city–state that he had fought for.

...

And if they were able to converse with one another, would they not suppose that they were naming what was actually before them?

GLAUCON: Very true.

And suppose further that the prison had an echo which came from the other side, would they not be sure to fancy when one of the passers-by spoke that the voice which they heard came from the passing shadow?

GLAUCON: No question, he replied.

To them, I said, the truth would be literally nothing but the shadows of the images.

GLAUCON: That is certain.

...

And suppose once more, that he is reluctantly dragged up a steep and rugged ascent, and held fast until he's forced into the presence of the sun himself, is he not likely to be pained and irritated? When he approaches the light his eyes will be dazzled, and he will not be able to see anything at all of what are now called realities.

GLAUCON: Not all in a moment, he said.

He will require to grow accustomed to the sight of the upper world. And first he will see the shadows best, next the reflections of men and other objects in the water, and then the objects themselves; then he will gaze upon the light of the moon and the stars and the spangled heaven; and he will see the sky and the stars by night better than the sun or the light of the sun by day?

GLAUCON: Certainly.

Last of he will be able to see the sun, and not mere reflections of him in the water, but he will see him in his own proper place, and not in another; and he will contemplate him as he is.

GLAUCON: Certainly.

He will then proceed to argue that this is he who gives the season and the years, and is the guardian of all that is in the visible world, and in a certain way the cause of all things which he and his fellows have been accustomed to behold?

GLAUCON: Clearly, he said, he would first see the sun and then reason about him.

And when he remembered his old habitation, and the wisdom of the den and his fellow-prisoners, do you not suppose that he would felicitate himself on the change, and pity them?

GLAUCON: Certainly, he would.

...

Imagine once more, I said, such an one coming suddenly out of the sun to be replaced in his old situation; would he not be certain to have his eyes full of darkness?

GLAUCON: To be sure, he said.

[And if he then tried to argue with his fellows about the falseness of what they saw and believed] with the prisoners who had never moved out of the den, while his sight was still weak, and before his eyes had become steady (and the time which would be needed to acquire this new habit of sight might be very considerable) would he not be ridiculous? Men would say of him that up he went and down he came without his eyes; and that it was better not even to think of ascending; and if any one tried to loose another and lead him up to the light, let them only catch the offender, and they would put him to death.

Plato advances a number of important points. First, Plato advances the argument that knowledge should be the basis of ruling. He makes this ever more explicit in the later sections of the Republic when he calls for rule by "philosopher kings." Second, he makes the observation that people will choose the comfort of their beliefs over truth when they are in conflict. When people confront someone who has truth on his side, Plato holds that they will kill in defense of their beliefs, even though their beliefs are delusions. Third, most people are quite comfortable living in a world of mythic traditions, in sum, delusion. It is only those few disciplined who strive to secure truth by leaving the social environment who can become philosopher kings. Because life in society compels acceptance of traditions and opinions as true, philosopher kings from a very early age must begin training, taken away from their families so they can be uncontaminated from extant traditions. Only if they are carefully selected as suitable, separated from their families, and trained for years, can they begin a rigorous exploration of the actual nature of things. Hence, fourth, and most basic, Plato distinguishes between knowledge and illusion, between truth and opinion.

Plato argued that to give the public a role in public affairs would introduce assertive opinion, what today's political psychologists would call "motivated reasoning" (Kunda 1990; Lodge and Taber 2000). Hence, it is no surprise that Plato predicted that when truth confronts belief, the result would be the killing of truth-sayers. Bear in mind that Socrates, Plato's teacher, was condemned to death by an Athenian jury, a jury elected by lot, for challenging the sacred beliefs of Athenians, therefore, do not take this allegory as merely fanciful.

Aristotle (1983) discussed the issue of how to obtain knowledge in a famous portion of his book, *The Politics*. And, as Aristotle was Plato's student, much as Plato was Socrates, this section can be understood as a conversation with his mentor as much as a lecture to others:

> The principle that the multitude ought to be supreme rather than the few best is one that is maintained, and, though not free from difficulty, yet seems to contain an element of truth. For the many, of whom each individual is but an ordinary person, when they meet together may very likely be better than the few good, if regarded not individually but collectively, just as a feast to which many contribute is better than a dinner provided out of a single purse. For each individual among the many has a share of virtue and prudence, and when they meet together, they become in a manner one man, who has many feet, and hands, and senses; that is a figure of their mind and disposition. Hence the many are better judges than a single man of music and poetry; for some understand one part, and some another, and among them they understand the whole. There is a similar combination of qualities in good men, who differ from any individual

of the many, as the beautiful are said to differ from those who are not beautiful, and works of art from realities, because in them the scattered elements are combined, although, if taken separately, the eye of one person or some other feature in another person would be fairer than in the picture. Whether this principle can apply to every democracy, and to all bodies of men, is not clear. Or rather, by heaven, in some cases it is impossible of application; for the argument would equally hold about brutes; and wherein, it will be asked, do some men differ from brutes? But there may be bodies of men about whom our statement is nevertheless true. And if so, the difficulty which has been already raised, and also another which is akin to it—viz., what power should be assigned to the mass of freemen and citizens, who are not rich and have no personal merit- are both solved. There is still a danger in allowing them to share the great offices of state, for their folly will lead them into error, and their dishonesty into crime. But there is a danger also in not letting them share, for a state in which many poor men are excluded from office will necessarily be full of enemies. The only way of escape is to assign to them some deliberative and judicial functions.

Aristotle believed that collective judgment could produce results superior to that offered by a singular, philosopher king. Aristotle also presaged the argument of Hobbes, that sovereign authority depended on the endorsement of the populace, for political, indeed all authority, depended on the audience's willing attention and acceptance. Aristotle defended democracy against the aristocratic critique that the public were too unstable to do the work of securing truth but he also changed what it meant to know. This debate can be clarified by focusing on points of agreement and disagreement.

For Plato the critical comparison is between truth, which describes the true nature of things, hence is universal, stable over time and space; and opinion, which is unstable and a distorted view of reality. So,

> Truth: *objective* (describes the true nature of the world), *stable* over space and time;
> Opinion: *subjective* (describes the shared beliefs and opinions of a community), *unstable* over space and time.

Hence, opinion is not enduring as it quickly adapts to meet various social requirements. It is easy to observe that people advance opinions that they expect will meet with the approval of others, indeed that is the principal task of politicians (as contrasted to statesmen who eschew the unstable public for presumed clear-eyed vision of the public good).[7]

Aristotle agreed that knowledge was the basis for sound judgment, but his view of what counted as knowledge expanded to include the subjective satisfactions that must be the goal of collective decisions. What does it matter if by some standard of truth an excellent meal is presented or some selection of poetry identified as the best, if those who are to consume the meal or listen to the reading of the poem find their taste ignored? Collective contributions from a diverse array of citizens will, Aristotle argued,

---

7. It is a common feature of political rhetoric for politicians to present themselves as being "of the people" when it serves but to also present themselves as statesmen, uninterested in the polls, a posture also often chosen for its current usefulness.

BOX 3.2 Rationality

This term is problematic as it has two different meanings: rationality as a *process* of decision making and rationality as a *result*, the best choice, however obtained. It is the former meaning that is usually applied in the formal comparison of reason and emotion though the second is also implied. If we reason to a decision we will be acting rationally and if we act rationally we will be securing the most rational outcome.

make for better meals, better poems, and better collective judgments, than reliance on the judgment of one, no matter how well trained that one individual might be. But, if you think through his examples, he did not accept Plato's notion of objective truth, at least in matters of political judgment. Is a good meal an objective truth in the manner that Plato construed? For Aristotle, no, because tastes matter and who is invited to attend a dinner will matter as each person will bring along a different array of tastes. Or, if one opts to go on a sea voyage, whether it be a voyage of settlement (Athenians sent out colonies to various locations around the Aegean sea) or of war (think of the Trojan war), how things will turn out is not able to be known in advance but will turn on many matters beyond the ken of those making the decision.[8]

Reason is most often taken as the foundation of judgment, but we also experience and are moved by passion. These separate faculties have long been understood as distinct. Hence, a common conception is that at any moment one or the other is dominant. The former, reason, is explicit and visible: When we reason, we have before us all the components: our reasons, our evidentiary claims, and logical operations that make explicit the recommendation that presents the best result for achieving our stated intention. So, if asked, we can reveal how we reasoned to a judgment (whether we choose to be honest or dishonest is another, but here, unimportant matter).

Passions, on the other hand, while visible in their expression, arise seemingly unbidden and mysterious. The word "instinctive" is often linked to emotion in a way that is never applied to reason. Notice that the contrast implies a spatial metaphor: Reason is an act of thinking that takes place in our conscious mind while feeling is an act of the body. The spatial metaphor, thinking in one's "head" and feeling in one's "heart" or "gut" is a trope of longstanding. We cannot readily access the true sources of our own feelings, let alone observe the sources of the feelings of others. Moreover, and more crucial, emotions are not rational.

This then raises a central theme: How to deal with the mysteries and power of emotion, a topic of such important that Nussbaum (1986, 1994) argued that it gave rise to philosophy. Mastering the emotions, as the stoics sought, would be another,

---

8. Unlike the Spartans, Plato's favorites, the Athens made its empire by its command of the seas. Most served in one capacity or another on the triremes. They knew war. They knew a good beginning may well end in disaster or victory. They knew that a voyage began in the harbor, began blind as to what lay ahead. They knew, as they left the harbor, their homes would sink below the horizon, leaving them blind to their home (and what lay in the past) and blind as to what they would find on their arrival, if they arrived. As their ships left all would wonder, do storms await; will they come across a turncoat who will give them important secrets; will they confront, unexpectedly, two enemies just joined in alliance; or a serene and smooth trip? It is beyond a sailor's craft to foretell what will happen (Thucydides 1996).

BOX 3.3   Modern conservatism

Embracing the discipline of the market, a liberating idea, in as much as to make a system of market exchange work required established traditions to give way, for example, religious injunctions against usury or against valuing the pursuit of riches But, securing the freedom of market exchanges often led some economic conservatives to weigh against government regulation. A position that differentiated them from others equally attracted to the liberating promise of progress, but who saw in a government a liberating force resulting from unconstrained democratic rule including the oversight of the economies of market exchange.

---

perhaps the most important, item on the discipline's agenda. And, mastering the emotions requires that we turn to and rely on reason to execute its careful, visible, construction of judgment.

If we translate these topics into the language of modern political psychology, the ancients were deeply interested in theories of personality (who has the capacity to rule), socialization (what could be done to train those who can rule), institutions (what arrangements could strengthen public judgment), and the psychology of decision making. Justifying who should rule depends primarily on who has the ability to make sound decisions. For Plato the answer was found in aristocratic rule, rule by the best. For Aristotle, the answer was found in collective judgment by the many; rule by democracy (though he acknowledged that entailed the risk of folly).

The notions of reason and emotion are also affected by the idea of progress. Previously, reason and passion were understood as unalterable aspect of our nature. But if time marks progress rather than cycles, then perhaps the two-fold taxonomy, reason and emotion, is alterable. And, indeed enlightenment scholars developed a new taxonomy to replace the old. The full story is well told by Albert Hirschman (1977). In the modern taxonomy, a third category was invented and inserted between reason and passion: interest. Interest was understood as a calculating emotion, either selfish or generous our usage: "self-interest" and "public interest." Here interest is our attachment, emotion, to a goal. Interest as an emotion has the ability to move us to action, something that reason famously lacks. But as linked to some end, our "interest" can attach to a thing, say one's farm; an activity, such as one's profession; some intention, such as protecting one's family; or as patriotism, protecting one's nation. Interest becomes rational by linking means and end with motive because the goal disciplines otherwise unruly emotion.

Adam Smith (1986), with the help of others, used the notion of interest in his theory of the market economy.

Markets would enable interest bearing individuals to interact by mutual exchange and with felicitous benefit. Hence, interest and markets would produce an auspicious future, the ever expansive commonwealth. This new taxonomy envisioned a new world that would expand free exchange to yield an ever more inclusive and beneficent society. Only a conception of time as progress would make such a vision prophetic and realistic. Had the conception of time as cyclical remain embedded in the thinking of Condorcet (1795), Adam Smith, and others of the time of the enlightenment, it is quite unlikely that they would have envisioned these developments for doing so time as cyclical would prevent such developments.

The enlightenment also changed the notion of knowledge. No longer were reason and passion the sole mental states that humans experienced. The taxonomy was changed to include a third mental category, interest. Table 3.1 shows the old and new taxonomies.

The language of interest permeates the modern discussion of politics. We have "special" interests. Among these are the organized efforts of various economic sectors, such as mineral extraction corporations to seek advantage. Added to this example are other "special interests," organized groups, such as unions, professions, or various groups, defined by some common beliefs or values, among them dealing with sexual orientation, age, or regional loyalties. We also have the "public" or "common" interest, those shared interests that are presumed to unite a community, state, or nation. We have warring interests as when we speak of our "economic interests" as adverse to our "social interests." It is common to proclaim that "interest groups" are the core of democratic politics (Truman 1951).

Because interests do not reside in the self-aware mental region, in which conscious reason resides, we may not even know what our "interests" are. This then gave birth to the notion of "false consciousness"; that is, we have interests but we misconstrue what they are, instead adopting some views that will not serve us as well. And, because individuals may not know their interests, we as scholars, or as pundits or just observers can ascribe on to others what we hold what their "real" interests must be. We can say someone has a "vested" interest in some affairs (as when we might consider a politician, judge, or bureaucrat to be corrupted by virtue of some "interest" that we assert alters the appropriate decision-making process). Hence, interests provide a potent and highly useful concept to explain political judgment and behavior with the added advantage (or disadvantage) of being somewhat elusive.

However this tripartite taxonomy of reason, interest, and passion, is not the last taxonomic effort to understand mental states. While table 3.1 outlines the major comparisons, and commonalities in premodern and modern conceptions, there is one implicit presumption that joins this particular modern conception with the premodern and that has to do with the focus on locations of reason and emotions as an essential point of demarcation. It is not just that emotion and reason have different qualities

Table 3.1. Old and new taxonomies of mental states

Mental states				
Premodern		Postenlightenment		
Reason	**Emotion**	**Reason**	**Interest**	**Emotion**
Located in the mind with weak control over body; too easily pushed aside by passion, but able to assess and make reasoned decisions	Located in the body; very powerful, direct control over the body; turbulent, often irrational	Located in the mind with weak control over body; too easily pushed aside by passion, but able to assess and make reasoned decisions	Neither mind nor body; but a distinct combination of calculating emotion, enduring, powerful, and rational	Located in the body; very powerful, direct control over the body; turbulent, often irrational

(particularly with respect to their different levels of strength, i.e., relationship to action and rationality, i.e., one is and one is not). It is that each has a spatial locale.

Neuroscience, making using of a variety of tools to investigate mental states, offers a new path to understand our mental states. These investigations have revealed new roles for emotion and indeed, for reason. I investigate these insights in chapters 4 and 5. Here I want to make a more basic point about conceptions of time and how they enable and constrain.

Human Nature and Conceptions of Time

Much as time as cycle imports normative judgments, so does the conception of time as progress. Let me offer examples taken from the literature on personality to make the point. One of the most enduring topics of focus in psychology and political psychology has been the rejection of democratic rule. In the aftermath of World War II, one of the more perplexing issues that arose in the social sciences was why many residing in democratic nations in Europe, even though under the duress of a world wide depression, the recent influenza pandemic, and the destruction caused by World War I, gave substantial support to the overthrow of their democratic institutions and gave support to authoritarian regimes: to Franco in Spain, to Mussolini in Italy, and, of course, to Hitler in Germany and Austria. This question led to one of the most influential studies to explain which types of people would eschew democratic politics for authoritarianism, *The Authoritarian Personality* (Adorno et al. 1950).

The logic of time as progress suggests that progress should be most revealed in the most developed of societies, those with the longest experience with progress and the wealth it yielded. Hence, it was deeply upsetting to see even in the face of the grave challenges facing European nations in the 1920s and 1930s to have fascism so evidently receiving a warm welcome. From the progressive perspective, authoritarianism is understood as pathology, both because it is understood as a historically archaic inclination and because it is at least partially responsible for the grave evils of fascism. And, this has shaped how some political psychologists understand conservatism.

Psychologist John Jost (Jost et al. 2003, 342) gave a widely adopted definition: Conservatism has "two core dimensions—resistance to change and acceptance of inequality." If change is the essential natural feature of time and if equality is, as de Tocqueville argued, a natural consequence of the trajectory of human nature through time, then of course conservatives are futilely braying against the inevitably of progress, much as ancient King Canute futilely directed the ocean tides to withdraw.

BOX 3.4 Omniscience redux

It is often argued by critics of collective judgment, such as Plato, that reliance on experts will achieve better results. At the core, this is the essential argument against democracy; whether those experts are monarchs or aristocrats—the learned of whatever training. As Philip Tetlock (2005) recently showed the ability of experts to use their expertise to predict the future and therefore to have a basis for authority over collective judgment is not sustained by evidence (see Tetlock 2005).

If conservatives are motivated to resist change and to value inequality, it follows that liberals are motivated to endorse change and to value equality. Recall that political psychology relies on thin description of variables and dimensions. If ideological predilection is a basic dimension of personality, as Jost and others hold, we can each be located somewhere along a dimension that arrays us depending on how much resistance to change we endorse. Great repugnance to change would anchor the conservative end, neutrality in the middle, and great enthusiasm for change at the other, liberal end. Because progress, we moderns presume, leads to a better future, then resistance to change would seem to be an archaic and counterproductive orientation. A comforting presumption if one is a progressive liberal, as many social scientists are. Not such a welcome conception if one is a conservative.

Perhaps we should be cautious in attributing this normative cast to this conception. Some of us will, so the data shows, resist change; others will be more inclined to embrace change. We discuss the issue of personality more fully in chapter 7, but let me offer here the obvious point that although sexual reproduction guarantees that children will share some of their parents' qualities, they also will be somewhat distinct. Why then has this distribution of differential orientation to change been preserved in our genes as evidence now suggests (Alford et al. 2005)? Perhaps the answer is that in any given case, our species is better off for having both orientations distributed among us than having just one modal position.

Imagine, as a thought experiment: Imagine that we are members of a small tribe living in a valley that has nice land and water to sustain us. Some of the tribe speculates that conditions in the next valley may be better. Others argue that going to another valley will expose the tribe to unknown dangers, perhaps dangerous predators or diseases. Two possible errors await them. If the first group persuades the tribe to go across and if dangers await them, the entire tribe faces possible doom. But if the second group is the more persuasive, a lush and more life sustaining valley is going to be left to others to exploit to the tribe's disadvantage. So risks await no matter which option we choose. We might forgo a rich reward by cautiously staying close to home; we might get into a horrible mess by wandering too far from home. The challenge we all have is to make is

---

BOX 3.5 **Example**

Groupthink, a term developed by Irving Janis (1982), depicts a pathological inclination of groups to display solidarity to a viewpoint, most often that of a leader (if you read his book with the same title you will have to go a considerable way within the book to find the desired alternative, he called it *vigilant appraisal* by which he meant an open-minded consideration of all possibilities). In his chosen case studies Janis argued that groupthink is a dangerous pathology, risking dangerous undertakings and overlong commitments to courses of action that have failed.

It is plausible to argue that solidarity has its uses as in the case of allies in World War II to defend and then defeat Nazi Germany, Imperial Japan, and their allies. They chose groupthink rather than to individually consider invitations to negotiate an earlier end. And, I note that the War on Poverty in the United States was abandoned not because it failed, it cut the rate of poverty in half, but because opponents persevered while supporters lost heart and abandoned the effort.

BOX 3.6   Examples of psychoanalytic approaches

Given their clinical training that scholars who applied psychoanalytic approaches to politics it should not be surprising the leaderships studies dominated. For two examples, see Alexander and Juliette George (1998) and Walter Langer (1972).

the decision of whether to stay in our familiar valley or leave for perhaps a better result "over the next hill." On balance, our species seems to have a bias toward approaching the new as a likely rewarding result (Axelrod 1983; Cacioppo, Gardner, and Berntson 1997), but some of us are more eager to explore the novel.

It is often pointed out that humans are bad scientists. Most of us are not good at numbers or good at statistical judgments or good at assaying the probabilities of events in the world at large (Nisbett and Ross 1982; Kahneman et al. 1982). But when we go into the next valley, we do not want to walk there one hundred times to judge how likely we are to find danger awaiting us. We are concerned with a point estimate, will we confront a bear this time, the risks of getting it right or wrong are not symmetric!

Hence particulars are very important, and the value of a distribution of orientations is to secure our ability as a group, whether a family, tribe, clan, or nation, to have a variety of orientations available. The perpetuation of both orientations suggests, as Aristotle did, that collective judgment depends on having a distribution of views brought to public discussion. In my view, then, the inclination to pathologize by treating a property, as archaic and dysfunctional is a presumption that we should eschew.

First, focusing on one quality, here why people are conservative, ignores the full range across the property, leaving unexamined why people are liberal or middle of the road moderates. Second, by considering the full range of variance, some are inclined to be conservative and others are inclined to be liberal, we might then go on to more thoughtfully consider the functional value of each orientation.

Let's consider a second example. As noted earlier, the ancient Greeks began philosophizing as they considered how to deal with what seemed to them to be an intractable conflict between their emotional natures and their rational abilities. In premodern thinking, this conflict was a central and hence unavoidable element in our natures. Perhaps some would have better ability to master the conflict but the conflict was inherent, natural. In modern thinking, the enlightenment notion of progress would foresee emotion becoming less potent as was the thinking about conservatism, faith, and passion would be left behind as reason's role expanded. Hence, apart from those who adopted psychoanalytic, that is, Freudian approaches, emotion was largely ignored.

Psychoanalysis was largely marginalized in academic psychology departments. In the United States psychoanalysis found its home in separate psychoanalytic institutes and in the humanities departments of universities. The greater enthusiasm in at that time was for so-called cognitive approaches: the study of beliefs, values, attitudes, schemas, ideological predilections, and other categorical labels for what people think and believe. This dual focus, eschewing emotion as a scientific topic and embracing cognition, was consistent with a deeper and widely embedded agenda that sustained all of the social sciences, political psychology included. Progress would make some traits diminish while other traits would strengthen. Happily given the presumptions in place in our two examples, the traits that would decline (conservatism and emotion's potent impact) while the traits that would strengthen (liberalism and the role and force of reason) fit into the normative narrative story of progress. Progress becomes not just an empirical story but a moral tale as well.

This practice of focusing on the presumed problematic feature, here conservatism and emotion, limits our imaginations. It may also distort our research. I strongly encourage you to develop a nose for catching such instances of pathologizing as you read the literature. First, it is often the case that instances of normative disparagement are implicit rather than explicit. Excavating the underlying presumptions is a great way to discover the implicit notions that are so deeply embedded that we take them for granted that they are invisible even to those who rely on them.

Second, once you have identified such an instance, you also will have also created a new research opportunity. Once you find a presumption, you can turn it into an explicit theoretical question and devise a research project needing an answer. If conservatism is a functional adaption, at least in some instances, as my argument above holds, then a research project should find that conservatism is manifestly advantageous is some circumstances. In a similar fashion, if progressivism, that is, liberality, is manifestly advantageous in other circumstances, then that too should be demonstrable in empirical research.

However there are still yet other reasons to make our presumptions explicit. It would seem apparent that if one understood the trajectory of time as a passage from docile subordination to tradition and faith to individual autonomy and self-reliance on reason then early intervention in the life of children would augment this process. Progress, the capacity for self-rule, is a consequence of the increased availability of education in and reward for the shift to reason and self-reliance. Criminality and other forms of poor behavior would likely be reduced if society made early education and early support more available. That assumption was behind the Cambridge-Somerville Youth Study. That study recruited over six-hundred young boys, most beginning before they were about twelve years old, half of whom were randomly assigned to a treatment program to prevent delinquency (Powers 1949; Powers and Witmer 1951) that lasted approximately five years (1939–1944). The young boys in the treatment group, $N = 325$, were given special and personal attention from teams of social workers and trained professionals, including psychiatric and medical care as necessary. Most were sent to summer camps as well as visited in home and school during the school year. Of course this intervention was expected to yield positive benefits to those who participated. The boys in the treatment group were matched to a control group of about 325 boys. Some years later a review of the results indicated that there was no decline in the rate of delinquency among the boys in the treatment condition compared to those in the control condition (Powers 1949). Some thirty years after that study another researcher (McCord 1978) revisited the research by tracing the participants and obtaining all the available public records. The retrospective subjective assessments by those who received its benefits suggested that the intervention had been helpful, indicating it was a success. However, objective measures tell a quite different story. The treatment group was significantly *more* likely:

- to commit a second crime;
- report signs of alcoholism;
- show signs of serious mental illness;
- die younger (of those who died);
- have at least one stress-related illness;
- lower occupational status;
- and report work as not satisfying.

Neither the original study nor the follow-up study that reported the above effects raised much attention beyond the juvenile delinquency subfield. Yet, unless a flaw in the research is revealed, it raises a question of the sort that conservatives are likely to make but liberals are likely to ignore: Can progress, especially when made a matter of social policy, prove successful?

I do not raise this point to challenge liberal orthodoxy, but rather to note that ideological commitments do not qualify as social science evidence. In a similar fashion, proclaiming President Lyndon Baines Johnson's War on Poverty program to be a failure, as conservatives have claimed, is more a case of political rhetoric than fact (in fact, the War on Poverty was not a failure, having halved the rate of poverty in during it history. Much of it was abandoned when conservatives replaced liberals in Congress and stopped funding the programs).

It is important to understand how these often unstated presumptions shape the discipline in political psychology. If you examine these presumptions, making them visible, you can then make prudent choices as to your own research agenda. But, before I turn to these presumptions, those that shape the field, there are more pragmatic concerns that should shape your research.

III. THE MODERN DILEMMA: THE UNEXPECTED TRAJECTORY OF PROGRESS

The enlightenment anticipated a path from past to future in which the blessings of trade, the spread of equality, and the rule of democracy would generate a "cosmopolitan peace" (Kant 1970b, 1970a, 1970c), a united world of beneficent self-government. The social sciences was not long after confronted by the unexpected popularity of authoritarian regimes in Spain, Italy, and Germany that emerged in Europe after World War I. This "escape from freedom," to use the wonderful title of Erich Fromm's (1965) important book cast doubts on the enlightenment promise of unabated progress toward a

---

BOX 3.7 **Research**

This shift *toward* the values of order and security produced by threat and stress has been documented by research at the microlevel—individuals will value order more and liberty less—and at the macrolevel—societies will value more conservative and more authoritarian leadership when under stress. For examples of microlevel research see, Stanley Feldman (2003), Stanley Feldman and Karen Stenner (1997), Mark Landau et al. (2004) and for examples of macrolevel research see, Richard Doty, Bill Peterson, and David Winter (1991), Stewart McCann (1997), and Stephen Sales (1973).

time of beneficence, peace, and democratic rule. The 1920s and the 1930s, when this retreat to authoritarian regimes took place, were marked by extraordinary stress. World War I caused approximately thirty-seven million casualties. The influenza epidemic immediately after took some twenty-seven million additional lives worldwide. And, of course, the Great Depression shrank economies all over the world leaving many without work and impoverished. These reversals away from democratic aspiration and toward the comforting assurance of authoritarian rule are perhaps not so surprising, nor are they necessarily evidence of the falsity of the enlightenment hypothesis.

The trajectory of progress was, after all, premised on material advancements. So, if material conditions collapse as they did in the '20s and '30s then that offers an explanation that can be dealt with by economic and social recovery.

In contrast, conditions in the United States immediately after World War II were by all accounts conditions that should have favored the achievement of enlightenment expectations. After World War II, economic conditions in the United States were robust, not the least because of the wartime destruction of most of the industrial capacity of the United States' economic competitors in Europe and in Asia. Although the United States suffered many casualties during World War II, these numbers (in absolute and in percentage terms) were quite modest compared to those suffered by other competitor nations. The United States also benefited by the widespread expansion of public education, advanced by the GI Bill, which gave considerable financial support to soldiers and sailors returning to civilian life, enabling them to go to university rather than return to work. It was in this largely beneficent situation, a period of peace and economic growth, that American social scientists began to study voters with new tools at their disposal.

The emergence of survey methodology in the mid-twentieth century gave scholars the ability to study the "average man." Social scientists then (Berelson, Lazarsfeld, and McPhee 1954; A. Campbell et al. 1960) and since (Delli Carpini and Keeter 1996) have eagerly used surveys to produce generalizations about the American electorate.

Collectively, the great weight of research on the American electorate has concluded that the public is largely disengaged, ill informed concerning matters of politics and incoherent in its opinions. As a consequence, "stronger" versions of democracy that rely on electorate driven politics must be understood as utopian perhaps even dangerously so. Here again social science has largely contributed to the conservative critique of the modern, finding that citizens are too ignorant, too lazy, and too emotional to play a responsible role in governance.

BOX 3.8 Comment

We should not leave aside the literature generated by social psychologists on power of belief. I previously noted the work of Solomon Asch (1951), Muzafer Sherif (1958, 1966), Stanley Milgram (1974), and Philip Zimbardo (Haney, Banks, and Zimbardo, 1983), among others. Their work warns of dangers that echo those advanced by Thomas Hobbes (1968).

People are too easily seduced to undertake actions that they would not do if they were more resistant to external blandishments and if they were more capable of sustaining their moral autonomy.

BOX 3.9 **Place to start**

On heuristics in politics, a good place to start is Samuel Popkin (1991), *The Reasoning Voter*. And in psychology the following are useful: Galen Bodenhausen and Robert Wyer (1985); Shelly Chaiken and Durairaj Maheswaran (1994), Gerd Gigerenzer, Peter Todd, and ABC Research Group (1999).

To the general portrait of voters as largely bereft of information and organized attitudes we should note more recent work has largely added to that conclusion:

- Many in the public fear the responsibilities of democratic politics.
- Many are ill motivated to engage the demands of time and effort that are prerequisite to being informed about the messy details of policy, programs, and politicians.
- And many are uncomfortable with the face-to-face confrontations that agonistic politics compels (Hibbing and Theiss-Morse 2002; Mansbridge 1980; Mutz 2006).

We are seemingly left with an electorate passive, empty of political convictions, and uncomfortable with the conflict of ideas that is inherent in multiparty democracies. Of late there has been an effort to vouchsafe the democratic electorate by research that shows that citizens rely on "heuristics" to make political decisions.

Heuristics are guides that people can rely on, such as party loyalty ("I am a member of the center-right party so I will cast my ballot marked for all center-right party candidates") and ideology ("I am a liberal, so I shall support all liberal-minded candidates, and all liberal causes seeking my support"). Relying on heuristics is very efficient as it enables one to avoid the burden of collecting a lot of information about each of the candidates and the policies they advocate, avoids the task of weighing the validity thereof, and avoids the task of making a comparative assessment among the alternatives.

Another effort to find a way out of this seemingly intractable portrait of electorate incapacity has been the effort by James Fishkin (1991) to construct deliberate environments in which people can and will perform up to expectations.

He begins by summarizing the current state of affairs (Fishkin 1991, 21): "First, the deliberative competency of mass publics is suspect. It is a dubious accomplishment to give power to the people under conditions where they are not really in a position to think about how they are to exercise that power. Second, aroused publics might, on occasion, be vulnerable to demagoguery. They might be stirred up to invade the rights or trample on the essential interests of minorities." You should note that Fishkin

---

BOX 3.10 **Deliberative democracy**

In addition to Fishkin's work, you can find useful discussions in Seyla Benhabib (1996), James Bohman and William Rehg (1997), and Jon Elster and Adam Przeworski (1998).

---

repeated the charges advanced by Plato and Hobbes. From Plato, the public is to be judged on their ability to think clearly and from Hobbes, on their ability to resist the rhetorical power of emotion elicited by overly persuasive leaders. His solution was to create deliberative forums where randomly selected citizens could gather and adjudicate the competing alternatives in a protected environment among themselves. In this environment protected from rhetoric directed at them by solicitous politicians and supported by experts, they can reason; they serve as a form of citizen jury. Only thereby can citizens competently function.

Relying on heuristics, although efficient, is not an acceptable alternative to reasoning by citizens in democratic politics. Relying on deliberative forums that engage only a small group of citizens will not easily sway the larger electorate to accept the legitimacy of its decisions. Democracy, unlike other forms of governance, depends on collective judgment of the entire electorate. Collective persuasion produced by elite cues, convenient reliance on heuristics, or by a small, even if randomly selected, citizen jury will not suffice. The legitimacy of collective judgments comes from. First, the public construction of public policy that in turn entails the public presentation of reasons and of evidentiary claims so that contending claims can be both seen and weighed. Second, the display of reasons and evidence must be all encompassing for all citizens to have the opportunity to contribute their concerns, doubts, and considerations. Third, the ability of collective judgments to gain legitimacy, and thereby to become authoritative, depends on the palpable reasonableness of the laws and of the manner of their generation in the eyes of the public (Tyler 1990). Laws implemented by brute force of numbers—that is, without a rationale that is perceived as reasonable, its intentions expressly connected to the purpose of securing an acceptable goal—will not be judged legitimate (Tyler 1997).

The conclusion that follows is that the public is largely incapable of serious consideration of collective matters and places politics in the hands of the few.

BOX 3.11   Mass opinion

The phrase "mass opinion" is derogatory. It draws on a supposed analogy between public affairs and the realm of physics and Newton's laws of motion. Force, external to the object, a mass, explains movement. And absent external force, an object remains unmoved, if still, or if moving continues along its trajectory. And as a "mass" nothing of the contents of the public neither beliefs, values, nor desires explains movement.

Hence, the attraction of the term *mass* for it obliterates interest in the public, which becomes an inert material to be moved about by external force. And what force? The practiced skills and judgment supposedly natural to elites. This reduces the public's role to the limited and modest task of "consenting" to rule by their betters. The phrase, "manufacture of consent" comes from Lippmann (1922, 158). The insight was used by Ginsberg (1986) to advance the claim that popular sovereignty is largely a fabrication of the political regime.

In a similar fashion, "opinion" draws on Plato's simile of the cave. As you recall, opinion was contrasted with truth. Opinions are just shadows, only vaguely linked to real objects they purport to depict. Hence, they are airy things, readily pushed around and of course, are "merely" opinions.

These presumptions are central in John Zaller's (1992) magisterial, *The Nature and Origins of Mass Opinion.*

If the public cannot reason, either from reluctance or from incapacity, it follows that we must settle for "mass" politics and the "manufacture of consent" rather than a democracy of collective purpose and direction. Democracy's enemies, and now its friends, have concluded that the public is feeble in its political faculties. It follows that reliance on public direction is not only misconceived but also doomed to a predicted fate. Perhaps the certainty accorded to this portrait is, even with the accumulation of some fifty years of scholarship, premature.

Before a valid assessment of civic competence can be derived it would seem essential to begin with a clear and appropriate understanding of democratic politics. It is impossible to draw a conclusion about the level of competence of any agent, individual or collective, unless one has some definition of what constitutes competence. Using a misconstrued standard combined with a misunderstanding of the complexity of democratic politics generates conclusions that are neither accurate nor revealing. It is important to emphasize that "facts" are meaningful not in and of themselves. Facts become meaningful when located in a theoretical framework that gives them definition and significance. Here are two examples to illustrate that point.

In an often told story, George Washington, following his two terms as president of the United States, went out horseback riding during a rainstorm. He arrived home with a fever from an infected throat. He was soon under the care of doctors. But, through being bled of four quarts of blood to reduce the infection, he died. Why was he bled? Because for thousands of years, reliant on the dominant theory developed by the Greek physician Galen, doctors believed that the health of humans is the result of the proper balance of the four "humors." It was believed that each one of four fluids had to be in proper balance to sustain health. Yellow bile explains when and why people are "bilious" or "choleric." Lymph fluid explains when and why people are sluggish or dull. Blood explains when and why people are "sanguine" or passionate. And, finally, black bile explains when and why people are melancholic or depressed. Because the balance of these four fluids is the basis of health, imbalance, excessive fluid of one type or another, explains illness. It is not surprising then that medical treatment of fever associated with the infection directed attention to the cause, an excess of blood. And the doctors took what they understood was the best corrective action, reduce the excess blood.

The death of this august patient, as in many other circumstances when current belief confronts failure, had no consequence on medical practices. Nor would future

---

BOX 3.12 **Comment**

The failure of therapeutic intervention to succeed could either be explained by malpractice, the frailty of their patient, or by questioning the theory of medicine. That this death, as with so many others, did not lead to questioning the validity of the humors theory of health can be understood as a case of *motivated reasoning* a theory of decision making (Kunda, 1990). The theory of motivated reasoning argues that

reasoning is largely used to defend existing commitments and beliefs.

In this case the doctors did not question their diagnosis even as their patient died. Perhaps not surprising as their status was based on their expertise and that expertise in turn derived from the theory of humors. Questioning that theory would undermine their claim to expertise and status.

failures by themselves cause doctors to change their medical practice. Until the discovery of germs and their role in generating illness and the acceptance of that discovery, medical practice remained reliant on the theory of humors.

Students of social psychology will not any surprises in this tale as the ability of people to hold fast to beliefs in the face of contrary observations has been amply documented.

My next example, coming as it does from a time of war, also shows the persistence of faith, but more significantly it offers a second lesson. During the Vietnam War, "body counts" of enemy kills was advanced by the US military as a core metric to mark the success of their efforts to overcome an intransigent and resilient enemy.

If one believes that the more of the enemy one kills the better, then if follows that the higher the body count the better. The interpretation of enemies killed as a mark of success depends on the encasing presumption of a limited supply of enemy combatants. But if the number of enemy kills marks the ability of the enemy to increase its commitment and to continue to increase the supply of soldiers devoted to the effort then increased casualties, takes on a quite different meaning. An enemy that can throw platoons into the fight likely anticipates casualties in modest numbers. An enemy that has the capacity to commit divisions, and then armies, anticipates far greater casualties. Higher casualties may measure the enhanced resources of the enemy, their ability to recruit, lead, and field ever larger armed forces.

The number of casualties is a fact. A "fact" is clearly empirical and when reliably determined by objective criteria facts, observations, then that becomes "data." But data obtain meaning only when facts are tied to some implicit and/or explicit conceptual structures. Different conceptual structures can attend to the same datum. And, different conceptual structures can radically alter the normative meaning of "results."

Science begins with taxonomic structures to define the designated properties, what science describes as factors, dimensions, variables, or concepts. Taxonomies simplify the descriptive process by identifying a parsimonious number of descriptive properties, and thereby enabling us to ignore all other properties as not pertinent. And more important, taxonomic structure provides the meaning of those properties.

The enlightenment period, particularly with its normative presumptions, has largely shaped the debate in ways that remain largely unexamined even as they are largely accepted as received wisdom (Marcus 2008). To be specific, if democracy is the natural expression of progress then the shift from reliance on tradition and on hierarchy to reliance on democratic deliberation should increasingly become expressed, by more and more people. Attentiveness, willingness to engage in the public debate and explicit open-minded consideration of alternative policy prescriptions, and alternative leadership teams should increasingly become evident.

One foundation of this summary assessment of modern citizens in America is found in the well-established taxonomy of reason and emotion. Here again Plato largely set the framework: reason as the path to truth and emotion as the source of delusion. To speak of emotion in any other way would be nonsensical. All emotions share common features: They are powerful. They are hidden in their sources, and they are at best nonrational if not irrational.

Reason has its properties defined as well. But what we mean by the use of reason to being rational is complicated by two meanings that are each associated with the phrase "being rational." This can lead to a confused discussion. Rationality sometimes means one thing, sometimes the other, and sometimes both. First, rationality is understood as a *process of reaching* a decision. A *rational process* involves collecting evidence, making a logical connection between means and goals such that the respective benefits and costs of alternative courses of action can be explicitly and expressly weighed. Second, rationality is understood as a *postdecision result*. The challenge is that the best result is only determinable in retrospect. A rational result is one that is the best result. And, rationality often implies an empirical relationship between the process and the outcome: *If* one uses a rational process *then* one will secure a rational result.

Even those who praise emotion as superior to reason, who value emotion, agree on the basic terms of the contrast. Reason and emotion are distinct. If there is a disagreement as to which is the better basis for judgment, it is agreed that citizens must choose one or the other—to choose between being rational or being emotional. It would seem that citizens must align with Galileo or align with Goethe.

Perhaps this opposition between reason and emotion depends more on the presumptive psychology that informs this view of their empirical and normative qualities. An important element in the assessment of citizenship is the role of emotions. If citizens are supposed to be rational and if being emotional is distinct and antagonist to reason then we have a twofold agenda. First, we should look for evidence of citizens thinking and acting rationally. Second, we should look for evidence that reliance on emotion is declining to provide space for reason to come into its own. As reviewed earlier, little evidence has been found to confirm these expectations.

However, the specific insights of neuroscience that I review in the chapter that follows radically challenge conventional wisdom of the nature of knowledge, emotion, the functions of emotion, the nature, capacity, and purposes of consciousness and rationality. The neurosciences alter the relationships of time, reason, and emotion, and of knowledge. These fundamental reconceptions have proved in the short time that neuroscience has contributed to new understandings of key components of political psychology: knowledge, reason, emotion, the mind (consciousness), and how judgments are formulated. If we draw on neuroscience we can derive new understandings that can shed fresh light on the old enduring problems of ignorance and folly in human affairs.

IV. CONCLUSIONS

Blindness to the constraints induced by progressive convictions is not limited to political psychology. Economics, especially the classic orientation of the discipline, has bound itself to a theory of human action premised on rationality that so far has proved to be largely chimerical. Sociology, and social psychology, has wedded themselves to largely pathological views of social actions, born of and with the continuing influence of studies purporting to show how the public is largely incapable of self-control, eschewing individual autonomy for the safety of collective acquiescence. A more positive view of collective membership is offered by Henri Tajfel (Tajfel and Turner 1979) who argued that groups sustain us and hence are, in the main, positive resources that are formed when members find a common interpretation and common cause. I return to this aspect of human and political affairs in later chapters, but let me end on this point. The problem of explanation without a clear recognition and understanding of the normative foundations of political psychology (the enlightenment and with it the commitment to a conception of human nature and progress) will limit the value of our research to show us what is and what is not plausible, let alone possible.

EXERCISES

Select a recent article from the journal *Political Psychology*. Perform two operations. First, if, as is commonly the case, the dependent variable is labeled by its "high value" (as a scale of conservatism is named so that high scores are the most conservative), reflect the numbers and the name. If the author does not make it clear what an individual with a low score would be labeled (e.g., in this example, what is a person who has low scores on the conservatism items), provide an apt conceptual name based on what the hitherto low scorers responses measures. Then, second, rewrite the abstract with the variable now renamed. Do the findings make the same points?

In that same, or if you prefer another, article, what are the normative implications? If you had the power to be a social engineer, what policies would you adopt to make use of of these findings? Would a liberal agree to the policies you applied? Would a conservative? Write what you think would be the likely response of a typical liberal or conservative. Reading parts of cognitive psychologist George Lakoff's (2002) book, *Moral Politics*, may be helpful in this exercise.

Do a Google Scholar search for a social science article with the phrases "affect and cognition" or "affective and cognitive" in the title. Then generate a simple taxonomy contrasting affect with cognition. Add to the taxonomy the features, stated or implied, about affect and about cognition therein. Does the research demonstrate these features or does it presume them?

REFERENCES

Adorno, Theodor, Else Frenkel-Brunswick, Daniel Levinson, and R. Nevitt Sanford. 1950. *The Authoritarian Personality*. New York: Harper and Row.

Arendt, Hannah. 1968. *The Origins of Totalitarianism*. New York: Harcourt Brace.

Aristotle. 1983. *The Politics*. Translated by T. A. Sinclair. New York: Penguin Books.

Asch, Solomon E. 1951. "Effects of Group Pressure upon the Modification and Distortion of Judgment." In *Groups, Leadership and Men: Research in Human Relations*, edited by Harold Guetzkow, 177–90. Pittsburgh, PA: Carnegie Press.

Axelrod, Robert. 1983. *The Evolution of Cooperation*. Cambridge, MA: Harvard University Press.

Benhabib, Seyla. 1996. "Toward a Deliberative Model of Democratic Legitimacy." In *Democracy and Difference: Contesting the Boundaries of the Political*, edited by Seyla Benhabib, 67–94. Princeton, NJ: University of Princeton Press.

Berelson, Bernard R., Paul F. Lazarsfeld, and William N. McPhee. 1954. *Voting: A Study of Opinion Formation in a Presidential Campaign*. Chicago: University of Chicago Press.

Bodenhausen, Galen V., and Robert S. Wyer, Jr. 1985. "Effects of Stereotypes in Decision Making and Information-Processing Strategies." *Journal of Personality and Social Psychology* 48:267–82.

Bohman, James, and William Rehg, eds. 1997. *Deliberative Democracy: Essays in Reason and Politics*. Cambridge, MA: MIT Press.

Burke, Kenneth, and Stanley Edgar Hyman. 1964. *Perspectives by Incongruity*. Bloomington: Indiana University Press.

Cacioppo, John T., Wendi L. Gardner, and Gary G. Berntson. 1997. "Beyond Bipolar Conceptualizations and Measures: The Case of Attitudes and Evaluative Space." *Personality and Social Psychology Review* 1:3–25.

Campbell, Angus, Philip E. Converse, Warren E. Miller, and Donald E. Stokes. 1960. *The American Voter*. New York: Wiley.

Campbell, Donald T. 1960. "Blind Variation and Selective Retention in Creative Thought as in Other Knowledge Processes." Psychological Review 67:380–400.

———. 1988. *Methodology and Epistemology for Social Science*. Chicago: University of Chicago Press.

Chaiken, Shelly, and Durairaj Maheswaran. 1994. "Heuristic Processing Can Bias Systematic Processing: Efforts of Source Credibility, Argument Ambiguity, and Task Importance on Attitude Judgment." *Journal of Personality and Social Psychology* 66:460–73.

Condorcet, Jean-Antoine-Nicolas de Caritat. 1795. *Outlines of an Historical View of the Progress of the Human Mind*. London,: Printed for J. Johnson.

Darwin, Charles. 1966. *The Origin of Species*. Cambridge, MA: Harvard University Press.

Delli Carpini, Michael X., and Scott Keeter. 1996. *What Americans Know about Politics and Why It Matters*. New Haven, CT: Yale University Press.

de Tocqueville, Alexis. 2000. *Democracy in America*. Translated, Edited, and with an Introduction by Harvey C. Mansfield and Delba Winthrop. Chicago: University of Chicago Press.

Doty, Richard M., Bill E. Peterson, and David G. Winter. 1991. "Threat and Authoritarianism in the United States, 1978–1987." *Journal of Personality and Social Psychology* 61:629–40.

Elster, Jon, and Adam Przeworski, eds. 1998. *Deliberative Democracy*. New York: Cambridge University Press.

Feldman, Stanley. 2003. "Enforcing Social Conformity: A Theory of Authoritarianism." *Political Psychology* 24:41–74.

Feldman, Stanley, and Karen Stenner. 1997. "Perceived Threat and Authoritarianism." *Political Psychology* 18:741–70.

Festinger, Leon. 1956. *When Prophecy Fails*. Minneapolis: University of Minnesota Press.

———. 1957. *A Theory of Cognitive Dissonance*. Stanford, CA: Stanford University Press.

Fishkin, James. 1991. *Democracy and Deliberation*. New Haven, CT: Yale University Press.

Frazer, Michael. 2010. *The Enlightenment of Sympathy*. New York: Cambridge University Press.

Fromm, Erich. 1965. *Escape from Freedom*. New York: Avon.

George, Alexander L. and Juliette L. George. 1998. *Presidential Personality and Performance*. Boulder, CO: Westview.

Gibbon, Edward. 1900. *The Decline and Fall of the Roman Empire*. New York: Knopf.

Gigerenzer, Gerd, Peter M. Todd, and ABC Research Group. 1999. *Simple Heuristics that Make Us Smart*. New York: Oxford University Press.

Ginsberg, Benjamin. 1986. *The Captive Public: How Mass Opinion Promotes State Power*. New York: Basic Books.

Haney, Craig, Curtis Banks, and Philip Zimbardo. 1983. "Interpersonal Dynamics in a Simulated Prison." *International Journal of Criminology and Penology* 1:69–97.

Hegel, Georg, Wilhelm Friedrich, and J. B. Baillie. 2003. *The Phenomenology of Mind*. Mineola, NY: Dover.

Hegel, Georg, Wilhelm Friedrich, and S. W. Dyde. 2005. *Philosophy of Right*. Mineloa, NY: Dover.

Hibbing, John R., and Elizabeth Theiss-Morse. 2002. *Stealth Democracy: Americans' Beliefs about How Government Should Work*. Cambridge: Cambridge University Press.

Hirschman, Albert O. 1977. *The Passions and the Interests: Political Arguments for Capitalism before Its Triumph*. Princeton, NJ: Princeton University Press.

Hobbes, Thomas. 1968. *Leviathan*. London: Penguin Books.

Janis, Irving L. 1982. *Groupthink*. Boston: Houghton Mifflin.

Jost, John T., Jack Glaser, Arie W. Kruglanski, and Frank J. Sulloway. 2003. "Political Conservatism as Motivated Social Cognition." *Psychological Bulletin* 129:339–75.

Kahneman, Daniel, Paul Slovic, and Amos Tversky. 1982. *Judgment Under Uncertainty: Heuristics and Biases*. Cambridge: Cambridge University Press.

Kant, Immanuel. 1970a. "An Answer to the Question: 'What is Enlightenment?'" In *Kant's Political Writings*, edited by Hans Reiss, 54–60. Cambridge: Cambridge University Press.

———. 1970b. "Idea for a Universal History with a Cosmopolitan Purpose." In *Kant's Political Writings*, edited by Hans Reiss, 41–53. Cambridge: Cambridge University Press.

———. 1970c. "Perpetual Peace: A Philosophical Sketch." In *Kant's Political Writings*, edited by Hans Reiss, 93–130. Cambridge: Cambridge University Press.

Kunda, Ziva. 1990. "The Case for Motivated Reason." *Psychological Bulletin* 108:480–98.

Lakoff, George. 2002. *Moral Politics: How Liberals and Conservatives Think*. Chicago: University of Chicago Press.

Landau, Mark J., Sheldon Solomon, Jeff Greenberg, Florette Cohen, Tom Pyszczynski, Jamie Arndt, Dale T. Miller, Daniel M. Ogilvie, and Alison Cook. 2004. "Deliver Us from Evil: The Effects of Mortality Salience and Reminders of 9/11 on Support for President George W. Bush." *Personality And Social Psychology Bulletin* 30:1136–50.

Langer, Walter. 1972. *The Mind of Adolf Hitler*. New York: Basic Books.

Lippmann, Walter. 1922. *Public Opinion*. New York: Macmillan.

Lodge, Milton G., and Charles Taber. 2000. "Three Steps toward a Theory of Motivated Political Reasoning." In *Elements of Political Reason: Understanding and Expanding the Limits of Rationality*, edited by Arthur Lupia, Mathew D. McCubbins, and Samuel L. Popkin, 183–213. New York: Cambridge University Press.

Madison, James, Alexander Hamilton, and John Jay. 1961. *The Federalist Papers*. Cleveland: World Publishing.

Mansbridge, Jane J. 1980. *Beyond Adversary Democracy*. New York: Basic Books.

Marcus, George E. 2008. "Presidential Address—Blinded By the Light: Aspiration and Inspiration in Political Psychology." *Political Psychology* 29:313–30.

Marx, Karl, and Friedrich Engels. 2002. *The Communist Manifesto*. New York: Penguin Classics.

McCann, Stewart J. H. 1997. "Threatening Times, 'Strong' Presidential Popular Vote Winners, and the Victory Margin, 1924–1964." *Journal of Personality and Social Psychology* 73:160–70.

McCord, Joan. 1978. "A Thirty-Year Follow-Up Study of Treatment Effects." *American Psychologist* 33:284–9.

Milgram, Stanley. 1974. *Obedience to Authority*. New York: Harper and Row.

Mutz, Diana Carole. 2006. *Hearing the Other Side: Deliberative versus Participatory Democracy*. Cambridge: Cambridge University Press.

Nisbett, Richard, and Lee Ross. 1982. *Human Inference: Strategies and Shortcomings of Social Judgment*. Englewood Cliffs, N.J.: Prentice-Hall.

Nussbaum, Martha Craven. 1986. *The Fragility of Goodness: Luck and Ethics in Greek Tragedy and Philosophy*. Cambridge: Cambridge University Press.

———. 1994. *The Therapy of Desire: Theory and Practice in Hellenistic Ethics*. Princeton, NJ: Princeton University Press.

Plato. 1974. *The Republic*. New York: Penguin.

Popkin, Samuel L. 1991. *The Reasoning Voter: Communication and Persuasion in Presidential Campaigns*. Chicago: University of Chicago Press.

Porter, Roy. 2001. *The Enlightenment*. New York: Palgrave.

Powers, Edwin. 1949. "An Experiment in Prevention of Delinquency." *The Annals of the American Academy of Political and Social Science* 261:77–88.

Powers, Edwin, and Helen Leland Witmer. 1951. *An Experiment in the Prevention of Delinquency: The Cambridge-Somerville Youth Study*. New York: Columbia University Press.

Rokeach, Milton. 1964. *The Three Christs of Ypsilanti: A Psychological Study*. New York: Knopf.

Sales, Stephen M. 1973. "Threat as a Factor in Authoritarianism: An Analysis of Archival Data." *Journal of Personality and Social Psychology* 28:44–57.

Sherif, Muzafer. 1958. "Group Influences upon the Formation of Norms and Attitudes." In *Readings in Social Psychology*, edited by Eleanor Maccoby, T. M. Newcomb, and E. L. Hartley, 219–32. New York: Holt.

———. 1966. *Group Conflict and Competition*. London: Routledge & Kegan Paul.

Smith, Adam. 1986. *The Wealth of Nations* (Books I–III). New York: Viking.

Tajfel, Henri, and John C. Turner. 1979. "An Integrative Theory of Intergroup Conflict." In *The Social Psychology of Intergroup Relations*, edited by W. G. Austin and S. Worchel, 33–47. Monterey, CA: Brooks/Cole.

Tetlock, Philip. 2005. *Expert Political Judgment: How Good Is It? How Can We Know?* Princeton, NJ: Princeton University Press.

Thucydides. 1996. *The Landmark Thucydides: A Comprehensive Guide to the Peloponnesian War*. Translated by Robert Crawley. New York: Free Press.

Truman, David Bicknell. 1951. *The Governmental Process; Political Interests and Public Opinion*. New York: Knopf.

Tyler, Tom R. 1990. *Why People Obey the Law*. New Haven, CT: Yale University Press.

———. 1997. "The Psychology of Legitimacy: A Relational Perspective on Voluntary Deference to Authorities." *Personality and Social Psychology Review* 1:323–45.

Zaller, John R. 1992. *The Nature and Origins of Mass Opinion*. New York: Cambridge University Press.

CHAPTER 4

Neuroscience and Political Psychology

We found ourselves at the end of chapter 3 with a dystopian assessment of democracy, an apparent ill-suited match between the mental apparatus of the public and the high-minded requirements of democracy: People should be well informed about politically significant matters, but they are not. People should think rationally, but they most often do not. People should deliberate over political choices, but they rarely do (not to mention yet other standards often applied). The progressive hopes of the enlightenment confronts what is at best a mixed bag of results.[1] The modern world evolved because events and changing understandings combined to generate new possibilities, but those new possibilities have not unfolded in the beneficent fashion predicted. Modernity seemingly brought war on a far grander scale than ever before, the unexpected continuing appeal of authoritarianism, and a public ill informed, easily manipulated, and ill at ease with the responsibilities of democratic governance in the new dynamic cosmopolitan world.

In this chapter I present an argument that neuroscience belongs as one of the primary sources of theoretical and empirical insights for political psychologists. As I noted in earlier chapters political psychologists have long borrowed from other disciplines. The theory of rational choice arrived from classical economics. Theories that explain how groups interact and impact individuals arrived from sociology, social psychology, and anthropology. So did theories about the role of "structure," of culture and institutions. Therefore, looking elsewhere is a long-established practice. In that tradition then, adding neuroscience is merely continuing in much the same vein. And, as an added incentive, neuroscientists bring with them new methodologies that enable us to peek inside the workings of the human brain. But how is that going to help us confront the

---

1. On one side of the ledger is the expansion of the nominal democracies in the world, the successful return to democracy from dictatorial rule, Portugal, Spain, Argentina, and Chile, to name but four. On the negative side is the public distrust and ignorance of science, among the other unexpected features of modernity as outlined in the previous chapter.

modern challenges that seem to portray the public as ill adapted to politics and the obligations that come from popular governance?

Neuroscience provides new perspectives into how humans understand, how people experience, and how humans make decisions, these new insights enable us to reinvigorate the old and, in the main, stagnant arguments between those who argue for popular government and those who argue for elite-run government. And, with particular reference to the debate about knowledge, neuroscience has a lot to offer about what constitutes knowledge. And, as knowledge is, in the modern world, the road to power, new understandings of knowledge will have political consequences. And therein lays its most valuable contribution.

The chapter is organized into four sections. In the first section I report that neuroscience offers as a new take on the role of time and mental states. Once again I discuss time but not at the daily, monthly, annual, and century time frames of premodern cycles or the long trajectory of modern conceptions of time. Here the time ranges I consider are in milliseconds. And, I revisit our old friends, reason and emotion and find them redefined as well.

In the second section I examine neuroscience and the *natures* of knowledge (the plural spelling of nature is meaningful). In both premodern and modern conceptions knowledge is a product of reason. Neuroscience will expand our notions of knowledge far wider than the conventional notions of knowing. I discuss the processes of acquiring knowledge and its multiple forms.[2] In the third section, after I examine how neuroscience has examined time and knowledge, I discuss what neuroscience tells us about action, all types of actions, but most important for political psychologists, political actions. Neuroscience is not the only modern science that has dealt with these topics. And, while I greatly value the new insights that neuroscience offers, other approaches, in other disciplines, should not be ignored. Therefore, in the final section, I provide a summary of a parallel attempt to understand knowledge, more specifically, the effort of psychologists to grapple with emotion as a form of knowledge.

I. NEUROSCIENCE AND TIME

In chapter 3, I examined how the conception of time shapes our understanding of the world, ourselves, and what is possible. Here, a focus on time again enters to alter our understanding of familiar terms, emotion and reason. Neuroscience is a relatively young discipline but even so its volume of research has grown at an impressive pace. So much so that I discuss only the most important discoveries pertinent to political psychology. For those of you who want to learn more, you can find more on the subject: Marcus (2002) and Nørretranders (1998).

In the familiar debates as to mental states, there are two or three types of mental states to consider: affect and reason; or after the enlightenment, affect, interest, and reason. The most common way of considering these mental states has been to locate them (Damasio 1994). Emotion has long been associated with the heart (or "gut"). Reason

---

2. In the enlightenment period, one of the first undertakings was to create an encyclopedia that would contain all knowledge so that enlightenment could be spread far and wide (Diderot, d'Alembert, and Mouchon 1778). Education would produce the literate population that could have access to reason's product (Locke 1996; Gutmann 1987).

BOX 4.1   Social neuroscience:

A new area in neuroscience has emerged called social neuroscience. Largely lead by neuroscientist and social psychologist John Cacioppo, this subfield is devoted to considering the more "macro" impacts of neuroscientific research. Some citations are appended in the suggested readings for this chapter.

is located in the mind (though interestingly, "interest" has not been given any definitive locale). All of this matters because most scholars, and most of us, think that we should make decisions, especially in politics, by making *reasoned* decisions. That presumes not only that the claim is valid—true—but also that is it possible. And, here, the common conventional presumption that emotions come from somewhere "outside our heads" and make us act irrationally, is clearly implicated in the most often defamatory claim that the public is too emotional to be entrusted with the responsibility to govern (Herzog 1998; Le Bon 1986; Sartori 1987).

The most common way to distinguish between affect and cognition, between emotion and reason, is to rely on spatial metaphors, as in Freud's (1971) construction between the *subconscious* and *consciousness*, the former the "location" of passion lying hidden *below* in the subterranean reaches and pushing *up* into the conscious mind, the location of reason. One therapeutic benefit of this conception is that, presumably if we try, we can build a barrier that will protect the thinking space from invading emotion. We will "keep our heads" rather than "losing our minds."

As we shall soon see this fundamental presumption has been shown by neuroscience to be false. The important difference between the feeling and thinking is temporal not spatial.[3] And that means that much of what we have long believed about our mental states and what best suits politics is based on a false foundation of claims.

Science attempts to avoid confusions over meaning by requiring concepts, variables, to be limited to a single property, a property that varies (minimally to a simple dichotomy, e.g., voting [yes, no]; or, more usefully, to a continuous range, e.g., partisanship—from those who are inattentive to political party membership through increments to stable fervent party loyalists). When scientists may begin with everyday terms, such as emotion and reason, they have to convert these lay terms, which often have multiple and variant meanings to scientific terms meant to be more amenable to scientific clarity. So, the lay term *emotion* became *affect*. And, the lay term *reason* became *cognition* (from the Latin, to cogitate, to ponder, to think).

As we shall see, relatively new discoveries in neuroscience have made the term *cognition* problematic for its continued use in political psychology. That is because cognition came to be defined in the social sciences as "information processing" rather than its ancient meaning: cogitating, expressly thinking about some matter. And, as explained later in this chapter, information processing is what the brain does, so much so that it is hard to exclude *any* neural activity in the brain as not involving *cognition*, so defined. To avoid confusion I refer to the operations of the brain by using the phrase, or various equivalents, as for example, when I say the brain.... And, I

---

3. All mental states arise, no surprise, in the brain.

shall refer to the mind when I am speaking about the subjective experience known as conscious awareness. Finally, when I say "we," "you," or "I," I am referring again to the available, to us, world of the mind, the subjective experience of immediacy in which we can report to ourselves or others, what we consciously see and hear, taste, smell, and touch, and what we think.

The first, and most consequential, insight is that consciousness is not instantaneous. Things "out there" that we see and hear do not happen as we see and hear them. It takes time for the brain to generate consciousness.[4] Although we experience our conscious awareness as if it is a real-time display of the world and the events occurring therein, it is actually a representation that takes five-hundred milliseconds to generate (Libet 1985, 2004; Libet et al. 1983; Libet et al. 1979). Indeed, one aspect of consciousness is the ability of the brain to fool the mind into thinking that its subjective state is both veridical and instantaneous. And, as we shall see both of these qualities are, in important ways, confabulations.

And, most important, research has shown that the brain does not wait for consciousness to act. Figure 4.1 shows the role of time in preconscious processing and the appearance of consciousness. In sum, most of the time the brain acts and the mind most often observes.

Subjective experience seems to appear instantaneously. We see someone enter a room, though the actual sight of the person appeared in the back of our retinas some five-hundred milliseconds earlier. It takes the brain about five-hundred milliseconds to process the electrical signals that arrive from the two retinas via the optic nerves to the brain. The end result is conscious vision—sight. The same time lag is true for the other sensory streams that enter the brain. Electrical signals from our ears arrive via the auditory nerves; taste and touch also arrive as electrical signals. It is interesting that what appears to be our oldest sense, smell, is the one sensory mode in which the brain actually touches directly.[5] It takes five-hundred milliseconds for each of these sensory streams to be encoded, and then combined into the multimodal representation we experience as consciousness.

Another of the qualities we accept is that conscious representation is truthful, that we are *just* observing; our brain is passively recording the world out there. I do not expect you to accept the truth of these claims merely based on trust or authority. After all, the primary illusion of consciousness, that we have complete, instantaneous, and veridical access to the world, is very thoroughly engrained in our subjective experience. So, what should you believe: Your history of experience or these new and unexpected claims? To show you that your sense of consciousness is sometimes false consider the exercises described next. They are designed to show you how the brain and the mind interact. I have chosen some examples that, while not political, are straightforward so as to demonstrate how our brains shape consciousness in an active manner. And, while

---

4. The how of this has spawned considerable research and hardly a day goes by without some new research hoping to gain some purchase on the matter. And, hardly a day goes by without a popularizing book being published presenting the latest speculations and evidence of how the human brain constructs the subjective state of consciousness.
5. The olfactory bulb is a part of the brain that projects into the sinus cavities. Molecules in the airstream land on the bulb their shapes being sensed and interpreted as smells (Rolls, Kringelbach, and de Araujo 2003; Shepherd 2007; Zou, Li, and Buck 2005).

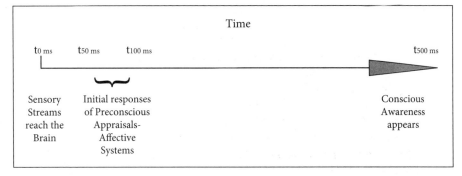

Figure 4.1 Preconscious Processing and Conscious Awareness

these are not political examples, the same processes that shape our grasp of the physical world are just as much in play in the political world. You will have some experiences to puzzle over.

Figure 4.2 presents two horizontal lines of equal length. They are equal in length, and, if you have normal vision, you will see them as equal in length.

Two equal length lines, no problem. What we see on the page in front of us, is what we see. Now, without changing anything about those two lines, I show them again, but with added information. And with that added information, let's look at those lines one more time (see figure 4.3).

If you have normal vision, most of you will see these same two lines as *not* being equal, the line below appears to most of you as shorter than the line on the top. Yet they are equal in length. Many other visual illusions also have this ability to distort our perception. What is happening here?

One of the tasks of our visual system is to locate ourselves within the world, to place us in the spatial geography we inhabit. The brain begins processing sensory information very early soon after the electrical signals arrive via the optic nerves. The brain's visual system creates a third dimension, depth, using a variety of analyses (Zeki 1993). We need to locate things including ourselves, not just in relationship to up and down and left and right, but how close to us, foreground and background, and whether approaching us or moving away. And we need to know as soon as possible. Waiting a half second might seem to be a small price, but it leaves us very vulnerable. And, not surprisingly, evolution presses for the earliest analysis of object identification, location, and movement.

In this instance, in figure 4.3, the two angles lines are interpreted by the visual system as a plane that recedes toward a far horizon. So, instead of seeing a flat vertical page, your brain constructs an image that has depth, a foreground, at the bottom, and a

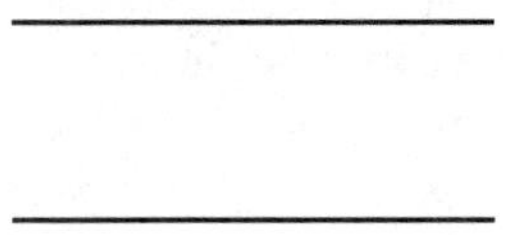

Figure 4.2 Two Equal Length Lines

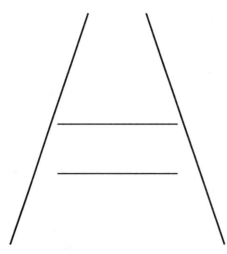

Figure 4.3 Two Equal Length Lines with Two Additional Lines

distant horizon, at the top. The visual system interprets the diagonal lines to identify a horizon (which is far away) and to distribute the two horizontal lines in that now available dimension of depth.

Here two equal length horizontal lines are placed into a plane with a foreground at the bottom and background at the top. By adding its constructed depth of field the bottom horizontal line must be closer to us and the upper horizontal line must be farther away. And, as that line must be farther away, it must be longer. The vision system then adjusts our conscious perceptions of their lengths to be consistent with this imposition of depth depicted in figure 4.3. All of this happens very quickly and is intended to make the conscious experience of vision more useful. The illusion occurs because the brain adjusts our conscious experience to be consistent with its *preconscious* analysis.

Here is another example. Take off one of your shoes. Then, close your eyes. Then, *at the same moment*, touch one finger of one hand to your nose and one finger of your other hand to one of your toes. Most of you will experience these two sensations, touching your toe and touching your nose, as simultaneous. But, that is not how the brain experiences the two sensations. Because the distance one electrical signal has to travel, that from the toe to the brain, is considerably longer than the distance the other electrical signal has to travel, from nose to brain, the brain receives the sensation from the nose earlier than the sensation from the toe. The brain then makes an adjustment so that the conscious experience of the two events is experienced as simultaneous. Another observation about these two examples: We experience the world as immediate, but as these two examples demonstrate, the brain is doing work before "we," our conscious selves, consciously perceive the world. In the first example, the preconscious brain does so by generating depth perception and in the second example the preconscious brain does so by modifying the time flow of two events so that the conscious illusion of immediacy is maintained.

A third and final example: Have something handy that you can read. It can be this page, or it could be a credit card or a newspaper page. Before you do so, look up and around you. Observe how much you see. If you have been to an eye clinic or doctor's office to have your vision checked, you might have been asked to extend your two hands in front of you and then move them to the sides, stopping when you can still just see them both. This is a means to measure your peripheral vision. So, try that yourself noting how much of the ceiling, if you are inside, and the floor you can see without moving your head and how far to each side you can also see, again without moving your head or your eyes in the eyeball sockets. Note all the many objects you readily see around you.

Now, bring up that paper to read and as you read note the extent of your vision: the top, the bottom, and the sides.

What do you see? Again, assuming normal vision, you will see little outside of the limits of the page. What happened to the rest of the world out there?

In brief, the brain, knowing that reading is a very intensive activity, opts to remove extraneous information. The brain shrinks the periphery of conscious vision to just the page. Reading is a challenge as there are many small items that are very similar, ... a e c o ... for example, that must be differentiated, grouped into pairs, then into words, phrases, sentences to determine meaning (Dehaene 2009).

The eyes, as they normally do, are still focusing light onto the back of each retina where the cells that respond to light continue to function. Each cone and each rod generating an electrical signal that are then passed to the two optical nerves where they travel onto and into the brain's visual processing regions (one optic nerve for each eye). The brain still has the full visual field available, but during the period when you are reading the brain limits the visual representation in conscious awareness to the narrowed visual field that contains just what is needed to read. If you stop and lift up your head from the page you will see the full visual field "instantly" reappear. Here again is an example of the brain doing important work during the interval between the arrival of sense data to the brain, and five-hundred milliseconds later, when consciousness arises, when "we" become present. The brain shapes our conscious state to fit the task demands of the moment.

However, this tranquil example is not the only instance of the brain acting swiftly.

If you reflect on the point that consciousness takes five-hundred milliseconds before you see, hear, touch, and so forth, then something should to occur to you. If you waited so the conscious "you" can see or touch, you would not be able to operate effectively in the world. A soccer player kicks the ball toward you, a tennis player serves, a baseball

---

BOX 4.2 Comment

There is one more qualifying element. If you are in a normal and quiet situation then this description is likely to be accurate. But if something unusual intrudes, a whiff of a strange smell, an unexpected noise, or just friends making a lot of noise, then you are likely to find it difficult to read. The brain is also noting how safe the environment is for the activity at hand—in this case reading what is on the page.

If that appraisal is "just a normal quiet situation" then the brain generates that appraisal as a state of calmness, and allows the narrowing of the field of vision. If that appraisal yields a conclusion of "something unusual here" the brain generates a state of increasing anxiety, widens the field of vision, and shifts attention in the direction of the intrusion.

Here is the first hint that emotion is being recast in functional terms.

BOX 4.3   Comment

A pitcher in baseball stands on the pitching mound some 60″ 6″ (or 18.39 meters) from home plate. At ninety miles an hour the ball reaches home plate in about four-hundred milliseconds. Assuming the batter's eyes detects the ball at the moment it leaves the pitcher's hand, how can the batter "see the ball" then determine whether it will be a strike or ball, and if the batter determines it to be a good pitch, initiate a swing that will begin a trajectory of the bat to a calculated spot where the batter can then drive the ball into the field of play?

The answer is that the batter cannot wait until conscious vision is available. Happily, in this as in many other tasks, the brain does all of this *before* conscious awareness.

---

pitcher throws a fastball at a speed of some ninety to one-hundred miles an hour to home plate or a politician interacting with supporters or opponents at a rally. But it takes you five-hundred milliseconds before you can consciously see the soccer ball, see the serve, see the baseball, or visualize the face of a stranger. If you had to rely solely on conscious awareness to identify and then to react you would find yourself largely helpless in any situation that requires swift comprehension and a fleet and deft response.

As neuroscientist Joseph LeDoux (1996, 2000) showed with respect to conditions of threat and fear, the brain is continuously processing incoming sensory streams for the earliest indication that something unexpected or dangerous is present: a whiff of smoke, a sudden rustle of sound underfoot, or a sudden movement at the periphery of vision. And the brain begins in the first one-hundred milliseconds of arrival of the various sensory streams. The brain is designed to determine the import of such signs as quickly as possible and also to initiate appropriate actions to manage the circumstances. It does this appraisal and initiation of action well before the brain is able to represent (some of) that information in conscious awareness (Armony and LeDoux 1997). If that whiff is really smoke then we had better get up and look around, if that rustle of sound is a snake then we better look down and get ready to move, and if it is a sudden movement we better quickly to turn to see what it is. Waiting half second is a luxury that many dangerous situations will not reward. And, our brains have evolved to not wait for or rely on consciousness.

We rely on our brains not only to construct the physical world in which we move and operate, we also rely on our brains to construct the social world, as we engage, sometimes cooperatively and sometimes antagonistically with others. We are social creatures, so it not just lines, shapes, and objects that the brain perceives in this early preconscious realm. The brain uses our senses to guide how we interact with each other, with those like us and those not like us. These social interactions are just as fully engaged by these preconscious processes. As we shall see later, our prejudices, positive and negative are not "buried below" in some "subconscious" part of the brain, they are engaged *early* not *below*. Here again, it is timing that matters, not location. If we want to understand how, when we think, and to what effect; and how, when, and to what effect, we feel, we need to turn to neuroscience to explain preconscious neural processes.

What is the brain doing before we are aware? What does it know and how does it know it?

Table 4.1. Processing capacities of preconscious systems and conscious awareness

Sensory system	Brain bandwidth (bits/second)	Conscious awareness bandwidth (bits/second)
Visual	10,000,000	40
Auditory	100,000	30
Touch	1,000,000	5
Taste	1,000	1
Smell	100	1

II. NEUROSCIENCE AND KNOWLEDGE

Knowledge in its conventional sense means what can be depicted in semantic form, facts, descriptions, conclusions, and the like. But if consciousness takes five-hundred milliseconds to generate, what are we to make of the brain's "knowing" in the preconscious period? The first thing we can say is that the brain has far more knowledge of the world than does the conscious mind.

Zimmermann (1989) measured the capacity of the brain to process sensory information. He then went on to ask: How much of that information appears in conscious awareness? He determined that there is an extraordinary difference in the capacity of the brain to process sensory information and its capacity to display that sensory information in the conscious mind. As it turns out, what "we" see, hear, touch, taste, and smell is a very small portion of what the brain knows about the external world. Table 4.1 displays the real-time processing capacity in bits per second of the five sensory systems for the brain and for conscious awareness.

Our brains know far more than our conscious minds know. And, our brains actively use what it knows before consciousness can get into the act. In the range of forty to 120 milliseconds, a number of preconscious systems—some of them affective systems— are active.

Unlike representation in consciousness where the external world is presented as a vivid portrait of that world that we take to be veridical (i.e., a one-to-one exact representation), preconscious appraisals are often expressed as affective states, emotional feelings that convey the ongoing assessments of the brain.

As I noted at the beginning of this chapter, as neuroscientists examined how active the brain is in processing information, they expanded the term cognition to mean *any* information processing whether taking place in consciousness or in preconscious information processing. But every time a nerve cell sends a neurotransmitter (a chemical such as dopamine or serotonin) across a nerve synapse to a nearby nerve cell it is communicating,

---

BOX 4.4 Comment

Visual representation is not really veridical in another aspect. Color does not exist in the world; rather it is a way the brain has of representing differences in wave length and other features of the external world. Some species share with humans this ability to apply color to visualize representations, other species do not.

sending information, does that mean cogitation is taking place? If affective processing is examining the sensory information that arrives in the brain to ascertain the nature of the world then affective processing is also information processing. But that means that emotions are cognitive given this definition of cognition, indeed it means all neural activity is information processing. This new definition obliterates the distinction between cognition and affect. Further, there is a loss in expanding the term cognition in this fashion: As the term evolved to apply to thinking and as explicit thinking plays a special role in democratic politics using the term "cognition" as neuroscientist has blurs the distinction between thinking in consciousness and preconscious information processing.

There are a number of preconscious appraisal systems and neuroscience has only begun to identify and map their functions, interactions, and how they shape consciousness (Panksepp 1989, 1998). There was an early effort to identify a unified "limbic system" that controlled all emotion; however, that effort was soon abandoned as it became clear that the effort to create a unified neurological analog to the established tradition of emotion as a homogenous property was misguided (LeDoux 1991). There is another aspect of neuroscience that has revised thinking about the brain and conscious mind.

It turns out that we do not have one memory system; neither do we have the two most often described as long-term and short-term working memory systems. We have at least three systems of memory and each serves different functions (Mishkin and Appenzeller 1987; Squire 1987; Rolls 2000; Stanton 2000). The memory system for the preconscious realm is separate from the memory systems that support conscious awareness. The former is called procedural (or sometimes associative) memory. The two that support consciousness are called semantic (or declarative memory) and working (or short-term) memory.

How does the brain initiate actions to manage actions, such sudden unexpected signs of threat, and the many familiar tasks of daily life such as walking or reading? The answer is that the brain uses preconscious *affective* processes. Rather than the semantic character of consciousness, preconsciousness uses an affective language with its own syntax, structure, and dynamic features to interpret and represent. These preconscious affective appraisals operate at a cycling capacity about five times faster than conscious awareness. Emotional processes, preconscious affective appraisals are thus earlier and faster than consciousness. These qualities enable us to function in a dynamic and fast changing world and with each other.

III. NEUROSCIENCE AND ACTION

How does the brain manage to initiate and control actions, the types of actions that we use to manage the common affairs of our lives? The basic answer is that we have two routes to action, including decisions. The so-called "dual process" model arose in the 1980s (Petty and Cacioppo 1986). Here again, at that earlier stage, before neuroscience fully engaged the issue, the language of description in social psychology was spatial rather than temporal. One route was called "peripheral processing," neural processing that took place "outside of awareness" and "central processing, neural processing that took place "inside" the mind (Chaiken and Trope 1999). The dual model view of neural states is now well established (Evans 2008).[6]

---

6. Which is not to claim that this is the final word: As with all scientific knowledge, it only the most current provisional view.

Early brain processing executes all tasks that fall within its range of capacities. Those challenges that are not well executed by rapidly affected controlled processes are conveyed to the slower and cruder processes that are available to us within consciousness. While consciousness is slow and has limited access to the sensory stream, having a late and incomplete understanding of the world, it provides an alternative "workspace" in which issues can be represented, semantically grasped and communicated, and alternative responses contemplated. While the preconscious systems can initiate action and have deft control of them, the limited ability of consciousness to initiate and control action is actually an important survival advantage. If every thought gave rise to action we could not consider and compare alternative courses of action, rather each thought would be converted into action. The weakness of linkage between thought and action allows us to formulate, ponder, deliberate, reflect, and reconsider. Further, we can engage each other and using semantic formulations express options we are considering to others, here and grasp their views, we can engage in collective deliberation, all and fully before acting.

Most habituated actions are executed without requiring an active role of consciousness (Bargh and Pietromonaco 1982; Changeux 1986; Bargh et al. 1992; Jeannerod 1997; Bargh and Ferguson 2000). Habits are executed by continuously matching learned actions as they are executed, such as playing a sport, by relying on fast preconscious affective appraisals of the continuous sensory stream, what is going on out there, and to somatosensory streams, what is happening with the body. And, here again, affective feedback and feedforward provides nonvivid representation of success or failure of the unfolding habit. In the case of hitting a baseball arriving at some ninety miles an hour, these fast appraisals can manage both the external speed of the ball and the controlled movements of the body to, at least on occasion, strike the ball. Consciousness goes along for the ride, observing. The brain often generating a sense of subjective control, this gives "us" the sense of executive control, but most of the time this subjective sense is itself a construction of prior nonconscious processes (Wegner 2002).

Although the precise details of how habits are learned and how and when they are expressed in action is now being explored in neuroscience, that habits are potent has long been understood. Aristotle, Edmund Burke, Isaiah Berlin, and William James, to pick but four scholars, all emphasized that the role of sentimentally entrenched habits were central to social and political judgment and action (Aristotle 1983, 1985; Berlin and Hardy 1991; Burke 1973; James 1890). Rather than seeing reliance on habits as a poor alternative to reason, as some would have it (Popkin 1991) and as we shall see, reliance on habits while not based in explicit reason are, nonetheless, often—but not always—more efficacious than reliance on reason.

BOX 4.5   Comment

Perhaps the most remarkable evidence of the nonessential role of consciousness in most action is that demonstrated by Lawrence Weiskrantz (1986, 1997). Using people who have a blind area in their field of vision but who can nevertheless locate and grasp objects placed before them in a location where they cannot consciously see them. He calls this phenomenon "blindsight."

These discoveries change the discussion about emotion and reason. First, instead of thinking about them in spatial terms, we have to think of them in temporal terms. Preconscious affective changes impact on what we do and how we think. Second, we have many emotional states, for example, happiness and sadness. Although these are quite different as we all know, these two, as is the case with many emotions, are not so much different in kind, but rather more different in degree. We need to understand that we are experiencing a variety of simultaneous and shifting emotional states that convey important functional information about both external and internal states of affairs. In the case of happiness and sadness, these are emotions, and the words we use to label them, are different appraisals of how well things are going. When things are going well we feel happier, when things are going less well we feel less happy, or, sad: differences in degree. Third, rather than thinking of emotion and reason as mutually exclusive and antagonistic, we need to think about the effects that preconscious affective processes have on "downstream" states of consciousness, tuning the latter so that states of consciousness are modified to meet the then current tasks demands.

Procedural memory stores the routines we have learned enabling us to confidently and capably walk, run, write, play the piano or tennis, or drive a car. Semantic memory stores and brings forth our visual and semantic memories such as recalling the color of the shirt we wore yesterday, personal and place names, salient dates, numbers, and the like.

The examples given should not be taken to mean that habituated actions do not include social behaviors such as conversations and other joint activities with others, both friend and foe. Our habits deal with the social and the political just as they do with respect to physical movements. These systems work seamlessly together to support our ability to navigate ourselves, with others and out and about in the world. Working and semantic memory have very limited access to procedural memory. Hence, although "we" know that "we" can write, we have no direct conscious access to the memory system that stores the actual programs that control arm, finger, and hand movements that guide a pen or pencil across to page to produce letters or diagrams (Milner and Goodale 1995).

Knowledge, thus, has two quite different forms. One is the familiar kind of knowledge that is encased in semantic information. It is familiar because it is represented in conscious awareness. We can recall the experiences of our lives available in semantic memory. We can and often do describe them. On the other hand, the second form of knowledge, procedural information that guides our habits, is largely inaccessible to conscious awareness. Habituated knowledge is information that although not readily available to introspection is nonetheless the basis for most of our actions. This inaccessibility has one obvious consequence. When we consciously try to account for our actions, our preferences, we often get it wrong in as much as are attempting to gain access to information that is most often consciously inaccessible.

Social psychologist Timothy Wilson (2002; Wilson and Dunn 1986; Wilson et al. 1989; Wilson and Schooler 1991) performed extensive studies over the years. His work showed that when asked people will give explanations for why they like this or that, this person or that person, but asking preferences can often lead to speculations that are false rather than accurate. He used a wide variety of stimuli, asking subjects about posters that people might put on the wall, or various jams, to take the less political

BOX 4.6 Confabulation

Neuroscientist Michael Gazzaniga (1985) studied patients suffering from epilepsy, patients who because of serious recurring bouts of grand mal seizures had their corpus callosum severed. The corpus callosum is a bundle of nerve fibers that connect the left and right side of the brain. As each optic nerve is evaluated by the visual system on the other ventricle then the two visual fields are distinct, the left eye visual field is constructed by the right brain's visual system and the right eye's visual field is constructed, seen, by the left visual system.

Gazzaniga made use of the fact that language ability, our ability to comprehend and speak language, is located on the left side of the human brain to conduct some interesting experiments. By putting up a barrier so that the patients could only see what was in each eye's visual field, Gazzaniga chose to study what patients would say about objects placed in front of their left eye but not visible to the right eye. Because the corpus callosum had been severed on left side of the brain, the seat of consciousness and language could not see and report on what the left eye was seeing. So, what did these patients report? They confabulated—they made up stories about what they were seeing. I highly recommend that you read his important work. Perhaps we all confabulate more than we think!

examples, but the breadth of his research applies to all types of things and people we evaluate. We swiftly react to people those reactions often occur before we consciously come to know, thus much of the time our reactions seem "automatic" and we often cannot accurately explain them to ourselves no less than to others, as psychologist Patricia Devine's (Devine 1989; Devine et al. 1991) research into prejudice and stereotypes showed. And, given our lack of conscious awareness of our own prejudices, we often misstate whether we hold them or what they contain.

These insights suggest ways in which the standard approaches in social science have miscast the task of understanding the relationships between thoughts, feelings, and action. First, most political psychology methodologies collect data that is derived from subjects who rely on their recall, rely on semantic memory, and these are often incomplete and biased. Thus the cognitive appraisal theory of affect can tell us something about the introspective reports that humans generate to explain their emotional states and their intuitions about what caused them to themselves and to others. But the cognitive appraisal approach, being reliant on retrospective and partial accounts, cannot provide a general and fully accurate account.

Further, explicit descriptive accounts, by which I mean the statements people generate when asked to describe the world, themselves, their actions, and the actions of others, often presume that these accounts precede and explain their action. If that assumption is accurate then a competent map of the conscious environment will explain how our beliefs, values, and preferences shape the actions that follow. Because this perspective misses the relatively recent discovery of the "automaticity" of most actions, actions that unfold and are controlled "automatically," research that depends on individuals to explain their actions based on self-generated values, preferences, motives, or other stated reasons, will be seriously compromised. The term automaticity should not be taken to mean that these routines are rigid and mechanical. For stored in procedural memory are all the branchings that enable familiar variations to be mastered as when we use our vocabulary to cover many topics with many individuals easily adapting to changing themes and participants. Some preconscious appraisal processes always remain outside of conscious awareness. For example, the amount of light that the pupil allows into the retina is dynamically and swiftly controlled. The ongoing adjustments do not intrude into consciousness. Other preconscious appraisals do intrude into consciousness most notably when increasing anxiety warns "us" that something is amiss.

All of this is not to say that all actions arise outside of conscious control. For if consciousness offered no executive purpose why did it evolve? Jeffrey Gray (2004) argued that consciousness evolved as an error correcting space. When reliance on automatic, swift and sure habituated actions would prove problematic, then consciousness is available to take over executive (i.e., deliberative) control.

The important point is that these models identify a dynamic capability that all people have: We can rely on heuristics and we can rely on deliberative processes. And it is this dual capacity that has been largely missed in the past half century of research on citizens and citizen competence. I develop this point more fully in later chapters. Here it is sufficient to posit that this capacity to shift the strategic resources from peripheral (or partisan) to central (or deliberative) identifies a flexibility that reveals an expanded range of human abilities.

The tradition of research on citizenship generally begins with an array of performance standards that are thought to be ubiquitously applicable. These standards are derived from the presumption that citizens should be rational. If that presumption is reasonable then the failure of citizens to display rationality in each and every circumstance convicts them of incompetence. If, on the other hand, rationality is only sometimes a useful decision strategy then a more complicated set of standards needs to be applied.

And, dual processes models suggest that we have evolved a flexibility such that deliberation and automaticity are each useful adaptations best articulated in specific but not universal circumstances. Automaticity might well be more efficient than rationality in familiar circumstances, having the advantage of speed and proven ability. On the other hand, in novel or perplexing circumstances, deliberation might be invoked to make use of conscious flexibility and openness to new outcomes. If different decision strategies are best suited for some but not all circumstances, then the standards of citizenship maybe more complicated than thought. Further, in as much as preconscious affective processes are engaged in both decision strategies that suggest that the traditional juxtaposition, both empirical and normative, of reason against emotion should be retired. If nothing else would come from neuroscience research this alone would be sufficient to justify its expanded role in political psychology. But we can expect even more from neuroscience.

Political psychologists are paying more attention to shifts from automaticity to awareness control, and back, a topic I discuss in the next chapter. A full account of citizenship will take into account more dynamic and nuanced features that result from a fuller understanding that the "self" extends beyond what introspectively generated reports make available. But to fuel the research agenda political psychology will need to map the preconscious affective appraisals that generate our fuller understanding of self, others, and our actions. Furthermore, we need to study the memories of our store of patterns of behavior embedded in procedural memory, both norm compliant and norm violating. This enables research to study the interactions that take place between preconscious appraisals and the affective systems that generate them, on the one hand, and the conscious awareness and decision-making capacities that reside within. Consciousness is the constructed representation of reality in which our subjective experience resides but often is not the domain within which decisions and behavioral control are initiated and controlled. As sometime executive control shifts from nonconscious to conscious mechanisms, and further, this shift is largely controlled by preconscious affective systems that adds to the complexity that flows from these insights from neuroscience.

IV. PSYCHOLOGY AND KNOWLEDGE

In psychology after some period of disinterest, emotion attracted attention. Emotion became an interesting topic in academic psychology. Even so, emotion, relabeled as affect, was examined as an adjunct to the presumed dominant role of cognition. We can summarize various phases in the evolving conceptions as the valence conception, the discrete (or appraisal) conception, and more recently, the dimensional conception. Although these are often seen as mutually exclusive conceptions, in my view, they are not.

Valence Conception

Through the 1950s to the 1980s affect was thought to be the second component in the definition of an attitude (Ajzen and Fishbein 1977, 1980). Attitudes had a "what" component (i.e., the cognitive aspect, the descriptive), an evaluative component (i.e., the affective component, the like–dislike, or "affect" tag), and a do component (i.e., the behavioral disposition associated with that attitude). Therefore, for voters, with an attitude, say to President Obama, the cognitive component is the depiction of who he is (which can of course vary from that given by "birthers" to that held by loyal Democrats, and can be very rich or thin as knowledge will vary across individuals). The "affect tag" (Fiske 1981) associated with the attitude toward President Obama was understood as an evaluative appraisal, functioning to resolve the approach–avoidance issue. And, the structure of that appraisal was as a single, valence dimension, that is, approach (very positive) through neutral to avoid (very negative). Finally, the two prior components, the descriptive and evaluative, inform the behavioral component. Having a positive (or negative) attitude, here towards President Obama, would incorporate and explain the various behaviors those holding positive, or negative, attitudes would likely enact.

In political science then, and since, numerous surveys included "feeling thermometers" designed to capture the affect tag component of attitudes toward all types of targets. The American National Election Studies (ANES) had, and have, feeling thermometers toward presidential candidates, social groups, organizations (e.g., labor unions), and more. In the typical application subjects are asked to think about some target, say a particular candidate or a policy position, and asked to choose a value along a range from 0 to 100 "degrees" indicating how "cold" (0) or "warm" (100) they feel toward that target. All well and good if feelings toward that, or any target, are in fact, a simple matter of liking or disliking.

Indeed, this conception of "affect" fits the enlightenment program quite well. The presumptions of the valence model are that evaluation follows knowing. Further, not only is "cognition" primary in a temporal sense, we must know before we can evaluate, but also primary in a foundational sense as affect is reduced to a passive and memory role (in which the "affect tags" passively store evaluative conclusions). Sad to say, this conception's empirical foundations collapsed in the 1980s. I turn to that collapse after considering a parallel conception of emotion, discrete or appraisal approaches.

Discrete or Appraisal Conceptions

Cognitive appraisal theories rely on a core assertion. Unlike the valence approach, appraisal theories of various stripes hold that feelings are not a simple matter of like–dislike, approach–avoidance. Rather, feelings arise from a series of cognitive appraisal considerations that generate a variety of separate affective states. Hence, appraisal theories hold that feelings result from and via a cognitive interpretative stage (Ortony, Clore, and Collins 1989; Parkinson and Manstead 1992; Roseman 1979, 1984, 1991; Scherer, Schorr, and Johnstone 2001; Scherer, Dan, and Flykt 2006). This has a lengthy tradition as it dates back at least to William James (1883, 1894). An example might go as follows: Something bad happens to you, but you cannot determine what to feel unless you identify the cause. What just happened? That question must be answered before you can know how to feel.

If you are the cause then you are likely to feel guilty. If you view someone else as the cause, you are likely to feel anger. Moreover, the word discrete is used to suggest that cognitive appraisals generate, at any given moment and circumstance, essentially one affective state. That is each "discrete" emotion is a separate and distinct state from other discrete emotions.[7]

What if cognitive engagement is irrelevant as people confront the task of making a decision? What if engaging one's preferences to make a choice takes place without conscious involvement? One of the first psychologists to advance this possibility that affective responses arise before and therefore independent of conscious consideration was Robert Zajonc who in 1980 published a very influential article, "Feeling and Thinking: Preferences Need No Inferences" in the American Psychologist. The article (Zajonc 1980) remains worth reading. Zajonc's claims have since been amply sustained by research. But the reception that the article received is also worth considering. The reaction was, in the main, hostile. Journals were soon publishing attacks and defenses of the argument that affective responses arose independent of cognitive processes (Lazarus 1984; Tsal 1985; Zajonc 1984).

No doubt, apart from the normal scrutiny that any new claim should provoke, a claim that people make decisions without explicit deliberative consideration would seem to imply that citizens are not acting in a responsible fashion. Reason in collective action, in politics, is the presumptive way to reach the rational, that is, optimal, result, and reasons are the substance language of the public discussion over what should take place. If preferences arise without the engagement of reason then reason is at best a

---

7. There are different sets of "discrete" emotions depending on which theorist one adopts as authoritative (Marcus 2000).

spurious distraction from the actual means by which people, as private actors or as citizens make choices.[8]

The development of cognitive appraisal theories were made independent of and well before the neuroscience investigation of emotion began. And, they were well established in psychology by the time that Robert Zajonc advanced his challenging alternative view. Cognitive appraisal theories have only lately begun to consider the role of preconscious processes as it relates to cognitive appraisal conceptions of emotion (Storbeck and Clore 2007). And, even at this late date, when the temporal difference between affective and conscious appraisals has been clear for some thirty years, there are scholars using neuroscientific methods (such as fMRI) who still ignore the temporal dimension, referring to "top-down" meaning cognitive appraisal and "bottom-up" meaning affective appraisals (Ochsner et al. 2009).

This apparent disinterest or disregard by cognitive appraisal theorists, in the main, may reflect on the extent to which how well conception of "affect" fits the enlightenment program. The presumptions of cognitive appraisal theories, much like the valence model, hold that evaluation follows knowing. Thus, as with the valence model, cognitive primacy is protected and emotion subdued by its supposed receptiveness to prior cognitive appraisal. As with the valence model, the expectations of cognitive appraisal theories to provide an accurate and comprehensive explanation for affective responses that people experience was to prove disappointing.

Let me say that I think it is quite likely that cognitive interpretations *augment* preconscious appraisals downstream. And, when I return in chapter 5, to an explanation of the theory of affective intelligence, I show that there are predictable circumstances when preconscious affective controls over political judgment and behavior are inhibited so that cognitive processes can be dominant. It is hard to imagine how, given the temporal sequence of neural processes, cognitive appraisals can explain preconscious modulations of feelings in as much as cognitive appraisals arise after preconscious appraisals. Hence, research that applies cognitive appraisals to the explanation of affective states, and the role of cognitive appraisals on affect and thereafter on political decision and behavior, has to contend with an alternative explanation. Cognitive appraisals may often be spurious, downstream retrospective elaborations that arise from preconscious appraisals. To use Gazzaniga's (1985) formulation, cognitive appraisals may most often be confabulations that provide self and public accounts in lieu of otherwise inaccessible preconscious processes.

To discount that alternative account, a fuller model is needed to undergird cognitive appraisal research. Such a model would include both preconscious appraisals and postawareness reflection, so that one could conclude whether cognitive appraisals have any, let alone, robust effects on the formation of political judgments or modify political behavior above and beyond the effects attributable to preconscious processes. To

---

8. And, there is a further motive for the negative reaction. Those committed to cognitive appraisal approaches confronted two conclusions if Zajonc was proven right. First, at least a major class of choice, if not all, is independent of cognitive appraisal. And, if that is true, it follows, second, that the importance of cognitive appraisal theories is sharply reduced. The result will likely provoke a hostile response from cognitive appraisal theorists.

my knowledge, at this juncture, no such studies have been conducted with the results published.

Dimensional Conceptions

A third approach to emotion in social psychology arose unexpectedly from a study intended to go beyond the valence approach reliant on feeling thermometers by reliance on a cognitive appraisal theory of emotion (Abelson et al. 1982). It is worth examining this particular research in some details both because it informs as to the validity of the valence and cognitive appraisal conceptions and because the timeframe of the research had a detrimental impact on subsequent research.

Robert Ableson, Don Kinder, and Mark Peters of Yale, and Susan Fiske, then of Carnegie Mellon conducted two national surveys of American voting age subjects. They relied on Ira Roseman's (1979) then current formulation of discrete appraisal theory of the structure of affect. The specific way in which the subjects were instructed is worth attending to carefully. As reported in their article (Abelson et al. 1982, 621–2):

> "Now I want to ask you about (candidate). Think about your feelings when I mention (candidate). Now, has (candidate)—because of the kind of person he is or because of something he has done—ever made you feel: Angry?…Happy?…
> .Hopeful? …" and so on through a list of affects. For each affect term, the interviewer recorded a simple Yes or No response.

Before I turn to the list of affects, the above summary of the method is itself quite revealing. First, if valence theory were correct then no matter which feeling is on the list, the results would support treating each of them as equivalent ways of assessing whether the subject in question liked a candidate. The words, happy, hopeful, or indeed any another positive term would do just as well as any other. They would be redundant repetitions of the essentially same query: Do you like this candidate? In the same way, whether we disliked a candidate can be assessed by using any negative term, angry, mad, or any other negative term would function just as well as any other negative term. Second, note that the instructions probed for a simple "yes" or "no" to the query "has (candidate)…ever made you feel [feeling term]"? Why did they opt for "a simple yes or no"? This is actually somewhat unusual as researchers normally want to increase variance and therefore typically ask how much not just whether or not. A "simple yes or no" is a very limiting approach to ascertaining variance within and across subjects. Far more typical is offering subjects a response rating that spreads out the possible responses. For example, by asking "how angry does [candidate x] make you feel" and providing responses across a range from not at all to extremely with a number of intermediate response options.

The authors did not say why they opted for a simple dichotomy. But, I can draw a reasonable inference that it was because of their reliance on cognitive appraisal theory. I surmise that doing so led them to focus on their effort to support appraisal theory as superior to valence theory. Valence can easily accommodate a list of feelings if those feelings demonstrate that they are equivalent to liking, for the positive terms, and disliking for the negative terms. Cognitive appraisal theory, on the other hand treats feeling states, at least the "basic affects" as separate. That is, if one is feeling this feeling state, then following the logic of appraisal theories, one should not report feeling other affect states. This is because each feeling results from appraisals that differentiate the circumstances that give rise to each distinct and separate feelings. As in the example I gave earlier, if one attributes blame to another one should feel anger but not other negative affects. If one is uncertain about whom to attribute the punishing circumstance then that uncertainty should lead to anxiety, but not to anger nor to guilt. Given this either/or logic a simple "yes/no" response makes sense.[9]

In the first, smaller study the data included twelve named feeling terms: *afraid, angry, disgusted, disliking, frustrated, sad, uneasy, happy, hopeful, liking, proud,* and *sympathetic*. In the second, larger study a smaller set was used, parsing down to a set of seven named feeling terms: *afraid, angry, disgusted, uneasy, hopeful, proud,* and *sympathetic*. They reduced the feeling terms in the list to anticipate the following discussion because they found that the five dropped items did not apparently add anything useful to their analyses.[10]

Hence, we have two predictions, one from each of the then available theories. Analysis of the data, should the valence theory prove an apt account, would result in the negative terms (afraid, angry, disgust, dislike, frustrated, sad, and uneasy) should all be equivalent as should the positive terms, happy, hopeful, like, proud, and sympathetic. And further, all twelve in study 1 or seven in study 2, should fall along a single dimension ranging from the most positive to the most negative. In the case of the feeling thermometers, numbers are used to measure how much we like a candidate (or person, group, or whatever), with 80 to 100, meaning we like them very much; 40 to 60, not so much; and 0 to 40, not at all. But we can use words rather than numbers so that proud is equivalent to 100 or another very high number, and angry to 0, we do not like that person at all (using the words as "markers" noting where on the feeling thermometer to locate how we feel about that individual). Here, words or numbers, can equivalently be used to enable subjects to tell us how much they like or dislike, in this instance, candidates.

On the other hand, if cognitive appraisal theory is correct, then subjects should cluster into twelve (study 1) or seven (study 2) groups according to which feeling is predominant. Subjects should have generated a pattern of responses of lots of "noes" (they didn't feel that way about that candidate) and only one (or perhaps at the margin, a second) feeling. If they relied on cognitive appraisals to identify the specifics of the situation then only one reported feeling would be the result, hence, a single yes and a lot of noes.

However, Abelson and his colleagues (and ever study since) found instead that that the feeling responses did not follow along a single dimension. Nor, did subjects use these words to differentiate their affective responses into seven or more discrete states, as cognitive appraisal theories hold.

---

9. One detrimental consequence of applying such logic was that for decades following the ANES data that included these measures for evaluating presidential candidates, from 1980 to 1996, retained this dichotomous response format even though the Abelson report clearly showed the underlying logic to be incorrect.

10. This proved to be a second detrimental consequence. Dropping items to get to parsimony delayed the identification of an important dimension of affective appraisal of presidential candidates for over a decade and a half (Marcus et al. 1995; Marcus et al. 2006).

Instead, they found that people used the words that they had on hand to make but two sorts of appraisals. One was a "positive" appraisal defined by any array of positive affect terms would fall (whether happy or elated, hopeful or proud, or any other positive feeling word). The second appraisal was labeled "negative" and as with the positive appraisal, selecting just about any of the negative affect word seemed to suffice. The resulting two-dimensional structure emerged for both studies, no matter the candidate (multiple Republican and Democratic presidential candidates were used) and no matter the partisan status of the subject, whether Republican or Democrat. You might misunderstand this summary to mean that they found people using these emotion words much as expected by valence theory—people like or dislike a candidate. But that is not what they found. Rather than making one like–dislike assessment, people made two simultaneous appraisals, a positive appraisal and a negative appraisal. I have more to say on this later.

This is an excellent case of social science research, and a good case study for why political psychologists and scholars in general do such work. Data can surprise us and lead to new understandings. Abelson and colleagues did not make an available conceptual and measurement conclusion. If having multiple feeling terms available to probe subjective feeling experiences reveals two dimensions, what should one make of a feeling probe that compels a single valence that precludes revealing multiple dimensions? To put the matter more bluntly, feeling thermometer measures prevent subjects from reporting what the availability of multiple measures clearly demonstrates, that a single valence measure confounds, that is, combines two different properties into one single measure (Marcus 1988).

As noted throughout this book, science requires that all variables be defined both conceptually and empirically as single properties. That is, each variable can take on values, high or low, on a single facet or feature. Confounded properties violate this requirement in as much as we cannot determine in confounded variables whether the scores vary because one of the confounding terms is varying, because the other confounding term is varying, or because both are varying. This is highly problematic because the inability to identify the source of variance prevents scientific analysis.

In any case, the data collected by Abelson and colleagues (1982) found their evidence did not support a single evaluative dimension that valence theory expected, or the separate discrete feeling states that cognitive appraisal theories predicted. Instead from these data they proposed a new model. Two rather independent dimensions account for the responses to almost any array of events, groups, individuals, or circumstances (Mayer and Gaschke 1988).[11]

Putting the matter another way, when people confront a situation, person, group, or for that matter reflect on themselves and their lives, they have two basic concurrent affective appraisals. One view, largely advanced by psychologist James Russell (Barrett and Russell 1998; Russell 2003; Russell and Barrett 1999; Russell and Carroll 1999; Russell, Weiss, and Mendelsohn 1989) argues that the two appraisals report on the valence (i.e., how positive or negative a feeling state is being experienced) and how intensely felt is the feeling state. The alternative conception is that advanced by psychologists

---

11. The two dimensions are generally not "orthogonal," that is to say; those who feel more positive to a candidate (or anything else) is unrelated to how negative they feel. The two dimensions are most often moderately negatively correlated.

Auke Tellegen and David Watson (Tellegen 1985; Tellegen, Watson, and Clark 1999; Watson and Tellegen 1985) that rotates these two dimensions so they form the positive and negative dimensions much as Abelson's team presented.

Early

Through the twenty-year period following 1980 the general finding of two dimensions was repeatedly replicated by numerous studies, using data from many cultures, and with different teams of scholars (Russell 1980, 1983; Watson, Clark, and Tellegen 1984; Mayer and Gaschke 1988; Russell, Lewicka, and Niit 1989; Russell et al. 1989). The principal psychologist at the center of this activity has been David Watson (Watson et al. 1984; Watson and Tellegen 1985; Watson 1988b, 1988a; Watson, Clark, and Tellegen 1988; Watson and Clark 1994; Watson and Tellegen 1999; Watson 2000). All well and good, science moves forward. Many others also contributed to this seemingly robust result (Bradley and Lang 2000; Ito, Cacioppo, and Lang 1998; Lang et al. 1993; Russell and Bullock 1985; Yik, Russell, and Barrett 1999).

In this last account it would seem that swift affective responses are two dimensional, one a positive dimension and one a negative dimension that co-occur. This then led to the work with my colleagues, Michael MacKuen and W. Russell Neuman (MacKuen et al. 2007; Marcus 1988; Marcus and MacKuen 1993; Marcus, Neuman, and MacKuen 2000), which we subsequently labeled the theory of affective intelligence. The task of this theory was then, and is now, to identify the likely antecedent conditions that prompted changes in affective responses. And what consequential impacts on political judgment and behavior resulted therefrom. In our work with ANES data, the data series of national election surveys that now contained the feeling items that Abelson and colleagues generated, we found, in the main, the same two dimensions in the 1980–1996 series (Marcus et al. 2000).

Current

More recent research has suggested that at least three dimensions are needed to describe the concurrent emotional responses that people commonly experience. Many studies using multiple feeling terms, found that all positive feeling terms defined one positive dimension, and all negative feeling terms defined a single negative dimension. But the distinction between the physiology of anger and fear is well-known (Ax 1953). My colleagues and I (Marcus et al. 2000; Marcus 2002; Marcus et al. 2006) and psychologist Jennifer Lerner (Lerner and Keltner 2000, 2001; Lerner et al. 2003) found that under certain conditions, specifically when subjects were exposed to an aversive stimulus, an anger dimension emerged, a second negative dimension. When people confront circumstances that are absent a punishing, threatening situation (a hated candidate, an offensive policy position, or a threatening group or enemy), then just two dimensions emerged, one positive and one negative. But when an aversive situation is evident then just one negative dimension no longer simply and uniquely summarized peoples' affective responses. Rather, one negative dimension measuring uncertainty or risk and a second negative dimension measuring aversion or anger emerged. Hence, we have at the moment fairly robust evidence that three dimensions are often, especially in political circumstances, minimally required to account for the concurrent affective experience. To avoid confusion with valence theory, we use, and recommend using, enthusiasm to describe the positive dimension, and anxiety and aversion to refer, respectively, the two negative dimensions.

It is quite plausible that further research will lead to greater elaboration of the dimensional structure of emotion. And, as noted earlier, it is likely that an integration of theories of preconscious affective appraisal with theories of postawareness cognitive appraisal will emerge in the years ahead.

Still awaiting is the integration of a large and growing body of research on "moral emotions" such as guilt, shame, and disgust to the more general research literature on affective responses (de Hooge, Zeelenberg, and Breugelmans 2007; Greene et al. 2001; Haidt 2001; Borg, Lieberman, and Kiehl 2008; Moll and de Oliveira-Souza 2007; Moll et al. 2007; Oakley 1992; Petersen 2010; Tangney 1991; Tangney et al. 1996; Tangney, Stuewig, and Mashek 2007).

The historical trajectory of work on emotion in psychology has been a focus on affective responses with limited attention to the neural structures that subserve these responses. The historical, if brief, trajectory of work on emotion in neuroscience has been a focus on the neural structures that subserve affective processes. As these trajectories merge a richer and more robust array of research will emerge building on the work that has begun (Adolphs et al. 1996; Campbell, 1960; Adolphs 2009; Ashby, Isen, and Turken 1999; Berntson, Boysen, and Cacioppo 1993; Cacioppo et al. 1993; Cacioppo, Berntson, and Crites 1996; Gray 1987, 1990; Hsu et al. 2005; Weber and Johnson 2009; Zahn et al. 2009; Izard 2009; Lewis, Haviland-Jones, and Barrett 2008).

V. CONCLUSIONS

Other political psychologists will argue with my summary of scholarship, perhaps arguing that there is no need to attend to neuroscience formulations or research. Indeed quite a lot of political psychological research makes no mention of neuroscience. And, it is safe to say that in the near-term and perhaps the longer term more research will not take any note of or make any use of neuroscience. Many political psychologists are neither trained in nor interested in neuroscience.

Still, it is my view that the turn toward neuroscience research has already had a profound impact on the psychological understanding of human nature. First, neuroscience research has shown that although we experience consciousness as instantaneous, this is not actually when we experience consciousness. And, second, before our brain constructs the subjective experience of consciousness it is actively considering where we are, the nature of the world, and executing the many tasks that enable us to function in the world, governing many appraisals, decisions, and actions, all before consciousness awareness is generated. Third, neuroscience research has established that the preconscious knowledge of self, of available actions and how to execute and modify them, as well as of the external world, is richer than the knowledge available within consciousness. Fourth, we have multiple memory systems, one of which serves the preconscious and is not accessible by consciousness, and two of which, long-term and working memory, do serve consciousness. The latter is largely sustained with semantic language and syntax, the former is not. Fifth, the transformation of the psychology of emotion and reason from reliance on spatial metaphors—down versus up, inside versus outside, central versus peripheral, or body versus mind—to a temporal framework in which preconscious response reported as affective dimensional responses to provide swift and dynamic abilities to respond efficiently in the preconscious stage, as well as to impact on conscious awareness, opens up new possibilities for political psychology. And, finally, emotion, understanding how and when we feel, becomes a vital center of a new theory of democratic and nondemocratic politics. No longer can a reason-centered view of human nature be the normative ideal. How that is a topic we accept as a challenge in chapter 5.

EXERCISES

Select some visual illusions (there are many sites on the web just use any search engine to find them). Investigate why that illusion "works." Why does the brain process that image and come to a nonveridical solution? (A useful example of such an analysis is offered in Campbell, Brewer, and Collins 1981).

Select some articles that contain the words *affect, affective, feeling,* or *emotion* and either *cognitive, cognition, thinking,* or *reason* in their titles. As in the exercise at the end of chapter 3, you can use Google Scholar to conduct this search. Categorize whether the researchers use a temporal or a spatial dimension to contrast the qualities of the affect and the cognitive. Further, assess what functions are assigned to each. Finally, what is the implicit or explicit normative status with respect to humans' ability to engage in self-regulation and collective deliberation of affect and cognition?

REFERENCES

Abelson, Robert P., Donald R. Kinder, Mark D. Peters, and Susan T. Fiske. 1982. "Affective and Semantic Components in Political Personal Perception." *Journal of Personality and Social Psychology* 42:619–30.

Adolphs, Ralph. 2009. "The Social Brain: Neural Basis of Social Knowledge." *Annual Review of Psychology* 60:693–716.

Adolphs, Ralph, Hanna Damasio, Daniel Tranel, and Antonio R. Damasio. 1996. "Cortical Systems for the Recognition of Emotion in Facial Expressions." *Journal of Neuroscience* 16:7678–87.

Ajzen, Icek, and Martin Fishbein. 1977. "Attitude-Behavior Relations: A Theoretical Analysis and Review of Empirical Research." *Psychological Bulletin* 84:888–918.

———. 1980. *Understanding Attitudes and Predicting Social Behavior.* Englewood Cliffs, NJ: Prentice-Hall.

Aristotle. 1983. *The Politics.* New York: Penguin Books.

———. 1985. *Nicomachean Ethics.* New York: Odyssey Press.

Armony, Jorge L., and Joseph E. LeDoux. 1997. "How the Brain Processes Emotional Information." *Annals of the New York Academy of Sciences* 821:259–70.

Ashby, F. Gregory, Alice M. Isen, and And U. Turken. 1999. "A Neuropsychological Theory of Positive Affect and Its Influence on Cognition." *Psychological Bulletin* 106:529–50.

Ax, Albert. 1953. "The Physiological Differentiation between Fear and Anger in Humans." *Psychosomatic Medicine* 15:433–22.

Bargh, John A., Shelly Chaiken, Rajen Govender, and Felicia Pratto. 1992. "The Generality of the Automatic Attitude Activation Effect." *Journal of Personality and Social Psychology* 62:893–912.

Bargh, John A., and Melissa J. Ferguson. 2000. "Beyond Behaviorism: On the Automaticity of Higher Mental Processes." *Psychological Bulletin* 126:925–45.

Bargh, John A., and Paula Pietromonaco. 1982. "Automatic Information Processing and Social Perception: The Influence of Trait Information Presented Outside of Conscious Awareness on Impression Formation." *Journal of Personality and Social Psychology* 43:437–49.

Barrett, Lisa Feldman, and James A. Russell. 1998. "Independence and Bipolarity in the Structure of Current Affect." *Journal of Personality and Social Psychology* 74:967–84.

Berlin, Isaiah, and Henry Hardy. 1991. *The Crooked Timber of Humanity: Chapters in the History of Ideas*. New York: Knopf. Distributed by Random House.

Berntson, Gary G., Sarah T. Boysen, and John T. Cacioppo. 1993. "Neurobehavioral Organization and the Cardinal Principle of Evaluative Ambivalence." *Annals of the New York Academy of Science* 702:75–102.

Borg, Jana Schaich, Debra Lieberman, and Kent A. Kiehl. 2008. "Infection, Incest, and Iniquity: Investigating the Neural Correlates of Disgust and Morality." *Journal of Cognitive Neuroscience* 20:367–79.

Bradley, Margaret M., and Peter J. Lang. 2000. "Affective Reactions to Acoustic Stimuli." *Psychophysiology* 37:204–15.

Burke, Edmund. 1973. *Reflections on the Revolution in France*. Garden City, NY: Anchor Books.

Cacioppo, John T., Gary G. Berntson, and Stephen L. Crites, Jr. 1996. "Social Neuroscience: Principles of Psychophysiological Arousal and Response." In *Social Psychology: Handbook of Basic Principles*, edited by Tory E. Higgins and Arie W. Kruglanski, 72–101. New York: Guildford.

Cacioppo, John T., David J. Klein, Gary G. Berntson, and Elaine Hatfield. 1993. "The Psychophysiology of Emotion." In *The Handbook of Emotion*, edited by R. Lewis and J. M. Haviland, 119–42. New York: Guilford.

Campbell, Donald T. 1960. "Blind Variation and Selective Retention in Creative Thought as in Other Knowledge Processes". Psychological Review 67:380–400.

Campbell, Donald T., Marilynn B. Brewer, and Barry E. Collins. 1981. *Scientific Inquiry and the Social Sciences*. San Francisco: Jossey-Bass.

Chaiken, Shelly, and Yaacov Trope, eds. 1999. *Dual Process Models in Social Psychology*. New York: Guilford.

Changeux, Jean-Pierre. 1986. *Neuronal Man*. Oxford: Oxford University Press.

Damasio, Antonio R. 1994. *Descartes' Error: Emotion, Reason and the Human Brain*. New York: Putnam.

Dehaene, Stanislas. 2009. *Reading in the Brain: The Science and Evolution of a Human Invention*. New York: Viking Adult.

de Hooge, Ilona E., Marcel Zeelenberg, and Seger M. Breugelmans. 2007. "Moral Sentiments and Cooperation: Differential Influences of Shame and Guilt." *Cognition and Emotion* 21:1025–42.

Devine, Patricia G. 1989. "Stereotypes and Prejudice: Their Automatic and Controlled Components." *Journal of Personality and Social Psychology* 56:5–18.

Devine, Patricia G., Margo J. Monteith, Julia R. Zuwerink, and Andrew J. Elliot. 1991. "Prejudice With and Without Compunction." *Journal of Personality and Social Psychology* 60:817–30.

Diderot, Denis, Jean Le Rond d'Alembert, and Pierre Mouchon. 1778. *Encyclopédie, Ou Dictionnaire Raisonné Des Sciences, Des Arts Et Des Métiers*. Geneva: Pellet.

Evans, Jonathan St. B. T. 2008. "Dual-Processing Accounts of Reasoning, Judgment, and Social Cognition." *Annual Review of Psychology* 59:255–78.

Fiske, Susan T. 1981. "Social Cognition and Affect." In *Cognition, Social Behavior, and the Environment*, edited by J. Harvey. Hillsdale, NJ: Erlbaum.

Freud, Sigmund, and James Strachey. 1971. *The Complete Introductory Lectures on Psychoanalysis.* London: Allen & Unwin.

Gazzaniga, Michael. 1985. *The Social Brain: Discovering the Networks of the Mind.* New York: Basic Books.

Gray, Jeffrey A. 1987. "The Neuropsychology of Emotion and Personality." In *Cognitive Neurochemistry*, edited by S. M. Stahl, S. D. Iversen, and E. C. Goodman, 171–90. Oxford: Oxford University Press.

———. 1990. "Brain Systems That Mediate Both Emotion and Cognition." *Cognition and Emotion* 4:269–88.

———. 2004. *Consciousness: Creeping Up on the Hard Problem.* Oxford: Oxford University Press.

Greene, Joshua D., R. Brian Sommerville, Leigh E. Nystrom, John M. Darley, and Jonathan D. Cohen. 2001. "An fMRI Investigation of Emotional Engagement in Moral Judgment." *Science* 293:2105–8.

Gutmann, Amy. 1987. *Democratic Education.* Princeton, NJ: Princeton University Press.

Haidt, Jonathan. 2001. "The Emotional Dog and Its Rational Tail: A Social Intuitionist Approach to Moral Judgment." *Psychological Review* 108:814–34.

Herzog, Don. 1998. *Poisoning the Minds of the Lower Orders.* Princeton, NJ: Princeton University Press.

Hsu, Ming, Meghana Bhatt, Ralph Adolphs, Daniel Tranel, and Colin F. Camerer. 2005. "Neural Systems Responding to Degrees of Uncertainty in Human Decision-Making." *Science* 310:1680–83.

Ito, Tiffany A., John T. Cacioppo, and Peter J. Lang. 1998. "Eliciting Affect Using the International Affective Picture System: Trajectories through Evaluative Space." *Personality and Social Psychology Bulletin* 24:855–79.

Izard, Carroll E. 2009. "Emotion Theory and Research: Highlights, Unanswered Questions, and Emerging Issues." *Annual Review of Psychology* 60:1–25.

James, William. 1883. "What is Emotion?" *Mind* 9:188–204.

———. 1890. *The Principles of Psychology.* Cambridge, MA: Harvard University Press.

———. 1894. "The Physical Basis of Emotion." *Psychological Review* 1:516–29.

Jeannerod, Marc. 1997. *The Cognitive Neuroscience of Action.* Cambridge, MA: Blackwell.

Lang, Peter J., Mark K. Greenwald, Margaret M. Bradley, and Alfons O. Hamm. 1993. "Looking at Pictures: Affective, Facial, Visceral and Behavioral Reactions." *Psychophysiology* 30:261–73.

Lazarus, Richard. 1984. "On the Primacy of Cognition." *American Psychologist* 39:124–29.

Le Bon, Gustave. 1986. The Crowd: A Study of the Popular Mind. London: Unwin.

LeDoux, Joseph E. 1991. "Emotion and the Limbic System Concept." *Concepts in Neuroscience* 2:169–99.

———. 1996. *The Emotional Brain: The Mysterious Underpinnings of Emotional Life.* New York: Simon & Schuster.

———. 2000. "Emotion Circuits in the Brain." In *Annual Reviews Neuroscience*, edited by W. Maxwell Cowan, Eric M. Shooter, Charles F. Stevens, and Richard F. Thompson, 155–84. Palo Alto, CA: Annual Reviews.

Lerner, Jennifer S., Roxana M. Gonzalez, Deborah A. Small, and Baruch Fischhoff. 2003. "Effects of Fear and Anger on Perceived Risks of Terrorism: A National Field Experiment." *Psychological Science* 14:144–50.

Lerner, Jennifer S., and Dachere Keltner. 2000. "Beyond Valence: Toward a Model of Emotion-Specific Influences on Judgement and Choice." *Cognition and Emotion* 14:473–93.

————. 2001. "Fear, Anger, and Risk." *Journal of Personality and Social Psychology* 81:146–59.

Lewis, Michael, Jeannette M Haviland-Jones, and Lisa Feldman Barrett. 2008. *Handbook of Emotions*. New York: Guilford.

Libet, Benjamin. 1985. "Unconscious Cerebral Initiative and the Role of Conscious Will in Voluntary Action." *The Behavioral and Brain Sciences* 8:529–66.

————. 2004. *Mind Time: The Temporal Factor in Consciousness*. Cambridge, MA: Harvard University Press.

Libet, Benjamin, Curtis A. Gleason, Elwood W. Wright, and Dennis K. Pearl. 1983. "Time of Conscious Intention to Act in Relation to Onset of Cerebral Activity (Readiness-Potential)." *Brain* 106:623–42.

Libet, Benjamin, Jr., Elwood W. Wright, Bertram Feinstein, and Dennis K. Pearl. 1979. "Subjective Referral of the Timing for a Conscious Sensory Experience." *Brain* 102:1597–600.

Locke, John. 1996. *Some Thoughts Concerning Education*. Indianapolis, IN: Hackett.

MacKuen, Michael, George E. Marcus, W. Russell Neuman, and Luke Keele. 2007. "The Third Way: The Theory of Affective Intelligence and American Democracy." In *The Affect Effect: The Dynamics of Emotion in Political Thinking and Behavior*, edited by Ann Crigler, George E. Marcus, Michael MacKuen, and W. Russell Neuman, 124–51. Chicago: University of Chicago Press.

Marcus, George E. 1988. "The Structure of Emotional Response: 1984 Presidential Candidates." *American Political Science Review* 82:735–61.

————. 2000. "Emotions in Politics." In *Annual Review of Political Science*, edited by Nelson W. Polsby. Palo Alto, CA: Annual Reviews.

————. 2002. *The Sentimental Citizen: Emotion in Democratic Politics*. University Park: Pennsylvania State University Press.

Marcus, George E., Don Kinder, Michael MacKuen, Wendy Rahn, and Lisa D'Ambrosio. 1995. Measuring emotional response in the 1995 pilot. Proposal to the 1995 ANES Pilot Planning Committee, Berkeley, CA.

Marcus, George E., and Michael MacKuen. 1993. "Anxiety, Enthusiasm and the Vote: The Emotional Underpinnings of Learning and Involvement during Presidential Campaigns." *American Political Science Review* 87:688–701.

Marcus, George E., Michael MacKuen, Jennifer Wolak, and Luke Keele. 2006. "The Measure and Mismeasure of Emotion." In *Feeling Politics: Emotion in Political Information Processing*, edited by David Redlawsk, 31–45. New York: Palgrave Macmillan.

Marcus, George E., W. Russell Neuman, and Michael B. MacKuen. 2000. *Affective Intelligence and Political Judgment*. Chicago: University of Chicago Press.

Mayer, John D., and Yvonne N. Gaschke. 1988. "The Experience and Meta-Experience of Mood." *Journal of Personality and Social Psychology* 55:102–11.

Milner, A. D., and Melvyn A. Goodale. 1995. *The Visual Brain in Action*. Oxford: Oxford University Press.

Mishkin, Mortimer, and Tim Appenzeller. 1987. "The Anatomy of Memory." *Scientific American* 256:80–89.

Moll, Jorge, and Ricardo de Oliveira-Souza. 2007. "Moral Judgments, Emotions and the Utilitarian Brain." *Trends in Cognitive Sciences* 11:319–21.

Moll, Jorge, Ricardo de Oliveira-Souza, Griselda Garrido, Ivanei E. Bramati, Egas M. A. Caparelli-Daquer, Mirella L Paiva, M. F., Roland Zahn, and Jordan Grafman. 2007. "The Self as a Moral Agent: Linking the Neural Bases of Social Agency and Moral Sensitivity." *Social Neuroscience* 2:336–52.

Nørretranders, Tor. 1998. *The User Illusion*. New York: Viking.

Oakley, Justin. 1992. *Morality and the Emotions*. London: Routledge.

Ochsner, Kevin N., Rebecca R. Ray, Brent Hughes, Kateri McRae, Jeffrey C. Cooper, Jochen Weber, John D. E. Gabrieli, and James J. Gross. 2009. "Bottom-Up and Top-Down Processes in Emotion Generation: Common and Distinct Neural Mechanism." *Psychological Science* 20:1322–31.

Ortony, Andrew, Gerald L. Clore, and Allan Collins. 1989. *The Cognitive Structure of Emotions*. New York: Cambridge University Press.

Panksepp, Jaak. 1989. "The Neurobiology of Emotions: Of Animal Brains and Human Feelings." In *Handbook of Social Psychophysiology*, edited by H. Wagner and A. Manstead. Chichester, England: Wiley.

———. 1998. *Affective Neuroscience: The Foundations of Human and Animal Emotions*. New York: Oxford University Press.

Parkinson, Brian, and A. S. R. Manstead. 1992. "Appraisal as a Cause of Emotion." In *Emotion*, edited by Margaret S. Clark, 122–49. Newbury Park, CA: Sage.

Petersen, Michael Bang. 2010. "Distinct Emotions, Distinct Domains: Anger, Anxiety and Perceptions of Intentionality." *Journal of Politics* 72:357–65.

Petty, Richard E., and John T. Cacioppo. 1986. *Communication and Persuasion: Central and Peripheral Routes to Attitude Change*. New York: Springer-Verlag.

Popkin, Samuel L. 1991. *The Reasoning Voter: Communication and Persuasion in Presidential Campaigns*. Chicago: University of Chicago Press.

Rolls, Edmund T. 2000. "Memory Systems in the Brain." *Annual Review of Psychology* 51:599–630.

Rolls, Edmund T., Morten L. Kringelbach, and Ivan E. T. de Araujo. 2003. "Different Representations of Pleasant and Unpleasant Odours in the Human Brain." *European Journal of Neuroscience* 18:695–703.

Roseman, Ira. 1979. "Cognitive Aspects of Emotion and Emotional Behavior." Paper presented at the Annual Meeting of the American Psychological Association, New York, NY.

———. 1984. "Cognitive Determinants of Emotions: A Structural Theory." In *Review of Personality and Social Psychology*, edited by P. Shaver. Beverly Hills, CA: Sage.

———. 1991. "Appraisal Determinants of Discrete Emotions." *Cognition and Emotion* 5:161–200.

Russell, James A. 1980. "A Circumplex Model of Affect." *Journal of Personality and Social Psychology* 39:1161–78.

———. 1983. "Pancultural Aspects of Human Conceptual Organization of Emotions." *Journal of Personality and Social Psychology* 45:1281–88.

———. 2003. "Core Affect and the Psychological Construction of Emotion." *Psychological Review* 110:145–72.

Russell, James A., and Lisa Feldman Barrett. 1999. "Core Affect, Prototypical Emotional Episodes, and Other Things Called Emotion: Dissecting the Elephant." *Journal of Personality and Social Psychology* 76:805–19.

Russell, James A., and Merry Bullock. 1985. "Multidimensional Scaling of Facial Expressions: Similarity From Preschoolers to Adults." *Journal of Personality and Social Psychology* 48:1290–98.

Russell, James A., and James M. Carroll. 1999. "On the Bipolarity of Positive and Negative Affect." *Psychological Bulletin* 125:3–30.

Russell, James A., Maria Lewicka, and Toomas Niit. 1989. "A Cross-Cultural Study of a Circumplex Model of Affect." *Journal of Personality and Social Psychology* 57:848–56.

Russell, James A., Anna Weiss, and Gerald A. Mendelsohn. 1989. "Affect Grid: A Single-Item Scale of Pleasure and Arousal." *Journal of Personality and Social Psychology* 57:493–502.

Sartori, Giovanni. 1987. *The Theory of Democracy Revisited*. Chatham, NJ: Chatham House.

Scherer, Klaus R., Elise S. Dan, and Anders Flykt. 2006. "What Determines a Feeling's Position in Affective Space? A Case for Appraisal." *Cognition and Emotion* 20:92–113.

Scherer, Klaus R., Angela Schorr, and Tom Johnstone. 2001. *Appraisal Processes in Emotion: Theory, Methods, Research*. Oxford: Oxford University Press.

Shepherd, Gordon M. 2007. "Perspectives on Olfactory Processing, Conscious Perception, and Orbitofrontal Cortex." *Annals of the New York Academy of Sciences* 1121:87–101.

Squire, Larry R. 1987. *Memory and Brain*. New York: Oxford University Press.

Stanton, Mark E. 2000. "Multiple Memory Systems, Development and Conditioning." *Behavioral Brain Research* 110:25–37.

Storbeck, Justin, and Gerald L. Clore. 2007. "On the Interdependence of Cognition and Emotion." *Cognition and Emotion* 21:1212–37.

Tangney, June Price. 1991. "Moral Affect: The Good, the Bad and the Ugly." *Journal of Personality and Social Psychology* 61:598–607.

Tangney, June Price, Rowland S. Miller, Laura Flicker, and Deborah Hill Barlow. 1996. "Are Shame, Guilt, and Embarrassment Distinct Emotions?" *Journal of Personality and Social Psychology* 70:1256–69.

Tangney, June Price, Jeff Stuewig, and Debra J. Mashek. 2007. "Moral Emotions and Moral Behavior." *Annual Review of Psychology* 58:345–72.

Tellegen, Auke. 1985. "Structures of Mood and Personality and Their Relevance to Assessing Anxiety, With an Emphasis on Self-Report." In *Anxiety and the Anxiety Disorders*, edited by A. H. Tuma and J. D. Maser. Hillsdale, NJ: Erlbaum.

Tellegen, Auke, David Watson, and Lee Anna Clark. 1999. "On the Dimensional and Hierarchical Structure of Affect." *Psychological Science* 10:297–303.

Tsal, Yehoshua. 1985. "On the Relationship between Cognitive and Affective Processes: A Critique of Zajonc and Markus." *Journal of Consumer Research* 12:358–62.

Watson, David. 1988a. "Intraindividual and Interindividual Analyses of Positive and Negative Affect: Their Relation to Health Complaints, Perceived Stress, and Daily Activities." *Journal of Personality and Social Psychology* 54:1020–30.

———. 1988b. "The Vicissitudes of Mood Measurement: Effects of Varying Descriptors, Time Frames, and Response Formats on Measures of Positive and Negative Affect." *Journal of Personality and Social Psychology* 55:128–41.

———. 2000. *Mood and Temperament*. New York: Guilford.

Watson, David, and Lee Anna Clark. 1994. "The PANAS–X: Manual for the Positive and Negative Affect Schedule–Expanded Form."

Watson, David, Lee Anna Clark, and Auke Tellegen. 1984. "Cross-Cultural Convergence in the Structure of Mood: A Japanese Replication and a Comparison with U.S. Findings." *Journal of Personality and Social Psychology* 47:127–44.

———. 1988. "Development and Validation of Brief Measures of Positive and Negative Affect: The PANAS Scales." *Journal of Personality and Social Psychology* 54:1063–70.

Watson, David, and Auke Tellegen. 1985. "Toward a Consensual Structure of Mood." *Psychological Bulletin* 98:219–35.

———. 1999. "Issues in the Dimensional Structure of Affect–Effects of Descriptors, Measurement Error, and Response Formats: Comment on Russell and Carroll (1999)." *Psychological Bulletin* 125:601–10.

Weber, Elke U., and Eric A. Johnson. 2009. "Mindful Judgment and Decision Making." *Annual Review of Psychology* 60:53–85.

Wegner, Daniel M. 2002. *The Illusion of Conscious Will*. Cambridge, MA: MIT Press.

Weiskrantz, Lawrence. 1986. *Blindsight: A Case Study and Implications*. Oxford: Oxford University Press.

———. 1997. *Consciousness Lost and Found: A Neuropsychological Investigation*. Oxford: Oxford University Press.

Wilson, Timothy D. 2002. *Strangers to Ourselves: Discovering the Adaptive Unconscious*. Cambridge, MA: Belknap.

Wilson, Timothy D., and Dana S. Dunn. 1986. "Effects of Introspection on Attitude-Behavior Consistency: Analyzing Reasons Versus Focusing on Feelings." *Journal of Experimental Psychology* 22:249–63.

Wilson, Timothy D., Dana S. Dunn, Dolores Kraft, and Douglas J. Lisle. 1989. "Introspection, Attitude Change, and Attitude-Behavior Consistency: The Disruptive Effects of Explaining Why We Feel the Way We Do." *Advances in Experimental Social Psychology* 22:287–343.

Wilson, Timothy D., and Jonathan W. Schooler. 1991. "Thinking Too Much: Introspection Can Reduce the Quality of Preferences and Decisions." *Journal of Personality and Social Psychology* 60:181–92.

Yik, Michelle S., James A. Russell, and Lisa Feldman Barrett. 1999. "Structure of Self-Reported Current Affect: Integration and Beyond." *Journal of Personality and Social Psychology* 77:600–19.

Zahn, Roland, Jorge Moll, Mirella Paiva, Griselda Garrido, Frank Krueger, Edward D. Huey, and Jordan Grafman. 2009. "The Neural Basis of Human Social Values: Evidence from Functional MRI." *Cerebral Cortex* 19:176–283.

Zajonc, Robert B. 1980. "Feeling and Thinking: Preferences Need No Inferences." *American Psychologist* 35:151–75.

———. 1984. "On the Primacy of Affect." *American Psychologist* 39:117–23.

Zeki, Semir. 1993. *A Vision of the Brain*. Oxford: Blackwell Scientific.

Zimmermann, Manfred. 1989. "The Nervous System in the Context of Information Theory." In *Human Physiology*, edited by R. F. Schmidt and G. Thews, 166–73. Berlin, Germany: Springler-Verlag.

Zou, Zhihua, Fusheng Li, and Linda B. Buck. 2005. "Odor Maps in the Olfactory Cortex." *Proceedings of the National Academy of Sciences* 102:7724–29.

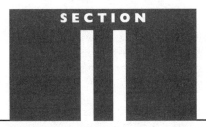

SECTION

II

Political Psychology

CHAPTER 5

Brain and Conscious Mind

In the chapter 4, I presented some of the important insights neuroscientists have produced about the brain and the mind. In this chapter I show how these insights provide a new foundation for political psychology, joining the ranks already provided by other social sciences. In section 1, I elaborate on those insights. In section 2, I present a provisional theory that incorporates preconscious and postawareness dynamics of neural process. And, finally, in section 3, I develop the political implications of those insights. Although neuroscience is still in its infancy, we have learned enough to fundamentally challenge older conceptions of human nature. The theory of affective intelligence is one of the few attempts to address the radical implications of these insights.

I have emphasized that what is meant by the word *knowledge* must now take into account the broad expanse of preconscious knowledge that the brain uses to comprehend and act in the world. Conclusions limited to what people consciously know will apply only to that subset of knowledge that is available to the mind and semantic memory. Claims about what people know and what that knowledge is used for will be distorted if that is the only variant of knowledge that is taken into account. I have emphasized that rather than thinking and feeling as being spatially distinct—emotions in the heart and reasons in the mind or placing emotion in some other place, for example, a supposed "subconscious" place, a place that is believed to lie *under* the conscious mind—we should attend to their temporal relationship.

I have emphasized that some neural tasks are performed and under full control of preconscious processes. But, as I discuss later in this chapter, one task of preconscious is to determine when the "automatic" controls (i.e., preconscious processes that do not rely on conscious engagement) are set aside for deliberative processes. These and other insights compel us to reconstruct political psychology—to develop a new science of psychology and politics.

There is an even larger consideration before us. The centrality of "cognition"—the theater of the mind in which contemporary experience and our capacity to express ourselves semantically coexist in a seemingly vivid, comprehensive, instantaneous, and veridical fashion—holds a justifiably privileged place in psychology and politics. By privileged I mean that psychology and political science each hold that cognition is an essential quality of human nature most especially because conscious control of what we know and how we act is vital to the plausibility of governance of, for, and by the people. The argument that affect arises before and independent of conscious awareness threatens not only our scientific understanding but also threatens our aspiration for a politics of thought, judgment, and deliberated action.

The challenge of studying ourselves is great because we are flawed observers. Even as we try to be scientific, to be objective, we often fail because we judge our efforts, and we judge them in self-interested ways. We fail because our brains have evolved in such a fashion as to hide from us the actual means by which brain, mind, feeling, thinking, and acting are executed. The brain has evolved to give us a subjective world that has all the appearances of being comprehensive. What we have before us seems to be the entire world in all its glories. The brain also has evolved to give us the illusion that what we see and hear is instantaneous—that when we see and hear a political figure give a speech, we are seeing and hearing what is being said in "real time," therefore any conclusions and reactions are responses that require conscious awareness (for how could we respond to a speech that we have not heard or seen).

The sense we have that the world we inhabit is immediately and comprehensively before us, we move and see others move instantaneously, is a powerful sensation, one that our brains carefully and artfully recreate from instant to instant. How the brain accomplishes this is not yet well understood. What is known is that this subjective experience is itself a confabulation. One, however, that is so potent, so persistent, that we can see it only in the fringes of experience. For example, in the dusk of the day, colors start to disappear and the world becomes marked by grays of lighter and darker shades. Colors do not appear and disappear in the world; rather the cone cells in our eyes and our brains together can construct colors when there is enough light. But the brain cannot construct colors when the light levels fall below a specific threshold. How these illusions work is itself most interesting but more important is the impact those illusions have had in shaping our grander understandings of self, social experience, and politics. As neuroscience reveals the fuller scope of these illusions and reveals the realities that lie hidden, psychology, political science, and political psychology need to make major changes in our empirical understandings and perhaps make new normative models to guide our aspirations for freedom, sociality, and politics.

Let's turn to psychology first.

I. THE PSYCHOLOGY OF MIND AND BRAIN

For many years, centuries, and millennia, scholars could at best observe human behavior and ponder how the brain might make it all happen. And many did to support their speculations about the brain and its operation. The mind, on the other hand, seems readily apparent, vivid even. How are the two related? It has even been suggested that they are only weakly related. The notion of "free will," so central to western thought and

BOX 5.1   *Ghosts, spirits, ghouls, specters, wraiths, angels, devils,* **and** *demons*

These are some of words that express the deeply entrenched hope for life outside, or beyond, a hope that animates many aspects of cultures, secular and religious.

our conception of ourselves as freely thinking and freely acting individuals, seemed to require some substantial independence of mind from brain. It has been thought that if the brain directs the mind than our thoughts are not free; and, if our thoughts are determined by biology than our actions must also be directed by biology.

The conceit that our thoughts give rise to action is achieved by a mind–body dualism. In this view, each—the brain and the mind—have their separate realms.

Now that neuroscience and cognitive science have been pursuing this for a while we can gain some purchase on the ways in which brain and mind function. The principal insight is not so much in the location of brain function, which is where in the brain are various faculties located, but in the timing of brain processes.

The most important point about the timing of brain processes is shown in figure 4.1, that consciousness takes about five-hundred milliseconds of brain activity to generate. The second point is that the brain does many things in the period *prior* to conscious awareness. The third point is that the brain confabulates so that this time delay is obscured so that our conscious lives are not generally aware of this time delay. And, that these three insights fundamentally alter what we have as the central agenda for psychology and political psychology. Indeed, the brain's development resulted in specific confabulations. I mentioned the time shifting as one of these. The brain enables us to inhabit consciousness with the conviction that what we subjectively experience is contemporaneous, instantaneous with objective events. Figures 5.1 and 5.2 later, give an exercise for you access to the sensation of time in consciousness. Figure 5.1 shows seven color words, red, green, blue, purple, black, orange, and yellow.

As you can see, the color of the words matches the name of the word; the word red is displayed in red letters. The colors and words are harmonious. For most of us, at least those of us that are not color blind, we can swiftly, instantaneously see the colors and read the names.

Let's do a simple experiment that exposes the ability of the brain to generate this sense of immediacy by changing one aspect of the above display. Figure 5.2 displays the same words, in the same locations. However this time, the names and colors of the words do not match.

BOX 5.2   **Faculty and location in the brain**

Neuroanatomy has located specific areas of the normal human brain that sustain specific faculties, for example, the various regions that are essential in sustaining conscious vision, speech, or memory, and so on. These have obvious importance in clinical practice. And identifying these areas is a critical initial step in understanding how the brain and consciousness function. But, it is the dynamic interactions of all these areas that we most need to understand.

Because the semantic labels, the color words no longer match, word and colors conflict—the word *blue* is written in red letters—reading becomes difficult, especially if we are tasked with identifying the word meaning and ignoring the word's color (this conflict is the basis of what is called the Stroop task, named after a graduate student, John Stroop, who developed it in his 1935 PhD thesis). Word recognition takes mental processing and this is normally very rapid. Indeed so rapid that, apart from the occasional stutter that can afflict us, it seems instantaneous, see an object or think of an object and the word is retrieved and enunciated, it flows. See the word *red* or see a red object, and out comes the right word. By creating a conflict between the recognition of color, the actual color, and the meaning of the word, red as the name of a color, the brain has to take more time to resolve the conflict and subjective time slows down. Because resolving the name and colors requires mental effort, we can experience the mental effort that now intrudes on the otherwise swift and seamless identification of names and objects. Our brains could have evolved in a different fashion, of course, and one of the alternatives could have made that time lag of five-hundred milliseconds apparent rather than hidden. I suspect that most of us would not enjoy that evolutionary alternative with what the obvious differences in subjective experience of actual and subjective time. But no matter, our brains have evolved to hide those two different time courses from us.

Some political ramifications of the Stroop test: What does the issue of time have to do with politics? Or for that matter our ability to identify a color word slows down when the color word does not match the color of the text? The above example conveys certain implications. These are:

First, we act more swiftly, and accurately, when we confront familiar experiences (the word *red* is itself colored red). Therefore, we are more vulnerable when we find ourselves confronting something unusual or unexpected. We have a stake in the skills learned, and those skills work best when they are practiced in familiar settings. It has long been observed that humans regularly hold a positive view of their own group and are likely to form negative attitudes to other groups (Linville and Jones 1980; Pettigrew and Tropp 2006; Sherif 1958; Struch and Schwartz 1989). This dynamic develops very early and seems to be quite ubiquitous (Aboud 1988). Perhaps that predilection is routed in the difficulty humans have of applying known skills that work in familiar settings to unknown groups and in unfamiliar settings.

Second, there is a further ramification. If familiarity is a requisite of mastering skills, much as athletes may perform better at home in familiar settings than "on the road," so too in politics, we may find ourselves better able to communicate, understand, and engage with those who are familiar to us. Because we have practiced skills of identification and engagement that, much like the result of the Stroop test research, work better when the expected and familiar match. Familiarity is a marker of certainty and efficiency. When we feel safe and in familiar circumstances humans function best because the inventory of skills acquired works best within bounded domains we have learned to master (Gould 2003).

I used vision and touch to illustrate some of the functional features of the brain, but there are other senses. And, these senses display the same requirement that the brain plays an active rather than a passive recording role. Let's turn to another sensory stream, hearing. Hearing gives us access to valuable information about the world. We sense

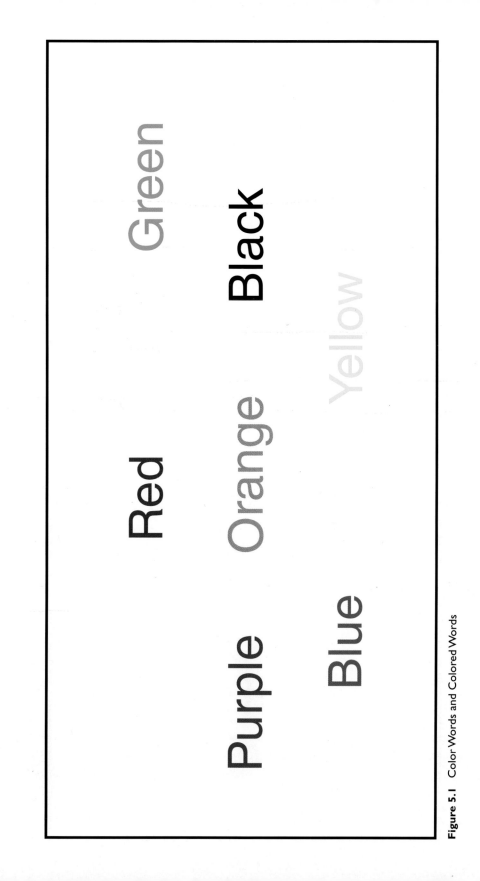

Figure 5.1 Color Words and Colored Words

Figure 5.2 Color Words and Colored Words Redux

whether something is important from its sound. And, sound conveys more than the importance of some event. We can learn something further about its nature: Was that sudden sound noise, thunder, a backfire, a gun shot, or a door slamming? Moreover, having two ears allows the brain to compare the auditory signals enabling us locate sound in space so we can judge whether it is close or far, whether it is to our right or left, in front or behind. The changing pitch of a sound can also identify the speed of the object generating the sound as well as its trajectory relative to our location. All of this is very useful. Here again, a brain function is achieved by misrepresenting the world. One might want to use a microphone and recording studio as an analogy but that would mischaracterize how the brain deals with sounds that reach the inner ear to generate electrical signals, which then travel to the auditory regions of the brain. The brain does not act as a microphone, passively listening and recording the sounds out in the world. The human body generates a lot of noise, for example, the beating heart, blood moving through arteries and veins, lungs expanding and contracting, the stomach digesting food, and more dramatically, snoring. Yet, the brain has learned to screen out these noises from the sensory stream. What we "hear" has had these sounds eliminated so that although these sounds exist, and add to the electrical signals that move to the brain, the brain actively filters out these "distractions." This then has the beneficial result of allowing our hearing to be restricted to external, the internal sources of sound being purged.

Some political ramifications of the brain's purging of internal sounds: Let me restate this result in a way we might see around us. The brain "knows" that the internal sounds of digestion, the circulatory system, and so on, are normal and can safely be ignored. Therefore, the brain removes these sounds so they do not distract us in the conscious experience of hearing. The brain is actively sorting out what our minds should address by purging out "irrelevant" sounds. Does this sound very normal?

Humans have a general capacity to ignore "irrelevant" information. What gets defined as irrelevant is less significant, although of course important, than another principle. For the brain to function it must impose prior knowledge, what is irrelevant (the internal sounds of the normally functioning human organism, a noisy enterprise) to preserve its capacity to attend to and address the external world. As I mentioned earlier, psychologist Milton Rokeach began his career with a project that involved bringing together three patients into recurring group therapy sessions. Each of these patients believed they were the messiah come back to earth (Rokeach 1964). Yet each was able to easily come to the conclusion that the others were frauds without any apparent reflection on their own veracity. And, while there are, no doubt, individual differences in how much we each remain open to conflicting information (Rokeach 1960; Festinger 1957) there is the broader pattern I am emphasizing.

We are all reliant on brains that construct and restrict the conscious experience so that it attends to what the brain has previously learned about the external world and how best to function therein. And, in the pervasive realm of stereotypes we can observe the same dynamic: prior knowledge is automatically impelled by the brain to make sense of the external world (Bodenhausen 1988; Bodenhausen and Lichtenstein 1987; Devine 1989; Macrae, Milne, and Bodenhausen 1994; Rahn 1993; Valentino, Hutchings, and White 2002; Vinacke 1957).

The active involvement of the brain in determining what "we see" is also true. Rather than passively recording information about the world, the brain is dynamically

Figure 5.3 Rubin's Vase Figure

involved in constructing the image of the world using its prior understanding of the world as it decodes the electrical impulses received from the eyes through the optic nerves.

Vision illusions are many and I discuss one more example here to demonstrate how the active brain is involved in shaping the visible, the visual component of our conscious experience. This last example is called Rubin's vase (named after Danish psychologist Edgar Rubin). This example reveals a critically important insight into the normal function of the human brain. We see the brain involvement in Rubin's vase, figure 5.3. The image can be seen either as a vase or as two faces. That ambiguity is also shaped by our consciousness as we can "flip" what we see from vase to faces and back. Focus on the black, two faces; focus on the white, a vase. But this image cannot be three faces nor can it be a cigar. So, the ambiguity is limited. More important, the specific plasticity, faces or a vase, applies more generally to other and to less ambiguous images. We need to know before we can see. Or, to put it another way, our brain applies a theory about what we are seeing in order to see. Change the theory and we see something different. But, what we see is not totally dependent on our theory, our expectations.

What we see depends on the flow of electrical signals. Therefore, seeing is dependent on empirical data, the ability of the eyes to capture, focus, and translate light into electrical signals. Then, those signals are transmitted via the optic nerve to the brain. Change the light that strikes the rods and cones, and the flow of electrical signals will be different and what we see also will be changed. The brain applies its own information, its own knowledge, to shape the ultimate representation that is the conscious visual field.[1] To accomplish all of this, the brain needs to anticipate what is out there so it can assess and combine all this contemporary sensory flow into a coherent multimodal

---

1. There is one sense that is not mediated: smell. The sense of smell, perhaps our oldest sense, is produced by the brain actually touching external objects. A part of the brain, the olfactory bulb, extends into the sinus cavities. There it waits for molecules wafted into these cavities and as these objects touch the bulb, the brain tries to make sense of how the molecules "fit" as they rest on the brain. The brain then deciphers them, generating the sensation of smells that repel or attract. The magnitude of the perfume industry worldwide shows the potency of this primal knowledge.

experience that we call consciousness. In the five-hundred milliseconds that begin when these signals arrive at the brain, various parts of the brain attend to different analyses. For example, one of the visual centers in the brain searches for lines so not only near and far can be identified but also to identify objects. And, prior knowledge, memories of prior stimuli and their features stored in the brain, can greatly speed up these processes so that objects and their significance can be distinguished as swiftly as possible. All of this is largely completed before consciousness and indeed is essential to the creation of consciousness.

It has been common to point to illusions to make the general point that we are fallible, that we often misperceive the world. And, that assertion is often true. Humans are fallible and often misperceive the world. But, I want to use these examples to make a quite different point. The brain is actively involved in the construction of reality; indeed without that active engagement we would not be able to perceive the world at all. Perception is more than the passive recording of sense-data. Perception is the joint result of sensory data and an active and theorizing brain. The two elements combine so that the brain can generate the subjective experience of reality we experience as consciousness. Changing either changes our conscious perceptions. There is one more feature of the active brain that we need to grasp to fully understand the relationship between preconscious brain activity and the subjective quality of conscious experience.

Some political ramifications of brain's ability to shift perspectives: The Rubin's vague figure is clearly not in and of itself political. So, we see two faces or we see a vase. In a more general fashion, the ability of the brain to shift how we understand what we see by altering the theoretical interpretation, the same external material taking on different meaning depending on what meaning we ascribe to it, has generated a lot of research into what we call "framing." To take but one example in the domain of political tolerance: Research has shown that if a conflict dilemma that engaged the issue of tolerance is presented as within the context as an issue of safety, people used the description of the situation with a bias to restrict political rights of those they detest in the interest of security. On the other hand, when subjects were presented the same information—similar to Rubin's vase—but in a context of when we invoked the positive features of democracy and tolerance, then people used the description of the situation with a bias toward securing the right of those they deteste (Marcus et al. 1995). In a more general vein, there is a wealth of research on framing that shows how robust the effects that expectations, prior theories in effect, have on political judgments. Change the frame of reference, and as in our ability to see either a face or a vase, friend or foe, we can alter what we see politically (Bazerman 1984; Berinsky and Kinder 2006; De Martino et al. 2006; J. N. Druckman 2004; J. Druckman 2001; Kahneman and Tversky 1984; Kühberger 1998; Neale and Bazerman 1985; Nelson, Clawson, and Oxley 1997; Ryan 2004).

In broad perspective, the brain's ability to shift its understanding of the circumstances by shifting from one interpretation to another is a capability that sustains the flexibility to alter our course of action from one value, policy, or ideological, perspective to another. If there was a rigid unshakable linkage between our perceptions of the world and an embedded understanding, then our political alternatives, our capacity to understand the alternatives and to shape our future from among imaginative alternatives would be severely restricted. As Hobbes (1968) noted, our capacity to imagine reflects again a looseness between the external world and our internally generated representations thereof. If we could not imagine something other than the exact reality we inhabit, we would be entrapped by the inability to see something different, something better.

Split Brain Experiments

Consciousness provides us with a subjective arena in which we experience our purpose and executive control. If consciousness depends, in part, on the dynamic combination of prior knowledge and contemporary sensory experience what happens when one of those components is missing? In chapter 4, I made a brief mention of the important experiments of neuroscientist Michael Gazzaniga (1985, 1998). He used an important feature of the organization of the human brain. Some of the brain's functions are lateralized. Some functions occur on the left side of the brain and some on the right. For example, each eye sends its electrical signals down the optic nerve and into the brain. The optic nerves, one from each eye, arrive in the brain and each connects to the brain's many visual centers, but the optic nerves cross so that the left eye's optic nerve connects to the right hemisphere while the right optic nerve connects to the left hemisphere. The left eye's electrical signals are processed by visual centers in the right side of the cortex (the surface mantle of the brain), while the right eye's signals are processed on the left side visual cortex regions.[2]

In the normal state of affairs, we experience the integrated consequences of these diverse and distributed processes. But for people with bad cases of epilepsy, where grand mal seizures incapacitate the brain, doctors have developed one way to limit the spread of these electrical storms. The two hemispheres of the human brain, left and right are connected by a large bundle of nerves, called the corpus callosum. Cutting this bundle prevents the two hemispheres from "talking" to each other and therefore prevents grand mal seizures that begin on one side of the brain from spreading to the other side. This operation gives some relief from the worst seizures that, when spread to both hemispheres, incapacitates by overwhelming the brain.

As I briefly noted in the last chapter, Michael Gazzaniga was able to make creative use of these patients. Because language is a lateralized function (our speech centers are on the left side of the brain), what would patients who were shown something only to the left eye say about what they saw? As Gazzaniga (1998) told it, the left side is not only where our language centers are located but also where our ability to make conscious sense of things is located. It is where we explain to other and ourselves what we experience, and what we do. Split brain patients enabled Gazzaniga to study what happens when the brain knows something solely through the left eye. He placed patients before something but with a barrier set up so that the right eye could see one visual field but not what was being shown to the left eye. As a result, the right side of the brain knew what the left eye saw but because the corpus callosum had been cut the right side of the brain could not communicate that information to the left side of the brain, the side

---

2. There are distinct visual processing centers for movement, color, and so on; each sending signals to other centers and finally converging into two regions at the back of the brain, called V1, where the subjective construction of consciousness arises.

that has language. What did the patients tell Gazzaniga when asked what they could see when shown something in their left visual field? If our brains were designed so that we would be objective observers, reporting no more, no less than what we actually see, these patients would have reported back, "we can see nothing" because the information obtained from the left eye is blocked from passing to the language centers. But that is not what happened.

The patients' brains inferred that what their right eye was seeing was probably similar to what the left eye was seeing (it was not). That inference led their brains to confabulate. The patients comfortably and with confidence reported a plausible story generated by the left brain, the language interpreter even though the actual content of the left visual field conflicted with the story. The inarticulate right side of the brain, which could see what the left eye saw, could not intervene because it had no means of communicating with its left side partner. The more important point to make about these studies is that they demonstrate our active eagerness to explain, an eagerness so potent that it operates even when it relies solely on speculation and treats this specula-tion as certain "fact." We are designed to rely more on our confident explanations than on our sense-datum. And so, even when we have no sense-datum, we are eager to see and report what we see with great confidence.

The discipline of psychology is only beginning to take full note of these findings and has not refocused itself to address the roles of brain and mind. Most of psychol-ogy is concerned with the mind, the attitudes, the beliefs, the stream of consciousness taken largely in isolation from the study of other brain processes (though of course, recognizing the role of "unconscious cognitive processes"). Studying the brain is vital to grasping the relationships of mind, brain, and time.

As consciousness is a slow developing experience and is highly dependent on and influenced, shaped, by faster preconscious systems, including the various systems of memory, to understand consciousness requires taking into account what is happening in and outside of the brain before consciousness. The existing formulations acknowl-edge the obvious. There are aspects of mental life that arise in consciousness and we can describe them, variously, as perceptions, beliefs, attitudes, opinions, preferences, values, and so on. And, further, there are mental processes that take place outside of consciousness. If you read that last sentence carefully you should note that it uses a spa-tial metaphor. "Inside" is consciousness, "outside" is somewhere else. The reliance on spatial metaphors is deeply embedded in past and current thinking in psychology.

Here are some additional commonly used spatial metaphors in psychology to explain how humans operate. Sometimes we engage in "top-down" reasoning, and in other occasions, "bottom-up" reasoning. Or, sometimes we engage in "central process-ing" while in other instances we rely on "peripheral processing." Or, sometimes we engage in "implicit" reasoning while at other times we rely on "explicit" reasoning. It is important to say these distinctions are real. We have alternatives ways of responding to political and moral choices. There are different modes of reasoning, behaving, and decision making. But relying on spatial metaphors misconstrues the real difference.

The real difference between "in" and "out" is not one of space. And, in a related fash-ion to search for brain regions where certain functions seem to be located is distorted to the extent that we anticipate there is a one-to-one correspondence between location and function. Identifying brain regions with brain functions is a useful preliminary

BOX 5.3   **Spatial and temporal metaphors redux**

It is very common in the research literature to see work reporting on *subliminal* effects. Here can we see the reliance on spatial metaphor in full reveal. The projects explore how sensory information supposedly *below* the level of conscious awareness impact conscious perceptions and judgments. But when you examine how these projects are executed you will find that the most common operational procedure is to show subjects a fleeting stimulus *before* the target task. Conscious awareness does not have the capacity to present briefly presented sensory stimuli but the critical step is the temporal ordering, preliminal exposure occurs before not concurrent with exposure to the target task.

step. But it is a preliminary inquiry to the more searching inquiry of how and when different brain regions and functions interact to sustain the complex and dynamic processes that make us human.

II. TIME AND BRAIN FUNCTIONS

The important difference between consciousness and those brain functions that are nonconscious begins with the critical point that there are temporal differences, with some processes taking place *before* consciousness and some processes taking place *during* and *within* consciousness.

Therefore, the differences in processing reflect fast processes that enact without the intercessions of the slow processes that sustain consciousness they not only enact these processes but also interact dynamically to shape consciousness in a variety of ways. That fundamental reconceptualization means that much of what is conventional wisdom, which presumes that studying the content, structure, and dynamics of consciousness can be undertaken in isolation from the wider and prior array of neural processing, is wrong and incomplete. This can be quite exciting as a rather dormant discipline, relabeling ideology to attitudes, and relabeling attitudes to schemas, and so on, can generate a new and wide agenda that focuses on:

- The limitations of mind and the multiple brain controls of behavior: Rather than treating the mind as the core of executive control, recognizing that this control function is a sometime role initiated under specific circumstances. The mind has limitations. It is slow, it provides a biased and crude portrait of the world and of ourselves; it often represents distorted understanding as noted previously. These limitations are not debilitating however, because preconscious processes are most often managing the direction of our actions. Studying consciousness in isolation from these other operant systems overstates the consequences of "biases" in conscious representation and in conscious decisions that have been identified by scholars such as Kahneman and Tversky (Kahneman, Slovic, and Tversky 1982; Kahneman and Tversky 1984). Placing the study of consciousness within a larger context of nonconscious, or more precisely, preconscious, systems of representation and control is a far more challenging agenda but one that has great promise.
- The limited access of awareness to the operations of the brain: Conscious awareness is a wondrous but often illusional system of representation. It is now well

established that consciousness engages in potent time shifting and representational distortions. The word *representation* warrants some attention—to represent means that what we see, feel, hear, taste, and smell are re-presentations. Or to be more precise, interpretations of the "thing" being depicted. Smell is quality generated by a brain that touches molecules and comes to a conclusion about the character and value of that molecule that it has just "smelled," and so it represents that class of molecules by a system of "smells." The molecules do not have smells, our brain describes them by associating each molecule with a brain generated sensation we call smell. The generated system of representations—smells—constitute assessments of external stimuli. As well is taste. Color, one feature of the visual field, is also a representation generated by the brain from electrical signals. That is, colors are generated by the brain. Colors are used to convey, to re-present, information about the electrical impulses arriving down the optic nerve. More important, one of the important limitations of consciousness is that it has access primarily to just one memory system, most of labeled *declarative* or *semantic* memory (and, of course, to *working* or *short-term* memory). But much of what we do, when we walk or talk for example, is not guided by this memory system. What we learn to do is stored in another memory system, most often called *procedural* or *associative* memory. And, our consciousness has very limited access to the information stored in this second memory system. We know we can walk, we know we can talk (at least most of us). But we do not know how the body and brain makes these actions happen (what nerve pathways are used, what somatosensory and sensory mappings are dynamically linked so balance and action unfold smoothly and rapidly). Indeed if you take a moment and ask yourself how you get out of a chair, a simple task that the able bodied among you will have done thousands of times, you can construct a broad but largely incomplete account (derived from either observing yourself or others) of the action. But you cannot be specific as to which muscles, nerves, and tendons are engaged let alone in what sequences they are involved.

- The importance of understanding the brain and mind distinction and relations (mapping the dynamic of preconscious control systems and the role of emotion therein): The fuller agenda I promote here would attend to the interplay of preconscious and conscious systems, as well as putting the role of *procedural* memory on par with *semantic* memory in ongoing research on how people rely on past experience in guiding current behavior.

- Shifting allocation of cognitive resources (e.g., attention) and shifting decision strategies: And, of course, studying thinking has long been a, perhaps even, *the* focus of human inquiry. To think, to cogitate (the root word, from Latin, from which we derive the word *cognition*) has long been a central focus of human study. We all know that ancient precept: to know thyself. But, knowledge has both conscious and nonconscious aspects and by focusing only on the content available to us when we "think" or when "we remember" is focusing far too narrowly, and fails to capture how the brain acts when it stores, recalls, and interacts with the environment, both the body in which it rests as well as the larger environment, the outside world. The word *cognition* is often defined in cognitive neuroscience as "information processing" but this definition conflates and hence confuses by obscuring quite different neural processes. Thinking is a way of information processing. Although we can use the alternative term, cogitation, to stand in as a more elegant formal term, to expand the related term, "cognition" to cover the broader realm of all neural mechanisms for conveying and processing "information" misleads by presuming that we take for thinking inside of consciousness is also happening "outside" of consciousness. At some point in the future, as we gain a better understanding of how neural systems function, we may come to the conclusion that all neural systems that "process information" do so in a similar fashion. At this moment, that is not known and it would be best to conclude that neural mechanisms convey information within each and from one process to another without also presuming that each of these processing systems do so in a common fashion. For example, we know that the electrical signals from the optic nerves come to the thalamus and then to the amygdala, and to other regions of the brain, eventually to be represented as vision but also to generate the current feeling states characterized as feelings or mood states. Are each of these stages reliant on some common "cognitive" processes? Perhaps, but it is far too premature to use some overarching term, cognition, to depict some commonality. If we are all, in a fashion, studying "cognition" then we are either studying thinking, and only that, or we are studying an entire cosmos of disparate and often quite distinct systems that may have far less in common than what they share. Perhaps it is best to avoid the confusion by limiting the term, cognition, to its older and if more narrow but more coherent meaning, thinking.

- The task of integrating the multiple systems of memory: working, procedural, declarative. Although we have full access to what we remember in working and also to a great extent of what we have learned and stored in declarative memory, we do not have conscious access to procedural memory. Even though we rely on it far more intensely and continuously than we do declarative memory. As we type away on our keyboards, as we walk, talk, run, and execute all the sundry simple and complex acts of ordinary life we are drawing on procedural memory's ability to swiftly and deftly execute the habitual actions that make up our repertoire of learned action. Without conscious intervention we readily adapt to writing with chalk on a blackboard; a magic marker on a white board; or on a package awaiting a label to be completed with a pencil, or ballpoint, or fountain pen, on a very wide array of surfaces whether level or upright or slanted. Each requires different degrees of pressure and movement. None of us but those who are expert on the neuroscience of movement knows how our brains direct the subtle movements of finger, wrist, and arms so that letters smoothly flow from instrument onto whatever surface we have before us. And, while the role of habit and procedural memory is itself become an important area of work in psychology, largely due to the work of Jon Bargh and his colleagues (Bargh et al. 1992; Bargh and Chartrand 1999; Bargh and Pietromonaco 1982), the larger impact remains unfulfilled. The multiple systems of memory and their disparate but linked relationship to habituated and intentional actions remain before us a vital and central topic of research. Focused research that isolates each, habit and action, conscious intention and judgment, and so on, presumes that findings will be unaffected by a larger vision that seeks to understand their dynamic interplay.

These memory systems and their functional characteristics have differential relationships to awareness, judgment, and action (and to each other). Taking each system in isolation will produce findings that are distorted by their inattention to the dynamic ways these multiple systems expand the collective adaptive capacity of human action and (Baumeister, 2011).

The seductive and potent experience of consciousness lies behind the language choices psychologists have adopted. The subjective dominance of consciousness is revealed by the terms used to describe what humans do "inside" consciousness as "central" or "top," and all other neural processes—some that are far more vital, far more constantly engaged in our ability to function—are depicted as "peripheral," "below," or "outside." Language choices reflect deeply embedded presumptions. And, these presumptions, by encouraging the false expectation that studying the "inside" without taking consideration of other neural dynamics, will generate findings that are neither reliable nor valid.

The discipline of psychology has only lately obtained the tools and intellectual focus to actually have insight into how the brain functions. Indeed Sigmund Freud began his training as a neuroscientist but, judging the field too young to be productive, turned to inventing psychoanalysis as a better approach. The shift to studying all neural processes is greatly aided by the advances in neuroscience since Freud's time.

Understanding the full array of neural processes can of course shed light on the mind, and that remains a vital topic (Dehaene 2001). But the mind is only one product generated by an array of neural processes that sustain our freedom to feel, act, and on occasion, think. Political psychology needs a psychology that accounts for all neural processes, those that sustain consciousness to be sure, those that enable consciousness, those that work with but outside of consciousness, and those that work outside of consciousness sustaining other essential functions. For absent this fuller account, our research and our understanding will rest on partial, and hence, distorted theories; theories that will misunderstand how, when, and why we feel, think, and act. That psychology is now being constructed. Rather than awaiting its production by scholars in psychology, welcome as that is, neuroscientists and political psychologists have much to contribute in the development of that psychology and in exploring the ramifications thereof for our understanding of politics. This is a moment in which doing political psychology is needed more than ever before.

III. A PROVISIONAL BEGINNING: THE THEORY OF AFFECTIVE INTELLIGENCE

How then should the temporal relationship of preconscious neural processes and the later and more limited array of conscious processes be integrated? How can "dual process" routes be integrated to choice and action? One effort at integration has been attempted by Michael MacKuen, W. Russell Neuman, and me (MacKuen et al. 2010; Marcus 1988; Marcus 2002; Marcus and MacKuen 1993; Marcus, Neuman, and MacKuen 2000; Neuman et al. 2007). In brief here, and elaborated in the chapter that follows, the preconscious formulates an understanding of the world and uses that understanding as well as the immediate goals to initiate and adapt behavior to achieve those goals. Its deft integration of neural maps of the body enables it to have deft control over our skeletal and musculature movements. Affective processes offer swift assessment of the success and failure of the unfolding of action and provide necessary feedback to the dynamic interplay of action and external consequence.

The value of the historic information, the information encoded in procedural memory, is that it retains how we have done things that successfully achieve our recurring goals. But this value is diminished considerably when circumstances are novel. Indeed relying on familiar habits in novel circumstances may prove disastrous. To handle that circumstance, when we face situations we are ill prepared to master requires that we have a swift means for identifying novelty. And as it happens, we have a dedicated neural system to continuously evaluate the incoming sensory stream for the earliest possible assessment of the familiarity of the contemporaneous situation (Gray 1985).

The outputs of this system are multiple and complex. First, it generates its appraisal by modulating the affective state of anxiety. The anxiety appraisal is expressed as a dimension that ranges from calmness, signaling a match between expectations and the familiarity of external environment, to increasing levels of anxiety when comparing expectations against the data of the sensory stream generates a mismatch. As anxiety increases the system initiates a number of neural processes. The surveillance system inhibits the ongoing action, we stop our ongoing activity. The surveillance system also, simultaneously, shifts attention toward the identified discrepant source (e.g., if a sound, we turn toward, if a smell, we lift our heads, widen our nostrils and take in more air to get more information, etc.). In sum, the surveillance system is designed to detach us from our normal reliance on extant dispositions to resolve the many recurring tasks of life. It is designed to direct our attention to the unusual. And, the surveillance system directs the brain to gather more specific information about the contemporaneous situation as soon as possible after a mismatch circumstance has been swiftly identified. And, the surveillance system does all this well before we are consciously aware.

The most interesting aspect of the surveillance system is that it also performs a further task. When activated by a novel stimulus or circumstance, after inhibiting our normal reliance on the established array of previously mastered tasks, the surveillance system passes executive control from preconscious neural processes to the slower and later state of conscious awareness. Thus, consciousness is given special responsibility to formulate a new understanding, rather than rely on preconscious maps of representation. It is given responsibility to consider alternatives without being limited to or favoring the historical orientations that normally direct our choices, and to rely on explicit deliberative choices within conscious awareness. As conditions return to familiar normality, executive control shifts back to preconscious processes and conscious awareness returns to its normal state of observer status.

Some political ramifications of the theory of affective intelligence: There has long been an ongoing debate as to whether citizens have the array of skills necessary to the tasks of governing (Dahl 1992; Elkin and Soltan 1999; Kuklinski and Quirk 2001; Lane 1999; Rosenblum 1999; Smiley 1999). One implication of the theory of affective intelligence is that the terms of this debate should be changed. The value of skills is dependent on the task those skills are meant to accomplish.

More important, the tasks of familiarity are quite different from the tasks of dealing with novel circumstances. And, democracies, as do all regimes, have to be successful at both, the familiar recurring tasks but also the unusual, unexpected, novel situations that arise as traditions fade or are attacked; as policies fail to achieve anticipated results; or as the environment, social, economic, and natural, changes in unfamiliar ways. When H1N1 flu arrives, when a bloated economy rife with excess collapses, when a surge of immigrants arrive from a new source in numbers large enough to disrupt the familiar (in the United States, the arrival of Chinese laborers imported in the 1800s to work on building transnational railroad or in the 1960s when largely upper class Cubans fleeing the revolution arrived; in Europe, the eastern migration of laborers looking for work in Europe after the eastern expansion of the European Union, to give but a few examples) these events are going to cause some, or even many, to feel anxious. The people who make up a populace find strangers among them and this novelty is initially experienced as heightened anxiety.

When large numbers of people feel anxious, that in turn leads to a shift in the psychological foundations of citizens, and leaders, from that which is "normal," the comfortable reliance on established patterns of understanding and judgment. In familiar circumstances citizens rely on what psychologists call "heuristics" to guide their actions. When anxious, when in novel circumstances, citizens will set aside their defended reliance on extant convictions, the heuristics of ideological and partisan values, and consciously investigate, learn, consider their options, and make explicit deliberate choices reliant on unfettered consideration of the now and newly available choices. And because the surveillance system when it confronts novelty, when it signals with heightened anxiety, inhibits reliance on existing heuristics and on existing habits of thought and action (Brader, Valentino, and Suhay 2008).

[margin note: shift away from heuristics]

I have not used the familiar tropes of reason and emotion as these terms are too redolent of spatial and normative presumptions. This is also the case for their quasi-scientific terms, cognition and affect. That terminology is now very problematic. For preconscious processes are very much functioning in ways equivalent reason, though absent the involvement of semantic and conscious machinery that we normally attribute to the use of reason (i.e., "reasons" and "reasoning"). Hence, affect is "cognitive." Moreover, the familiar tropes of reason and emotion obscure the different types of knowledge that each has available. Moreover, the complexity of the dynamic and conjunctive interplay of preconscious and postawareness processes does not fit either the premodern taxonomy of reason and emotion or the enlightenment expansion to reason, interest, and emotion. The static features of these familiar taxonomies ignore the situational interaction of novelty and familiarity and the temporal flow of events that is characteristic of neural processes. Citizenship then should be redefined as a shifting array of skills, one set of which are mobilized in familiar settings and one set of which are arrayed in novel settings. This leads to a challenge to all of us to rethink the nature of the democratic citizen (Marcus 2002), an important task that has yet to fully be taken up by the discipline.

There are five major tasks awaiting the further testing and development of the theory of affective intelligence.

First, as with any theory its tenants will be challenged, especially by those wedded to established conceptions (Ladd and Lenz 2008). This is normal and to be expected.[3] Theoretical claims may prove to be sustained by empirical work, or if not, claims can be

3. And, of course, challenges will be accepted (Brader 2011; Marcus, MacKuen, and Neuman 2011).

adjusted in light of new(er) work, or if not, different theoretical claims will be advanced and gain support. This is all normal science.

Second, to date, the levels of anxiety examined have ranged closer to the calm to moderate end of the spectrum than to the upper reaches. This leaves unexamined whether the relationships between anxiety and its various downstream effects are linear or curvilinear. It is possible that at the upper reaches other outputs may be generated such as panic. We do not know.

Third, research to date has largely focused on the changes that arise as anxiety is invoked (Brader 2006; Brader et al. 2008). Less examined is whether these changes return to baseline after anxiety recedes.

Fourth, cognitive appraisal theories hold that our cognitive interpretation of circumstances gives rise to affective states. This view has largely not integrated the role of preconscious processes in the shaping of affective states. When and under what circumstances interpretations of affective states arise and further, may prove salient and consequential remains and as of this moment is not theorized. Cognitive appraisal theories presume cognitive appraisals are always determinative of affective experience. But, taking into account of the early upstream role preconscious processes in shifts in affective states, the role of cognitive appraisals must be limited, in the main, to modifying earlier affective states. And still further, the theory of affective intelligence's dual process view suggests further that the role of cognitive appraisal will be quite different in states of high(er) anxiety than in states of calmness (i.e., low anxiety). Integrating the downstream role of cognitive appraisal remains an as yet unrealized task.

Fifth, as noted earlier in this chapter, the earliest formulation of the theory of affective intelligence conceived of preconscious affective processes as defined by two appraisals, one dealing with the success (or failure) of ongoing familiar tasks and one dealing with the identification of novelty (Brader 2005; Marcus 1988; Marcus and MacKuen 1993). The theory has expanded more recently to consider a third occasional appraisal, aversion, that is held to appraise the success (or failure) of ongoing familiar tasks that deal with familiar but punishing circumstances (MacKuen et al. 2010; Marcus 2002). It is highly likely that further expansion and modifications await.

IV. THE POLITICS OF MIND AND BRAIN

The challenge for politics is to fit the special role that the mind plays in our conceptions of politics, generally, and democratic politics, more specifically. The role of individual autonomy lies at the center of the justification for democratic regimes. If the people are to be the basis of politics, again using President Abraham Lincoln's formulation (1953), "government of the people, for the people, and by the people," then we must have some credible basis for the people's competence in matters of self and collective rule. And, the role of reason rests at the center of all justifications for rule, whether democratic, aristocratic, or monarchial.[4] If rulers cannot reason well, if they cannot demonstrate their supposed special ability to reason, then they cannot substantiate their claims to enlightened statesmanship. For the general capacity to reason is the foreground on which the

---

4. Here I set aside the case of theocratic rule in which some other intelligence augurs the actions to take, communicating these directions through some intermediary, be that a priestly class or a monarch ruling on the claim of a divine entity.

more rarified ability to reason on behalf of all rest. So, absent the capacity to reason undermines their claim to legitimate authority.

Autonomy and reason then each have a special status for if rulers fail on the grounds of unreason, and if the public fails on the grounds of failure to sustain their autonomous judgment, then politics fails. If citizens act by the submissive direction of others then the normative and empirical basis for democracy fails. It is for these reasons that scholars of politics have focused on the apparent fragility of individual autonomy. The work of scholars such as Erich Fromm (1965), Leon Festinger (1956), Milton Rokeach (1960), Solomon Asch (1951), and Muzafer Sherif (1966; Sherif and Hovland 1961) are so central to the social science enterprise. In each of these and other scholars, the breach of autonomy for submission to group or leader is the problematic challenge that gravely threatens democratic rule. Fear of the demagogue and fear of the great charismatic leader has long raised the principal doubts that individual citizens will resist the impulse to defer to others, to alienate themselves from their own use of reason. Now we find that reason is not normally the dominant and autonomous faculty that controls judgment and action, even for those who among us who most indulge and who have the talent to reason, a course of events that philosopher Hannah Arendt (1963) labeled "the banality of evil.[5]

Perhaps the most representative and influential of this concern for the ease with which people are alienated from reliance on their own judgment is the array of studies conducted by Stanley Milgram (1974). Milgram arrays the standard fears of democratic governance that the people, rather than staying true to their convictions, would be easily transformed into compliant automatons willingly enacting the apparently obvious evil and destructive desires not by adoption of the aims of those giving the orders, but even more disturbing, by merely following instructions. From the point of view of our aspirations for democracy, and for a democracy built on the expressed capacity of citizens to make meaningful decisions, to rely on the public's capacity to be guided by moral principles, to be thoughtful and thereby self-directed, it is not just worrisome that study after study has suggested that such moral autonomy is lacking. It suggests that rather than being the scientific judge, citizens are not, in the main, willing or able to defend their autonomy of judgment from outside forces, whether they be charismatic leaders, demagogic speakers, or even just seemingly "normal" orders by people at middle-level positions of authority. We do not act with common purpose because we have first thoughtfully considered the reasons and evidence in the light of the moral ends and plausible promise of realizing the public purpose. Rather, we too often seem to act with common purpose *because* we have abandoned thoughtful and critical consideration.

Thus, the findings of neuroscience show that explicit use of reason is just one facet of neural activity and that the use of reason unfolds dependent on many neural processes. Further that reason, at best, on occasion has executive capacity, all of this suggests that earlier worries of democratic excess and turbulence may have more merit than democratic enthusiasts might wish to acknowledge.[6] All of this suggests that the

5. For others who also have pursued this trajectory of concern, read (Becker 1975; Browning 1992; Hare 1993; Hilberg 1992; Lifton 1986; Staub 1989; Waller 2002).
6. David Wegner (2002) went further arguing that the subjective sense of intention is itself an illusion generated by other neural processes outside of consciousness.

dream of democratic rule may in reality become a dystopia. And, for political psychology, this means the search for autonomy remains at or near the top of the discipline's scholarly agenda. Of course, from this central concern many other topics flow. What role does personality have in overwhelming autonomy? This might seem like a strange question to raise, but we often explain why our enduring personality might disengage us from thoughtful deliberation. That is the central insight that has generated a new fifty plus year search for the authoritarian personality (Adorno et al. 1950). And, there has been a larger sweep to that focus. The search for submission has generated interest in social dominance orientation (Pratto et al. 1994; Sidanius and Pratto 2004), and into ideological predilections that are held to be antagonistic to autonomous reason (Jost et al. 2003). At this juncture, I am not concerned with the empirical merit of the research, but rather its normative entanglement with the presumption that the prospect for democratic regimes is contingent on individual autonomous use of and reliance on explicit deliberation guided by autonomous judgment.

In the West, the conception of "free will" has its special place in democratic politics. The idea that humans have a disembodied, and thereby, free will has shaped our understanding of our place in the natural world and shaped the religious conceptions as well as humans seek to have some unique quality that "frees" us from the natural laws that govern all else in the natural order. The notion that freedom depends on some disembodied consciousness has had a perverse but profound impact on western thought. It has led freedom to be rather narrowly defined as freedom from constraint. And, in the West, one of those "constraints" is that we are embodied, that is, physical creatures. That conception, when joined with a conception of the body as obedient to the physical laws that governs us all, leads to the mind–body split. In this view, our "spirit" or "soul" was understood as disembodied and hence free from the constraint of those laws. The mind–body division has had a long run and remains deeply embedded to pernicious effect by obscuring a far more useful, and plausible, conception of freedom.

Being free, as Isaiah Berlin (1969) argued, is better thought as having two quite different components, neither disembodied. Being free, depends on the absence of some tyrannical, that is, exterior, barrier. This form of freedom Berlin (1969) depicted as "negative" liberty, the absence of coercion. A tyrannical ruler, a set of cultural norms that repress expression, or laws that seek to repress vice, are all examples of constraints that wisely or not, limit what we can do through one or another form of coercion. The second dimension of freedom, Berlin called positive freedom, depends on our talent and discipline to express our abilities and talents. This variant of freedom is the use our talents in and on the world. As he argued, the notion of disembodied reason as the fundamental conception of freedom ensures that the real phenomenon and agency of freedom is ignored for some cultural fantasy. Hence, the unconscious—again note the spatial metaphor as unconsciousness lies below—rather than being a source of the imaginative, becomes a shackle binding us to some nonconscious and hence external uncontrolled influence. Being embodied is essential to our status as free agents. Understanding that consciousness is partnered with other neural processes and that these processes are robust both as to the impact they have on shaping consciousness but also in generating feeling and action is a theoretical formulation that political psychology needs to enthusiastically embrace.

Further, a disembodied "I" also blinds us to the communal, social, character of human experience. Autonomy is a vital faculty but it is not the sole faculty. To treat conforming to obedience as pathological, and to treat unity in thought and action is a form of subservience, are each problematic for in democratic societies collective action is how democratic politics most often takes place. We often forget that deliberation is touted as a central value in democratic thought because it supposedly adds value to our capacity to question and fully consider the option *before we act*. But if we do not act, then deliberation adds little or no value. So, we need theories of action for without collective action there is little that any system of politics can accomplish. That action might be part of the normal array of conventional politics, voting, talking with friends, or organizing neighborhood parties in support of a cause or a candidate. Actions also may be novel and demanding, as it was many decades ago when rebelling colonialists in Massachusetts assembled to toss imported tea into Boston Harbor, or to assemble on Lexington and Concord commons to confront British troops, or not so long ago when Americans marched in Washington, DC to promote civil rights and to protest an increasingly unpopular war. Deliberation without action is time wasting and of little consequence for politics however valuable it might be as central to the process of creativity in the arts and sciences.

In the domain of democratic politics, deliberation can be a pathological activity. Deliberation is dysfunctional when it is not married to effective action. Deliberation is dysfunctional when it is invoked as a tactic designed to gain delay or to generate division. Deliberation, then, is not apt for every political circumstance. Most circumstances are familiar and already have an apt behavioral response readily and quickly at hand, habits that can be deployed to achieve their predictable and useful results. The core agenda for political psychology thus begins with the recognition that deliberation is the specific political response that consciousness makes available for those circumstances that are beyond the swift but limited skills of preconscious neural systems.

There are of course many substantive topics that have yet to fully integrate the recent attention to this human dual ability, swift but preconscious reliance on existing heuristics and slow but thoughtful consideration of expressly described choices in conscious consideration. Work has been done, but it is preliminary at best, and in many areas of politics much remains to be done.

Among some of the topics that may benefit from applying a dual model conception and research design are:

Elite psychobiography—the enduring interest in leadership, its training for beneficent, and for pathological purposes. By and large the view of leadership is monochromatic, although see Blight (1990) for an important exception. Also, *elite decision making*—such topics as "groupthink" and "vigilant appraisal," terms proposed by Irving Janis (1982) depicting what he took to be, respectively, ineffective and effective leadership decision-making dynamics; interstate negotiation especially during times of threat and war as well as enduring intrastate conflicts such as civil war and demands for autonomy by subnational regions.

In addition, *voter decision making*—including but not limited to such issues as the role of dispositional and situation factors. For the former, such issues as political socialization, the role of partisan and ideological affiliation, group identities (whether issue, religious, regional, or class oriented), the inclination of obedience to authority, which has given rise to the interest in authoritarianism, social dominance orientation, and the like. For the latter, issues such as the role of imminent threat, campaign ads, candidate and leadership attractiveness (i.e., charisma), issue appeals, the rise and fall of economic conditions whether normal or unexpected, and so on, although see (Marcus et al. 2000).

Similarly, *group dynamics* both within (the ability of groups to sustain but also to repress individual autonomy) and group to group (such issues as stereotypes and ethnic and racial violence or tolerance), applicable to both elite and citizen dynamics.

Related to group dynamics is the topic of hierarchy. Humans, social creatures that we are, find themselves organized most often in hierarchies, with some holding superordinate positions (i.e., giving orders to others) and many holding subordinate positions. This is the common pattern in families, with males and older individuals having positions of authority over females and younger individuals, in work with formal charts of organization as well as in many if not all social organizations (Pratto et al. 1994; Sidanius and Pratto 2004). In the political realm, hierarchy often finds experts and the powerful authority over others, but democracy promises a more equalitarian relationship. How does our dual capacity to shift from *automaticity* to *deliberation* and back, relate to the often sudden appearance of change in regimes, as in the recent Arab spring, the earlier instances in the Ukraine, or for that matter, the still earlier revolutionary changes? What happens to authority patterns when large numbers of people feel change, feel anxious? Neuroscience has begun to examine how the human brain manages hierarchy, how we know our place (Zink et al. 2008), but as yet we do not have the research that links this work to circumstances when authority and existing hierarchy shift or even collapse, how do people shift from one system of hierarchy to another? Much remains to be known.

The potent modern rise of nationalism, augmenting or replacing earlier ethnic, clan, dynastic, and religious bonds of attachment. The more recent development of supranational projects (e.g., the Soviet Union and the European Union): This topic looms as vital to better achieve success in the effort to counter "ethnic cleansing" and advancing nation building (although see Schatz and Staub 1997; Schatz, Staub, and Levine 1999; Staub 1997).

As these topics are all approached from the perspective of psychology they each touch on psychological processes: personality, perception and persuasion, alienation and engagement, and as already discussed, "cognition" and "affect," among many more. What makes these topics so common is that they are each, in various ways, concerned with how political regimes, leaders and followers and the system of institutions particular to each variant and cultural practices engrained in each locale form the context in which politics plays out.

In sum, the search for static relationships—what role do identified personality traits play in shaping leadership success, or what impact does external threat have on public opinion, to take but two examples—must be reformulated to take into account the dynamics that alter the roles these factors play and when and to what effect. The primary message for political psychologists going forward is that the multiple neural systems, those that support consciousness in its passive and in its active modes, as well as those that sustain neural processes outside of consciousness, evolved so as to interweave their abilities. Hence, interactive models, models that can properly specify the dynamic shifts in role and process, that can properly outline how and when neural processes work with other neural processes, and that can properly outline which processes and which circumstances these linkages are strengthened and inhibited (for activation is only half of the neural story, inhibition being the other equal partner) is the future of the discipline.

Consider that humans have evolved as a species with abilities that have enabled humans to flourish even as conditions change, as the human species flowed out of Africa, as it changed from a largely nomadic and hunter gathering way of life, through the development of agriculture and ever larger cities, from ruling by clans and tribes, to nation states, and even multistate organizations. So, presumably we have a repertoire of abilities that enabled this adaptability.

Why do we have the particular array of adaptations we have? Why do we have two eyes and not three, perhaps locating a third in the back of the head so that we could see what might be sneaking up behind? Why do we have automatic habits and reflexes? Because evolution has made them available and their availability enables us to function swiftly and effectively. Neural mechanisms, many that act outside of conscious control and outside of awareness, give us a fuller array of adaptive means, that would result if we had to rely solely on consciousness. For example, the dilation and contraction of the pupils in our eyes, to let in more or less light, is a nonconscious assessment, a choice, that is efficient and "automatic" and requires no conscious attention or consideration. We have many systems that work quite well and do so by working outside of consciousness. Conscious representation does not have the precision to identify viruses and bacteria that can cause illness and death. Happily evolution provided us with quite a few mechanisms that protect, none of which depend on cognition or conscious awareness. This seems as an obvious point, and unrelated to political psychology. But I raise it because it reinforces the central point of this chapter, that focusing only on what is conscious is sufficient to define the boundaries of political psychology. It is not.

We have both an immune and an autoimmune system; human skin evolved to repel infection; the sneeze reflect also designed to repel infection from airborne agents; the disgust reflex to rapidly disgorge something foul we have ingested; and, the blood brain barrier designed to protect the brain against infection and disease. Our health can, of course, be enhanced by explicit decisions we make, to live a healthier life by useful exercise and diet, but our health primarily depends on nonconscious mechanisms. All of this is quite a good thing as during most our recent history humans misunderstood the conditions of illness, relying for millennia on a theory of "humors" that had little to do in protecting health. It was not until quite recently in the life of our species, after many millennia, that the disease theory was created, identifying bacterial and virus infections as well as defects in our DNA instructions as the principal causes of illness. Had we as a species been solely or even primarily reliant on what we conscious understood to maintain our health, and had we not had the benefit of these nonconscious protective systems, we would have long ago become extinct.

In a similar way, conscious awareness has given us extended capabilities, but these augment other defenses that protect us. It is true that these extensions are critical to democracy in particular the Center for Deliberative Democracy (http://cdd.stanford.edu/) provides a window into the literature that documents the various contributions of deliberation. But deliberation is not always possible—and even when it is—it is not well suited (for reasons given earlier) to handle the swift recurring tasks that make the familiar tranquil and efficient. Our preconscious neural mechanisms are also a mix of abilities and limitations. In one study, social psychologist Keith Payne (Cameron and Payne 2011; Payne 2001) showed that white Americans are more likely to mistakenly construe a tool as a weapon when held by a black male than when held by a white male. With the swift and deftness that comes with "automaticity" also comes often unstated presumptions that embed a large array of traditions, many of which will inure us to the harm caused thereby (Cameron and Payne 2011). We are freer because we are embodied with biological mechanisms that enable freedom, freedom not only to rely on the past and the skills that have mastered the familiar but also the freedom to abandon them for new possibilities. One of the consequences of that embodiment is that we have physical and mental faculties that enable us to function in the world and on it. Conscious awareness is but one of the mental faculties we rely on.

These dynamics at the neural level have their parallels at the societal level. Modern representative regimes are often married to liberal economics. And, in such states, the notion of freedom is casually taken to be the negative variant, the absence of constraint. The freest markets, and hence the freest of societies, are those that offer the greatest array of choices without restriction or state imposition. But, just as neural basis for conscious choice rests on the full array of neural mechanism, so to the fuller array of choices for individuals in society rests on established societal practices and institutions on which political choice rests. Just as we rely on our immune systems to protect out health, we rely on state's regulating restaurants by health codes and regular and uncorrupted health inspections so that we can focus on the menu for choices of taste and not whether we confront the dangers of ill-stored or ill-prepared food. Building codes, insurance mandates, sewage systems, well-designed roads, and many more are examples of the positive evolution of mechanisms that parallel those of our physical inventory. Extending the fantasy of disembodied will to society by promoting an ideology of "maximal" freedom has its appeal but it distorts the agenda of political psychology by discouraging interest in the mechanisms that sustains the social and the political.

States generate markets to afford choices in consumption and production as well as in the creation of culture. But states also seek to prevent markets most often by making those they wish to discourage by making them illegal. Labor laws often prevent markets in child labor, or preclude certain types of labor contracts, such as indentured servitude (or slavery). And, states act to limit the actions of markets. Thus, pharmaceutical industries are required to demonstrate the safety and efficacy of most medicines before they can introduce them to the health market. Regulations mandate how to go about testing drugs before designating some of them as safe and ready for sale to anyone who might wish to buy them (e.g., aspirin). Other drugs require a doctor's approval (and often approval by others, typically those who pay the freight), while yet other drugs are strictly illegal under any circumstances. Limiting choices goes hand in hand with the ability of markets to extend choice. Unhindered markets would of course extend choices. But societies' value eliminating some choices so that we can feel free to act without constraint. Hence, if drug testing regimes are effective, then we can take drugs, both prescription and over the counter variants, without excessive concern for their potency and ill effect (history tells us that the key word in that sentence is *if*). Because we can take that array of considerations for granted, we do not have to invest attention and strategic ability over the concern that drugs might kill us, much as health department inspections of restaurants free us from doing our own inspections or observing who gets ill at which restaurants to avoid eating at places that may make us ill or even kill us. We would be better guided by adopting the presumption that such offloading of responsibility increases our freedom to the extent that such alternative mechanisms are effective, and history tells us, they are generally but not universally so.

The extraordinary array of topics that fall within the scope of political psychology range, temporally, those that unfold in nanoseconds to those that play out over millennia, from those that take place with a single individual to those that engage billions of people. Political psychology must extend its interest in freedom by understanding that "constraints" sometimes also enable, that extending choice can overwhelm, and that we have evolved to benefit from resolving the many challenges of life by embedding solutions embedded in our DNA, in various memory systems, in our cultural practices, in our society norms and political institutions. But we must begin with a full and accurate comprehension of politics. Politics is enacted in many ways. Deliberation is but one form of politics and that form is not universally relevant or even apt. Individual autonomy is a core value of liberal societies and an essential underpinning of democratic agency and legitimacy. But individual autonomy is not the sole or universal state of citizenship let alone social experience. Collective action and action based on solidarity are also essential features of democratic agency and legitimacy. Neither is universally applicable. Again, as with many other features of political psychology, how and when people are drawn to collective action, with both beneficent and pernicious consequences must be matched with the same seriousness and consideration as is the search for better explanations for when and how people seek and protect their individual autonomy, and again for consequences sometimes beneficial and sometimes detrimental. The continuing legacy of the enlightenment that reason is the singular route to individual autonomy and to freedom is a legacy to be valued. To rely solely on that legacy excludes understanding how positive freedom is no less vital (Bargh et al. 1992; Burke 1973; Haidt 2001) for a political psychology that begins with a sound understanding of how politics, democratic politics in particular, unfolds.

V. CONCLUSIONS

Darwin (1966) began with understanding that life confronts a changing world, a world that also presented competitors and dangers. As such, every species relies on means to survive and procreate that not only fit the particular time and space, the environmental niche they inhabit, but to evolve so that as the world changes, they can adapt. For if they do not, they face extinction when the array of abilities is inadequate in confronting new competitor species or new environmental circumstances, climatic change being but one such.

Every species has the dual challenge of preserving what has worked and introducing novel mechanisms that can either augment or replace extant means. As is well-known, Darwin found the dynamic that drove evolution to be in random mutations. Some, most, of these would be unsuccessful and pass into oblivion, but few would provide an advantage and through reproduction become a continuing part of that specie's arsenal.

Psychologist Donald T. Campbell (1960; 1986) argued that knowledge advances much as Darwin applied to the evolution of physical qualities. The success or failures of ideas depends on what they contribute to the robust experience of human life. We may generate the ideas, but reality decides whether they are any good. This suggests that we will gain most advances by encouraging more to participate. It also suggests that you will more likely come up with good ideas if you come up with more ideas. And, most important, that you do not let your natural anticipation of failure or embarrassment lead to self-censorship (any more than your natural inclination to self-aggrandizement might lead to you to overweening confidence that what you have just thought must be so). Relax, generate as many ideas, then do the scholarship to let reality tell you, and us, what works and what does not.

Not surprising in light of the events of the early twenty-first century—war, illness, economic disorder, each examples of grave violence on the rise—the concept of threat has become a vital topic infusing a wide array of domains: tolerance and intolerance, terrorism, ethnic cleansing, civil war, immigration, poverty, HIV/AIDS, H1N1 flu, global climate change, and more. These are, of course, apt and vital topics for political psychology. Applying Darwin's approach can enrich the notion of threat. All species must defend their environmental niche or abandon them in the hope that by moving they can find a better or safer locale, but to do so they must have the ability to correctly identify that which threatens.

The threats we face can find some commonality as examples of the special problem of contamination. Contaminants are those objects that can threaten our continued existence. Given the range of sensory information that can be represented in consciousness, we tend to think of "threat" as those external challenges that we see, hear, smell, taste, or feel, that can punish and even kill. But the fuller consideration of the dilemma of threat is that which can punish and kill can come from many sources. Threats present themselves at every level from the most "micro" to the most "macro." Consider that extinction can come from within the range from viruses and bacteria, at one smallest end of the scale, to climate changes that can take place over centuries and great expanses of territory, at the other end (Diamond 1997, 2005).

We have evolved multiple neural systems for identifying and addressing such threats, of which conscious awareness and deliberation constitutes just one array of faculties. These multiple systems, including the immune and autoimmune systems; the disgust system; sneezing; fear reactions to darkness, snakes, and loud noises among many others, have evolved and are deployed in various ways and in different circumstances. Some of these we can consciously experience and control, as when we opt to negotiate or go to war when confronting invasion or social disorder, or when we invest in medical technologies, but we also depend, heavily, on these many systems, systems that has evolved to work outside of consciousness, to keep us safe. This expanded view of threat identification and response exemplifies the need to have a far wider consideration of what it means to be human and what is required to sustain human society than the conventional focus on beliefs, values, perceptions, and other elements of thought, and a wider notion of action rather than a notion restricted to actions seemingly under conscious control.

EXERCISES

The theory of affective intelligence identifies three dimensions of affective appraisal, *anxiety* (how much novelty is evident), enthusiasm (how well is the goal-seeking task at hand performing), and aversion (how much are we being challenged by a familiar foe or threat). How would you augment this theory to take into account such social and moral emotions as empathy or disgust?

Design a research project to explore the following social patterns—xenophobia, benevolence, and other possible group experienced emotions. When and why do groups share a common affective response? When may they not?

Read the following article and then develop a theory of how anxiety may alter the neural processes described within. Source: Caroline F. Zink, Yunxia Tong, Qiang Chen, Danielle S. Bassett, Jason L. Stein, and Andreas Meyer-Lindenberg (2008). "Know Your Place: Neural Processing of Social Hierarchy in Humans." *Neuron* 58:273–83.

REFERENCES

Aboud, Frances. 1988. *Children and Prejudice*. Oxford: Basil Blackwell.

Adorno, Theodor, Else Frenkel-Brunswick, Daniel Levinson, and R. Nevitt Sanford. 1950. *The Authoritarian Personality*. New York: Harper and Row.

Arendt, Hannah. 1963. *Eichmann in Jerusalem: A Report on the Banality of Evil*. New York: Viking.

Asch, Solomon E. 1951. "Effects of Group Pressure upon the Modification and Distortion of Judgment." In *Groups, Leadership and Men: Research in Human Relations*, edited by Harold Guetzkow, 177–90. Pittsburgh, PA: Carnegie Press.

Bargh, John A., Shelly Chaiken, Rajen Govender, and Felicia Pratto. 1992. "The Generality of the Automatic Attitude Activation Effect." *Journal of Personality and Social Psychology* 62:893–912.

Bargh, John A., and Tanya L. Chartrand. 1999. "The Unbearable Automaticity of Being." *American Psychologist* 54:462–79.

Bargh, John A., and Paula Pietromonaco. 1982. "Automatic Information Processing and Social Perception: The Influence of Trait Information Presented Outside of Conscious Awareness on Impression Formation." *Journal of Personality and Social Psychology* 43:437–49.

Baumeister, Roy F., E. J. Masicampo, and Kathleen D. Vohs. 2011. "Do Conscious Thoughts Cause Behavior?" *Annual Review of Psychology* 62:331–61.

Bazerman, M. H. 1984. "The Relevance of Kahneman and Tversky's Concept of Framing to Organizational Behavior." *Journal of Management* 10:333–43.

Becker, Ernest. 1975. *Escape From Evil*. New York: Free Press.

Berinsky, Adam J., and Donald R. Kinder. 2006. "Making Sense of Issues Through Media Frames: Understanding the Kosovo Crisis." *The Journal of Politics* 68:640–56.

Berlin, Isaiah. 1969. "Two Concepts of Liberty." In *Four Essays on Liberty*. London: Oxford University Press.

Blight, James G. 1990. *The Shattered Crystal Ball: Fear and Learning in the Cuban Missile Crisis*. Savage, MD: Rowman & Littlefield.

Bodenhausen, Galen V. 1988. "Stereotypic Biases in Social Decision Making and Memory: Testing Process Models of Stereotype Use." *Journal of Personality and Social Psychology* 55:726–37.

Bodenhausen, Galen V., and Meryl Lichtenstein. 1987. "Social Stereotypes and Information-Processing Strategies: The Impact of Task Complexity." *Journal of Personality and Social Psychology* 52:871–80.

Brader, Ted. 2005. "Striking a Responsive Chord: How Political Ads Motivate and Persuade Voters By Appealing to Emotions." *American Journal of Political Science* 49:388–405.

———. 2006. *Campaigning for Hearts and Minds: How Emotional Appeals in Political Ads Work*. Chicago: University of Chicago Press.

———. 2011. "The Political Relevance of Emotions: "Reassessing" Revisited." *Political Psychology* 32:337–46.

Brader, Ted, Nicholas A. Valentino, and Elizabeth Suhay. 2008. "What Triggers Public Opposition to Immigration? Anxiety, Group Cues, and Immigration Threat." *American Journal of Political Science* 52:959–78.

Browning, Christopher R. 1992. *Ordinary Men: Reserve Police Battalion 101 and the Final Solution in Poland*. New York: HarperCollins.

Burke, Edmund. 1973. *Reflections on the Revolution in France*. Garden City, NY: Anchor Books.

Cameron, D. Daryl, and Keith B. Payne. 2011. "Escaping Affect: How Motivated Emotion Regulation Creates Insensitivity to Mass Suffering." *Journal of Personality and Social Psychology* 100:1–15.

Campbell, Donald T. 1960. "Blind Variation and Selective Retention in Creative Thought as in Other Knowledge Processes". Psychological Review 67:380–400.

———. 1986. "Science's Social System of Validity-Enhancing Collective Belief Change and the Problems of the Social Sciences." In *Metatheory in Social Science: Pluralism and Subjectivities*, edited by Donald W. Fiske and Richard A. Shweder, 108–35. Chicago: University of Chicago Press.

Dahl, Robert. 1992. "The Problem of Civic Competence." *Journal of Democracy* 3:45–59.

Darwin, Charles. 1966. *The Origin of Species*. Cambridge, MA: Harvard University Press.

Dehaene, Stanislas. 2001. *The Cognitive Neuroscience of Consciousness*. Cambridge, MA: MIT Press.

De Martino, Benedetto, Dharshan Kumaran, Ben Seymour, and Raymond J. Dolan. 2006. "Frames, Biases, and Rational Decision-Making in the Human Brain." *Science* 313:684–87.

Devine, Patricia G. 1989. "Stereotypes and Prejudice: Their Automatic and Controlled Components." *Journal of Personality and Social Psychology* 56:5–18.

Diamond, Jared. 1997. *Guns, Germs, and Steel: The Fates of Human Societies*. New York: Norton.

———. 2005. *Collapse: How Societies Choose to Fail Or Succeed*. New York: Viking.

Druckman, James N. 2004. "Political Preference Formation: Competition, Deliberation, and the (Ir)Relevance of Framing Effects." *American Political Science Review* 98:671–86.

Druckman, Jamie. 2001. "Evaluating Framing Effects." *Journal of Economic Psychology* 22:91–101.

Elkin, Stephen L., and Karl Edward Soltan, eds. 1999. *Citizen Competence and Democratic Institutions*. University Park: Pennsylvania State University Press.

Festinger, Leon. 1956. *When Prophecy Fails*. Minneapolis: University of Minnesota Press.

———. 1957. *A Theory of Cognitive Dissonance*. Stanford, CA: Stanford University Press.

Fromm, Erich. 1965. *Escape From Freedom*. New York: Avon.

Gazzaniga, Michael. 1985. *The Social Brain: Discovering the Networks of the Mind*. New York: Basic Books.

———. 1998. *The Mind's Past*. Berkeley: University of California Press.

Gould, Roger V. 2003. *Collision of Wills: How Ambiguity About Social Rank Breeds Conflict*. Chicago: University of Chicago Press.

Gray, Jeffrey A. 1985. "The Neuropsychology of Anxiety." In *Stress and Anxiety*, edited by C. D. Spielberger, 201–27. Washington, DC: Hemisphere.

Haidt, Jonathan. 2001. "The Emotional Dog and Its Rational Tail: A Social Intuitionist Approach to Moral Judgment." *Psychological Review* 108:814–34.

Hare, R. D. 1993. *Without Conscience: The Disturbing World of the Psychopaths Among Us*. New York: Simon & Schuster/Pocket.

Hilberg, Raul. 1992. *Perpetrators Victims Bystanders*. New York: Harper Collins.

Hobbes, Thomas. 1968. *Leviathan*. London: Penguin Books.

Janis, Irving L. 1982. *Groupthink*. Boston: Houghton Mifflin.

Jost, John T., Jack Glaser, Arie W. Kruglanski, and Frank J. Sulloway. 2003. "Political Conservatism as Motivated Social Cognition." *Psychological Bulletin* 129:339–75.

Kahneman, Daniel, Paul Slovic, and Amos Tversky. 1982. *Judgment under Uncertainty: Heuristics and Biases*. Cambridge: Cambridge University Press.

Kahneman, Daniel, and Amos Tversky. 1984. "Choices, Values, and Frames." *American Psychologist* 39:341–50.

Kühberger, Anton. 1998. "The Influence of Framing on Risky Decisions." *Organizational Behavior and Human Decision Processes* 75:23–55.

Kuklinski, James H., and Paul J. Quirk. 2001. "Conceptual Foundations of Citizen Competence." *Political Behavior* 23:285–311.

Ladd, Jonathan M., and Gabriel S. Lenz. 2008. "Reassessing the Role of Anxiety in Vote Choice." *Political Psychology* 29:275–96.

Lane, Robert E. 1999. "The Joyless Polity: Contributions of Democratic Process to Ill-Being." In *Citizen Competence and Democratic Institutions*, edited by Stanley L. Elkin and Karol Edward Soltan, 329–70. University Park: Pennsylvania University Press.

Lifton, Robert Jay. 1986. *The Nazi Doctors: Medical Killing and the Psychology of Genocide*. New York: Basic Books.

Lincoln, Abraham. 1953. *The Collected Works of Abraham Lincoln*. New Brunswick, NJ: Rutgers University Press.

Linville, Patricia W., and Edward E. Jones. 1980. "Polarized Appraisals of Out-Group Members." *Journal of Personality and Social Psychology* 38:689–703.

MacKuen, Michael, Jennifer Wolak, Luke Keele, and George E. Marcus. 2010. "Civic Engagements: Resolute Partisanship or Reflective Deliberation." *American Journal of Political Science* 54:440–58.

Macrae, C. Neil, Alan B. Milne, and Galen V. Bodenhausen. 1994. "Stereotypes as Energy-Saving Devices: A Peek inside the Cognitive Toolbox." *Journal of Personality and Social Psychology* 66:37–47.

Marcus, George E. 1988. "The Structure of Emotional Response: 1984 Presidential Candidates." *American Political Science Review* 82:735–61.

———. 2002. *The Sentimental Citizen: Emotion in Democratic Politics*. University Park: Pennsylvania State University Press.

Marcus, George E., and Michael B. MacKuen. 1993. "Anxiety, Enthusiasm and the Vote: The Emotional Underpinnings of Learning and Involvement during Presidential Campaigns." *American Political Science Review* 87:688–701.

Marcus, George E., Michael B. MacKuen, and W. Russell Neuman. 2011. "Parsimony and Complexity: Developing and Testing Theories of Affective Intelligence." *Political Psychology* 32:323–36

Marcus, George E., W. Russell Neuman, and Michael B. MacKuen. 2000. *Affective Intelligence and Political Judgment*. Chicago: University of Chicago Press.

Marcus, George E., John L. Sullivan, Elizabeth Theiss-Morse, and Sandra Wood. 1995. *With Malice Toward Some: How People Make Civil Liberties Judgments*. New York: Cambridge University Press.

Milgram, Stanley. 1974. *Obedience to Authority*. New York: Harper and Row.

Neale, M. A., and M. H. Bazerman. 1985. "The Effect of Framing of Conflict and Negotiator Overconfidence on Bargaining Behavior and Outcome." *Academy of Management Journal* 28:34–49.

Nelson, Thomas E., Rosalee A. Clawson, and Zoe M. Oxley. 1997. "Media Framing of a Civil Liberties Conflict and Its Effect on Tolerance." *American Political Science Review* 91:567–83.

Neuman, W. Russell, George E. Marcus, Ann Crigler, and Michael MacKuen. 2007. "Theorizing Affect's Effects." In *The Affect Effect: Dynamics of Emotion in Political Thinking and Behavior*, edited by W. Russell Neuman, George E. Marcus, Ann Crigler, and Michael MacKuen, 1–20. Chicago: University of Chicago Press.

Payne, Keith B. 2001. "Prejudice and Perception: The Role of Automatic and Controlled Processes in Misperceiving a Weapon." *Journal of Personality and Social Psychology* 81:181–92.

Pettigrew, Thomas F., and Linda R. Tropp. 2006. "A Meta-Analytic Test of Intergroup Contact Theory." *Journal of Personality and Social Psychology* 90:751–83.

Pratto, Felicia, Jim Sidanius, Lisa M. Stallworth, and Bertram F. Malle. 1994. "Social Dominance Orientation: A Personality Variable Predicting Social and Political Attitudes." *Journal of Personality and Social Psychology* 67:741–63.

Rahn, Wendy M. 1993. "The Role of Partisan Stereotypes in Information Processing About Political Candidates." *American Journal of Political Science* 37:472–96.

Rokeach, Milton. 1960. *The Open and Closed Mind*. New York: Basic Books.

———. 1964. *The Three Christs of Ypsilanti: A Psychological Study*. New York: Knopf.

Rosenblum, Nancy L. 1999. "Navigating Pluralism: The Democracy of Everyday Life (and Where It Is Learned)." In *Citizen Competence and Democratic Institutions*, edited by Stanley L. Elkin and Karol Edward Soltan, 67–88. University Park: Pennsylvania University Press.

Ryan, Michael. 2004. "Framing the War against Terrorism: Us Newspaper Editorials and Military Action in Afghanistan." *International Communications Gazette* 66:363–82.

Schatz, Robert T., and Ervin Staub. 1997. "Manifestations of Blind and Constructive Patriotism: Personality Correlates and Individual-Group Relations." In *Patriotism in the Lives of Individuals and Nations*, edited by Dani Bar-Tal and Ervin Staub, 229–45. Chicago: Nelson Hall.

Schatz, Robert T., Ervin Staub, and Howard Levine. 1999. "On the Varieties of National Attachment: Blind Versus Constructive Patriotism." *Political Psychology* 20:151–75.

Sherif, Muzafer. 1958. "Group Influences upon the Formation of Norms and Attitudes." In *Readings in Social Psychology*, edited by Eleanor Maccoby, T. M. Newcomb and E. L. Hartley, 219–32. New York: Holt.

———. 1966. *Group Conflict and Competition*. London: Routledge & Kegan Paul.

Sherif, Muzafer, and Carl Hovland. 1961. *Social Judgment*. New Haven, CT: Yale University Press.

Sidanius, Jim, and Felicia Pratto. 2004. "Social Dominance Theory: A New Synthesis." In *Political Psychology: Key Readings*, edited by John T. Jost and Jim Sidanius, 315–32. New York: Psychology Press.

Smiley, Marion. 1999. "Democratic Citizenship: A Question of Competence?" In *Citizen Competence and Democratic Institutions*, edited by Stanley L. Elkin and Karol Edward Soltan, 371–83. University Park: Pennsylvania University Press.

Staub, Ervin. 1989. *The Roots of Evil: The Origins of Genocide and Other Group Violence*. New York: Cambridge University Press.

———. 1997. "Blind Versus Constructive Patriotism: Moving From Embeddedness in the Group to Critical Loyalty and Action." In *Patriotism in the Lives of Individuals and Nations*, edited by Dani Bar-Tal and Ervin Staub, 213–29. Chicago: Nelson Hall.

Stroop, J. Ridley. 1935. "Studies in Interference in Serial Verbal Reactions". Journal of Experimental Psychology 18:643–62.

Struch, N., and S. H. Schwartz. 1989. "Intergroup Aggression: Its Predictors and Distinctness From in-Group Bias." *Journal of Personality and Social Psychology* 56:364–73.

Valentino, Nicholas A., Vincent L. Hutchings, and Ismail K. White. 2002. "Cues That Matter: How Political Ads Prime Racial Attitudes During Campaigns." *American Political Science Review* 96:75–90.

Vinacke, Edgar W. 1957. "Stereotypes as Social Concepts." *Journal of Social Psychology* 46:229–43.

Waller, James. 2002. *Becoming Evil: How Ordinary People Commit Genocide and Mass Killing.* Oxford: Oxford University Press.

Wegner, Daniel M. 2002. *The Illusion of Conscious Will.* Cambridge, MA: MIT Press.

Zink, Caroline F., Yunxia Tong, Qiang Chen, Danielle S. Bassett, Jason L. Stein, and Andreas Meyer-Lindenberg. 2008. "Know Your Place: Neural Processing of Social Hierarchy in Humans." *Neuron* 58:273–83.

CHAPTER 6

Political Action

The Uses and Limits of the Mind

My focus in chapters 4 and 5 was to demonstrate that the brain is engaged in active "information processing" that occurs before conscious awareness. For most of human existence, insofar as the action of the brain was understood as separate from the mind, the distinction between brain and mind was understood as spatial.[1] The mind was the center, what happened elsewhere was "outside" or "below" the subconscious, still in the brain or further outside in the heart or "gut." This understanding has both an empirical aspect and a normative aspect. The empirical aspect is the belief that the mind is where "we" reside. We inhabit consciousness where we look about, observing all that we see, hear, touch, taste, and smell, both about the world we inhabit and how we regard ourselves. However, this understanding was also a normative view as well. It is in the mind where we *should* locate the decision to take action.

These understandings have implications for politics in all its forms. In politics, as in many other areas of life, people make decisions. Some are leaders; some are bureaucrats or have advisory, staff roles. Many are active citizens, engaged in various ways beyond just voting, by attending to political affairs, participating in political discussions with friends, families, and coworkers. All who live in a political community, local, state, or national have their lives impacted by the decisions made, either with or without their involvement. How decisions are made, both individually and collectively, have always been at the heart of arguments about who should rule. Our empirical beliefs about the how decisions are made, in particular who makes good decisions and who does not, influences our judgment as to who should rule.

Democratic politics has long depended on the validity of a particular normative view and its empirical underpinnings. Representative politics rests on the claims that:

---

1. A common approach has been to divide the brain into three portions, with the "oldest" in the core; the more advanced "layers" built on "top" of, the *triune* brain (MacLean, 1990). Hence, "thinking" was assigned to the top layer, the "cortex" with more the more "basic," and crude functions buried "deep" within.

1. The public can observe the claims others are making, and ascribe plausible motives for the claims they are advancing (transparency; although of course people can and do lie).
2. Pubic conflict enables people to test the claims and various proposals, both pro and con, of the leadership abilities of representatives, executive, legislative, and judicial.
3. The public can assess the claimed linkages that join stated reasons, the justifying reasoning, and actions meant to realize the aims advanced.
4. The leaders and followers know their own mind (by which we normally mean that people can be fairly, if not always, trusted to act to make sound judgments as to what is in their self-interest, and as to what they wish for the collective, public interest).

As citizens we *should* listen to proposals that politicians advance to preserve or to "reform" this or that aspect of our lives, we *should* read news accounts of speeches that we were not present to hear, we *should* observe and participate in debates as to which course of action seems most promising. Doing so allows us to examine the merits, weigh the pros and cons, make comparisons, judge prospective claims against the historical record (has cutting taxes raised economic well-being, has increasing regulation made food safer, and so on).

How could representative politics be justified if we cannot accurately observe and publicly and privately, weigh, discuss, and judge the leadership abilities of our leaders? What if the leaders themselves are equally misguided? How can the accomplishments or failures of government actions be judged if we do not transparently assess and collectively debate the likelihood of success or the causes of failure of this or that policy? How can policy analysts serve us by presenting their work in testimony or written reports on why a policy under public scrutiny succeeds or fails? How could democratic politics take place in any way other than before us within the observable world of consciousness?

The issue of misperception has long been studied by political psychologists (Jervis 1976; Stein 1988). But rather than understanding misperception as an occasional if serious aberration, scholarship in neuroscience presents us with a number of critical insights that suggest conscious perception is often misperception. The first being that brain processing "outside" of conscious awareness is not *out* but *before, during,* and *after* consciousness. That insight has largely escaped the attention of many political psychologists.

The second insight that also has largely gone unattended is that the preconscious has its own memory system, one that is largely inaccessible from and by conscious introspection. Most of the important actions of the active brain are temporally prior to conscious awareness. Most of the knowledge we have about ourselves, actions mastered, and the ways those actions are initiated and adapted to achieve a wide variety of goals across most circumstances is similarly inaccessible to conscious introspection. This too has largely escaped that attention of many, but not all, political psychologists. Of course, most political psychologists know there is something more than consciousness: Freud's work among others before and since generated attention to the *unconscious*. But as long as the spatial metaphor continues to dominate the dynamics of the dual model approach to decision and action in human affairs generally, and politics, more specifically, will be missed. My purpose in this chapter is to reinforce the claim that this fundamental shift from spatial to temporal relationships requires a new political psychology.

This chapter has four sections. In the first, I briefly summarize what is now known about the capabilities, respectively, of the preconscious brain and of the conscious mind. This is daunting because we are at the beginning of this effort at this juncture. As I mentioned above, political psychologists have long know that neural processes "outside" the mind have to be taken into account. Various efforts have arisen to formulate theoretical approaches that address that insight. In the second section, I examine how political psychology has wrestled with the *unconscious*. As we shall see some of the inadequacies of those solutions can be resolved by integrating the insights of neuroscience. I describe in the third section, how the relationships between preconscious brain activity and conscious awareness display a very dynamic interplay. I outline what is now known about those dynamics. Finally, in the last section, I outline the shape of the next political psychology.

I. THE LIMITS OF THE MIND, THE BLIND SPOT OF POLITICAL PSYCHOLOGY

It has been very common, as noted in earlier chapters, to segregate "affect" and "cognition." The phrase, "cognitive and affective factors in …" is common in titles of published articles in political psychology (you will find many examples if you search the literatures of psychology, political science, and political psychology). Here is one example:

In exploring patriotism, a team of political psychologists have found what they believe are two versions of patriotism. Moreover they believe that each is independent of the other. One is "blind" patriotism by which they mean an emotional variant. The other is "constructive" patriotism by which they mean a cognitive version (Schatz, Staub, and Levine 1999; Staub 1997). In this example, and in most other such cases, the two facets are treated as concurrent—the possibility of a temporal relationship is ignored. And, of course, the normative implications are, here, explicit. The emotional patriotism is blind, unseeing, and hence a source of irrational action, whereas the cognitive patriotism is reason based, and therefore, capable of supporting rational uses.

The tools that enabled neuroscientists to discover and explore the preconscious are very recent. But, the subjective experience of consciousness has been with us for a very long time. Therefore, it is not surprising that most of the historical work on self and collective governance holds that knowing means knowing as that which is available to us in conscious awareness. Hence, whether one takes knowledge as semantic and conceptual, much as Plato did, or as prudential and experiential as did American philosopher and educator John Dewey (Dewey 1910, 1925; Dewey and Bentley, 1949) knowledge is widely understood as put into these semantic terms: Newton describing gravity, Einstein the relationship between energy and mass, Louis Pasteur on germs and illness, economists on the relationship between supply and demand, and so on. Knowledge is understood as what is available to consciousness and represented largely in words.

Of course, we can also speak of knowledge as depicted in visible images and auditory sounds not just as words. In politics, we see, know, and understand the flags, bunting, and banners often displayed at political rallies. We also see and remember images of political leaders or of political events and these have meaning as well. The role of symbols has been an important topic in research about how people are reached and moved (Edelman 1964; Elder and Cobb 1983). We hear debates and speeches. We hear, observe, note, and respond. Thus a straightforward account of how this would seem to be: We perceive, make a decision, and then, we act. But a political psychology that ignores the role of the preconscious will be misleading. In the language of science, excluding factors that have causal import will yield theories that are misspecified and underspecified. Such theories that misidentify which variables are the real causes of what we do.

As I discussed in prior chapters, consciousness is an artful and often deceitful phenomenon. Our experience in consciousness is in many ways a charade. We are conscious of a world that seems instantaneous even though it is a delayed representation. Our brains construct the quality we call color, to distinguish different wave lengths of electrical signals received and processed by the brain.[2] Our conscious state is constructed to give us the impression that consciousness is all that we have of the world we inhabit and of ourselves. But preconscious representations abound and they have quite different qualities and capabilities than conscious perception.

An Overview of Preconscious Appraisal and Action
My focus in chapters 4 and 5 was to explore the various limitations of conscious awareness. Happily, the brain has not one system of perception, conscious awareness, but also has a rich and potent system of apprehension, of perception that takes place in the temporal window that resides between the arrival of sensory and somatosensory signals into the brain and conscious awareness. Within that five-hundred millisecond window, the brain is actively decoding and encoding those signals. Our brains identifies the gender of person within eighty milliseconds from the moment when the sensory signals from the eyes arrive via the optic nerves, even though we do not consciously see the person until five-hundred milliseconds have passed. Our brains can identify an object approaching us within forty to fifty milliseconds of the visual signals arriving into the brain even though we, residing within the realm of consciousness, cannot consciously see the object until a further 450 milliseconds have passed.

Although we experience consciousness as comprehensive and instantaneous, this moment always being this moment when all that is can be observed, that is not how the brain understands. I have mentioned in chapters 4 and 5 that vision begins soon after the electrical signals arrive in the brain's visual processing regions. These signals are first deciphered to identify objects. Consider that the optic nerves convey millions of nerve signals, from each of the rod and cone cells that lie on the surface of each eye's retina. Each of these signals must be analyzed so that groups of signals can be identified as cohering thereby identifying a single object from the broader array of signals. One of the ways this is done is by finding evidence of straight lines. Only thereafter can the movement of objects be accomplished because discerning movement requires identification of objects and background. Thereafter, in a separate visual processing region in the brain, color is assigned as an attribute of objects by making use of the wavelength

2. Although the brain can do this only if there is enough light to stimulate both the rod and cone cells in the eyes. As light falls, at dusk, color disappears and we see the world in shades of gray.

of the electrical signals. All of these occur at different times as the processing regions begin, complete their work, and pass their work to other regions for further processing, finally culminating, at a region identified as V1, where conscious vision is generated.

These neural abilities enable us to take action at the earliest possible moment. We duck or move out the way well before conscious awareness has any inclination that something of concern is salient. These capabilities obviously give us considerable adaptive benefit over what would occur if we had to await the full five-hundred milliseconds for conscious awareness to unfold. Assessing and acting at the earliest possible moment offers far faster and enables more fluid movements including not only interactions with objects but more importantly with people.[3]

Attending to the characteristics of the preconscious systems gives us insight to how we preconsciously perceive and often act before we are aware. One insight is that the brain has multiple systems concurrently processing, activating, and inhibiting various downstream processes. In sum, although we experience consciousness as a unified representation in which sight, sounds, taste, smell, and touch are all integrated into a seamless dynamic portrait, the brain processes these different sensory streams separately, acting swiftly on the basis of these early representations.

The use of technologies such as fMRI enables neuroscientists to map the specific brain processes giving us some insight into where these brain process are located.

Using this and other techniques, such as positron emission tomography (PET) scans, some that enable researchers to monitor specific neurons, some that make use of patients who have had lesions in specific locations of their brain—lesions are damaged areas, damaged by diseases, such as a viral infection or a stroke—neuroscientists have been attempting to map which brain regions are dedicated to such tasks as procedural memory; semantic memory; speech recognition; speech generation;

BOX 6.1 fMRI

One of the major techniques available to neuroscientists, and increasingly to scholars from other disciplines, is functional magnetic resonance imaging (fMRI). This technique allows scholars to record which areas of the brain are active while the subject is engaged in a given task. It accomplishes this by measuring the uptake of oxygen that follows when nerves are active, needing nurturing.

I set aside the technical issues (the technique does have a temporal delay as the uptake of oxygen is not instantaneous with neural activity; the spatial accuracy is approximate rather than precise; is limited to small numbers of subjects as each subject must be tested in a laboratory setting). A more serious issue is that brain activity tells us only half of the story of how neural networks function. Yes, activation of a region implies that that region is involved in the processing of neural information for a given task, but the nature of neural systems is that work by activation and by inhibition.

The fMRI does not give any insight as to which regions are inhibited for a system to function and which regions are inactive because they have no role in the task at all. This is an important limitation as inhibition is an important way that the brain functions, activation is but part of the story of neural processes.

---

3. Erving Goffman (1959, 1963, 1971, 1981, 1982, 1986a, 1986b) was an inspired observer of these preconscious actions.

representation of motor actions; representations of the various sensory streams; deliberation; and such responses as disgust, the startle reflex, among many others. One line of investigation has explored the division of tasks in the brain, into left and right side asymmetries. Neuroscientists Michael Gazzinga (1977; 1985; 1992) and Richard Davidson (1995), among others, focused on the work of the left language brain and the work of the heuristic and holistic right side. Neuroscientist Jill Bolte Taylor (2009) offers a vivid first-person account of what it is like to experience a stroke in her left brain.

The preconscious has some global capacities and these differ from those available in conscious awareness. Representation is one of those primary differences. Table 6.1 compares the two systems of representation.

It is crucial to identify the various differentiated processes that make up preconscious appraisal. More important, these preconscious processes shape conscious awareness to serve the goal-action plan then in place. For example, we have two blinds spots in the visual field, called *scotomas*. These blind spots exist because at the spot in the back of our eyeballs, where the optic nerves leave the eyeball, there are no cone and rod cells, the cells that react to the light entering the eye. The brain "paints" in those spots

Table 6.1. Preconscious and conscious representation

Information availability	Preconscious perception: Less than 500 milliseconds	Conscious awareness: No earlier than 500 milliseconds
Sensory reports: Information sent by the sensory apparatus of eyes, tongue, ears, olfactory bulb, and skin to the brain	• Full access to all sensory information streams • Appraisals available much sooner than consciousness • Very fast cycling of information; largely devoted to normative actions, for example, how to recognize a friend, or a stranger, or foe, how to hug a friend, how to punch a foe, how to turn a page, converse with family, friends, strangers, run, walk, stumble and recover, and so on • Fluid and multiple sequences concurrently active	• Very limited as controlled by preconscious appraisals (e.g., attention, in the case of the visual field, information intake is either defensive or broad open search depending on preconscious appraisals) • Very slow cycling (which is why at 24 frames per second we observe static images as smooth movement) • Representation is integrated into a holistic representation in which all modes (visual, auditory, etc.) are seamlessly linked
Somatosensory reports: information sent by muscles, skin, and joints that have nerve receptors ensuring that the brain gets information about various aspects of the body, including temperature, position, movement, and difficulty (expressed in pain)	• Detailed and precise access to and control of muscles and skeletal positioning • Dedicated to serving the normative integration of goals and coordinated learned actions hence bidirectional (to and from the body)	• General and remote—largely unconnected to procedural memory (the memory system where actions in all their learned permutations are retained)
Learned plans/goals/actions	• Detailed and precise control over integrated deft muscular skeletal movements with appropriate use of the autonomic, sympathetic, and parasympathetic systems—largely nonsemantic with historical experience as action stored in procedural memory	• General and abstracted—semantic in character with historical experience stored in declarative memory

so well that we have before us the full frontal image as if complete and real. The size of those blind spots is about palm size when you hold your arms extended out.

Here is yet another example of the preconscious shaping consciousness. The body produces a lot of noise (blood pumping through arteries and veins, the heart makes noise pumping, the digestion system makes noise as well) but the brain screens out much of the noise so that we can focus on sounds "out there" (couples, one of whom or both, might snore, often get into arguments, "stop snoring" "I am not snoring" largely because the person snoring is not conscious of the sound, their brain filters the noise out as irrelevant). But these limitations of conscious awareness pale in importance when it comes to how the brain handles action.[4]

We know we can, to take two mundane examples, reach out and turn a page so we can continue reading, or lift a glass of water to our mouths to take a drink. But our conscious brain does not have the ability to judge the precise distance between where the hand is nor how to calculate the velocity and trajectory of movements so that the hand is moved properly to the appropriate location. Nor how to access the proper muscles so they are tensed and relaxed in the proper sequence to generate the fluid movement the action requires. Nor how to shape the fingers to suit the task; nor how to vary the grip depending on the tactile feedback; nor how to prepare the mouth for either a lick of the fingers to better allow the page to be turned; nor how the lips should be pursued just so in preparation for managing the flow of liquid into the mouth.

These action sequences are highly normative and integrate not only with respect to sensory information but also with respect to somatosensory information. Further, with respect to the dynamic linkages between these movements and the learned patterns of action and goals stored in procedural memory. For it is in procedural memory where the entire repertoire of learned actions, each and every one, are retained as learned sequences integrating perception, sensory, and somatosensory, and the goals they are meant to obtain.

These sequences are highly normative in that they are goal seeking and hence require real-time feedback on the success or failure of execution so as to judge the step-by-step coordination of actions and reactions as well as the need to, on occasion, shift from one permutation of action to another. And, it is the role of affect to provide these ongoing representations assessments. These fast cycling processes of deft action, cascading sequences of movements, the unfolding of goal-seeking action, rely on matching of action and expectation so that adjustments, including abandonment if failure is imminent, can be made. Preconscious affective appraisals provide these swift assessments so that upstream and downstream adjustments can be made.

The examples, earlier, in the main deal with physical movements that seem apolitical but the same processes apply when we interact with people. People recognize friends and foes very early in the visual processing sequence. And, because the mechanisms of identification are stored in procedural memory, where the precise and varied ways that enable us to deal with friends and how to deal with foes lies beyond our conscious access, some of us will have learned to treat some people as foes even as we describe ourselves as open-minded and tolerant (Devine 1989). Hatred toward others

---

4. I will not go into the details of neurobiology in action. Here I want to focus on the general principles. Good places to start can be found in Changeux (1986); Jeannerod (2006); Milner and Goodale (1995).

is not just an emotional experience that identifies who is the enemy (object identification) and why they are the enemy (historical experience, direct or acquired through learning). Hatred toward some despised person or group is also a set of likely actions including facial displays; it is also a set of expectations of mutual support from people we have come to rely on and an array of other actions, beliefs, and verbal expressions that fit the various occasions that then fit into the familiar circumstances when hatred is a core element. Just as we know how to lift a cup of water, we know how to hate. Just as we know how to turn a page, we know how to love and be benevolent toward others.

We rely on these preconscious processes and we do so with very limited direct conscious knowledge that they are working, let alone how they do their work. And, when these systems fail either through accident, disease, or aging, we quickly become self-conscious when either of these systems goes awry, when the vestibular system becomes dysfunctional we experience a wave of vertigo—how many of you know what the vestibular system is, let alone what it does, and how it does it? If we had to rely on the slow and non-normative forms of representation available to us in conscious awareness we would find our movements slow, clumsy, stumbling, and largely incompetent.

How the brain accomplishes this is complex and requires many appraisal systems from each of the sensory modes all integrated with somatosensory inputs into the learned patterns and goal storing regions of the brain. Rizzolatti and Sinigaglia (2008) in a fine account, offer a nice balance of the neurobiological details in an accessible manner. Suffice it so say that in most actions, the conscious mind is a casual and tardy observer.

It has been the visible role of emotion that has commanded the attention of thinkers for many eons. What we observe in others, their postures, their facial displays, and gestures, and what we experience as "feelings" have defined the domain of emotion (Darwin 1998; James 1883, 1894). But, neuroscience research has established that these aspects of affect and emotion are a very small and biased aspect of emotion's role in human behavior. These forms of emotion are but the most persistent and robust of the ongoing affective appraisals that are selected for representation in consciousness (revisit table 4.1 in chapter 4; the brain "downsizes" thereby selecting what external and

---

BOX 6.2 Sophistication

When political scientists examined the American voter, using surveys that enabled them to interview thousands of adult citizens, they soon found that all voters were not alike. Some voters were highly attentive and engaged in politics, others far less so, indeed, some were not engaged at all. The principle explanation for differences between those who citizens who are most active and those least is that the "politically sophisticated" have more knowledge of the political system, current events, political issues, and the like (Delli Carpini & Keeter, 1996). Those who were actively engaged, know more, and thus were characterized as politically sophisticated (Luskin 1987, 1990).

However reflecting on the role of habits suggests another conception of sophistication, one that is rooted in the ability to master through habituation, a range of tasks, and not semantic in character. The singular focus on semantic knowledge as the single criterion for who is a better citizen will miss the other dimension of competence, the ability to achieve deft, fluid, and easy engagement with task characteristic of politics.

internal representations are appropriate for re-representation in conscious awareness). In sum, the full roles that affect plays in human affairs and in politics has largely been missed because its preconscious roles have been unavailable until the tools of neuroscience enabled scholars to reveal them.

II. POLITICAL PSYCHOLOGY WRESTLES WITH THE UNCONSCIOUS

Though not the first to do so, Sigmund Freud (1961, 1962) advanced the claim that something inchoate—understood as "repressed memories," "drives," and "passions"—existed outside of consciousness. Freud placed that "outside" *below* in our subconscious. His conception led to the further claim that these nonconscious impulses contained experiences from our earliest moments, memories not available, having been suppressed and "buried" below, in the subterranean reaches of the mind. Clinicians trained in Freudian psychodynamics offered relief, claiming they could help their patients discover this hidden aspect that would free them from the potent grip of these mysterious memories and forces because they were buried. This conception was used by the earliest political psychologists to argue that political choices were themselves driven by these hidden underpinnings (Lasswell 1930, 1948; Barber, 1985; George and George 1998).

The principal approach to the unconscious is the presumption that after we have experience some person, group, situation, or indeed anything sufficient to formulate an attitude the substantive elements in the attitude formation toward that stimuli fade as time passes. The basic and substance of our experience with the stimulus in question falls away, leaving behind just an evaluative component, an "affect tag" (Fiske 1981). Many of us come to think of ourselves as Democrats or Republicans, Social Democrats, or Tories, or as liberals or conservatives, but the basis of those dispositions will have been long lost, or so the long traditional view has it. Although we may not with any accuracy recall when, how, or why, we acquired these attitudes, we can, of course, generate contemporary justifications.[5]

There have been three closely related, indeed overlapping approaches to the nonconscious in psychology: stereotypes, heuristics, and implicit attitudes. Here, in the interest of parsimony I am going to focus on their common elements.

The concept of "heuristic" processing came into political science from social psychologists doing work on stereotypes (Bodenhausen 1993; Bodenhausen, Sheppard, and Kramer 1994; Bodenhausen and Wyer 1985; Chaiken, Liberman, and Eagly 1989; Chaiken and Maheswaran 1994). Psychologist John Bargh in turn generalized the formulation into the concept of "automaticity," which described the ability of people to rely on heuristics to guide actions without any active conscious engagement (Bargh et al. 1986; Bargh et al. 1992; Bargh and Chartrand 1999; Bargh and Pietromonaco 1982). Something in our brain, something not available to the conscious mind—the stored inclinations to favor or disfavor—provides efficient guides to choice and action. These have been called stereotypes, and when they are inclinations to disfavor, prejudice (as when we say this person is prejudiced against …) and heuristics.

Political psychologists came to describe people's reliance on their extant convictions to guide their political actions, "heuristic" processing (Kuklinski and Quirk

---

5. With but modest likelihood that the original grounds for the attitude formation will be compatible with the contemporary rationale we construct.

2000; Rahn 1993) to describe the quick and easy reliance on stereotypes and on self-identification with either party or ideological label to generate political judgments and actions. Political psychologists Rick Lau and David Redlawsk (1997, 2001) showed that reliance on heuristics often leads voters to the "correct" vote. Voters could do the extensive work of becoming fully informed to make responsible vote decision. And, if they did so they would live up to the many exhortations to be well-informed and thoroughly engaged in the democratic process. But, by relying on their "heuristics" voters have an alternative that is both more efficient and allows them to arrive at the same outcome as if they made the effort to be fully informed and fully engaged.[6] The claim that heuristics are generally efficient and rational, in result if not as a process of decision making, has received considerable support in psychology (Gigerenzer, Todd, and ABC Research Group 1999) and in political science (Popkin 1991).

The research on how stereotypes and heuristic are used by humans has largely focused on patterns of reliance on extant dispositions. Much of the work in this vein has been flawed. Although the research demonstrates that knowledge of stereotypes and prejudices are largely ubiquitous, reliance on them as guides to behavior is not omnipresent. As psychologist Patricia Devine (1989; Devine et al. 1991) showed with respect to racial prejudice, political scientist John Sullivan and colleagues showed with respect to political tolerance (Marcus et al. 1995; Sullivan, Piereson, and Marcus 1982; Sullivan et al. 1993), and others, including myself, my colleagues, and Ted Brader, showed with respect to voting (Brader 2006; Marcus, Neuman, and MacKuen 2000), heuristics are available to provide a swift response reliant on those convictions. But, this research also shows that reliance on heuristics is often abandoned. Thus, when and why heuristics matter; and when and why they do not has now become a most interesting question.

What stereotypes and heuristics have in common is that we can identify them to ourselves. Although we do not know or at least cannot recall how we acquired them, we can rely on them. All of this suggests that stereotypes and heuristics have a neural basis. But treating memory as a singular faculty in the brain, as classic psychology has, gives us little basis for saying how the brain and mind make use of heuristics and stereotypes. That becomes even clearer when we consider the notion of "implicit attitudes" (Bargh and Pietromonaco 1982; Greenwald, McGhee, and Schwartz 1998). Here the choice of words is informative. Why choose the word *implicit* to describe an attitude? Implicit attitudes are attitudes of a different sort. Unlike most attitudes, which are available to us and to scholars examining the beliefs of those they are studying, "implicit attitudes" are those that are not available to conscious recovery or introspection by the people who presumably hold them.

The Implicit Association Test was invented to measure implicit attitudes (Bargh and Pietromonaco 1982; Greenwald et al. 1998). Recall that the Stroop test demonstrated that we function swiftly when executing a familiar task, naming a color word presented in the same color as the named word (the word *red* presented in red). But, when the task is novel we perform more slowly (the word *red* presented in the color green or blue). The implicit association test (IAT) relies on that temporal difference; familiar tasks take less time than novel tasks. If we have a hidden attitude toward a stimulus,

---

6. To their credit, Lau and Redlawsk added the important qualification, "most of the time."

party, social group, policy, or so on, then we have a link between that stimuli and its evaluation. On the other hand a novel stimulus would require more and therefore, time consuming evaluation. The IAT explores whether we have such hidden, implicit, attitudes by matching two target concepts with an attribute. The two concepts are presented in a two-choice task (e.g., the words *black* and *white*) and an evaluative attribute (e.g., the words *pleasant* and *unpleasant*). The key variable of interest is how fast the subjects respond to the classification task (do these pairs match). Subjects are asked to respond as swiftly as they can to the task. For example, if subjects matched the words *pleasant* and *white* faster than the words *pleasant* and *black* they are presumed to have a positive "implicit attitude" that favors whites over blacks. This approach has been used to explore, among many other topics, ingroup–outgroup biases (Egloff and Schmukle 2002) and the approach–avoidance anger nexus (Wilkowski and Meier 2010).

However what are "implicit attitudes"? If one attends to the existence of procedural memory, a memory system that is not accessible to conscious introspection, we can move beyond the mystery. We know many things and how to do many things. This knowledge, although not semantic in character, nonetheless provides for quite and efficient management of recurring tasks. This knowledge is "automatic" (using the particular word that psychologist Jon Bargh applied) insofar as the involvement, indeed the awareness, of the mind is concern. But the use of this knowledge is not "automatic" as far as the brain's functioning is concerned. Rather, before conscious awareness arises, these stimuli are swiftly evaluated and cognitive and behavior responses are then generated by preconscious neural mechanisms (Ronquillo et al. 2007).

If, as I now recommend, we reformulate this work on "implicit attitudes" and the work on heuristics and stereotypes within a framework that provides for preconscious neural processes, where the work of "automatic" and "implicit" appraisal and response take place, we can get a more accurate understanding of how different memory and appraisal systems function. Moreover, we can obtain some insight into when preconscious and awareness neural processes hold sway and when and why each gives way. We turn to that elaboration in the next section.

The Preconscious and Politics

Many of the specific examples of actions under preconscious control in this chapter are of little importance in the realm of politics. But there are examples that do apply to politics. The work on "mirror" neurons is one such area of research. Mirror neurons are specific neurons in the brain that fire in correspondence when a person observes others performing a task that is within the subject's repertoire of learned actions (Rizzolatti and Sinigaglia 2008; Semin and Cacioppo 2007). Humans act on their own: but humans also act with and against others. We must have some neural capacities to model the actions of others so we can coordinate either cooperative or antagonistic actions. Mirror neurons provide some of the critical neural infrastructure that enables us to interact with others so that we have available habituated action sequences that enable us to achieve all that we need to master our environment, including working with or against others. Whether we are joining others to attend a political rally, or trying to "read" the intentions of the police as they gather to confront a demonstration, we need to have some capacity to know what others are doing and what they are intending to do. The work to date on mirror neurons seems to be central in that essential functionality. And, of course, we have no conscious experience of what our mirror neurons are doing at any given moment (though through them we gain "intuitions").

The work in neuroscience has extended our understanding of preconscious appraisals. Unlike representation in consciousness, preconscious appraisals are fundamentally normative and biased toward the space in which actions can take place. The nerves of the motor cortex integrate sensory data—what is there, out there—action modalities (what I can do to and with it) and goals (what's sought). Thus, stereotypes, which loom large in the history of social and political action, deserve new and expanded understanding.

The general concept of stereotype is applied to the mental image of a group or an individual. We observe someone and based on some feature, apparent ethnicity, gender, or age, rely on an available stereotype to infer who that person is and how we expect them to behave, friendly or antagonistic, subordinate or superordinate. A good deal of scholarship has been devoted to when and how stereotypes are used by people. It is a common aspiration that stereotypes, being automatic, fast, and thoughtless, could be suppressed or, even better, eliminated by an enlightened and reasoning public. But this review of the neuroscience of preconscious appraisal and its role in action suggests a different array of possibilities. We can, as we shall see, under certain conditions, set aside our preconceptions, our neural procedural maps of who we engage and what we expect when we do engage. But, we cannot act without the preconscious motor system's deft linkage of perception, internal means by which our actions are enacted, and goals as well as the preconscious system's ability to apply those same preconscious appraisals to the actions of others. Consciously seeing what actions others undertake is not a window into the somatosensory system and goals of others. It is the ability of our preconscious motor cortex ability to understand how that other person generates their actions, and to comprehend the intentions of those actions that is beyond what our conscious visual observations can provide.

A related point is also important, motor actions are not generalized, that is, here's how I lift [whatever], but rather here's how I lift a paper cup of a particular shape and size, as opposed to that glass or this plastic cup, each of which are different permutations, a range of permutations each having it's own motor sequences that then collectively make up the repertoire of learned actions, to my lips to drink, as opposed to passing it across the table to a friend.

I want to outline an important discovery in the neuroscience of action, the distinction that in preconscious appraisal systems is a motor action system that differentially encodes near—peripersonal—space from distant—extrapersonal—because action dynamically takes place only within the first. The survival value of mastering near space seems obvious. To take but one example, objects coming toward one, and entering peripersonal space, needs to be identified as quickly as possible and appropriate action initiated equally swiftly. Waiting a half second can be quite fateful. Is that person reaching toward me with a hand, is that hand open, the face smiling, or the hand grasping a knife and a face that glowers? Waiting for conscious awareness to represent these observations in vivid detail seems most imprudent, and so it is. The identification of objects, especially those moving toward us, but also of all objects, and then to be able to initiate strategic and tactical actions, these most often begin preconsciously.

This discovery of the differential treatment, in preconscious appraisals, of near and far, is also apparent in social behaviors. The favoring of the near, where our actions can make a space hospitable and secure, as against distance terrain in which the unknown lurks, is another way of noting the near universal bias toward ingroups, "us," our common membership, habits, traditions, and the like—and the negative bias against outgroups, "them," their habits, traditions, and the like (LeVine and Campbell 1972; Warnecke, Masters, and Kempter, 1992; Kinder and Kam, 2010). The preconscious appraisals systems are designed to favor the near space and its contents in which we act. It is not, therefore surprising, that our preconscious appraisal systems favor habits (for they integrate perception, goals, and the motor sequences that enact them) over slow and clumsy deliberative and self-conscious routes to action.

One of the earliest discoveries in the social sciences was the concept of "social distance" (Bogardus 1925). Though human society evolved from the family unit, in to larger social entities, clans, tribes, and empires, and from rural to more urban settings, thereby setting the stage for still larger forms of social organization, now national and supranational states, we still distinguish between and differentially respond to the near from that which lies afar (Stangor, Sullivan, and Ford 1991; Tesser and Collins 1988). And, the swift application of the prejudicial is a core feature of the preconscious appraisal systems (Devine 1989; Devine et al. 1991).

However, we can rely on more than just preconscious appraisal and action. The depiction of ourselves and the world we move in within consciousness awareness is designed to be what neuroscientist Jeffrey Gray called an "error correcting space" (2004). Conscious perception is less normative in its operation, its failure to have direct linkage at the level of neurons, between goals, perception, and action, is a strength. Consciousness can be more neutral in its appraisal of the external precisely because the preconscious has already coded the interplay of internal and external in the service of goal-seeking action. Note also this underscores Gray's point that consciousness is an error correcting space designed to resolve issues that are beyond the competency of the many systems that function before and outside the realm of consciousness.

Therefore, scientific discoveries such as those by Louis Pasteur that led to a fundamental change in medical treatment, discovering that germs cause illness, a discovery that in turn lead to the development of vaccines, augmented already existent human nonconscious systems designed to keep us safe from disease. A partial list of these nonconscious systems would point to: the immune system; the skin, which serves as a barrier against infectious disease as well as other pathogens; the disgust reflex, which expels foul tasting or smelling food hopefully before it can poison us; the genetically encoded fear of snakes; and nostril hairs and the sneeze reflex, which expel possibly dangerous airborne elements.

Ted Williams, relying on talent and discipline, could hit a one-hundred-miles-per-hour fastball or an eighty-miles-per-hour curve ball, with no reliance on the mathematics of quadratic equations, the use of which would also allow him to calculate where the ball and bat would best meet. Perhaps that is not a surprise given that the equations could not enable him to execute the actions that enabled him to be one of the best hitters in the game. Other examples abound. Italian painters in the renaissance (fifteenth and sixteenth century) discovered how to draw with perspective so that images they painted appeared with foreground and background. Our preconscious appraisals had long enabled us to move out and about in the world with an accurate sense of near and far. Preconscious appraisals decoding of electrical signals arriving from the optic nerves of the two eyes, along with the movement and angles of eyeballs in their sockets, and the vestibular system, also offered us the knowledge of where things are in the spaces depicted, foreground and background so we can correctly reach into the space and grasp, lift, hug, or attack as the circumstances warranted.

Having consciousness, an error correcting space, presumes a prior action directing ability, a neural capacity to move actions from the preconscious realm to the later domain of consciousness, another neural "space" within to consider and initiate actions. The slowness of consciousness, its inability to link detailed action with sensory information about the world and somatosensory information about ourselves, leaves it a poor domain in which to place universal responsibility for action. But consciousness provides a valuable addition to our repertoire because it affords a "second chance" to get it right, having either identified a mistake, to ponder it and come to a new decision, or if the early appraisals identify a task beyond the competence of the extant repertoire of learned actions, to shift executive control to conscious control. We have evolved so that our brains can relocate executive control from the preconscious to the awareness state we call consciousness. This shift takes place under certain circumstances. I turn to that dynamic next.

III. DUAL PROCESS MODELS—BRAIN AND MIND

One of the primary errors of continuing a cognitive focus is the false presumption that learning what takes place within the domain of consciousness can be accomplished without understanding this dual shift dynamic. It is not just that some actions are driven by "peripheral" or "automatic" processes and other "central" or "explicit" process drive other actions, it is that the brain shifts responsibilities from one to the other in a dynamic fashion.

In psychology the capacity to shift from brain to mind, from "peripheral" to "central processing" to use the terminology of one theoretical account (Petty and Cacioppo 1986), has been given the term "dual process" models (Chaiken and Trope 1999). Why might people shift from one to the other mode of action? There are some obvious classes of factors worth considering. First, people often subordinate executive control from themselves to some other person often within an institutional setting where subordination is expected. This pattern of deference has given rise to a major portion of the social psychology corpus of research (Asch 1951; Festinger 1956; Haney, Banks, and Zimbardo 1983; Milgram 1974; Pratto et al. 1994; Sherif 1958; Sidanius and Pratto 2004). In addition, as noted earlier, most learned behavior depends on the swiftness of execution available in preconscious reliance on extant learned habits. When do people shift from one modality to another, from preconscious to conscious control, or from conscious control back to preconscious control?

Deliberation is sometimes available because we need to rely on flexible wide-scanning consideration of new possibilities to replace or augment the old; sometimes new coalitions are needed rather than constant reaffirmation of old factional loyalties. This reliance on conscious awareness is enacted under certain, but not all, circumstances. Moreover, the preconscious appraisals systems of the brain recruit the conscious mode of executive control for just those circumstances when swift reliance on habituated patterns of behavior would be ill advised. The preconscious temporal space affords the comparison of external information flowing into the brain for ongoing and swift comparison against the stored expectations of what secure reliance on habits require. When these comparisons fit, when the most current information about the external world matches expectations, then safe reliance on extant habits, convictions, dispositions can proceed without disruption.

However, when that comparison identifies a mismatch then the preconscious brain generates at the earliest moments a rise on anxiety, signaling something awry, inhibiting the ongoing habituated action, stopping what John Bargh (Bargh and Chartrand, 1999) called "automaticity," shifting attention to the source of the novelty (or absent a clear direction, begins a scanning search to identify the cause), and finally, shifts executive control from preconscious to conscious modalities (Gray 1981, 1985, 1987a, 1987b; Marcus et al. 2000).

How and when people master political tasks, embedding them in habituated representations of sensory, somatosensory, and goals so they can be enacted prior to and independent of conscious engagement is a domain that has until lately been largely ignored in political psychology. That leaves an enormous array of topics that await research. How and when are these habituated actions acquired? And, once acquired, how and under what conditions are they modified, strengthened, weakened or abandoned, either for the circumstances at hand, or forever? Habits can appear to be consciously intentional, the many blogs and pundit shows on cable and network news amply demonstrate that political discussions often have a sealed, utterly self-contained, scripting that makes them no less habituated than physical movements. That these are evoked in conscious awareness makes them no less habituated. The dual process model invites application in political psychology so we can get a richer understanding of when deliberative processes augment or replace nonconscious reliance on habituated routines. Are the circumstances that prompt the shift universal or particular, applying to some but not all participants in some shared circumstance? It should come as no surprise that

---

BOX 6.3   Partial theories

Too many extant theories focus on too narrow a domain and therefore misconstrue what they depict. For example, the theory of motivated reasoning makes the usual observation that people often subordinate the validity of their beliefs to the defensive value of protecting their beliefs from external challenge. People, or so the theory holds, are motivated by reason to defend rather than test their beliefs. This then is taken as a biased form of reason, and evidence that humans are ill suited to reason with the care and objectivity, that, by comparison, scientists approach an issue.

Dual process models suggest that defending beliefs is but one of two possible responses when beliefs are challenged. For those circumstances when beliefs are defended scholars who treat motivated reasoning as evidence of bias and irrationality miss the strategic benefit of protecting beliefs that have proven valuable in the past. In familiar conditions defending what has proven successful is adroit and adaptive. But further, scholars of motivated reasoning tend to ignore the strategic abilities we each possess to abandon motivated reasoning when prompted by preconscious appraisals that identify conditions as unfamiliar. In such circumstances defense of extant convictions is both maladroit and maladaptive.

some are more "sticky" in their reliance on proven habits while others are more inclined to rely on deliberative approaches (Cacioppo and Petty, 1982). What reverses the shift, returning us from deliberative modes of thought and action to the comfort and mastery afforded by habituated control? These and other questions await answers.

IV. CONCLUSIONS

The agenda for political psychology has largely favored the development of models of thinking, cognitive models. The focus on consciousness is not surprising given the importance of reasons, excuses, explicitly stated goals and plans, programs, and policies for democratic policies. Without all of these available for transparent consideration, we cannot have debates about the explicit goals, thoughtful and collective discussion about their respective merits, or clarity of the linkages we surmise exist between causes and effects. And, in the absence thereof, how can the people govern themselves? Further, as consciousness is the arena within which we reside, it is the arena where we observe ourselves and others play out our various actions, what we say, what we hear and do, and what we observe others do.

Therefore a lot of scholarly attention has been devoted to the taxonomic categories we can use for dealing with the conscious field. Among those considered conceptions are the following.

- Attitudes are affective orientations linking beliefs and actions, normally measured by presenting statements for people to agree or disagree (e.g., on whether health care should be provided as a right by government or whether negotiation is the best way to resolve conflicts). How these are organized leads to the attempt to identify attitude "structures" and such questions as whether one set of attitudes "constrains" another so that people display some degree of consistency or not (Abramson 1993; Converse 1970; Eagley and Chaiken 1992; Fishbein 1967; LaPiere 1934; McGuire 1972, 1985; Zaller 1987).
- Beliefs are statements of observations that people may accept as true or false (e.g., the level of taxes are too high or too low; or that the level of support for war will generate more/less casualties). Here the concern is often over the plausibility of beliefs and the role of beliefs in informing political action (e.g., whether President Barack Obama is an American or Kenyan citizen; or whether the United Nations is planning a world government). The role of beliefs in political organizations, forming like-minded groups so that some basis for organization can be constructed is a core concern. Unlike attitudes that are normative dispositions for or against some politics, group, individual, or action, beliefs are more oriented to content (Bem 1970; Converse 1964; Fishbein and Ajzen 1975; Goertzel 1994; Huddy and Terklidsen 1993; Kinder 2006; Taber and Lodge 2006). And, as such they are also a core aspect of stereotypes (Bodenhausen and Lichtenstein 1987; Devine 1989; Huddy and Terklidsen 1993; Macrae, Milne, and Bodenhausen 1994; Vinacke 1957).
- Values are generalized valuations assigned to broad domains (e.g., whether one places more importance on security or on preserving civil rights). Here, as with attitudes, these are expressly normatively, but unlike attitudes, values are formulated in universal terms, held to be applicable to all situations unless constrained

by other, conflicting values (Alvarez and Brehm 2002; Chong 2000; Kahneman and Tversky 1984; Pollock, Lilie, and Vittes 1993; Schwartz and Bilsky 1987).

- Schemas are thought to be the semantic linkages that represent how the brain stores and connects various attributes (e.g., a cognitive item or element, the name Ronald Reagan links to the following elements: "actor" links to the concept of president as well as to the concept Republican and to other attributes such as "male," "white," "conservative," and so on; of course these attributes may also include images and sounds, of a particular speech or of his voice). It would be expected that some people will have "richer" schemas than others and depending on their predilections may have more depth and breadth to their "schemas" in some topic domains than in others (Conover and Feldman 1984; Lau 1986; Lodge and Hamill 1986; Miller, Wattenburg, and Malanchuk 1986).
- Ideologies were earlier understood as a hierarchical set of principles that explained and directed how various attributes of society function (e.g., Edmund Burke's view of community or Karl Marx's theory of capital and class conflict), but, more recently a set of semantic labels that brand a grab bag of policy beliefs and dispositions (e.g., in the American context, conservative: belief in free unregulated market and government support for traditional conventions of social norms).

These contending conceptions are too rarely considered collectively. Whichever taxonomic categories one applies, this focus on the semantic content led cognitive scientist George Lakoff (2002; Lakoff and Johnson 1999) to argue that however one characterized the organization of these cognitive elements, they accounted for and explained the political judgments and actions that people undertake, support, and oppose. These conceptions give us ways of defining, categorizing the content of conscious.

Groups of scholars have given considerable attention to one or more of these, some devoted to values (Shalom Schwartz and Milton Rokeach in psychology, Stanley Feldman, William Jacoby in political science for example), and these have led to fruitful debates: Are values organized in a strict hierarchy or loosely as in a distributed network with various links and nodes; are they stable over time or dynamically changing their relative status; are they contextually limited or applied in a universal fashion, and so forth. All to the good, but however we settle on the taxonomic structure and labels for the semantic stream we are focusing on only a small portion of the mental stream. Moreover, the mental stream that is represented in consciousness is both biased and limited. It is biased in that the stream has no direct access to somatosensory information. That is the conscious mental stream does not have access to the cortical mapping of the body and or the full sensory stream that depicts the external so that, for example, we can deftly move our fingers to pick up a coin on a desk, but the conscious mental stream is largely observant of the act and without insight as to the precise manner of its execution. It is in consciousness that we must make inferences from the limited and tardy observations available and to thereby surmise our intentions from the observed actions that might capture our attention that might call for some explanation, to ourselves and or to others.

However, these have very limited and often highly biased access to the preconscious. Having identified the preconscious and its many functions gives us insight into the extended capabilities that people have: People can and do rely on habituated procedures to handle tasks large and small that they face, but they also can abandon preconscious reliance when they confront "error" and shift to conscious deliberative processes. This has considerable implications for politics, especially for democratic politics.

As a result, our conceptions of democratic citizenship, of late, have been dominated by the failure of citizens to live up to the enlightened conception of citizens as thinking, informed, and deliberating individuals. First, this disappointment follows two claims: First, the premise that citizens *should* be thinking, informed, and deliberating when they engage in politics (Benhabib 1996; Fishkin 1991; Hanson 1993; Page 1996). Second, the data of over fifty years of research largely shows that they do not approach politics in this fashion (Converse 1964, 2006; Kinder 2006; Thompson 1970; Zaller 1992; Mueller 1999). As in any open discipline, some scholars have argued that this singular focus on thinking is misleading. Rather, they have argued that politics is about getting things done, achieving stated aims (Sanders 1997; Shapiro 1999). Each side of these contending views presumes their normative conception is universally applicable. But if people do both, steadfast reliance on extant habits and abandonment of habits for conscious reflection on and thoughtful consideration, then politics becomes both normatively and empirically far more complex.

Leaders who have firm goals will seek to find the slogans and phrases that will bind committed partisans to steadfast pursuit of victory so that those goals can be implemented. Leaders who seek power will often have to assemble new coalitions, or gain supporters so their ambitions can be secured by electoral victory, and to that end they need to turn disinterested citizens and engage them to link their fortunes with this new effort. But, in some circumstances leaders also will seek to disengage already committed citizens to back off from their prior convictions and consider new alliances, alliances that their convictions would seem to preclude. In a similar fashion, citizens will have an initial determination to make: Is this circumstance a familiar environment such that safe reliance on convictions of partisan, ideological, or ethnic (or still other) identifications, habits of understanding and action, can be relied on, or are these situations fraught with uncertain outcomes such that the thoughtless automatic reliance on habits seems ill advised and instead a turn to deliberation is called for? Preliminary work suggests that this dynamic is ubiquitous (Brader 2006; MacKuen et al. 2007; Marcus et al. 2000).

Politics becomes far more complex when leaders and citizens can each rely on either the modality of partisan solidarity (habitual reliance) or the modality of deliberation (thoughtful executive control). Each has its own presumptions about the proper interplay with others and with a sometimes compliant and sometimes harsh environment. Moreover, each modality has presumptions about the expected response of others and the environment. This further suggests that political psychology should study not only the internal dynamic that shifts citizens and leaders from one modality to the other and back but also the interplay between actors, leaders to leaders, citizens to citizens, citizens to leaders, and leaders to citizens when each relies on a different modality. What happens when one leader expects a situation to be one of mutual deliberation, setting forth the prospect of mutual accommodation, but finds instead the other side presenting their side in as steadfast and unthinking assertion?[7] What happens when an incumbent leader seeks to strengthen the resolve of his/her followers after various reverses? Does their resolve reaffirm or do they turn to deliberate over other, and to them, new alliances, new leaders, and new policies? When do deliberating citizens and deliberating leaders stop, embedding what they have learned into standing dispositions, habits so they can display the fluid efficiency that the costly route of deliberation precludes? A political psychology that is informed by neuroscience is far more likely to conduct the research that creates new answers and new understandings of how politics actually plays out in the world.

SUGGESTED FOUNDATIONAL READINGS IN NEURAL PROCESSES AND ACTIONS

Changeux, Jean-Pierre. 1986. *Neuronal Man*. Oxford: Oxford University Press.

Doidge, Norman. 2007. *The Brain That Changes Itself: Stories of Personal Triumph from the Frontiers of Brain Science*. New York: Penguin.

Dolan, R. J., G. R. Fink, E. Rolls, M. Booth, A. Holmes, R. S. J. Frackowiak, and K. J. Friston. 1997. "How the Brain Learns to See Objects and Faces in an Impoverished Context". *Nature* 389:596–98.

Jeannerod, Marc. 2006. *Motor Cognition: What Actions Tell the Self*. Oxford: Oxford University Press.

Milner, A. D., and Melvyn A. Goodale. 1995. *The Visual Brain in Action*. Oxford: Oxford University Press.

Ramachandran, V. S. 1992. "Filling in the Blind Spot." *Nature* 356:115.

Ramachandran, V. S., D. Rogers-Ramachandran, and S. Cobb. 1995. "Touching the Phantom Limb." *Nature* 377:489–90.

Rizzolatti, Giacomo, and Corrado Sinigaglia. 2008. *Mirrors in the Brain: How Our Minds Share Actions and Emotions*. Oxford: Oxford University Press.

Rolls, Edmund T., Fabian Grabenhorst, Christian Margot, Maria A. A. P. da Silva, and Maria Ines Velazco. 2008. "Selective Attention to Affective Value Alters How the Brain Processes Olfactory Stimuli." *Journal of Cognitive Neuroscience* 20:1815–26.

Taylor, Jill Bolte. 2009. *My Stroke of Insight: A Brain Scientist's Personal Journey*. New York: Plume.

Yang, Tony T., Gallen B. Schwartz, F. E. Bloom, V. S. Ramachandran, and S. Cobb. 1994. "Sensory Maps in the Human Brain." *Nature* 368:592–93.

EXERCISES

Read (DeSteno et al. 2004) and reframe as an exploration of preconscious processes.

Search for a political psychology article with the phrase, "affect[ive] and [or] cognition [or cognitive]" in the title. Then, evaluate whether the author(s) presume a temporal or spatial relationship between affect and cognition (they may do so explicitly). And, if they are using a spatial conception, reconstruct the theory to see how a shift to

---

7. Anecdotal examples are many: the West's recent efforts to engage the North Korean or Iranian leaderships to encourage them to abandon nuclear weapons development. Or, then British Prime Minister Blair's effort to move then President George W. Bush toward a negotiating stance toward the Iraq regime and its purported threat.

a temporal conception would alter the theory (i.e., how upstream affective responses arise and then shape downstream cognitive processes).

REFERENCES

Abramson, Paul R. 1993. *Political Attitudes in America: Formation and Change*. San Francisco: Freeman.

Alvarez, R. Michael, and John Brehm. 2002. *Hard Choices, Easy Answers: Values, Information, and American Public Opinion*. Princeton, NJ: Princeton University Press.

Asch, Solomon E. 1951. "Effects of Group Pressure upon the Modification and Distortion of Judgment." In *Groups, Leadership and Men: Research in Human Relations*, edited by Harold Guetzkow, 177–90. Pittsburgh, PA: Carnegie Press.

Barber, James David. 1985. *The Presidential Character: Predicting Performance in the White House*. Englewood Cliffs, NJ: Prentice-Hall.

Bargh, John A., Ronald N. Bond, Wendy J. Lombardi, and Mary E. Tota. 1986. "The Additive Nature of Chronic and Temporary Sources of Construct Accessibility." *Journal of Personality and Social Psychology* 50:869–78.

Bargh, John A., Shelly Chaiken, Rajen Govender, and Felicia Pratto. 1992. "The Generality of the Automatic Attitude Activation Effect." *Journal of Personality and Social Psychology* 62:893–912.

Bargh, John A., and Tanya L. Chartrand. 1999. "The Unbearable Automaticity of Being." *American Psychologist* 54:462–79.

Bargh, John A., and Paula Pietromonaco. 1982. "Automatic Information Processing and Social Perception: The Influence of Trait Information Presented Outside of Conscious Awareness on Impression Formation." *Journal of Personality and Social Psychology* 43:437–49.

Bem, Daryl. 1970. *Beliefs, Attitudes, and Human Affairs*. Belmont, CA: Brooks, Cole.

Benhabib, Seyla. 1996. "Toward a Deliberative Model of Democratic Legitimacy." In *Democracy and Difference: Contesting the Boundaries of the Political*, edited by Seyla Benhabib, 67–94. Princeton, NJ: University of Princeton Press.

Bodenhausen, Galen V. 1993. "Emotion, Arousal, and Stereotypic Judgments: A Heuristic Model of Affect and Stereotyping." In *Affect, Cognition, and Stereotyping: Interactive Processes in Group Perception*, edited by D. Mackie and D. Hamilton, 13–37. San Diego, CA: Academic.

Bodenhausen, Galen V., and Meryl Lichtenstein. 1987. "Social Stereotypes and Information-Processing Strategies: The Impact of Task Complexity." *Journal of Personality and Social Psychology* 52:871–80.

Bodenhausen, Galen V., Lori A. Sheppard, and Geoffrey P. Kramer. 1994. "Negative Affect and Social Judgment: The Differential Impact of Anger and Sadness." *European Journal of Social Psychology* 24:45–62.

Bodenhausen, Galen V., and Robert S. Wyer, Jr. 1985. "Effects of Stereotypes in Decision Making and Information-Processing Strategies." *Journal of Personality and Social Psychology* 48:267–82.

Bogardus, Emory S. 1925. "Measuring Social Distance." *Journal of Applied Sociology* 9:299–308.

Brader, Ted. 2006. *Campaigning for Hearts and Minds: How Emotional Appeals in Political Ads Work*. Chicago: University of Chicago Press.

Cacioppo, John T., and Richard W. Petty. 1982. "The Need for Cognition". *Journal of Personality and Social Psychology* 42:116–31.

Chaiken, Shelly, Akiva Liberman, and Alice H. Eagly. 1989. "Heuristic and Systematic Information Processing Within and Beyond the Persuasion Context." In *Unintended Thought*, edited by Jim S. Uleman and John A. Bargh, 212–52. New York: Guilford.

Chaiken, Shelly, and Durairaj Maheswaran. 1994. "Heuristic Processing Can Bias Systematic Processing: Efforts of Source Credibility, Argument Ambiguity, and Task Importance on Attitude Judgment." *Journal of Personality and Social Psychology* 66:460–73.

Chaiken, Shelly, and Yaacov Trope, eds. 1999. *Dual Process Models in Social Psychology* New York: Guilford.

Changeux, Jean-Pierre. 1986. *Neuronal Man*. Oxford: Oxford University Press.

Chong, Dennis. 2000. *Rational Lives: Norms and Values in Politics and Society*. Chicago: University of Chicago Press.

Conover, Pamela, and Stanley Feldman. 1984. "How People Organize the Political World: A Schematic Model." *American Journal of Political Science* 28:95–126.

Converse, Philip E. 1964. "The Nature of Belief Systems in Mass Publics." In *Ideology and Discontent*, edited by David Apter, 9–39. New York: Free Press.

——. 1970. "Attitudes and Non-Attitudes: Continuation of a Dialogue." In *The Quantitative Analysis of Social Problems*, edited by Edward F. Tufte, 168–89. Reading, MA: Addison-Wesley.

——. 2006. "Democratic Theory and Electoral Reality." *Critical Review* 18:297–329.

Darwin, Charles. 1998. *The Expression of the Emotions in Man and Animals*. New York: Oxford University Press.

Davidson, Richard J., and Kenneth. Hugdahl. 1995. *Brain Asymmetry*. Cambridge, Mass.: MIT Press.

Delli Carpini, Michael X., and Scott Keeter. 1996. *What Americans Know About Politics and Why it Matters*. New Haven, CT: Yale University Press.

DeSteno, David, Nilanjana Dasgupta, Monica Y. Bartlett, and Aida Cajdric. 2004. "Prejudice from Thin Air: The Effect of Emotion on Automatic Intergroup Attitudes." *Psychological Science* 15:319–24.

Devine, Patricia G. 1989. "Stereotypes and Prejudice: Their Automatic and Controlled Components." *Journal of Personality and Social Psychology* 56:5–18.

Devine, Patricia G., Margo J. Monteith, Julia R. Zuwerink, and Andrew J. Elliot. 1991. "Prejudice With and Without Compunction." *Journal of Personality and Social Psychology* 60:817–30.

Dewey, John. 1910. *How We Think*. Boston: Heath.

——. 1925. *Experience and Nature*. Chicago: Open Court.

Dewey, John, and Arthur Fisher Bentley. 1949. *Knowing and the Known*. Boston: Beacon Press.

Eagley, Alice H., and Shelley Chaiken. 1992. *The Psychology of Attitudes*. Orlando, FL: Harcourt Brace Jovanovich.

Edelman, Murray. 1964. *The Symbolic Uses of Politics*. Urbana: University of Illinois Press.

Egloff, Boris, and Stefan C. Schmukle. 2002. "Predictive Validity of an Implicit Association Test for Assessing Anxiety." *Journal of Personality and Social Psychology* 83:1441–55.

Elder, Charles D., and Roger W. Cobb. 1983. *The Political Uses of Symbols*. New York: Longman.

Festinger, Leon. 1956. *When Prophecy Fails*. Minneapolis: University of Minnesota Press.

Fishbein, Martin. 1967. *Attitude Theory and Measurement*. New York: Wiley.

Fishbein, Martin, and Icek Ajzen. 1975. *Belief, Attitude, Intention and Behavior: An Introduction to Theory and Research*. Reading. MA: Addison-Wesley.

Fishkin, James. 1991. *Democracy and Deliberation*. New Haven, CT: Yale University Press.

Fiske, Susan T. 1981. "Social Cognition and Affect." In *Cognition, Social Behavior, and the Environment*, edited by J. Harvey, 227–64. Hillsdale, NJ: Erlbaum.

Freud, Sigmund. 1961. *Civilization and Its Discontents*. New York: Norton.

———. 1962. *Totem and Taboo: Some Points of Agreement between the Mental Lives of Savages and Neurotics*. New York: Norton.

Gazzaniga, Michael. 1985. *The Social Brain: Discovering the Networks of the Mind*. New York: Basic Books.

———. 1992. *Nature's Mind: The Biological Roots of Thinking, Emotions, Sexuality, Language, and Intelligence*. New York: BasicBooks.

Gazzaniga, Michael S., Joseph E. LeDoux, and D. Wilson. 1977. "Language, Praxis, and the Right Hemisphere: Clues to Some Mechanisms of Consciousness". *Neurology* 27:1144–7.

George, Alexander L., and Juliette L. George. 1998. *Presidential Personality and Performance*. Boulder, CO: Westview.

Gigerenzer, Gerd, Peter M. Todd, and ABC Research Group. 1999. *Simple Heuristics That Make Us Smart*. New York: Oxford University Press.

Goertzel, Ted. 1994. "Belief in Conspiracy Theories." *Political Psychology* 15:731–42.

Goffman, Erving. 1959. *The Presentation of Self in Everyday Life*. Garden City, NY: Doubleday.

———. 1963. *Behavior in Public Places; Notes on the Social Organization of Gatherings*. New York: Free Press.

———. 1971. *Relations in Public*. New York: Basic Books.

———. 1981. *Forms of Talk*. Philadelphia: University of Pennsylvania Press.

———. 1982. *Interaction Ritual: Essays on Face-to-Face Behavior*. New York: Pantheon Books.

———. 1986a. *Frame Analysis: An Essay on the Organization of Experience*. Boston: Northeastern University Press.

———. 1986b. *Stigma: Notes on the Management of Spoiled Identity*. New York: Simon & Schuster.

Gray, Jeffrey A. 1981. "The Psychophysiology of Anxiety." In *Dimensions of Personality: Papers in Honour of H. J. Eysenck*, edited by R. Lynn, 233–52. New York: Pergamon Press.

———. 1985. "A Whole and Its Parts: Behaviour, the Brain, Cognition, and Emotion." *Bulletin of the British Psychological Society* 38:99–112.

———. 1987a. "The Neuropsychology of Emotion and Personality." In *Cognitive Neurochemistry*, edited by S. M. Stahl, S. D. Iversen, and E. C. Goodman, 171–90. Oxford: Oxford University Press.

———. 1987b. *The Psychology of Fear and Stress*. Cambridge: Cambridge University Press.

———. 2004. *Consciousness: Creeping Up on the Hard Problem*. Oxford: Oxford University Press.

Greenwald, Anthony G., Debbie McGhee, E., and Jordan L. K. Schwartz. 1998. "Measuring Individual Differences in Implicit Cognition: The Implicit Association Test." *Journal of Personality and Social Psychology* 74:1464–80.

Haney, Craig, Curtis Banks, and Philip Zimbardo. 1983. "Interpersonal Dynamics in a Simulated Prison." *International Journal of Criminology and Penology* 1:69–97.

Hanson, Russell L. 1993. "Deliberation, Tolerance and Democracy." In *Reconsidering the Democratic Public*, edited by George E. Marcus and Russell L. Hanson, 273–86. University Park: Pennsylvania State University Press.

Huddy, Leonie, and Nayda Terklidsen. 1993. "Gender Stereotypes and the Perceptions of Male and Female Candidates." *American Journal of Political Science* 37:119–47.

Jacoby, William G. 2006. "Value Choices and American Public Opinion". *American Journal of Political Science* 50:707–23.

James, William. 1883. "What is Emotion?" *Mind* 9:188–204.

———. 1894. "The Physical Basis of Emotion." *Psychological Review* 1:516–29.

Jeannerod, Marc. 2006. *Motor Cognition: What Actions Tell the Self*. Oxford: Oxford University Press.

Jervis, Robert. 1976. *Perception and Misperception in International Politics*. Princeton, NJ: Princeton University Press.

Kahneman, Daniel, and Amos Tversky. 1984. "Choices, Values, and Frames." *American Psychologist* 39:341–50.

Kinder, Donald R. 2006. "Belief Systems Today." *Critical Review* 18:197–216.

Kinder, Donald R., and Cindy D. Kam. 2010. *Us Against Them : Ethnocentric Foundations of American Opinion*. Chicago ; London: University of Chicago Press.

Kuklinski, James H., and Paul J. Quirk. 2000. "Reconsidering the Rational Public: Cognition, Heuristics, and Mass Opinion." In *Elements of Reason: Cognition, Choice, and the Bounds of Rationality*, edited by Arthur Lupia, Mathew D. McCubbins, and Samuel L. Popkin, 153–82. New York: Cambridge University Press.

Lakoff, George. 2002. *Moral Politics: How Liberals and Conservatives Think*. Chicago: University of Chicago Press.

Lakoff, George, and Mark Johnson. 1999. *Philosophy in the Flesh: The Embodied Mind and Its Challenge to Western Thought*. New York: Basic Books.

LaPiere, Richard T. 1934. "Attitudes vs. Actions." *Social Forces* 13:230–37.

Lasswell, Harold D. 1930. *Psychopathology and Politics*. Chicago: University of Chicago Press.

———. 1948. *Power and Personality*. New York: Norton.

Lau, Richard R. 1986. "Political Schemata, Candidate Evaluations, and Voting Behavior." In *Political Cognition*, edited by Richard R. Lau and David O. Sears, 153–82. Hillsdale, NJ: Erlbaum.

Lau, Richard R., and David P. Redlawsk. 1997. "Voting Correctly." *American Political Science Review* 91:585–98.

———. 2001. "Advantages and Disadvantages of Cognitive Heuristics in Political Decision Making." *American Journal of Political Science* 45:951–71.

LeVine, Robert A., and Donald T. Campbell. 1972. *Ethnocentrism: Theories of Conflict, Ethnic Attitudes and Group Behavior*. New York: Wiley.

Lodge, G. Milton, and Ruth Hamill. 1986. "A Partisan Schema for Political Information Processing." *American Political Science Review* 80:505–20.

Luskin, Robert C. 1987. "Measuring Political Sophistication." *American Journal of Political Science* 31:856–99.

———. 1990. "Explaining Political Sophistication." *Political Behavior* 12:331–61.

MacKuen, Michael, George E. Marcus, W. Russell Neuman, and Luke Keele. 2007. "The Third Way: The Theory of Affective Intelligence and American Democracy." In *The Affect Effect: The Dynamics of Emotion in Political Thinking and Behavior*, edited by Ann Crigler, George E. Marcus, Michael MacKuen, and W. Russell Neuman, 124–51. Chicago: University of Chicago Press.

MacLean, Paul D. 1990. *The Triune Brain in Evolution*. New York: Plenum.

Macrae, C. Neil, Alan B. Milne, and Galen V. Bodenhausen. 1994. "Stereotypes as Energy-Saving Devices: A Peek Inside the Cognitive Toolbox." *Journal of Personality and Social Psychology* 66:37–47.

Marcus, George E., W. Russell Neuman, and Michael B. MacKuen. 2000. *Affective Intelligence and Political Judgment*. Chicago: University of Chicago Press.

Marcus, George E., John L. Sullivan, Elizabeth Theiss-Morse, and Sandra Wood. 1995. *With Malice Toward Some: How People Make Civil Liberties Judgments*. New York: Cambridge University Press.

McGuire, William J. 1972. "Attitude Change: An Information Processing Paradigm." In *Experimental Social Psychology*, edited by C. G. McClintock, 108–41. New York: Holt Rinehart and Winston.

———. 1985. "Attitudes and Attitude Change." In *Handbook of Social Psychology*, edited by Gardner Lindzey and Elliot Aronson, 243–346. New York: Random House.

Milgram, Stanley. 1974. *Obedience to Authority*. New York: Harper and Row.

Miller, Arthur, Martin Wattenburg, and Oskana Malanchuk. 1986. "Schematic Assessments of Candidates." *American Political Science Review* 80:521–40.

Milner, A. D., and Melvyn A. Goodale. 1995. *The Visual Brain in Action*. Oxford: Oxford University Press.

Mueller, John. 1999. *Capitalism, Democracy and Ralph's Pretty Good Grocery*. Princeton, NJ: Princeton University Press.

Page, Benjamin I. 1996. *Who Deliberates? Mass Media in Modern Democracy*. Chicago: University of Chicago Press.

Petty, Richard E., and John T. Cacioppo. 1986. *Communication and Persuasion: Central and Peripheral Routes to Attitude Change*. New York: Springer-Verlag.

Pollock, Philip H., III, Stuart A. Lilie, and M. Elliot Vittes. 1993. "Hard Issues, Core Values and Vertical Constraint: The Case of Nuclear Power." *British Journal of Political Science* 23:29–50.

Popkin, Samuel L. 1991. *The Reasoning Voter: Communication and Persuasion in Presidential Campaigns*. Chicago: University of Chicago Press.

Pratto, Felicia, Jim Sidanius, Lisa M. Stallworth, and Bertram F. Malle. 1994. "Social Dominance Orientation: A Personality Variable Predicting Social and Political Attitudes." *Journal of Personality and Social Psychology* 67:741–63.

Rahn, Wendy M. 1993. "The Role of Partisan Stereotypes in Information Processing About Political Candidates." *American Journal of Political Science* 37:472–96.

Rizzolatti, Giacomo, and Corrado Sinigaglia. 2008. *Mirrors in the Brain: How Our Minds Share Actions and Emotions*. Oxford: Oxford University Press.

Ronquillo, Jaclyn, Thomas F. Denson, Brian Lickel, Zhong-Lin Lu, Anirvan Nandy, and Keith B. Maddox. 2007. "The Effects of Skin Tone on Race-Related Amygdala Activity: An fMRI Investigation." *Social Cognitive and Affective Neuroscience* 2:39–44.

Sanders, Lynn M. 1997. "Against Deliberation." *Political Theory* 25:347–77.

Schatz, Robert T., Ervin Staub, and Howard Levine. 1999. "On the Varieties of National Attachment: Blind Versus Constructive Patriotism." *Political Psychology* 20:151–75.

Schwartz, Shalom H., and Wolfgang Bilsky. 1987. "Toward a Universal Psychological Structure of Human Values." *Journal of Personality and Social Psychology* 55:550–62.

Semin, Gün R., and John T. Cacioppo. 2007. "From Embodied Representation to Co-Regulation." In *Mirror Neuron Systems: The Role of Mirroring Processes in Social Cognition*, edited by J. A. Pineda, 107–20. Totowa, NJ: Humana.

Shapiro, Ian. 1999. "Enough of Deliberation: Politics is About Interests and Power." In *Deliberative Politics: Essays on Democracy and Disagreement*, edited by Stephen Macdo, 28–38. New York: Oxford University Press.

Sherif, Muzafer. 1958. "Group Influences upon the Formation of Norms and Attitudes." In *Readings in Social Psychology*, edited by Eleanor Maccoby, T. M. Newcomb, and E. L. Hartley, 219–32. New York: Holt.

Sidanius, Jim, and Felicia Pratto. 2004. "Social Dominance Theory: A New Synthesis." In *Political Psychology: Key Readings*, edited by John T. Jost and Jim Sidanius, 315–32. New York: Psychology Press.

Stangor, C., L. A. Sullivan, and T. E. Ford. 1991. "Affective and Cognitive Determinants of Prejudice." *Social Cognition* 9:359–91.

Staub, Ervin. 1997. "Blind Versus Constructive Patriotism: Moving From Embeddedness in the Group to Critical Loyalty and Action." In *Patriotism in the Lives of Individuals and Nations*, edited by Dani Bar-Tal and Ervin Staub, 213–29. Chicago: Nelson Hall.

Stein, Janice Gross. 1988. "Building Politics into Psychology: The Misperception of Threat." *Political Psychology* 9:245–71.

Sullivan, John L., James Pierson, and George E. Marcus. 1982. *Political Tolerance and American Democracy*. Chicago: University of Chicago Press.

Sullivan, John L., Pat Walsh, Michal Shamir, David G. Barnum, and James L. Gibson. 1993. "Why Are Politicians More Tolerant? Selective Recruitment and Socialization among Political Elites in New Zealand, Israel, Britain, and the United States." *British Journal of Political Science* 23:51–76.

Taber, Charles S., and Milton Lodge. 2006. "Motivated Skepticism in the Evaluation of Political Beliefs." *American Journal of Political Science* 50:755–69.

Taylor, Jill Bolte. 2009. *My Stroke of Insight: A Brain Scientist's Personal Journey*. New York: Plume.

Tesser, Abraham, and James E. Collins. 1988. "Emotion in Social Reflection and Comparison Situations: Intuitive, Systematic, and Exploratory Approaches." *Journal of Personality and Social Psychology* 55:695–709.

Thompson, Dennis. 1970. *The Democratic Citizen: Social Science and Democratic Theory in the Twentieth Century*. New York: Cambridge University Press.

Vinacke, Edgar W. 1957. "Stereotypes as Social Concepts." *Journal of Social Psychology* 46:229–43.

Warnecke, A. Michael, Roger D. Masters, and Guido Kempter. 1992. "The Roots of Nationalism: Nonverbal Behavior and Xenophobia." *Ethology and Sociobiology* 13:267–82.

Wilkowski, Benjamin M., and Brian P. Meier. 2010. "Bring It On: Angry Facial Expressions Potentiate Approach-Motivated Motor Behavior." *Journal of Personality and Social Psychology* 98:201–10.

Zaller, John R. 1987. "Diffusion of Political Attitudes." *Journal of Personality and Social Psychology* 53:821–33.

———. 1992. *The Nature and Origins of Mass Opinion*. New York: Cambridge University Press.

CHAPTER 7

Personality and Political Psychology

Personality—temperament—is one of the oldest conceptions of human nature and has been the idea of temperament. Central to this idea is the notion that each of us has some stable and enduring features, we have character. And, it is these enduring and distinctive features that define our nature. A moment of courage in the past identifies a person as courageous. This identification of an event as a trait then leads to the expectation that because that person was courageous at an earlier time, they will act courageously again in future situations.

Wisdom, cowardice, laziness, or fastidiousness, these are just some of the many qualities that we identify as characteristics of a person. But making scientific sense of this concept is a challenging task. In this chapter I review the common approaches to personality in political psychology. I also cover the critical considerations you should apply to any personality approach, old or contemporary. Along the way, I examine how neuroscience and its related disciplines offer new tools and insights.

BOX 7.1 Stereotypes

It is common in all societies to assign temperamental qualities to groups as well as to individuals. Historically, such qualities have been ascribed to gender (men are...[fill in the qualities]; women are...[fill in the qualities]), sexual orientation (gays are..., straights are ...); to age (younger versus older); class (upper, middle, and lower); nationalities (the Swedes are..., the Russians are..., and so on); to religious communities (to Jews, or Protestants, who were thought to have the "Protestant ethic,"

and so on); to racial groups (race was and remains a popular if not especially scientific category, though many of the other categories are no less scientific).

How would you scientifically investigate this social practice? How do stereotypes get generated, how are they transmitted, when are they used, and when not? And is the use of stereotypes a matter of personality? Are some personality types prone to use stereotypes and others not?

People often treat those they interact with as if they have a stable nature that controls their behavior across time, then, now, and future. Indeed, a person who acted very unpredictably is likely to be described as "crazy." "There goes 'crazy Joe,' you never know what he's going to do next." Having a stable, and hence predictable, personality is of vital importance because we have every expectation that we and those we engage with live predictable lives. It is hard to imagine the development of complex social organization and culture without some temporal predictability. From that expectation derives such clichés as "once a coward always a coward".[1]

The notion of temperament has been from the very outset normative. The normative goal was to understand how and why people behaved in characteristic ways, and if their behavior changed, why? The theory of the four humors was developed by ancient Greek, Egyptian, and Roman physicians to describe both how and why people acted and to explain why people might depart from their "normal" selves. We begin our examination of personality with that ancient though now abandoned conception (though the terms for the four humors remain vital in our vocabulary). Examination of more modern conceptions, how they differ, how they advance our understanding, and their limitations follow.

Important throughout this chapter is the recognition that personality is not just a matter of scholarly interest. The ancients were interested in personality because they saw in temperament the answer to ill-health. It was physicians and those who sought their services, who early on had an interest in temperament. But, temperament was and also is a vital issue in politics. In ancient Athens, home to the first known democracy, Athenian citizens came together to elect those among them who would lead them in war or to lead critical diplomatic missions. Judging who would lead and achieve victory or forestall defeat was, and remains, a vital task for the city and for the nation. That belief in leadership as a skill presumes, of course, that not only do people have a temperament suitable for leadership, but further, that temperament actually controls behavior, and further still, that observers can accurately judge the temperament of those they need to work with or against.[2]

In matters of law, the issue of temperament comes up in many, if not all, instances of illegal conduct. One person kills another. For the law, in most legal systems, this is a matter of both judging the act and also, of judging the actor. If the killing took place as a person defended their family against robbers seeking to rape and pillage, a

---

1. Though we should note that ascribing a label, such as cowardice may prove to be more consequential than the temperament of the individual (Crane 2010).

2. Leaders have long recognized that they need to know the personality of the leaders they confront or those they contemplate collaborating with on some joint endeavor as Churchill, Stalin, and F. D. Roosevelt did after Pearl Harbor. It is common practice for the state security apparatus to generate personality profiles for their principals. Though even in democracies it is common practice for national leaders to keep these profiles secret, preferring instead to characterize those the favor in laudatory terms ("Uncle Joe" for Stalin while an ally) or as unadulterated evil when it is a leader of the enemy (Saddam Hussein went from "uncle" to evil after his decision to invade Kuwait but not after he gassed the Kurds during the Iraq–Iran war when he was "one of ours."). It would be pertinent to call for the public release of these these secret dossiers so citizens have the same information as their leaders. There are obvious reasons why these assessments are kept secret, among them that some the leaders of our allies are often found wanting in various ways both serious and just embarrassing, and it is the nature of international affairs that sometimes enemies become allies, and sometimes allies enemies.

jury might well find this the legitimate act of a courageous person, a case of justifiable homicide. Or, if a person while driving, kills striking another person. Is that an act of a drunk, or is this a person using his car to hit a person who, standing in the road, is using an automatic weapon to shoot pedestrians, or to make the matter of temperament irrelevant, striking a person who suddenly runs in front giving the driver no time to react?

The law confronts the issue of temperament in various ways, but rarely in isolation from two other considerations. First, is the consideration of the contemporary circumstance. And, second, is the consideration of whether the individual was able to control their behavior. In the hypothetical case of a driver and a deadly accident, perhaps the fault is not found in temperament, whether the driver was lazy, drunk, inattentive, or negligent, perhaps texting while driving, but in features of the circumstance, bad lighting, a broken traffic light, heavy rain, black ice, fog, or any of a number of other features that might explain an automobile crash.

Perhaps, the driver was not under volitional control of the situation, perhaps his doctor gave him the incorrect drug dosage causing his depth perception to fail, or his motor control to be less than normally deft. Perhaps, a carjacker jumped into the car and, putting a gun to the head of the driver said, "drive and drive fast." In these instances the law seeks to come to some judgment that takes into account each of these three elements: temperament, context, and volitional control. And, as we shall see later, political psychologists would be wise to do the same.

In our time, clinical interest in personality remains in full force. Psychologists and psychiatrists spend a consider part of their time on disorder identification, the assessment of its specifics into a diagnosis. But other institutions also have a strong interest in personality and administrators in these institutions also use an array of testing practices to do something quite similar, to examine some population, to identify some critical features, desirable or undesirable to help in the deciding who to let in, who to keep out, who to reward, and who to punish.

BOX 7.2 Entrapment

The law in many legal traditions provides the defense of "entrapment." This defense accounts for the temptation of law enforcement officers, who in the service of protecting the public and perhaps, gaining some renown or advancement, entice someone to do something illegal that they would not have done but for the inducements offered by the (typically) undercover police agent. It may well be the case that in such instances the person under indictment is a person of a criminal temperament but a criminal temperament is, generally, not sufficient to put someone in jail.

Joseph Conrad's masterful novel, *The Secret Agent*, gives a vivid portrait of how an agent provocateur can give birth to events that otherwise would have taken a different course (Conrad, 2007).

In the United States, some jurisdictions keep people in jail for certain sexual predatory crimes past their formal sentences. In these categories of crime, the law holds that certain criminals have a temperament, as judged by the courts' experts, that gives the court sufficient grounds to retain such criminals on the claim that they are protecting the public against future criminal acts.

BOX 7.3   **Seeing inside the black box**

Law enforcement officials have the task of determining the truth from suspects and witness. They have long sought "lie detectors" to ascertain the truthfulness of a witness or defendant. The various types have a dubious history and dubious scientific merit. In this effort they share the same challenge as conventional psychologists: What can we tell about what is true and what is not when we have little more than the verbal responses, facial expressions, and body posture to rely on.

Educational institutions use grading and testing with great abandon. In the United States, colleges and universities make extensive use of tests, such as the ACT, SAT, GRE, LSAT, and others to rank their applicants and to sort candidates into ranks of the less to the more "promising" students. The adjective, promising, is telling. Past test taking skill is expected to predict, if not future learning, at least future test taking ability.[3]

Most modern military services, at least in developed nations, also use testing to select the desirable applicants (whether volunteered or drafted) from those they believe, on the basis of the test scores, from those who would make poor soldiers. Soldiering, similar but differing in the particulars from being a good diplomat, requires certain specific personality qualities. Whether a test is a good way to identify these qualities, it is presumed that the assessment done as part of recruitment will predict future actions. Thus, in public service, as well as in private employment, there are exams for just about any job. There is an entrance examination for use in determining who to admit to the foreign service and for the secret services. In political campaigns, the public, as Athenian citizens centuries ago, observe the actions of candidates during campaigns so they can anticipate what if elected they will do once in office.

Administrative and clinical applications have long driven much of the research on temperament. For example, French psychologist Alfred Binet developed the Binet test, the progenitor of the Stanford–Binet intelligence test, to identify students who lagged behind their peers in cognitive development so they could be placed into special education programs. The development of tests, and their sale for use in various research, clinical, and administrative applications, has developed into a major industry in psychology. Many psychological tests, proclaimed as being reliable and valid provide measures of specific stable features of human temperament are sold as tools of the administrative and clinical trade. We swim in a world constructed on the premise that personality controls human behavior. What we are, it is believed, explains what we have done, and what we will do.

One approach to taking into account the past, temperament, and the present, context and volitional control, is to make a distinction between "trait" and "state." Traits are the stable components of our personality. We will see later various ways we can understand traits. On the other hand, states describe the momentary impact of context and

---

3. The latest research suggests test taking of this sort is correlated with academic performance most strongly in the first year of college, but that correlation declines with each year of college thereafter. That foretells a major point of this chapter, personality, however conceived and however measured, is far less informative about future behavior than most us believe.

thus enable us to consider how people respond to the contextual aspects of experience, why their traits might not control their response.

I argue that division of the sources of human behavior into "trait" and "state" is in and of itself too crude to be all that helpful. I also argue that doing political psychology requires some new conceptual tools to properly comprehend and thereby shape our understanding of the multiple aspects that shape political judgment and political action. Thus, and to that end, in this chapter I focus more on the historical conditions that shape political judgment and political action while in the next chapter I attend more to the various ways that contemporary conditions impact. But before we turn to the latest conceptions of personality, let's review the history of personality.

I. A VERY BRIEF HISTORICAL INTRODUCTION TO PERSONALITY

In this section I cover two topics. First, by reviewing some of the history of understanding personality, we can identify the conceptual tools that allow us to understand the scientific approach to personality. Second, in reviewing this history, we can follow the development of ideas, where the conception of personality begins, and how it has changed over time.

Personality has been conceptualized in three ways. The first conception is that of human nature, what we all have in common. James Madison, for example, chose human fallibility as a common feature easily observed in almost all human beings. He did, as we saw, accept as a rare occurrence the existence of enlightened statesmen who had the exceptional gifts, of foresight and of judgment unpolluted by selfish desires. But he also saw that such individuals were so rare that it would be best to plan our political regime without any acknowledgment of or reliance on such persons.

A second conception built on the first. We can note that although all of us might share in some basket of human qualities, we do differ in some fashion, one from another. That leads to efforts, such as the theory of four humors, to identify basic human *types*. In the various typologies the effort is to group people into some number of basic human personalities according to some core differences. We look at some of these typologies shortly. Here the idea is that there is some holistic dynamic that form theses basic types. In the theory of the four humors, it was thought that the relative predominance of the four bodily fluids generates four basic types of human personality. For example, blood, one of the four humors, was held to be responsible for bravery. The presence of ample blood is the basis for courage while its insufficient supply leads to cowardice. This leads to the frequent literary device of associating pallor with cowardice and a flushed face with aggression and willingness to confront danger, "his blood is up." But, as we shall see, is no agreement on what core qualities identify the essential human types so we have quite a number of contenders.

A third conception sets aside the holistic approach to personality—what we have in common is the effort to describe some small number of fundamental types to which we can each be assigned. In this alternative conception, the goal is to focus on some specific properties and to explore just these properties without any aspiration for being comprehensive. Earlier we reviewed a very important tradition in social psychology as researchers attempted to understand why people committed horrible acts of evil before and during World War II. That led to the property, *authoritarianism,* investigated by an entire generation of scholars, social scientists, and others including Erich

Fromm (1965), Theodor Adorno and his colleagues (Adorno et al. 1950), Else Frenkel-Brunswick, Daniel Levenson, and Nevitt Stanford, among many others. This type of focus does not give the entire picture of people's personality. Rather it is directed to a critical dimension, here authoritarianism, which is expected to explain why some people behaved in a specific way, here, in engaging in horrific acts toward others. This focus introduces the critical phenomenon of *individual differences*. Individual differences recognize that, given some defined dimension, people differ. Some are more authoritarian, some are less so. But to conduct research on individual differences first requires that we have some clarity on the properties we propose to investigate. If courage is a core trait, then some will be more courageous and others less so. What are the important properties or traits that people differ on? And, as with personality *types*, the array of personality *traits* or dimensions is quite large and growing.

Personality as Taxonomy—Personality as Types

We have already covered the idea of taxonomy: the conceptual categories that enable us to group like things and to distinguish unlike things. Four thousands of years, the agreed on taxonomy in the western tradition, harking back to ancient Egypt, Greece, and Rome was the four fold taxonomy known as the theory of humors. I begin with this taxonomy for two reasons: first, because it held sway for about two millennia. And, though no longer credible as biology, its influence lingers embedded in our language. Second, and more important, even though is is no longer a viable account we can sharpen our critical skills on it before turning to more contemporary formulations. Humans were grouped into one of four basic types based on the dominant fluid in their bodies. The theory of humors held that four fluids animate us: black and yellow bile, phlegm, and blood. The abundance or paucity of these fluids that "inflated" or "deflated" specific personality features.

The Four Humors

1. An abundance of black bile causes *melancholia*. Melancholia is expressed as sadness and depression.
2. An abundance of yellow bile causes *cholera*. The choleric personality is expressed as angry, aggressive, and ill-tempered.
3. An abundance of phlegm causes *phlegmatic* behavior. The phlegmatic personality is expressed as calm, steady, and imperturbable.
4. An abundance of blood causes *sanguinary* behavior. The sanguine express the qualities of courage and desire.

Physicians relied, for a very long time on the belief that illness arose from too much or too little of these four fluids. The normal, healthy, personality was one in biological balance. Too much yellow bile and one should observe someone who has an explosive angry nature. Too little blood, observable as someone with a pallid visage, will produce lack of courage. Though medicine, belatedly, abandoned this theory, during its long history, the theory of four humors gave physicians a therapeutic approach: Modify the fluids either by diet, or as we saw in the failed effort to bring the feverish George Washington back to health by bleeding him, by removing what the doctors believed was the "excessive" level of blood.

I end with this observation. It is easy now, in light of our current medical understanding, to understand disease as being the result of infection, trauma, or genetic failing (and their interactions). From that vantage point it is easy to see the humors explanation of personality as archaic. It is less easy to see that our contemporary accounts may at some future juncture be seen as no less archaic. If we all held a scientific orientation to theory, evidence, and belief, that would help us prepare for newer conceptions that might well serve us better than those now current. Science brings with it organized doubt and the reliance on formal collection and analysis of data. But holding a scientific orientation cannot prevent too much confidence that our current accounts are likely deficient and would best be replaced by something hopefully better.

Two current popular typologies demonstrate the continued appeal of "personality types." Popular treatments of research on brain organization focused on the discovery that some functional asymmetries exist between tasks served in the left and and those served in the right brain hemispheres. These brain asymmetries are real but in the normal brain these asymmetries work in harmony. Nonetheless popular readings of this research led to the claim that we each fall into one of two types based on which side of our brains are dominant. Some of us are are characterized as left brain thinkers and others and right brain thinkers. Those who are left brain thinkers focus on precise detailed analytic approaches to life. Whereas right brain thinkers tend to the overall integrity of experience, what is sometimes called a *gestalt* orientation (taken from the German, meaning overall, often taken to be more than the sum of the individual components of experience). Hence, if valid, we can all be readily placed into this two fold typology.

Another popular typology is the Myers–Briggs personality test meant to classify people into one of sixteen different personality types (Myers, McCaulley & Most, 1985). This personality taxonomy is based on four dichotomies, largely drawn from psychoanalyst Carl Jung's work. These dichotomies represent core preferences. The claim is that people are either extraverts or introverts; primarily prefer sensing or relying on intuition; prefer thinking or feeling; and, finally, prefer judging or perceiving. These four paired oppositional preferences generate the various combinations generate sixteen personality types.

You can take the Myers–Briggs to see which personality type you are within this particular formulation. An online version can be found at: http://www.humanmetrics.com/cgi-win/JTypes2.asp.

Table 7.1. Left and right brain typological descriptions of personality

Left brain thinkers	Right brain thinkers
Logical	Random
Sequential	Intuitive
Rational	Holistic
Analytical	Synthesizing
Objective	Subjective

Table 7.2. Jungian personality preferences

Extraversion	Introversion
Sensing	Intuition
Thinking	Feeling
Judging	Perceiving

How did you do? Most people will likely find their classification, in either of these schemes, left or right, or whichever of the Jungian sixteen personality types plausible. Not all that surprising as people themselves select the qualities that identify themselves and so the resulting classification has a measure of tautology. If you pick your own descriptive features, the collection is, not surprisingly, going to be familiar. However, that typological classification may tell us very little in the way of explanation of what we do in life. And, to return, yet again, to James Madison, we often find that many of us do not actually fit well in such schemes. Many of us have a mix of qualities and some these fall outside of the particular taxonomic categories. Where would we place ourselves if we were inclined to think and feel? What if most us use both left and right brain thinking styles? What if use neither? What if some, or many, of our actions do not depend on thinking at all?

These taxonomies were developed before neuroscience demonstrated that we have a rich range of skills and knowledge that is not accessible to us via self-reports. How can even a truthful subject report on the individual differences that no doubt exist when those differences are hidden from us?

Modern Research on Personality

There are three broad approaches to personality in the research literature: the psycho-analytic, the trait approach, and the identification of neural systems from neuroscience. Earlier I briefly touched on the Myers–Briggs typology, which depends on Jung's variant of the Freudian psychodrama. That typology provides an overall classification that assigns each of us to one of sixteen diagnostic types. Belonging to a type is explained by a distinct pattern of early life experience. It is in that early formative experience in which the formative issues of nurturance and punishment by parents shape not only the inner psychic life of the young child but persist to control the adult perceptions, expectations, and behavior.

Academic psychology has largely rejected Freud and psychoanalysis *tout court* (the influence of psychoanalytic approaches would find a more accepting welcome in the humanities divisions of American universities). Academic research in psychology turned its focus to specific properties identified as trait dimensions along which all individuals could be arrayed.

One of the early psychologists who took a trait approach to personality was Hans Eysenck (Eysenck, 1967, 1975; Eysenck and Eysenck, 1969, 1985). He began with a two trait conception of personality. The first, *extraversion–introversion* defines a dimension with the most extraverted at one end and the most introverted at the other end, with intermediate levels fleshing out the middle of the distribution. This approach has the advantage of allowing researchers to locate every individual they examine somewhere along the trait dimension. By assigning every research subject a value on this trait, each subject can be located somewhere on the trait using the many intervening values between the extremes. And, as it turns out, most of us are not highly extraverted or highly introverted.

In two ways this approach differs from the typological approach to personality. As in the Myers–Briggs example, types tend to make overall designations. We are "thinkers" or "feelers" or left brained or right brained. That we vary along a range with many intermediate values falling within a wide dimension is rather obscured. Moreover, the typological approach tends to the either or, whereas the trait-dimensional approach finds that, as a general rule, most of us fall closer to the middle of this, and indeed in any dimension. Research finds that as a general rule on most personality traits, the shape of the distribution is best described by the normal distribution (we can ignore the precise mathematics of this curve except to note that in normal distribution as seen in figure 7.1, its class is one of class of distributions that have this same general "bell" shape).

The height of the line reflects how many people one finds at that value of the dimension. And, as you can see, most people will find themselves closer to the middle. As with most personality traits, most of us are not located in the "tails" (or the extremes) of the space described by the normal curve but are in or near the middle.

Eysenck (1967) identified a second dimension labeled *neuroticism*. Eysenck defined neuroticism as the propensity to experience obsessions, phobias, and other neurotic tendencies. One reason I included Eysenck's first effort is that it draws attention to a very widespread pattern in psychology and political science. Unlike his first dimension, which clearly identifies each end of the dimension—extraverts preferring the social environment, finding it a more compelling environment, while introverts preferring the inner private life away from others—his second dimension's name, neuroticism draws attention to the one end of the dimension. So, the neuroticism dimension, unlike the extraversion–introversion dimension, tends to obscure or take for granted the other end. We can surmise that the other end of the neuroticism trait is emotional stability, and indeed of late it has become increasingly common to rename that trait *emotional stability*. But this habit of labeling some traits by naming one end of a distribution is a habit that you should note but yourself avoid for reasons I discuss a bit later in this chapter.

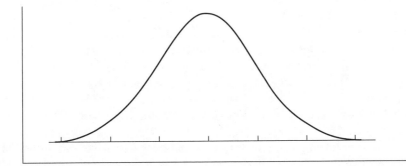

Figure 7.1 The Normal Distribution

These two dimensions are normally orthogonal, that is each trait is independent of the other. We each have a value of these two traits, and the value we have on one trait is not correlated with the value we have on the other trait. Extraversion–introversion and neuroticism are uncorrelated. If we turn from statistics to what this means in the language of spatial mathematics: two independent dimensions when located in a space define a two dimensional space, a space called a *circumplex*. The two dimensional space will form a large circle, which because it is a dense space allows for a quantity of variant locations distributed within the circle. This is an important difference from a taxonomic approach that would also describe a space. But that taxonomic space would have four "cells" that are produced if we divided people into high and low on each of the two dimensions. Though Eysenck rejected the four humors theory he did find a compelling parallel between his conception and that described by the four humors. Figure 7.2 shows how Eysenck drew that parallel.

You can examine how a trait and a typological approach are related by examining figure 7.2. Here Eysenck (1958) constructed a figure that displays his trait approach overlaying the four humors typology. The four humors are the four quadrants in the center. Note that these are solid as befits a typological approach. In the center are the four personality types: *melancholic, choleric, sanguine,* and *phlegmatic.* Around this inner circle is an outer ring with which Eysenck distributed a variety of names to identify the end points, these in capital letters: *EMOTIONAL UNSTABLE, EXTRAVERTED, EMOTIONALLY STABLE, INTROVERTED.* And, around the ring are additional labels that identified intermediate values resulting from the joint values cumulated as each individual will have a value resulting from their particular combination of trait values. So, someone who is *talkative* obtains this label by being both *Extraverted* and fairly *Emotionally Stable.* This contrasts with someone who is *impulsive,* someone who is also *Extraverted* but unlike the first individual, is less *Emotionally Stable.* Note also that Eysenck located his two traits at the boundaries, the trait *Neuroticism* lies between the melancholic and phlegmatic, on the left and between choleric and sanguine in the right. And *Extraversion–Introversion* lies between melancholic and choleric, on the top side, and between phlegmatic and sanguine on the bottom.

The principal methodology that allows researchers to assign people some value on a trait of personality has been and is to give a large number of lexical statements to some population of interest. These statements reflect some descriptions or preferences that are thought to be constituent elements of that trait of personality. People then rate each statement as "like" or "unlike" themselves.

Two factors shape how this research works. Much depends on the items, the statements, that make up the pool of statements presented to subjects to use to describe themselves. If there are no statements on whether one feels guilt, shame, or other moral feelings—such as if one feels guilty often or not at all, or if shame is important to them or not, and so on—it is not likely that the scholar will find a moral feeling trait in the resulting analysis. Statistical analysis cannot reveal a trait if the questions that could be used to identify a trait are not asked.

In addition, people cannot respond to items that they themselves cannot observe. And, as we have already seen in earlier chapters, much of the operation of the human brain is hidden to even the most astute observer. So, for example, most people cannot report whether their startle reflex is highly sensitive because the normal startle

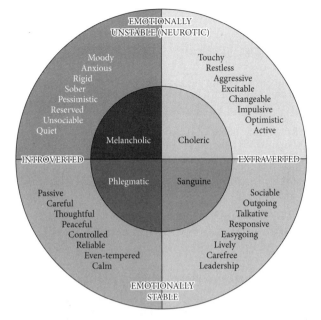

Figure 7.2 Hans Eysenck's Two Personality dimensions and the Four Humors
Source: Eysenck, H. J. and Eysenck, M. W. Personality and Individual Differences. Plenum Publishing, 1958.

reflex operates out of the normal state of consciousness. It is pointless to ask a question about whether they have frequent or intense experiences of eye blink startle. Or to offer another example, we can explore semantic memory by asking people what they remember but we cannot explore procedural memory by the same methodology of asking questions because introspection does not have access to the neural circuits that control physical action. But even qualities that are evident to consciousness often escape inclusion in such inventories. Most inventories do not include aspects that clearly impact on how humans make choices and engage in action. For example, I know of no wide-range personality inventory that explores whether people describe themselves as beautiful or ugly, or physically deft, athletic, or clumsy. Yet, the qualities of beauty and physical grace are clearly stable features of humans and they clearly shape human experience, including politics (Willis and Todorov 2006; Spezio et al. 2008).

However, there is another feature of that type of research that should give us some caution. The study of personality relies on presenting subjects with a battery of personality tests describing items in an "outside in" approach. We cannot see or observe the brain acting with, or without, for example intelligence directly, we infer its presence by the way people respond to questions. In a similar way, personality batteries give us no insight into how brains support social interaction, and how variations across brains lean us to either extraversion or introversion.

This then brings us to the third approach to personality, neuroscientific research and the related work on genetics. Neuroscience offers a variety of tools, including genetic analysis, twins raised together, twins raised apart, the analysis of DNA, that offer the promise of identifying the proteins that shape brain formation and function as well as of pathology. And, to that we can add the methodologies of lesion studies, single nerve cell recording technology, EEG, fMRI, PET scan, and more, all which give insight into the functional abilities and the individual differences in operation of the human brain. Rather than working "outside-in," using observations of how people behave, how they describe themselves or others, to advance hypotheses about how the brain and differences across brains produce the variety of behaviors we attribute to temperament, we can now work "inside-out," using research on brain function to account for the expression of personalities we observe. This approach is still early yet and it is premature to say we have a full understanding of brain function and individual differences in brain function. Joining both the inside-out and the outside-in methods will give us a way of triangulating research so that we are not dependent on the particular frailties of any given method or approach.

How does personality inform our understanding of politics? And, what does politics tell us about human personality? We turn to these questions next.

Personality in Psychobiography

A long popular application of personality to politics is to focus on the powerful. Particularly, but not exclusively, malevolent leaders, such as Hitler, Stalin, Pol Pot, Idi Amin, and others, have attracted considerable attention by scholars. Here again, the focus on pathology overwhelms any interest in the exemplary. There is a subordinate interest in benevolent leadership, but the dominant focus of research has been on the ways in which destructive violent leaders emerge and then impact their populations and too often the broader world. Hence, it has been common practice to research what is thought to be the psychic history, the psychobiography, of singular individuals to explain why they do what they do. Investigating the early formative years the psychobiographer seeks to identify the early interplay between child and mother, child and father, which is thought to form the way in which desires (the id) are shaped. And, to identify the particular ways the self, the conscious motives for success (the ego) navigates the world. And, finally, the psychobiographer seeks to identify the way in which the subject has internalized the demands of parents into a sense of conscience or obligation (the superego). The oedipal conflict, the assertive desires of the infant child blocked or frustrated by the parents is the foundation of adult personality (the name *oedipal* comes from the dramatic figure of Orestes, who murders his father and mother in various tellings by Greek tragedians) is held to be universal though variants abound. Alexander and Juliette George (1998) used this approach to craft a pyschoportrait of President Woodrow Wilson. Vamik Volkan and Norman Itkowitz (1984; Volkan, Itkowitz, and Dod, 1997) offered psychobiographies of the Turkish leader Ataturk and later, President Richard Nixon (as have many other psychobiographers). Erik Erikson (1958, 1969) offered psychobiographies of Gandhi and Luther. His approach extended the psychoanalytic framework to incorporate culture and context (E. Erikson, 1982).

Psychobiographies most often focus on major leaders, most often political, but in any case, the more influential. Core to the assertion is the dominance of history, the oedipal, early family, experience, over contemporary perception or contemporary deliberation. The essential hypothesis of psychoanalytic thinking holds that people determine the best course of action rely on historically formed convictions that meet their psychic needs whether normal or pathological. And further, that these inner needs can overwhelm consideration of and the influence of contemporary circumstances, the immediate external conditions of the world in which leaders operate.

A famous example of this approach was that provided by Cambridge (MA, USA) psychoanalyst Walter Langer. In 1942 the head of the OSS (the Office of Strategic Services, the precursor to the CIA), asked Langer to tell them as much as he could about Adolph Hitler. Langer interviewed those who had some personal experience with Hitler, colleagues and the former family doctor of Hitler, each then living either in Canada or in the United States, as well as read all of the documents he could find. Some months later he submitted his report to the OSS. Of particular note was his prediction that when, as by late 1942 seemed clear, the German effort to win the war would fail, Hitler would commit suicide rather than accept defeat. His report was later published as *The Mind of Adolf Hitler* (Langer, 1972), but you can find it on line at:

http://www2.ca.nizkor.org/hweb/people/h/hitler-adolf/oss-papers/text/profile-index.html

You can find a documentary made of this report at:

http://www.documentary-log.com/d92-inside-the-mind-of-adolf-hitler/

However, this was hardly the last such instance of expert leader profiles being generated by government use of psychoanalysts. Political psychologist Jerrold Post (then working for the CIA) prepared personality profiles of Anwar Sadat, president of Egypt and Menachim Begin, prime minister of Israel, for President Jimmy Carter in advance of the Camp David meetings. Psychobiographers have long been fascinated with leaders, especially those judged to be pathological given the psychoanalytic focus on obsession, compulsion, the persistent hardened approach to addressing life's challenges. Harold Lasswell (1930, 1948) applied these basic ideas to the broader public who he believed are no less driven by the early formative experiences of early childhood than elite leaders. LeVine and Campbell (1972) reported that one of the major theoretical approaches used to explain the ubiquitous propensity of humans to favor their group and to form antipathy to other groups, ethnocentrism, has its roots in the psychoanalytic presumption that conflict results from the projection of inner needs onto the external world leading to favoring oneself and those most alike, and expressing dislike, weakly or strongly, toward those perceived to be most unalike, a theme also developed by Vamik Volkan (1988) and Jerrold Post (Post and George 2004; Post 1993) among others. And, as noted earlier, the inquiry into the authoritarian personality, and the development of the scale

---

BOX 7.4 **Personality at a distance**

It is rare that scholars have direct access to the leaders they wish to understand. Walter Langer (1972) and Erik Erikson (1958, 1969) did not have any direct contact with their subjects.

Conducting a sound research program without direct access to your subject is a challenge: Research at a distance, whatever the theoretical focus requires special care. Political psychologist Jerrold Post published an excellent collection of articles by the leading practitioners of empirical research from a distance in a special issue of the journal *Political Psychology* in 2003. Among the scholars were political psychologists, David Winter, Meg Hermann, and Stephen Walker.

to measure, who has this personality, the F-Scale, was shaped by scholars deeply vested in the psychoanalytic approach to explanation (Adorno et al. 1950).

In their view, what happened between parents and child in the early formative years from birth through ages five or six, and you have the key to adult personality and thereby adult behavior. Vamik Volkan used the psychoanalytic perspective to focus on the role of narcissism in leadership. He elaborated the notion of narcissism to account for why some pursued a leadership role so they could express their need to be the focus of others, a need that evolved early in their childhood. He (Volkan and Itkowitz 1984; Volkan et al. 1997) also argued that some leaders express a beneficent variant of narcissism whereas others a malevolent variant. Another example of the recurring influence of the psychoanalytic tradition is found in the mortality salience theory. Accepting Ernst Becker's (1973) claim that the fear of death is one of core imperatives or drives that shapes all human personality, a group of social psychologists have been conducting a program of research to show the potency of this hypothesis (Landau et al., 2004).

In summary, psychobiography shares with the ancient Greeks, an interest in personality for its diagnostic value, for its ability to name, explain, and treat, various forms of pathology. Because it relies on detailed work on early childhood experience, psychobiography lends itself to case study analysis in which the cost and time to obtain detailed data on early childhood experience is more plausible than for large populations. The typical application of psychobiography is the analysis of specific members of the leadership elite. And, as such, it is not surprising, that is the more extreme leaders, Mao, Lenin, Stalin, Hitler, among others, those who have had both dramatic lives and destroyed more than they created, are the focus of attention.

Disease as evil is a common thread through this and other perspectives on personality. It is the deformed who do bad things. If nothing else this is a comfort to those who perceive themselves as having normal upbringings, as if this would distance "us" from the evil wrought by the presumed "others" who became the destroyers of life. That pathology explains evil as a belief that is interesting both as a claim about those who commit horrific crimes (a claim that is largely false) and as a self-serving assertion to create a psychic defense so we can feel apart from the evil that exists in the world.

BOX 7.5   Evil as pathology

Philosopher and then journalist, Hannah Arendt was sent to observe and report on the trail of Adolph Eichmann in Jerusalem (1963) coined the phrase the *banality of evil* to, erroneously, characterize Eichmann as a man of no imagination and evil intent, rather than merely doing what was expected of him. Historian Christopher Browning (1992) found that many of the men who went into the towns of Poland and slaughtered Jews were ordinary men of no clear ideological or independent intention other than to follow orders. And Stanley Milgram's (1974) as well as many of the classics of social psychology also find people willing to do what they are told even when their actions inflict clear harm on others. Although appealing, there is considerable evidence that personal pathology cannot be but a part of the explanation of evil and in some cases perhaps not even a part.

II. PERSONALITY IN POLITICAL PSYCHOLOGY

By rejecting the psychoanalytic approach, academic psychology had to find another way to approach personality and the predominant approach is the trait perspective. Individual traits are used by scholars to address the problem of explaining why and when people do harm to others. Among the traits that have been identified are: *authoritarianism, obedience to authority, ethnocentrism, dogmatism*, and many others. Still more traits—by now the list could go on for many pages—have been imagined, and many items have been written so that scales created with them allow researchers to assign numerical scores to research subjects. Psychologists have explored such traits as: *well-being* and *self-esteem*; *anxiousness, shyness*, and the like; *depression* and *loneliness* and the like; *alienation*; *locus of control*; *need for cognition*; and many more. John Robinson and colleagues (1991) published a collection of some of these trait measures in the volume, *Measures of Personality and Social Psychological Attitudes*.

The focus on traits generates research that is focused on one or, at most, a few identified specific aspects of personality. Each of these aspects understood as a trait, which is described as an enduring and stable disposition that explains some observed variation of behavior. With suitable measures, and typically a trait is measured by a series of statements shown to have some common meaning, we can measure and observe how people vary from low through middling to high on that quality. And, typically, the empirical data displays a normal distribution. It is not unusual for each trait to have ten, twenty, forty, or more items, each of which is intended to be a valid and reliable indicator of the trait. This poises a major barrier to research in political psychology as including a large array of traits in a study of public opinion or political behavior, or giving a large battery to some smaller group, say of candidates running for office, will certainly not be well received by those who are invited to participate as research subjects. Hence, some psychologists and political psychologists have developed "short forms" of these batteries reducing the number of items by half or less, so the burden on subjects is reduced sufficiently to gain a high(er) participation rate though this comes at the cost of scales that are less reliable.

The goal of obtaining reliable and valid measures of a personality trait is to identify a stable disposition, a disposition that explains the contemporary expression of that personality trait. That is but one account for why people behave as they do. There are a variety of theoretical approaches. Among these are the *behavioral approach* (Pavlov and B. F. Skinner). This approach holds that behavior is responsive to the regimen of rewards and punishments. Hence, this is a fully "state" approach as if one changes the mix of rewards and punishments then a change in behavior should rapidly follow. A different approach to predicting behavior is developmental theories that attempt to focus on the formation of personality. Important examples are Piaget's (1930, 1954, 1965, 1970) theory of cognitive development and Kohlberg's (1984) theory of moral development. Yet another class of personality theory is focused on beliefs that people hold, these theories seeks to explain how disparate beliefs can co-exist and how people resolve the antagonisms that contrary beliefs sometimes generate. Among these are the cognitive balance and dissonance theories of Heider (1958) and Festinger (1957), among others. Still yet another approach to explaining and understanding how consciousness is organized and expressed is the idea that the underlying structure of personality can be understood as a stable array of values. Core values motivate and structure personality (Maslow 1954). So

Table 7.3. Social dominance orientation battery items

1. Some groups of people are simply not the equals of others.	8. Increased economic equality.
2. Some people are just more worthy than others.	9. Increased social equality.
3. This country would be better off if we cared less about how equal all people were.	10. Equality.
4. Some people are just more deserving than others.	11. If people were treated more equally we would have fewer problems in this country.
5. It is not a problem if some people have more of a chance in life than others.	12. In an ideal world, all nations would be equal.
6. Some people are just inferior to others.	13. We should try to treat one another as equals as much as possible. (All humans should be treated equally.)
7. To get ahead in life, it is sometimes necessary to step on others.	14. It is important that we treat other countries as equals.

Note: Those given the questionnaire including these items, were given these instructions on how to respond: "Next to each item was a 1–7 scale, and the instructions read, 'Which of the following objects, events, or statements do you have a positive or negative feeling towards? Please indicate your feelings by circling the appropriate number alongside each item. Use one of the following responses. Remember, your first reaction is best. Work as quickly as you can.' The scale points were labeled *very negative* (1), *negative* (2), *slightly negative* (3), *uncertain or neutral* (4), *slightly positive* (5), *positive* (6), and *very positive* (7)."

Items 8 to 14 were reverse-coded.

Source: Pratto et al. (1994).

if we can measure and plot the structure of values we can then understand how people perceive and respond to the challenges, economic, social and political, they confront. Psychologists Milton Rokeach (1973, 1979) and Shalom Schwartz (Schwartz and Bilsky, 1987) are two of many who have pursued this approach to personality.

A major challenge to these theories, all of which locate the source of current behavior in stable dispositions or traits is that offered by Albert Bandura (1986). Bandura argued that most human behavior was socially learned. If he was correct this changes the causal explanation considerably. Bandura held that it is the current and recent expectations, derived from the immediate context, that largely shaped behavior. Hence, it is one's peers and colleagues and not one's parents that influence how we act. Psychologist Bob Altemeyer (1988, 1994, 1996) based on an extensive research program, argued that authoritarianism was not based in parental child-rearing practices, but following the view of Bandura, was found in cues taken from the contemporary social context.

Though the focus on specific traits is voluminous, empirical work has continued the attempt to characterize the whole personality. The most popular of these now current is the "the big five" (John 1990; McCrae and John 1992). Considerable work has gone in to developing the measurement (Eid and Diener 1999; Gosling, Rentfrow, and Swann 2003; John 1990; McCrae and John 1992; Rammstedt and John 2007). Research on the big five by psychologists Raymond Cattell (1946), Paul Costa and Robert McCrae (1985) and earlier models, such as Eysenck's as well as critiques of the "big five" has also been published (Block 1995).

The big five traits are: *openness to experience, conscientiousness, extraversion, agreeableness,* and *neuroticism* (now also frequently relabeled as emotional stability). Though hard to image, a five dimensional space would have five axes. Each axis would, if isolated from the other four, display a normal distribution, much like that shown in

BOX 7.6 Naming traits

When a trait has only one name attached, such as neuroticism, authoritarianism, openness to experience, social dominance orientation to offer just a small sampling, you should immediately ask: What is the appropriate name at the other end of the trait dimension? And what is the reason for being concerned only with one end of the distribution?

The best explanation I can offer is that some scholars seem to be interested in what they presume is a pathology. There are other counterexamples—openness to experience is one such example. But whatever the reason I believe it is a bad practice to focus on why people are at one end of a distribution rather than to ask why such a distribution exists at all.

---

figure 7.1. At one end would be those low on that dimension, for instance conscientiousness, while at the other end would be those high on that quality. And, as with most such personality traits, the bulk of the population examined would have middling scores. The reason I used the analogy of space and axes is that each axis is taken as independent of all the other dimensions. Hence, where one finds a person on the conscientiousness trait is independent of where that person might fall on agreeableness trait, or dimension. The technical term for this is that each of big five traits is *orthogonal* to the other four traits.[4] In part because the traits, apart from openness to experience, seem to have little obvious relationship to politics other than the more politically relevant traits of authoritarianism, social dominance orientation, or social conformity, they have only recently begun to be used in the analysis of political behavior. Especially noteworthy in these recent explorations is that research teams are attempting to incorporate the influence of context, that is to say environmental and situational factors, rather than rely on a series of hypotheses linking each simple trait to some facet of political behavior (Gerber et al. 2010; Mondak et al. 2010).

This model and others have their roots in the development of factor analysis, which enables a large pool of statements to be reduced to some core common qualities or dimensions. Psychologist and developer of factor analysis, Louis Thurstone (1947, 1938, 1939; Thurstone and Chave, 1929) saw in factor analysis the principal means to go from outside, statements that people accept or reject as self-descriptive; to inside, the identification of underlying traits of personality.

In sum, the study of personality in psychology is more inclined to the study of general populations, rather than the study of elites who engage psychobiographers. Further, the focus is on securing empirical measures most often by batteries of items meant to identify and assign scores to one of the following.

1. A broad inventory of the core traits of personality (e.g., the big five) that seeks to offer a comprehensive map of the dominant features of human personality.
2. Some specific traits that are not meant to collectively define a comprehensive personality but rather one or more traits that are pertinent to some specific

---

4. In correlational terms that means the traits are not correlated. In spatial terms it means that the axes are at right angles to each other (scores on one dimension can vary without also varying on any other dimension; the traits are independent of each other).

domain of behaviors (e.g., authoritarianism as a trait that predicts the articulation of authoritarian attitudes and behaviors or ideology as a trait that predicts policy and candidate preferences).

3. Find a measure to identify which of those intrinsic values that subjects rely on and then sort through various contemporary choices for comparison (e.g., those who value liberty over equality will opt to reject expansion of government programs or the values of democratic norms of security as contrasting values that impel people to make choices on such issues as civil liberties).

There are four major limitations in these strategic approaches to personality. Attention to these limitations and finding ways around them, can generate a considerable number of new research programs. Briefly, let us then take up each of these in turn.

Four Limitations of Trait Conceptions of Personality

First, the boundary challenge: Any battery of items is best suited to identify only such underlying dimensions as are represented in the items themselves. A large pool of items meant to identify who is drawn to authoritarian beliefs or behaviors can only identify traits that fall within that domain. What is left out might be more revealing, or enable scholars to extend the consideration to other traits but absent items. There is no technique of analysis that can wave a flag to the researcher say, "you've left something out." The impact of conservative critiques of democracy along with the evident appeal of totalitarian regimes of the left, or fascist regimes of the right, have clearly shaped the interest of scholars so there are innumerable items used to assess the attraction of non-equalitarian dispositions. But there is a relative dearth of items, and hence "traits" that explore the positive distributions which enable and exemplify people drawn to equalitarian relationships or who view the opportunity for public engagement in democratic conflict as a positive rather than obnoxious experience.

Second, the consequences of using specific statistical methods: The near universal adoption of factor analytic statistical analyses imposes patterns on the data. Factor analysis of pools of items presumes and requires that all people have some apt value on any and all the items and the universal relevance of traits. This results in people being arrayed along a dimension that ranges from very (for example) introverted to very (in this example) extraverted. Dimensions, identified by factor analysis, are presumed to apply to all people of all cultures, past, present, and future. The statistical method, factor analysis, imposes the presumption that traits are relevant to all possible subjects, each and every person. The scales are used to assign everyone a disposition value on that given trait or property, perhaps low in authoritarianism, perhaps middling, or perhaps high. But everyone gets an assigned score or value. But what if some traits, or dimensions, have only local rather than universal applicability? What if some traits are applicable to only some not all in the population of human beings? Consider that there are other statistical techniques, such as individual differences scaling (Carroll and Chang 1970; Tucker and Messick 1963) or Q-Sort (Brown 1980), that consider the possibility that some underlying traits are local, applicable to some set of individuals. Had these statistical approaches become the presumptive standard we would likely have a quite different inventory of personality traits, and a quite different view of whether such individual differences as we observe across individuals, is a reflection not of different values on some common array of traits, but rather, different clusters of traits being differentially dominant in different groups of people.

Third, is the timing problem: Researchers have control over what to include but they have less choice when it comes to when to measure personality. If some traits lay dormant, traits that do not become active unless some contextual cue primes the trait, then the responses given by research subjects may be shaped by circumstances of the moment they are obtained. If there are circumstances that leave some traits dormant while other traits are rampant, then the responses given will reflect not the enduring trait disposition, but rather overemphasize active traits and misrepresent by underscore the trait values of the then dormant traits. For example, political psychologists Stanley Feldman and Karen Stenner (1997) argued that the relationship between authoritarian dispositions and the articulation of authoritarian attitudes, authoritarian perceptions and authoritarian behaviors is not one of a direct relationship, in which those with an authoritarian disposition articulated authoritarian attitudes and behaviors. Rather, authoritarian dispositions lay dormant until subjects experience some societal threat that awakens these dispositions to play an active role as long as the threat remains. Scholar Noelle-Neumann (1984) argued for a similar dynamic also focusing on the capacity of perceptions of threat to have dynamic effects on otherwise stable individuals, individuals who in normal times appear and act quite normally.

However, here I want to advance a more general concern not just with respect to threat and authoritarianism. The interactive character of the relationship between traits and their expression in behavior may be a general pattern. If so, then the challenge of collecting data maybe considerable as the responses of subjects in research programs may be quite variant, the variation depending on what the triggering features of the context may be. Identifying these possible triggers is essential in as much as interactions do not self-identify themselves in data, rather researchers have to anticipate the relevant traits, the relevant possible environmental triggers, formulate these as testable hypotheses, and then collect data from people across variant contextual circumstances to have data of sufficient breadth to test such formulations. This is a daunting challenge but I predict that it will be prove to be a quite fruitful agenda.

Fourth, is the accessibility problem: Freud was neither the first nor the only one who surmised that the true sources of behavior are not accessible to people, whether they are dim, or are more self-aware and introspective. If so, and the discovery of preconscious neural systems certainly gives evidence to support that conjecture, then subjective self-reports will have access only to the content of that which flows through the stream of consciousness. And, to extend that metaphor, the stream may wander around and be driven by features of the brain without revealing what the operations of the brain are that control those meanderings.

Further, the interest in temperament, at least those aspects revealed in such trait batteries, is itself dependent on the presumption that those are the cause of, at the end of the day, behavior. But, as we have already seen in chapters 4 through 6, many behaviors are not much influenced by consciousness. Hence, finding ways of conceptualizing, theorizing, and then conducting empirical research on such nonconscious aspects of personality is a very important challenge to be addressed by personality psychologists and political psychologists.

BOX 7.7 **Racism**

At one time, at least in the United States as elsewhere, racist attitudes were socially acceptable in many communities. As times and attitudes changed it became increasingly unacceptable to state blatantly racist statements disparaging the intelligence or other normative features of liminal groups. Social scientists were quick to discover that although the public expression of such attitudes had diminished, for at least some of the public the underlying sentiments of prejudice remained. This led to the development of survey items that probed the existence of these prejudicial sentiments with items that did not in and of themselves express prejudicial assertions. Though whether any particular array of items allows to properly infer the endorsement of racial disposition can and has been contentious, the effort is one attempt to identify nonconscious aspects of personality. Sears and Henry (2003) offered one perspective on the effort.

We can observe some of the same patterns in political science. For example, the focus on political elites is reflected in the work of political scientist Fred Greenstein (1969, 1987, 1992) and James David Barber (1985). And, the interest in pathology is similarly evident in political science. The interest in psychology in the biological (Cloninger 1987; Gray 1970; Zuckerman 1991) and genetic bases of personality, often explored with twin studies (Tellegen et al. 1988), also passed into political science (Alford, Funk, and Hibbing 2005; Fowler and Schreiber 2008).

In political science, personality is more common in some substantive areas of research than in others. In the domain of terrorism in general and with specific attention to the phenomenon of suicide bombing personality is an approach to explain who engages in terrorism. The journal *Political Psychology* published a special issue on the topic, edited by Jerrold Post, including contributions by many of the leading scholars in the field, among them Martha Crenshaw, Jerrold Post, Alex Mintz, and others (the issue is volume 30, no. 3, 2009, covering pages 331–507). There, in addition to personality, they reported on research on the role of group dynamics, social identity, and context, as influential on recruitment to terror groups. A small number of political scientists have attempted to treat personality as central feature of explanations of politics, among these are Paul Sniderman (1975) and Shawn Rosenberg (1988). Personality has played an important role in research on political tolerance. Political scientist John L. Sullivan along various colleagues (Marcus et al. 1995; Sullivan, Piereson, and Marcus, 1982) used personality traits to account for why some people are more and others less politically tolerant. And, more recent, John Jost and colleagues (Jost et al. 2003; Jost, Nosek, and Gosling 2008; Carney et al. 2008; Jost, Federico, and Napier 2009) argued that ideological convictions, which in turn drive political preferences, judgments, and behavior, were themselves animated by a core ideology like personality trait that he called conservatism. Work on values, drawing on Rokeach and Schwartz also has been picked up by political scientists.

So, continuity is evident across the two disciplines. But political science in the main has evinced little interest in personality as such. Instead, the research agenda in political science early on focused on just one personality trait, *partisan identification*. As theorized by the Michigan research team of social psychologists and political scientists who joined to conduct the research that culminated in *The American Voter* (Campbell et al.

1960), partisan identification is an affective identification with a political party. Thus, people acquire a self-identification as a Republican or as a Democrat, or as a member in the Green, Peace, or whatever party. Who and when people acquire such identifications, if and when they change to a new party identification, or abandon an earlier identification, has dominated the research agenda of political science research on public opinion and political behavior. And, it has done so because the research shows that partisan identification, however measured—and by that read political scientists Francis Neely (2007) and Barry Burden and Casey Klofstad (2005)—party identification as it has become to be called has been shown to be the most potent of proximate causes of many forms of political behavior (Bartels 2000; Erikson, MacKuen, and Stimson 2002). More recently *ideological identification* has augmented the list of dispositions to number now two. These two variables, partisan identification and ideological identification, as in other forms of social, that is, group identification (see political psychologist Leonie Huddy 2001, 2003) are thought to be broad orientations that are acquired early in life, which apply to broad classes of political phenomenon, such as political preferences, political judgments and political behavior.

However, rather than turn to the more distal personality dispositions to augment this short list of factors, political scientists are more likely to explore more proximate factors by generating survey statements that can be combined to form issue scales to determine how people orient themselves on major issues of the day such as abortion, gay rights, and other social issues, as well as minimum wages, health care, and other economic issues. One can see this difference by comparing the measures contained in another handbook of measures, on political attitudes, which was produced by the team of John P. Robinson, Philip Shaver, and Lawrence Wrightsman (1999) *Measures of Political Attitudes*. This volume contains the attitudes that have engaged political

---

BOX 7.8 Conservatism

As political scientists developed batteries of issues to assess whether people adopted the liberal or the conservative position on any given array of issues they found something that seems, on its face, to challenge the single dimensional definition of ideology that psychological conceptions of ideology apply. It turns out that people, who adopt consistently conservative positions on social issues such as gay marriage, gun control, or abortion, do not also consistently endorse the conservative position on economic issues. In a similar way, liberals often divide into two groups: social liberals and economic liberals. Using issues to measure ideological orientation most often generates a two dimensional solution, not a one dimensional solution. At this juncture, this seeming discrepant set of results has not been reconciled.

This is hardly the only example of a trait defined in psychology as one dimensional turns out, when examined by political scientists, to be multidimensional. When political scientists imported the concept of efficacy from psychology, hoping that this new concept would help explain such political behaviors as political participation, they found that efficacy had two distinct components, internal political efficacy—how confident a person felt, they could make a difference—and external political efficacy—how responsive political leaders and institutions were perceived to be. This pattern has gone both ways, concepts believed to be one dimensional in one discipline are found to be multidimensional in another.

scientists interested in measuring the enduring dispositions thought to explain what people do as political actors. There is remarkably little overlap in the content between these two handbooks and that reflects the different approaches: psychologists concerned about personality while political scientists focused on substantive attitudes, typically toward politically salient objects (e.g., groups, issue positions, candidates, political symbols, and so on).

In sum, most, though not all, political scientists rely on partisan and ideological convictions to do much of the work of personality, of defining the way in which established convictions rule over contemporary patterns of thought and action. This is in part a consequence of the political science discipline's long reliance on publicly funded omnibus survey research, principally but no longer exclusively, the American National Election Studies. These omnibus surveys are rich in measures of political attitudes and quite impoverished as to personality measures.

A new discipline, neuroscience, offers new theoretical frameworks and new methodologies for understanding personality. It offers a new literature in which early promising findings are evident. I turn to that next.

III. NEUROSCIENCE AND PERSONALITY

Unlike psychoanalysis and academic psychological approaches to personality, neuroscience affords an inside out approach. Rather than inferring personality from what people do or say, neuroscience can observe how the brain is organized and how it functions. Therefore, we can understand how brain functioning generates how people act and converse.

Neuroanatomy, the study of the organization of the brain, is a complex and rapidly changing field. The principal focus has been on mapping where on the surface of the brain, the mantle layers of cells that form the cortex, do various functions seemingly reside. And, considerable progress has been made in marking out speech, verbal comprehension, motor movements as external actions and body movements as internal representations, visual, and other sensory processing. Each of these has some brain geographic location in the typical brain. Moreover, areas within, rather than on the surface of the brain also have been shown to be critical for such matters as the regulation of recurring tasks such as breathing, regulation of body temperature, as well as regions responsible for various types of memory and regions that engage in affective processes. Further still, at the level of nerve cells, considerable progress has been made on how brain nerves are grown, how they function, and the role of the various neurotransmitters in executing communications between nerves. You may have heard of dopamine and serotonin, two of the many neurotransmitters. All of these aspects are important. A sound training in neuroanatomy is a foundation that many political psychologists

---

BOX 7.9 Sources

A rich array of sources on neuroscience is available, free, on iTunes U. There you can find lectures that can be downloaded covering neuroimaging, neuroanatomy, and the many topics from the more basic to the intermediate.

would do well to obtain. In addition to learning what has been discovered, such training would also introduce the various methodologies available, how to use them, and their various strengths and limitations. But it is important to do more than obtaining a limited education. This is a fast evolving field. You need to learn where and from whom one can continue one's education. Which journals to scan and which to read more closely? Which scholars, which established research centers of neuroscience are most engaged in projects that could contribute to political psychology, and which conferences for training or exposure to the latest research, and what other nexus of reporting, should be monitored?

However, to move from inside to out we need to develop theoretical accounts that move from the microfocused domain of brain function to the more macrofocused of social and political action. Happily some scholars have already forged a path. Neuroscientist and psychologist John Cacioppo has long been committed to expanding the reach of neuroscience into the social realm. He fostered the name "social neuroscience" to mark this outward trajectory. He and his colleagues published a valuable collection of articles, *Foundations of Social Neuroscience*, which both prepare for and advance this effort to foster the broader contribution (Cacioppo 2002; Cacioppo and Berntson 2004a, 2004b). Focusing on the ways in which neuroscience can advance our understanding of politics, political scientist Darren Schreiber (Fowler and Schreiber 2008) and psychologists Drew Westen (2007) and Alexander Todorov (Todorov and Bargh 2002; Todorov et al. 2005; Willis and Todorov 2006) also have made material contributions, as have others.

Neuroscience offers a biological account to provide a basis for psychological accounts of personality. Neuroscientist Jeffrey Gray (1970), along with the more extensive presentation provided by Zuckerman (1991), showed how the principal two dimensions of millennial interest, introversion–extraversion and neuroticism, can be understood as the product of concurrently functioning dynamic neural systems that address management of reward, punishment, and surveillance. As such these systems are central in the processing of goals, learned practices to manage both reward and punishment, appraisals of external environments, and the integration of all these memory and contemporary appraisals so that coherent, tactical, and strategic actions can be undertaken, augmented, abandoned, modified, and finally, utilized to our advantage. Baseline differences of how and to what these systems respond then form the basis for the individual differences that we observe across individuals but are revealed in across different contexts.

Before we turn to that topic, it is important to grasp the fuller significance of the core discoveries reviewed in chapter 4. The understandings of personality have been constrained to apply to what can consciously observe and subjectively experience. That is so because we experience ourselves, the world we live in, and the people we interact with through the lens of conscious awareness. Yet, the core insight of neuroscience is that this is but one of multiple lens into and outside of ourselves. Moreover, the temporal displacement of these various lens and the capacity of these different systems of perception, appraisal, and functional control are different from the other. And, more important, consciousness offers neither the first understanding nor the fullest understanding. Hence, the prior and conventional understandings of personality have been limited to that which is consciously observed and which conscious humans have been, prior to neuroscience, observing and contemplating.

It is here that the theoretical insights and methodological tools of neuroscience are of greatest value. It is precisely because conscious awareness, introspection, what seems "clear to us" gives us no direct access to the nonconscious systems that include systems of memory not accessible by conscious introspection, and specifically procedural memory, nor access to multiple preconscious systems of appraisal, the systems that control and articulate much of our behavior. The natural blindness, due to the inability of consciousness to report neural processes that take place before as well as outside of conscious awareness, has led to vast unknown realm of neural activities that only recently are being mapped.

This blindness has been shown to exclude critical features important to political neuroscience and political psychology. For example, none of the major omnibus personality inventories explore sensitivity to hypnotic suggestion. Yet, at the same time, one of the core agenda issues that have dominated much of social psychology is compliance. Solomon Asch (1951), Muzafer Sherif (1958, 1966), Stanley Milgram (1974), Leon Festinger (1957), Milton Rokeach (1973, 1979), Philip Zimbardo (2008), Herbert Kelman (1989), Hannah Arendt (1963), Erich Fromm (1965), among other scholars have sought to explain what they take to be a maladaptive inclination for people with too much willingness to defer to others, to set aside moral considerations, to engage in thoughtless nonautonomous subordination to the commands of others. But because hypnosis seems to be so much out of the normal realm and violates the presumption of conscious control—I do what I want, I think, I act—people frequently deny they can be hypnotized. But this mental state of heightened suggestibility does occur (Spiegel and Spiegel, 2004). And, further, there are significant differences across individuals, some of us are very good candidates for hypnotic suggestion while others of are quite resistant. I am not suggesting here that hypnosis offers an answer to the human inclination to be compliant to authority, to the expectations of others. Rather, I am using it as an example of how scholars have focused on that which is consciously visible when we know things about the world, about others, about ourselves obtained by preconscious representations, many of which do not become represented in conscious awareness.

The varieties of neural systems operated in the preconscious temporal domain are beginning to be understood. And, further, the role of preconscious appraisals in their control of preconscious processes as well as their role in shaping conscious awareness is also beginning to be understood. The research agenda depends on having revised conceptions of personality conceptions, as well as measures, that incorporate the preconscious. This is so that preconscious dynamics and the ubiquity of affective appraisals and their baseline conditions as personality can be integrated with dimensions of personality that are applicable to consciousness dimensions of personality. Only then can we then go onto a comprehensive account of personality.

We now know that there are nonconscious visible aspects of personality, some behaviors are never under conscious control, and some behaviors are under conscious control. Although even here there are non- and preconscious neural processes that are essential to conscious control, and we know that some behaviors are sometimes under preconscious and sometimes under conscious control. This dual capacity, to engage and rely on habituated (preconscious) control and to disengage so that we can also sometimes rely on deliberative (conscious) control gives us new theoretical purchase on the core issues for political psychology.

Our nature prepares us for two primary adaptive stances, and we shift from one to the other and back so that we can be:

1. Either consciously reliant on attentive consideration of the contemporary context to achieve our goals, or reliant on history, via thoughtless reliance on habituated patterns. This duality raises the research agenda of: how, when, and why does this take place. And,
2. Either sensitive to collective purpose, oriented to solidarity, to working with others either in equalitarian or systems of super- and subordination, or we can eschew the influence of others for reliance on individual autonomy. This duality raises the research agenda of: how, when, and why does this take place.

Typical discussions of personality look for a one-to-one correspondence, between trait and state to explain human behavior. Here the task of understanding temperament is made more complex because this fluid dynamic of shifting is a normal part of the human array of abilities and applies no less to the baseline differences that describe the individual differences only some of which we have observed in the study of personality. Sometimes personality, as conventionally understood, matters, but sometimes it matters in ways not grasped because a critical component of human personalities is the ability to have this response flexible: habit or deliberation and individual autonomy or collective solidarity. But when and why personality matters, in the sense of the continuity of behaviors assigned to traits, is itself likely to be a matter of personality differences. To pursue that complexity requires reconceptualizing consciousness, or the role "state" influences on behavior. That we take up in the final section of this as well as in the next chapter.

Before we turn to that task, we need to revisit the issue of pathology that has dominated the domain of personality studies, the claim that humans are by nature enduringly inclined to undertake a variety of pathological behaviors that undermine individual and collective rationality and that too often get expressed as harm to others.

IV. PATHOLOGY AND RESEARCH AGENDA OF PERSONALITY IN POLITICAL PSYCHOLOGY

As I previously discussed, two factors drove the agenda in political psychology toward the pathological. First, the ancient world understood bad behavior within the framework of illness. The equivalence of evil with illness has been long enduring. We can readily understand its attractiveness, apart from its insightfulness.

If we can persuade ourselves that we, and those we trust, are well, and those we distrust or dislike, are ill, then we create a psychic distance that is clear, that is normally and morally satisfying. It is a very satisfying assertion to make, "those people are crazy!" Or to declaim to local acknowledgment, "Who but a crazy person would believe that?" Satisfying but perhaps the pathology and illness metaphors blind us to other explanations.

The second factor was the emergence of public support, whether passive or active, for fascist and totalitarian regimes. That this emerged in the twentieth century among literate and, at least in comparison to other regions of the world, among the best educated, cultivated, populations many with experience in democratic regimes (Germany, Austria, Spain, Italy, all had democratic regimes prior to fascist regimes that emerged in the 1930s and 1940s). Progress was supposed to bring us to cosmopolitan rationality, first among the more developed nations, and then later, extend to other nations as they advanced the predicted curve of progressive development.

One common answer for what hindered progress was the role of malevolent leaders. So, interest in the pathology of leaders has been a natural topic. How do such malevolent leaders such as Hitler, Lenin, Stalin, Mao, Pol Pot, among many others, arise? But the role of the public in following malevolent leaders has not passed without considerable research interest. The public's inclination to be submissive and participant in evil against others has clearly been the dominant agenda especially after the cry of "never again" pronounced after the Holocaust, and the Nuremberg trials, soon turned hollow, with Idi Amin in Uganda, Pol Pot in Cambodia, the ethnic violence launched in Rwanda, the numerous ethnic cleansing wars of the Balkans seemingly easily generated by a former Communist leader looking and finding a nonideological basis for generating public support for his leadership. All suggested that this focus on extremes of violence was not only of historic interest but remains a continuing issue of continuing central importance (Staub 1989). I want to make clear that this focus on the pathological as an explanation of evil is a potent tendency but not a universal pattern. Will many succumb to the temptation to explain the abhorrent as pathology some do resist? For example, political psychologist Jerrold Post (2007) found that pathology was not a useful explanation, that recruitment of terrorists was explained by local circumstantial factors that generated a broad shared view of anger that defined a norm rather than an extreme.

However, I want to suggest a heretical claim that the focused concerns on ethnic, religious, and group on group antipathy and violence, and the dangers of malevolent leadership, however vital, have cast a form of posttraumatic syndrome (PSD) on the agenda of political psychology. We need to solve other issues and the two I am going to present are no less vital if we want to understand how diverse, extended, democratic, enduring, and beneficent regimes can be secured. Each of the following issues, research agendas, is deeply enmeshed with the role of temperament.

First, how and why do people find life in cosmopolitan and heterogeneous communities appealing? The role of xenophobia and ethnocentrism is one end of the continuum. It is clearly a vital topic well worth examining (Kinder and Kam 2010). But what is happening at the other? And, what moves people from one to the other end of the distribution? Too often, the enlightenment's presumption that progress was a natural trajectory, that it was inevitable that the good future foreseen by progressives would unfold, has been shown to be false. Humans are living in wider and more diverse societies. And, with world trade, and cheaper forms of travel, more and more people are coming into contact with others quite unlike them in all the ways people may differ. New technological tools, such as the Internet, make interactions at a distance and the flow of information across vast distances more frequent and cheaper. The contact hypothesis is both highly simple, straightforward, and normally satisfying. Once different people interact, they come to find those interactions safe and of increasing value. It would be very nice if that were robust and ubiquitously true. It is not. Grievances live on differences and seemingly can exist, and flourish, quite well in the modern world. So, what enables us to live in a wider world of increasing heterogeneity, and volatile and rapid change? We don't know as much as we need to about this path.

Second, unlike its early creation in ancient Greece, modern democratic regimes rest on representative practices (however much some forms of direct democracy linger largely on the fringes). Modern democratic institutions must coexist with other and largely nondemocratic systems of authority. Thus, our temperaments must enable us to navigate politics at a distance and navigate within and across different forms of authority, democratic and nondemocratic. As we know, Plato, Hobbes, Lippmann, and others, all concluded that publics were ill-suited to politics for a variety of reasons: for Plato (1974), a too eager engagement in the world as it is rather than in the philosophical realm of truth, for Hobbes (1968) and Lippmann (1922), the issue was largely defined as a matter of gullibility, and for Madison, the danger was that of selfishness which mitigated against reaching for the public good or establishing justice. Unless we can identify a political psychology that provides a pathway through and past these challenges, democracy will lack a sound psychological footing.

Here I present two more modern critiques each in its own way setting forth the claim that however much danger fascism and totalitarianism present, representative democracies themselves present challenges that stand in the way of reaching their ennobling expectations. Political historian Richard Hofstadter (1965), in a famous essay, entitled *The Paranoid Style in American Politics, and Other Essays,* presented an important argument. Paranoia should be an expected feature of democratic regimes in extended modern societies. Changing his exposition from history, what he saw happening in the 1950s in the United States, into scientific language, the argument would be similar to the following:

> Modern heterogeneous societies that have democratic regimes confront three challenges that together tend to elicit the paranoid style of politics. First, people are asked to make ruling decisions by selecting this or that leadership candidate, or this or that political party to rule in their stead. Second, people are given accounts of what is happening, accounts that often must be trusted because individuals cannot themselves confirm the merits of the claims advanced. Third, even when relying on scientific knowledge, bad things happen. People are given vaccines, but some become ill and die. People vote for parties and candidates that promise great futures, but those futures elude them. People vote for parties and candidates that promise they will be responsible but then those parties or elected leaders seem to be inattentive and incompetent when terrorists pull off their latest exploits. Cities are destroyed by natural events, storms, fires, or earthquakes, even when governments have the means to protect and limit such damage. But, in democracies, government is our government. Democratic governments act in our name and on our authority.

Hence, Hofstadter's insight can be taken as a variant of the fundamental attribution bias, the pattern of giving ourselves credit for successes while allocating blame to others or to external circumstances for our failures. We could put the onus for these failures on ourselves. But it is far more congenial to blame "them," the others who oppose us. Moreover, it is even more useful to cast those others not only as malevolent but hidden and mysterious, ever available for use when circumstances merit. When things go great, the latest financial splurge is still in the uptick phase, or when government initiatives work as well or better than proclaimed, great, we can congratulate ourselves on the wisdom of our convictions, and celebrate the ennobling superiority of democracy. But what do we do when the government fails, whom do we blame then? Hence, the search for targets, scapegoats, to blame when we don't want to take ownership of the failures that grate on us. And, because the space between our lives and the actions of government are great, it is easy to fill that space with paranoid accounts. Rather than finding that we are our own worst enemy, thank you Walt Kelly, the explanation resides in some mysterious cabal, secret forces that have some mysterious hold on the levers of power to explain our powerlessness, to explain why our virtues do not produce virtuous results.

Political psychologists, John Hibbing and Elizabeth Theiss-Morse in two masterful programs of research (Hibbing and Theiss-Morse 2002, 1995) add more to this internal challenge to democracy. Well worth reading, as is the entire recommended reading list at the end of this chapter, they demonstrated that many show a natural inclination to eschew engagement in the actual practices of democratic politics. Even to the extent of the quite limited demands of the extended representative variant. Most people are ill suited and hence uncomfortable with the confrontation that milder forms of conflict that democracy requires. Hence, the ideal form of political engagement, of at least American citizens, is the search for some enlightened leader who can be trusted to accomplish good things for America without demanding anything more of citizens, the search for the "white knight" reducing the involvement of citizens to a minimum of knowledge, protected against the challenges of knowing details, however messy they may be, against the task of knowing the logic of policy appraisal and science of policy analysis, against the task of continual, if not continuous, monitoring of governmental actions and societal conditions.

The enlightenment's presumption expected that progress would "naturally" free people from traditionalism so they could then easily adopt a more cosmopolitan perspective. Progress, it was expected, would shift people from reliance on faith to reliance on reason. And that in turn, would lead people away from a deeply rooted commitment to continuity so that they could instead embrace dynamic changes that would introduce a better world. Finally, progress would diminish reliance on authoritarian submission, a normal practice in many social and economic settings, so that people could embrace democratic equalitarianism. There is much we do not yet know about how to encourage these shifts, and whether by doing so, we can make modern democratic regimes more fully democratic.

V. POLITICAL PSYCHOLOGY AND PERSONALITY GOING FORWARD

There are three elements that should be considered in exploring the role of personality in political psychology. Two of the three have to do with conceptions that should guide the research agenda of the field. The last has to do with the substantive agenda: What questions do we need answers to?

I already touched on the first element, the likelihood that we will increasingly find that interactions between various aspects of personality and context are the general pattern of how temperament influences political behavior and judgment. This was the route that the issue of nature versus nurture took: What roles do nature—our genes—and nurture—the environment—have in shaping who we are. For a long time a steady battle unfolded. On one side the gene proponents argued for the influence of genetic influences. On the other side the environmental proponents argued for the dominance of environment. Part of the explanation for the seemingly intractable nature of the argument was that each side were proponents, and acting as such, rather than as scientists seeking to rely on evidence to test alternative explanations. Also, each side had political commitments. The environmentalists were attractive to those who found in the environmental argument evidence to corroborate their conviction that by changing the environment one could improve the human condition. And, to the extent that environmental influences were found to be weak or intractable due to a dominant influence of genes then efforts to achieve social progress by modifying environmental conditions would be seen as doomed to irrelevance and hence at least wasteful and at worst encouraging hopes that could not be secured. Hence, some traditionalists found comfort for their political convictions corroborated by the genes control personality corroborated their political convictions. And, some progressives found comfort in the effort to deny that genes controlled personality because by diminishing the role of genes the role of environment, a more tractable set of levers to drive progress, could be strengthened. After a too long period of entrenched combat, the interaction model has come to replace the genes *or* environment with a genes *and* environment conception. After all genes survive by enabling their hosts to master and thrive in environments and so environments must matter. Genes are evolution's way of ensuring that environments matter and their character taken into account. Our biology is what enables us; better understanding of how is one of the critical paths that lie before us (Fowler and Schreiber 2008). The neuroscientific examination of how the brain functions is but one vital aspect of that agenda, understanding how our genes, and our environments interact is yet another. Given that the research (Alford et al. 2005; Tellegen et al. 1988) suggests that many, if not all, traits have a heritability impact on the order of fifty percent, including among others ideological inclination, then the fuller view of personality would invite genes, and early, later, and contemporary environmental influences.

Still yet another factor we should consider is what evolution tells us. One insight often missed and largely ignored in political psychology is that humans have two eyes, one nose, one spine, two ears, and so on. Many of our features are not variables but constants (but for very rare and often tragic events, joined twins sharing one heart or other organs, for example). Our genes are designed to create humans with a set of stable features: two legs, knees, feet, ten fingers, and ten toes and so on. Yet, with respect to temperament, our features are meant to vary. Unlike the number of toes, in which there is little or no variation, with respect to personality traits all of these show considerable variation. Whether the broad temperamental dimensions such as introversion–extraversion; the narrower traits, such as need for cognition, social dominance orientation, or conformity to obedience; or the political attitudes that most engage political scientists, such as social liberalism or economic conservatism, all of these show variation.

That raises the likely explanation that we have this variation because variations in some way make human nature more rather than less suited to exploit the environments in which our species finds itself. But this has a further implication. That implication suggests we should question the pattern of conceiving traits as having a desirably adaptive end and an undesirable and maladaptive end, as for example, neuroticism has most often been defined (Nettle 2006). Obedience to authority and its partner conceptions, authoritarianism, social dominance orientation, ethnocentrism, and need for cognition, are other examples of traits so conceived. And, if one applies a standard progressive agenda that designation is clear. We should be autonomous moral creatures not supinely passive doing whatever some authority figure demands of us. We should accept the equalitarian ideal of democracy and reject the appeal of certain table norms of tradition, we should rely on careful thought and not quick intuitive hunches, we should demand democratic practices not just in political institutions but everywhere else, family, religious, economic, and social institutions. But if so, why does our nature provide for wide distributions of these qualities so that some of us are more inclined to one end of the distribution whereas others are at the other? Before I offer any specific answers we need to consider the environments we travel through and how we come to know it and take its considerable variety into account.

That takes us to the issue of "state" influences on judgment and behavior, which I discuss next. If we can achieve theories of temperament that integrate genetic, prior environmental, and contemporary appraisals, as well modeling the likely interactions we find throughout, we can then discuss the substantive issues that modern representative societies will unavoidable present. I mentioned that modern democratic societies require that we move among strangers, for the diversity and size of even modest sized nations are too large and modern economic patterns too dynamic to allow us to live in communities of stable homogeneity as the common pattern. How does temperament enable us to manage in modern heterogeneous contexts? I also mentioned that the dominant pattern of modern democratic societies will be politics at a distance. We cannot directly know the broad pattern of past consequences of policies even long in place. Rather we must rely on others to provide either trusted or evidence based reports for us to consider. Most of any even the most educated and modern democratic electorates will not have the training or orientation to do the work of policy analysis ourselves. And, many of us will comfortably rely on extant convictions to sort what has worked and what will work if tried. And, the same challenges arise in the choice among contending parties and contending leadership candidates. Who has proved the best to lead, who will serve us best if elected? How does temperament enable citizens to sort through this challenge? How can temperament prepare citizens to work in both the equalitarian contexts defined by equal status and conflict as the common practices and in the hierarchical contexts defined by unequal status and stable relationships that use systems of superordination and subordination to preclude conflict? If we vary in our inclinations and our temperament and democratic practices of thought, sensibility, judgment, and behavior appeals more to some and less to others, how does democracy sustain itself? How can it if it ill suits some while matching the temperamental needs of others? These are the challenges that await us if we are to better understand how temperament can help us understand the modern condition.

SUGGESTED READINGS

Recent Reviews of the Literature

Carver, Charles S., and Jennifer Connor-Smith. 2010. "Personality and Coping." *Annual Review of Psychology* 61:679–704.

Heine, Steven J., and Emma E. Buchtel. 2009. "Personality: The Universal and the Culturally Specific." *Annual Review of Psychology* 60:369–94.

McAdams, Dan P., and Bradley D. Olson. 2010. "Personality Development: Continuity and Change over the Life Course." *Annual Review of Psychology* 61:517–42.

Mischel, Walter, and Yuichi Shoda. 2008. "Toward a Unifying Theory of Personality: Integrating Dispositions and Processing Dynamics within the Cognitive– Affective Processing System." In *Handbook of Personality Psychology*, edited by Oliver P. John, R. W. Robins, and L. A. Pervin, 208–41 . New York: Guildford.

Recent Application of Dual Model to Personality
Mukherjee, Kanchan. 2010. "A Dual System Model of Preferences under Risk." *Psychological Research* 177:243–55.

Recent Neural Network Approaches to Personality
Read, Stephen J., Brian M. Monroe, Aaron L. Brownstein, Yu Yang, Gurveen Chopra, and Lynn C. Miller. 2010. "A Neural Network Model of the Structure and Dynamics of Human Personality." *Psychological Research* 17:61–92.

Straube, Thomas, Sandra Preissler, Judith Lipka, Johannes Hewig, Hans-Joachim Mentzel, and Wolfgang H.R. Miltner. 2010. "Neural Representation of Anxiety and Personality during Exposure to Anxiety-Provoking and Neutral Scenes from Scary Movies." *Human Brain Mapping* 31:36–47.

RESOURCES

A Fresh Air (NPR) Podcast presents Neuroscientist Michael Gazzaniga discussing split brain studies. A very lucid and accessible introduction to brain function and how neuroscientists go about conducting their research (the opening 20 minutes of the show). Audio only. Available on iTunes.

A Ted lecture by neuroscientist Jill Bolte Taylor on her experience in going through a brain stroke. Video presentation—available at: http://www.ted.com/talks/jill_bolte_taylor_s_powerful_stroke_of_insight.html

EXERCISES

One of the most studied aspects of political character is ideology. For many years, ideology has been linked to a spatial metaphor, conservatives are described as "right" and liberals described as "left" (this coming from the French assembly where parties sat after the overthrow of the king). That implies there is a single dimension for ideology. In a recent issue of the journal *Psychological Inquiry* there were a series of articles that attempted to show what psychology could contribute to our understanding of politics. Three of the articles discussed the topic of ideology. One team, led by social psychologist John Jost argued that one dimension was sufficient to depict the ideological convictions of people. Another team, John Duckitt and Chris Sibly argued that two dimensions were needed. And, in the third article, political psychologist Karen Stenner argued that three different variants of conservatism existed (though it is not clear that this implies there are three variants of liberalism). Read these three articles (Jost et al. 2009; Duckitt and Sibley 2009; Stenner 2009). The easy exercise would be to evaluate which of the three is the more persuasive. A more challenging exercise would be to design a study that would gather the necessary data to test these three different accounts so that an empirical conclusion could be reached.

It is possible that all three of these accounts are, to some extent, false. What would a better account look like? It is possible that one of these accounts offers a sound and valid account (which one?). It is possible that two of the three can be integrated into a sound and valid account (which two?). I do not know (so this is not a "trick" question).

Develop a new trait measure of personality. For example, you might consider developing questions to measure how "graceful" people perceive themselves to be (questions about clumsiness would be useful to identify the low graceful end of the expected distribution). See if you can devise eight or more questions. Then, if conditions permit, ask thirty or forty subjects (fellow students, friends) to take your questionnaire. See if you find all of your items "work" (your professor can show you how to enter their responses into a statistical program and conduct the appropriate analyses.

Select some trait that has been named by one end of the distribution (e.g., authoritarianism). Formulate a clear conceptual name for the other end of the dimension (and, no, nonauthoritarianism is not going to cut it). Select some recently published research articles that use the common trait name. Revise the article abstracts, replacing the name of the trait with your alternative and then change the description of the findings to comport to your shift in focus. Are the normative implications of the studies the same?

REFERENCES

Adorno, Theodor, Else Frenkel-Brunswick, Daniel Levinson, and R. Nevitt Sanford. 1950. *The Authoritarian Personality*. New York: Harper and Row.

Alford, John R., Carolyn L. Funk, and John R. Hibbing. 2005. "Are Political Orientations Genetically Transmitted?" *American Political Science Review* 99:153–67.

Altemeyer, Bob. 1988. *Enemies of Freedom: Understanding Right-Wing Authoritarianism*. San Francisco: Jossey-Bass.

———. 1994. "Reducing Prejudice in Right-Wing Authoritarians." In *The Psychology of Prejudice: The Ontario Symposium Volume 7*, edited by Mark P, 131–48. Zanna and James M. Olson. Hillsdale, NJ: Erlbaum.

———. 1996. *The Authoritarian Specter*. Cambridge, MA: Harvard University Press.

Arendt, Hannah. 1963. *Eichmann in Jerusalem: A Report on the Banality of Evil*. New York: Viking.

Asch, Solomon E. 1951. "Effects of Group Pressure upon the Modification and Distortion of Judgment." In *Groups, Leadership and Men: Research in Human Relations*, edited by Harold Guetzkow, 177–90. Pittsburgh, PA: Carnegie.

Bandura, Albert. 1986. *Social Foundations of Thought and Action*. Englewood Cliffs, NJ: Prentice-Hall.

Barber, James David. 1985. *The Presidential Character: Predicting Performance in the White House*. Englewood Cliffs, NJ: Prentice-Hall.

Bartels, Larry M. 2000. "Partisanship and Voting Behavior, 1952–1996." *American Journal of Political Science* 44:35–50.

Becker, Ernest. 1973. *The Denial of Death*. New York: Free Press.

Block, Jack. 1995. "A Contrarian View of the Five-Factor Approach to Personality Description." *Psychological Bulletin* 117:187–215.

Brown, Steven R. 1980. *Political Subjectivity*. New Haven, CT: Yale University Press.

Browning, Christopher R. 1992. *Ordinary Men: Reserve Police Battalion 101 and the Final Solution in Poland*. New York: HarperCollins.

Burden, Barry C., and Casey A. Klofstad. 2005. "Affect and Cognition in Party Identification." *Political Psychology* 26:869–86.

Cacioppo, John T. 2002. *Foundations in Social Neuroscience*. Cambridge, MA: MIT Press.

Cacioppo, John T, and Gary G. Berntson. 2004a. *Essays in Social Neuroscience*. Cambridge, Mass: MIT Press.

———. 2004b. *Social Neuroscience: Key Readings*. New York: Ohio State University Psychology Press.

Campbell, Angus, Philip E. Converse, Warren E. Miller, and Donald E. Stokes. 1960. *The American Voter*. New York: Wiley.

Carney, Dana R., John T. Jost, Samuel D. Gosling, and Jeff Potter. 2008. "The Secret Lives of Liberals and Conservatives: Personality Profiles, Interaction Styles, and the Things They Leave Behind." *Political Psychology* 29:807–40.

Carroll, J. Douglas, and Jih-Jie Chang. 1970. "Analysis of Individual Differences in Multidimensional Scaling Via an N-Way Generalization of "Eckart-Young" Decomposition." *Psychometrika* 35:283–318.

Cattell, Raymond B. 1946. *The Description and Measurement of Personality*. New York: Harcourt Brace Jovanovich.

Cloninger, C. Robert. 1987. "A Systematic Method for Clinical Description and Classification of Personality Variants." *Archives of General Psychiatry* 44:573–88.

Conrad, Joseph. 2007. *The Secret Agent : A Simple Tale*. New York: New American Library.

Costa, Paul T., Jr., and Robert R. McCrae. 1985. *The NEO Personality Inventory Manual: Form S and Form R*. Odessa, FL: Psychological Assessment Resources.

Crane, Stephen. 2010. *The Red Badge of Courage*. New York: Library of America.

Duckitt, John, and Chris G. Sibley. 2009. "A Dual-Process Motivational Model of Ideology, Politics, and Prejudice." *Psychological Inquiry* 20:98–109.

Eid, Michael, and Ed Diener. 1999. "Intraindividual Variability in Affect: Reliability, Validity, and Personality Correlates." *Journal of Personality and Social Psychology* 76:662–76.

Erikson, Erik H. 1958. *Young Man Luther: A Study in Psychoanalysis and History*. New York: Norton.

———. 1969. *Gandhi's Truth: On the Origins of Militant Nonviolence*. New York: Norton.

———. 1982. *The Life Cycle Completed: A Review*. New York: Norton.

Erikson, Robert S., Michael MacKuen, and James A. Stimson. 2002. *The Macro Polity*. New York: Cambridge University Press.

Eysenck, Hans. 1967. *The Biological Basis of Personality*. Springfield, IL: Thomas.

———. 1970. "A Dimensional System of Psychodiagnostics." In *New Approaches to Personality Classification*, edited by A. R. Mahrer, 169–208. New York: Columbia University Press.

Eysenck, Hans J., and Michael W. Eysenck. 1985. *Personality and Individual Differences: A Natural Science Approach*. New York: Plenum.

Eysenck, Hans J., and S. B. G. Eysenck. 1969. *Personality Structure and Measurement*. London: Routledge and Kegan Paul.

Feldman, Stanley, and Karen Stenner. 1997. "Perceived Threat and Authoritarianism." *Political Psychology* 18:741–70.

Festinger, Leon. 1957. *A Theory of Cognitive Dissonance*. Stanford, CA: Stanford University Press.

Fowler, James H., and Darren Schreiber. 2008. "Biology, Politics, and the Emerging Science of Human Nature." *Science* 322:912–14.

Fromm, Erich. 1965. *Escape From Freedom*. New York: Avon Publishers.

George, Alexander L., and Juliette L. George. 1998. *Presidential Personality and Performance.* Boulder, CO: Westview.

Gerber, Alan S., Gregrory A. Huber, David Doherty, Conor M. Dowling, and Shang E. Ha. 2010. "Personality and Political Attitudes: Relationships across Issue Domains and Political Contexts." *American Political Science Review* 104:111–33.

Gosling, Samuel D., Peter J. Rentfrow, and William B. Swann, Jr. 2003. "A Very Brief Measure of the Big-Five Personality Domains." *Journal of Research in Personality* 37:504–28.

Gray, Jeffrey. 1970. "The Psychophysiological Basis of Introversion-Extroversion." *Behaviour Research and Therapy* 8:249–66.

Greenstein, Fred I. 1969. "The Benevolent Leader: Children's Images of Political Authority." *American Political Science Review* 54:934–43.

———. 1987. *Personality and Politics: Problems of Evidence, Inference and Conceptualization.* Princeton, NJ: Princeton University Press.

———. 1992. "Can Personality and Politics be Studied Systematically?" *Political Psychology* 13:105–28.

Heider, Fritz. 1958. *The Psychology of Interpersonal Relations.* New York: Wiley.

Hibbing, John R., and Elizabeth Theiss-Morse. 1995. *Congress as Public Enemy: Public Attitudes toward American Political Institutions.* New York: Cambridge University Press.

———. 2002. *Stealth Democracy: Americans' Beliefs about How Government Should Work.* Cambridge: Cambridge University Press.

Hobbes, Thomas. 1968. *Leviathan.* London: Penguin.

Hofstadter, Richard. 1965. *The Paranoid Style in American Politics, and Other* Essays. New York: Knopf.

Huddy, Leonie. 2001. "From Social to Political Identity: A Critical Examination of Social Identity Theory." *Political Psychology* 22:127–56.

———. 2003. "Group Identity and Political Cohesion." In *Oxford Handbook of Political Psychology,* edited by David O. Sears, Leonie Huddy, and Robert Jervis, 511–58. New York: Oxford University Press.

John, Oliver P. 1990. "The "Big Five" Factor Taxonomy: Dimensions of Personality in the Natural Language and in Questionnaires." In *Handbook of Personality Theory and Research,* edited by Lawrence A. Pervin, 66–100. New York: Guilford.

Jost, John T., Christopher M. Federico, and Jaime L. Napier. 2009. "Political Ideology: Its Structure, Functions, and Elective Affinities." *Annual Review of Psychology* 60:307–37.

Jost, John T., Jack Glaser, Arie W. Kruglanski, and Frank J. Sulloway. 2003. "Political Conservatism as Motivated Social Cognition." *Psychological Bulletin* 129:339–75.

Jost, John T., Margarita Krochik, Danielle Gaucher, and Erin P. Hennes. 2009. "Can a Psychological Theory of Ideological Differences Explain Contextual Variability in the Contents of Political Attitudes?" *Psychological Inquiry* 20:183–88.

Jost, John T., Brian A. Nosek, and Samuel D. Gosling. 2008. "Ideology: Its Resurgence in Social, Personality, and Political Psychology." *Perspectives on Psychological Science* 3:126–36.

Kelman, Herbert, and V. Lee Hamilton. 1989. *Crimes of Obedience.* New Haven: Yale University Press.

Kinder, Donald R., and Cindy D. Kam. 2010. *Us Against Them: Ethnocentric Foundations of American Opinion.* Chicago: University of Chicago Press.

Kohlberg, Lawrence. 1984. *The Psychology of Moral Development: The Nature and Validity of Moral Stages.* San Francisco: Harper & Row.

Landau, Mark J., Sheldon Solomon, Jeff Greenberg, Florette Cohen, Tom Pyszczynski, Jamie Arndt et al. 2004. "Deliver Us from Evil: The Effects of Mortality Salience and Reminders of 9/11 on Support for President George W. Bush." *Personality And Social Psychology Bulletin* 30:1136–50.

Langer, Walter. 1972. *The Mind of Adolf Hitler*. New York: Basic Books.

Lasswell, Harold D. 1930. *Psychopathology and Politics*. Chicago: University of Chicago Press.

———. 1948. *Power and Personality*. New York: Norton.

LeVine, Robert A., and Donald T. Campbell. 1972. *Ethnocentrism: Theories of Conflict, Ethnic Attitudes and Group Behavior*. New York: Wiley.

Lippmann, Walter. 1922. *Public Opinion*. New York: Macmillan.

Marcus, George E., John L. Sullivan, Elizabeth Theiss-Morse, and Sandra Wood. 1995. *With Malice Toward Some: How People Make Civil Liberties Judgments*. New York: Cambridge University Press.

Maslow, Abraham H. 1954. *Motivation and Personality*. New York: Harper.

McCrae, Robert R., and O. P. John. 1992. "An Introduction to the Five-Factor Model and Its Applications." *Journal of Personality* 60:175–215.

Milgram, Stanley. 1974. *Obedience to Authority*. New York: Harper and Row.

Mondak, Jeffery J., Matthew V. Hibbing, Damarys Canache, Mitchell A. Seligson, and Mary R. Anderson. 2010. "Personality and Civic Engagement: An Integrative Framework for the Study of Trait Effects on Political Behavior." *American Political Science Review* 104:85–110.

Myers, Isabel Briggs., Mary H. McCaulley, and Robert. Most. 1985. *Manual, a Guide to the Development and Use of the Myers-Briggs Type Indicator*. Palo Alto, CA.: Consulting Psychologists Press.

Neely, Francis. 2007. "Party Identification in Emotional and Political Context: A Replication." *Political Psychology* 28:667–88.

Nettle, Daniel. 2006. "The Evolution of Personality Variation in Humans and Other Animals." *American Psychologist* 61:622–31.

Noelle-Neumann, Elisabeth. 1984. *The Spiral of Silence*. Chicago: University of Chicago Press.

Piaget, Jean. 1930. *The Child's Conception of Physical Causality*. London: Harcourt, Brace.

———. 1954. *The Child's Construction of Reality*. London: Routledge & Kegan Paul.

———. 1965. *The Moral Judgment of the Child*. New York: Free Press.

———. 1970. *The Child's Conception of Movement and Speed*. New York: Ballantine.

Plato. 1974. *The Republic*. New York: Penguin.

Post, Jerrold M. 1993. "Current Concepts of the Narcissistic Personality: Implications for Political Psychology." *Political Psychology* 14:99–121.

———. 2007. *The Mind of the Terrorist: The Psychology of Terrorism From the IRA to Al Qaeda*. New York: Palgrave Macmillan.

Post, Jerrold M, and Alexander L George. 2004. *Leaders and Their Followers in a Dangerous World: The Psychology of Political Behavior*. Ithaca, NY: Cornell University Press.

Pratto, Felicia, Jim Sidanius, Lisa M. Stallworth, and Bertram F. Malle. 1994. "Social Dominance Orientation: A Personality Variable Predicting Social and Political Attitudes." *Journal of Personality and Social Psychology* 67:741–63.

Rammstedt, Beatrice, and Oliver P. John. 2007. "Measuring Personality in One Minute or Less: A 10-Item Short Version of the Big Five Inventory in English and German." *Journal of Research in Personality* 41:203–12.

Robinson, John P., Phillip R. Shaver, and Lawrence S. Wrightsman. 1999. *Measures of Political Attitudes*. San Diego, CA: Academic.

Robinson, John P., Phillip R. Shaver, Lawrence S. Wrightsman, and Frank M. Andrews. 1991. *Measures of Personality and Social Psychological Attitudes*. San Diego, CA: Academic.

Rokeach, Milton. 1973. *The Nature of Human Values*. New York: Free Press.

———. 1979. *Understanding Human Values: Individual and Societal*. New York: Free Press.

Rosenberg, Shawn W. 1988. "The Structure of Political Thinking." *American Journal of Political Science* 32:539–66.

Schwartz, Shalom H., and Wolfgang Bilsky. 1987. "Toward a Universal Psychological Structure of Human Values." *Journal of Personality and Social Psychology* 55:550–62.

Sears, David O., and P. J. Henry. 2003. "The Origins of Symbolic Racism". *Journal of Personality and Social Psychology* 85:259–75.

Sherif, Muzafer. 1958. "Group Influences upon the Formation of Norms and Attitudes." In *Readings in Social Psychology*, edited by Eleanor Maccoby, T. M. Newcomb, and E. L. Hartley, 219–32. New York: Holt.

———. 1966. *Group Conflict and Competition*. London: Routledge & Kegan Paul.

Sniderman, Paul M. 1975. *Personality and Democratic Politics*. Berkeley: University of California Press.

Spezio, Michael L., Antonio Rangel, Ramon Michael Alvarez, John P. O'Doherty, Kyle Mattes, Alexander Todorov et al. 2008. "A Neural Basis for the Effect of Candidate Appearance on Election Outcomes." *Social and Cognitive Affective Neuroscience* 3:344–52.

Spiegel, Herbert, and David Spiegel. 2004. *Trance and Treatment: Clinical Uses of Hypnosis*. Washington, DC: American Psychiatric Press.

Staub, Ervin. 1989. *The Roots of Evil: The Origins of Genocide and Other Group Violence*. New York: Cambridge University Press.

Stenner, Karen. 2009. "Three Kinds of 'Conservatism'." *Psychological Inquiry* 20:142–59.

Sullivan, John L., James Pierson, and George E. Marcus. 1982. *Political Tolerance and American Democracy*. Chicago: University of Chicago Press.

Tellegen, Auke, David T. Lykken, Thomas J. Bouchard, Kimerly J. Wilcox, Nancy L. Segal, and Stephen Rich. 1988. "Personality Similarity of Twins Reared Apart and Together." *Journal of Personality and Social Psychology* 54:1031–39.

Thurstone, Louis Leon. 1938. *Primary Mental Abilities*. Chicago: University of Chicago Press.

———. 1939. *The Reliability and Validity of Tests: Derivation and Interpretation of Fundamental Formulae Concerned With Reliability and Validity of Tests and Illustrative Problems*. Ann Arbor, MI: Edwards.

———. 1947. *Multiple-Factor Analysis: A Development and Expansion of the Vectors of the Mind*. Chicago: University of Chicago Press.

Thurstone, Louis Leon, and Ernest John Chave. 1929. *The Measurement of Attitude: A Psychophysical Method and Some Experiments with a Scale for Measuring Attitude toward the Church*. Chicago: University of Chicago Press.

Todorov, Alexander, and John A. Bargh. 2002. "Automatic Sources of Aggression." *Aggression and Violent Behavior* 7:53–68.

Todorov, Alexander, Anesu N. Mandisodza, Amir Goren, and Crystal C. Hall. 2005. "Inferences of Competence From Faces Predict Election Outcomes." *Science* 308:1623–26.

Tucker, Ledyard R., and Samuel Messick. 1963. "An Individual Differences Model for Multidimensional Scaling." *Psychometrika* 28:333–67.

Volkan, Vamik D. 1988. *The Need to Have Enemies and Allies*. Northvale, NJ: Aronson.

Volkan, Vamik D., and Norman Itkowitz. 1984. *The Immortal Ataturk: A Psychobiography*. Chicago: University of Chicago Press.

Volkan, Vamik D., Norman Itkowitz, and Andrew W. Dod. 1997. *Richard Nixon: A Psychobiography*. New York: Cambridge University Press.

Westen, Drew. 2007. *The Political Brain: The Role of Emotion in Deciding the Fate of the Nation*. New York: Public Affairs.

Willis, Janine, and Alexander Todorov. 2006. "First Impressions: Making Up Your Mind after a 100-ms Exposure to a Face." *Psychological Science* 17:592–98.

Zimbardo, Philip G. 2008. *The Lucifer Effect: Understanding How Good People Turn Evil*. New York: Random House Trade Paperbacks.

Zuckerman, Marvin. 1991. *Psychobiology of Personality*. Cambridge: Cambridge University Press.

CHAPTER 8

Political Psychology and Democratic Politics

Democratic politics allows most, if not all, adults—those designated as citizens—to shape collective decisions that govern the locale, district, or nation.[1] Citizens ought to do so by private reflection, collective deliberation, and rational consideration of the public good, or at least that is the ideal. Citizens can do so by turning to established traditions for guidance on such vital issues social, economic, and political. But it is often the case that there are different strands of tradition and, no doubt, some of these traditions will clash. Conflict often ensues over which tradition should be decisive when different strains of tradition demand that a public resolve conflicting sensibilities.

Collective discussions may lead instead to rejection of further reliance on traditions, however they are understood. The intent of democratic politics is to enable the broader public to consider, select, and then to empower those choices as authoritative for the community at large. Other regimes turn to religious figures or some designated individual (monarch), or some group (a class as in aristocracy or technocrats) and thereby seal off the public into at best the role of respectful and submissive audience; or, so nondemocratic regimes hope.

In this chapter I have one primary purpose. All politics deals with collective choices, choices that are variants of the following: What should the community do at this juncture? But only democratic politics provide for the great expanse of citizens to participate in that process, directly through town meetings or referenda or indirectly through elections and other representative institutions. But, as we have seen the public in democratic regimes often do not display the expected skills that scholars have long

---

1. Others not designated citizens can also impact collective decisions even those with little or no legal status. Prison rights for example, or, for another, in France demonstrations by personnes sans papiers.

believed were essential to sustain and legitimize democratic regimes.[2] This seems to lead to the conclusion—long advanced by partisans of aristocratic rule (Herzog 1998)—that citizens lack the wherewithal to participate in collective choices. My purpose in this chapter is to show that neuroscience offers more than just an added contributor to political psychology, joining with the other social sciences that have long contributed. Neuroscience offers alternative ways of understanding human nature that give us a more fruitful way of understanding the way in which democratic politics and human nature engage.

In chapter 7 I examined how humans rely on the past to guide their conduct in the present. The lessons of the past are encoded in genes, expressed in personality, and also encoded in habits acquired through experiences after birth. Collectively, these can be labeled "tradition." Many of these have to do with identifying regularized patterns of superordination and subordination, that is to say dominance and submission patterns. The most familiar of these have been: age, older over younger; gender, male over female; caste based on either religious, ethnic, language, or other range of social identities that place people within groups and places groups within a matrix of hierarchy. Modernity adds yet other hierarchies, notably those based on economic and social relationships.

Democratic politics adds a quite different array of authority patterns. Equality establishes a counterpoint to the embedded and widespread patterns of hierarchy. As citizens we celebrate our equal station as citizens. But, beyond that democracy expects more than that citizens respect their own authority, rather accepting the authority of others. But, in the consideration of citizenship capacities, much has been made of the supposed mismatch between actual patterns of democratic citizenships and those ideals held up by democracy's partisans. Instead of sustained attention to matters political empirical research finds torpor (Converse 1964; Ladd 1978; Doppelt and Shearer 1999; Thompson 1970). Instead of a public demonstrating political knowledge, empirical research finds ignorance (Caplan 2007; Erikson 2007; Delli Carpini and Keeter 1996). Instead of critical examination of policy and leadership choices, empirical research finds gullibility (Converse 2006; Frank 2004). Instead of rigorous investigation of policy and leadership choices, comfortable reliance on extant convictions (Campbell et al. 1960; Popkin 1991); and instead asserting democratic authority, too great a willingness to defer (Hibbing and Theiss-Morse 2002; Mansbridge 1980).

Of course democracy's defenders responded with measured enthusiasm (Fishkin 1991, 2009; Popkin 1991; Sullivan, Snyder, and Sullivan 2007). But the terms of this debate are based on presumptions of human knowledge, rationality, and action ancient in their conception. Neuroscience offers new understandings of these concepts, and these new understandings lead to research that fundamentally alters the debates about how democracy, citizens, and leaders function. Here I seek to show how much of a transformation of this debate neuroscientific political psychology has already achieved.

It has long been known that personality dispositions and habits serve as stable guides that enable us to again secure success in our various ventures. But, this benefit has promise only as long as current circumstances are quite similar to prior experiences.

2. There is, of course, a vigorous dissent to the conventional wisdom. Pateman (1970); Barber (1984); Gamson (1992); Key and Cummings (1966); and Schattschneider (1960) are among those dissenting from the dystopian description that has been for over sixty years conventional wisdom.

And, our species, as all living creatures, is born into a changing world that guarantees that we are likely to confront at least some experiences that are *not* comfortable continuations of past experience.

We can with certainty expect that the physical environments humans inhabit will change in ways not previously experienced. New species may appear. Some might prove beneficial, others dangerous. Old species may move away or become extinct. Humans are a mobile species and as we move around, most often in groups, from one place to another we will come into contact with new environments, new groups, possibly cooperating or possibly antagonistic. New technologies emerge, the result of science and imagination. These often alter the way humans live, providing for new possibilities both beneficial and malevolent in their consequences. Relying solely on the past, presuming the future holds no surprises, would leave our species vulnerable to novelties of all sorts. But novelty may challenge in a second way. If we are intractable in our reliance on past lessons, we may not be able to take advantage of new strategies that could improve our prospects.

Conveniently humans are equipped to do more than just rely on the past. Humans can modify or even set aside old lessons. Humans can acquire new lessons. In this chapter I lay out what we now know about when, how, and why reliance on the tried and true is set aside for new possibilities. This adaptability raises two questions. First, how does the brain adjudicate the ability to rely on prior knowledge and with its capacity put this knowledge aside for newly acquired knowledge? And, second, how does the brain adjudicate its ability to rely on swift "automatic" neural mechanisms and its ability to rely on explicit thoughtful deliberative processes to guide action? And, how does this all matter to democratic politics?

I. HOW DO WE KNOW?

We live within the subject realm of conscious awareness. Indeed the very phrase, conscious awareness is tautological. How can we be aware without consciousness? Here I want to emphasize the nonconscious mechanisms of awareness. I do so because we have very limited conscious access to our procedural memories, to the early and fast preconscious controls of most of the repertoire of learned behaviors. Yet, because we live within our subjective consciousness, reliant on the apparent immediacy that consciousness presents, it is hardly surprising that common sense and scholarship begins with the assumption of conscious awareness and conscious executive control of what we do.

Although consciousness offers us its version of the external world, a vivid and engaging representation of reality; it is only one of multiple means of knowing that humans have at their disposal. It is also one of two routes by which humans understand themselves, what they can do as well as how to do it. Moreover, although consciousness appears to provide a comprehensive, objective, and direct account of the external world, it actually is subject to many distortions as we have seen in chapters 4 and 5.

Consciousness, as numerous studies have shown and as Hobbes (1968) foresaw, enables us to place ourselves in many imaginative worlds, various admixtures of reality and mental construction. In actually, the sensible world of consciousness is not as tightly linked to reality as we think. Conscious awareness is a constructed world. A number of factors shape that construction. For example, our brains have to take the various sensory streams and make sense of them as distinctive streams but also to merge them into the single representation that is consciousness. This is an active process and requires that the brain use its foreknowledge to aid in that construction. Our individual experiences, as well as the specific culture we inhabit, contribute to the formation of that reality.

The basics of second path of perception, appraisal, and behavior, were introduced in chapters 4 and 5. To have a political psychology that has a full grasp of human nature, scholars need to grasp the significance of these two routes to knowing, generate the two domains of knowledge that the brain affords us. Although we have ready conscious access to just one, the other is far more important. But the issue is not which is more, or less important, but how we rely on both. Hitherto, political psychologists have largely explored the path of conscious awareness with modest and occasional delving into the, misnamed, subconscious. A comprehensive political psychology must explore both.

Let us begin with an analogy. In the early stages of World War II, naval vessels, warships, had sailors perched on high acting as lookouts, scanning the horizon for ships, for planes, and for changes on weather as best they could. Often with the aid of binoculars, they could see, daylight permitting, the sky and sea, birds and clouds, their shapes and colors. If objects appeared, lookouts would be able to see them, dimly at first, but with greater clarity as the object approached. They might eventually be able to see the flag of the vessel and so identify the ship as one of ours, or identify it as that of the enemy, or as unknown. Lookouts were given silhouettes of naval ships, both friend and foe, to help them identify what they could often but dimly see by shape alone. By practicing on these outlines of warships friendly and not, they hoped to be able to swiftly identify the class of vessel (destroyer, cruiser, PT boat; or if a plane, scout, fighter, torpedo bomber) and the nationality as well. They could discern, again light permitting, direction (heading toward or away, left or right). They could note the approximate altitude, the degrees above the horizon of a plane. They could make an approximate assessment of speed. Much depended on the alertness of the lookouts. Falling asleep while on duty, on watch, was one of the most serious offenses on a warship during war. The safety of the ship, all its crew, and their mission, hung in the balance.

If the lookout identified the object, ship or plane, as the enemy, the captain would be able to thwart the threat by taking evasive action, often with smoke machines to mask movement and to offer a place to hide, or by directing the ship's gunners to fire. The lookout's information gave the gunners the general location and approximate distance to search for the approaching enemy. Guns—aimed and fired by humans on a moving naval ship—confronted a great challenge. The task of aiming their guns and deciding when to fire them whether under attack is very difficult. For the shells of the guns fly from one moving platform toward other fast moving objects (naval warships could easily move at twenty knots an hour or more, warplanes at hundreds of miles an hour). The trajectory of the shells is affected by the movements of the ship, as it moved forward or backward at speed and as it was moved up, down, and side to side, by the sea, the shells' trajectories were also be impacted by gravity, as well as by the wind and other atmospheric elements. The time to reach the enemy and the distance that the enemy ship or warplane would move in the interval from firing to arrival all had to be taken into account. As a consequence the barrels of the guns had to be pointed not at the enemy, nor at the anticipated future position of the enemy, but at point where the arcing trajectory of the fired shells would, after their completed travel, likely strike their targets. The gunners had to rely on their judgment of wind, speed, and trajectory (their own as well as that of the enemy ship or plane). They hoped to use their training to save their ship and destroy their attackers. Sometimes they succeeded but more often than not they failed.

During World War II radar was quickly deployed both on land to warn of attacking bombers but also on naval warships. Developed most actively by the British, radar (radio detection and ranging), used transmitters to send out radio frequencies that would bounce off objects and then back to receivers. The time and angles of the radio waves enabled the objects that were struck to be identified. Moreover, radar also enabled the distance and speed of the objects to be precisely calculated. Early on in World War II, US warships operating in the Pacific, were equipped with the new radar technology. And, at the outset, warships made use of both lookouts and this new technology, radar, with radar operators sitting in small rooms near to the bridge and to the captain.

The ship's radar operator sat in front of a cathode tube screen. The green colored screen would show blips moving about, each blip representing a distinct object on the sea or in the sky. The green screen would in also display, next to each blip, numbers that represented the calculated speed, distance, and direction of each blip. The blips on the screens looked nothing like the objects they represented. They looked like blips. The blips did not show the colors of the objects, nor the clouds, or birds, or many other aspects of the environment around the ships, such as the sea. Radar also did not show whether the planes were fighters or bombers, whether the ships were destroyers, cruisers, battleships, or aircraft carriers. Radar gives a very impoverished image of the world around the ship. On that score lookouts are far superior.

However, compared to the information provided by the lookout, radar gives far more accurate readings of the speed, direction, and location of the objects they "saw." Moreover, of considerable benefit, radar could also "see" much farther than a human lookout even in the best of light and clear skies. And, radar can "see" in bad weather and can "see" without visible light. Radar, when linked to computers, can also calculate more exact assessments of speed and altitude. More important, because radar has a superior range, a ship with radar would alert the captain far earlier that there were possible threats even in fair weather but especially foul weather.

Not long after, naval radar was not only giving information on ships and planes in the area around the ship, it was also given the task of directing and firing the ship's guns. Linking radar to the ship's armament allowed the superior precision of radar to be programmed by computers to take into account the known characteristics of the guns, the effect of gravity, the current wind, and other pertinent information to aim and fire the shells with greater accuracy and efficiency. Because human gunners, on moving ships, had limited ability to properly calculate where to aim and when to fire, the general practice was to fire a hail of shells to generate a wall of shells in the hope that the approaching plane or ship would be hit. As radar directed guns would fire shells with better aim the guns could manage with fewer firings and yet cause greater damage on their targets. Given the choice between two ways of knowing—conscious observation provided by lookouts and that offered by radar—radar had a compelling array of advantages even if radar could not tell the color of the flag on the approaching vessel or observe the national symbols on the wings or flank of the approaching fighter.[3]

The relationship of preconscious perception and appraisal to conscious awareness is much like that between radar and human lookouts. Conscious vision is a remarkable faculty, but conscious awareness has its limitations. It is slow because it takes the brain five-hundred milliseconds to integrate the various components of vision, among them object identification and color imputation (you remember that all the brain receives are electrical signals that come from rod and cone cells that send these signals down the optic nerves to the brain). The brain also must integrate vision with the other sensory modalities so we can locate sounds, touches, tastes, and smells in the visual field. We hear a sound and we know where to turn to find the source of the sound. Moreover, conscious awareness is largely concerned with providing a comprehensive image of the world rather than a detailed portrait that is useful for action. Finally, because the precision required for deft and timely action is largely handled by preconscious perception, conscious awareness can "off load" the challenge of controlling action to the earlier, swifter, and more precise controls available in the preconscious affect enabled systems.

The analogy of the human brain to a wartime naval vessel with radar and human lookouts is not so strange. Neuroscientist Joseph LeDoux (1996) mapped how our preconscious appraisal neural apparatus provides very swift appraisal of the sensory stream. Neuroscientist Alexander Todorov (Engell, Haxby, and Todorov 2007; Willis and Todorov 2006) demonstrated that humans have their own "radar." Within one-hundred milliseconds, humans on viewing human faces arrive at a decision whether that person is trustworthy. And, in a similar fashion, the triggers in the environment that lead to an aggressive response are swiftly processed without conscious engagement (Todorov and Bargh 2002). Who we trust and distrust and the decision as to whether circumstances require an accommodating or an aggressive response are made well before consciousness has the opportunity to participate.

Further, and again like radar and weaponry, preconscious perception evolved to support the tight integration between ourselves as acting machines and the objects in the world we want to act on or with. The action supporting knowledge of where objects are, what they are like, and how to interact with them is stored in a separate system of memory, procedural memory (LeDoux 2000; Kim and Baxter 2001; Stanton 2000; Squire and Kandel 1999; Sherry and Schacter 1987). We have two ways of knowing, each of which has different properties.

The preconscious route is focused on the execution of learned tasks, habituated actions. As shown in figure 8.1, the preconscious systems of sensory, somatosensory perception, appraisal, and behavioral control operate far closer to the actual events being perceived and cycle before and faster than consciousness. Moreover, preconscious systems have direct access to the additional knowledge that is not available in semantic memory or available in conscious awareness. That knowledge is precise and

---

3. This problematic limitation of radar was solved by putting special electronic transmitters on "our" planes so that friendly planes could be identified. These so called IFF transmitters, identification friend or foe, actually only identified friends, but enabled deduction of approaching planes or ships not transmitting the proper friend identification signals to be the enemy. Even so, "friendly fire" often was directed at misidentified targets, a factor that remains a source of fatalities in war today.

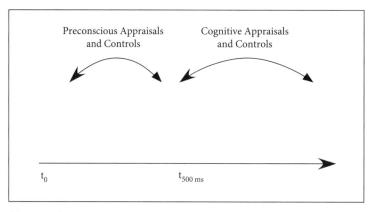

Figure 8.1 Time and Multiple Perceptual – Control Systems

detailed information about our bodies, skeletal, muscular, nerve speed, and muscular response.

It requires mastery of the body so that its specific muscular and skeletal components can be recruited to successfully accomplish any learned task. We know subjectively and consciously that we have nerves, skeletons, tendons, and muscles. But, we do not have access consciously to the specific somatosensory streams that flow from and to the various muscle and skeletal sensors from and to the brain and spine. This somatosensory data stream flow must be matched with specific information about the specific surround, the environment in which the action is to unfold. The preconscious appraisal systems make good use of their swift access to enable the deft control and ongoing adjustment of unfolding actions so that subtle "upstream" and "downstream" adaptions can be implemented. All these abilities are not within the range of capabilities of conscious awareness. Conscious awareness gives us a very

---

BOX 8.1 **The autonomic system**

The realm of the preconscious includes the various control systems such as the three subsystems that make up the autonomic system: the sympathetic, parasympathetic, and enteric systems. Humans have three major demands on the oxygen provided by the circulation of blood: digestion, physical activity such as running, and the brain. But the capacity of the blood-oxygen delivery system is such that it can only fully handle two of these three demands if they operate at full bore. The brain obviously requires precedence. Happily, the sympathetic and parasympathetic systems adjudicate this fight over limited resources. The sympathetic system gives physical movement precedence by increasing the heart rate, dilating the pupils so more light enters the eye, inhibiting digestion, inhibiting the liver, kidneys, and gall bladder among other actions. The parasympathetic system works to engage digestion by lowering the heart rate, contracting the pupils, increasing saliva, stimulating the liver, kidneys, gall bladder, among other activities. All these take place before and outside of conscious awareness. This is but one of many examples of the ongoing preconscious appraisals, both sensory and somatosensory, that lead to both activation and inhibition of vital systems, neural and physical.

BOX 8.2 **Visual illusions**

A useful Internet site for viewing a wide variety of visual illusions can be found at http://www.123opticalillusions.com/. Segall, Campbell, and Herskovitz (1966) made use of visual illusions to measure the impact of culture on visual perception.

---

crude grasp of our bodies. We observe ourselves self-consciously. We know how we feel, good or bad, but we do not have conscious access to specific muscles, nerves, or skeletal statuses. Our consciousness does not provide real-time access to the external world although our brain generates the illusion of immediacy thus hiding that insufficiency from us.

Neuroscientists Salvatore Aglioti, Joseph DeSouza, and Melvyn Goodale (1995) designed a very clever study that demonstrated that preconscious perception functions differently and better than conscious visual awareness. Before I discuss the study, a brief introduction: Aglioti and colleagues used visual illusions—a class of instances when the visual system generates misrepresentations of reality. I used some visual illusions in prior chapters. Here is another example of a visual illusion. But first, we begin with two identical size circles, side-by-side, as shown in figure 8.2.

Most of us, I hope, readily see these two circles as equal. That is not surprising because they are equal. The visual perception system is designed so we can extract meaning, to orient us in the world that we engage. As we navigate in the world we are often making comparisons. Which of various objects do we like (e.g., do we prefer this candidate or that)? Or, which of two items look more appealing? Comparison is a core competence to enable us to understand and to make explicit judgments. Hence, conscious awareness, in the visual presentation of the world, has us standing apart so that our conscious observation can identify discrepancies and give us the opportunity to "make sense" of what we observe.

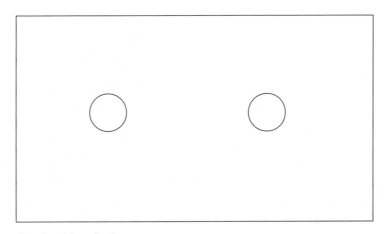

Figure 8.2 Two Equal Size Circles

On the other hand the perceptive system that serves the preconscious demands of action has a different functional design. Rather than disengagement, the action system requires the linking of our actions as they engage the external environment. The action system requires deft and swift mastery of action and deft and swift coordination of action with and in the immediate environment. Thus, detailed and precise recognition of objects and deft and swift location of objects enables fluid, swift, deft, and dynamic interplays between initiated actions and external objects. Hence, rather than comparison, the preconscious sensory systems are intended to allow us to function, to place our feet on the ground, to duck objects heading our way, to lift a pen, to converse in real time with a friend or a stranger. This focus on precision suggests that the preconscious route is less susceptible to visual illusions than is conscious awareness. And, it is that hypothesis that led Aglioti and colleagues to conduct their study.

Let's begin by noticing what happens when we add additional information to these two identical circles, as in figure 8.3. The original circles are the same as in figure 8.2. All that has changed is the addition of some circles surrounding the two circles. In the case of the left circle, very small circles were added forming a halo around the left circle. In the case of the right circle, much larger circles form the halo. As a consequence most people now perceive the two (inner) circles to be of different sizes. To most, the left circle appears to be larger than the the right circle.

The conscious visual perception system is influenced by the misleading local information, the two different sized halos that surround the two circles. The smaller circles surrounding the left circle and the larger circles surrounding the right circle, creates the impression that the circle on the left is larger than the circle on the right. This illusion is called "Titchener circles."

Aglioti and colleagues (1995) used this class of illusions to see if the conscious visual system had different properties than the preconscious visual system. First, they enlarged the circle on the right in small increments. As the actual size of the right circle increased, at some point it becomes large enough to overcome the illusion. They found that adding 2.5 millimeters to the diameter of the right circle was enough to make them appear to be of equal size. Thus, although the circles were not the same size, they

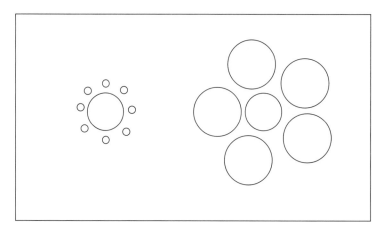

Figure 8.3 Tichenor Circles

appeared to be to the subjects in their study. You might replicate their study by redrawing the circles to see if you can also find how much larger the right circle needs to be to overcome the illusion.

Here is the very clever aspect of their study. They made wooden circles, much like poker chips of various sizes so that when they were placed on the printed images of the circles each chip fit precisely on the printed image. Imagine that they had these wooden circles, the "poker chips" that can be place directly on to the two circles as you see them in figures 8.2 and 8.3. But because the circle on the right, in figure 8.3 was then made larger to overcome the effect of the surrounding circles, the poker chip for that variant of the study was also made larger than its companion chip on the left. In the study, subjects were shown two versions of the illusion (figure 8.3). In one version the circles were as shown in figure 8.3 that is actually the same size, but perceptually different (the one on the left looking larger). In the second version they were shown the 2.5 millimeter enlarged right circle. In this circumstance, although in fact larger, the right circle is perceptually the same size as that on the left.

Subjects were randomly shown one or the other set for about three seconds and then given the following instruction: "if you think the two discs are the same size, pick up the one on the left; if you think they are of different size, pick up the one on the right" (they also reversed the instruction so that they were sometimes asked to pick up the disc on the left in the discs looked the same).

This procedure provided Aglioti and his colleagues with a useful validity check. The subject's response to the question, which circle seemed to them larger, gave clear indication that the visual illusion was effective. But what they were actually interested in was the grasping motion of the right hand as it reached for one, or the other, of the two poker chips, the disks. As we reach to pick up something, we normally extend our hand, rotating the palm so that it faces down, while spread our thumb and first fingers to prepare to place these fingers on either side of the object we plan to grip. These coordinated movements are controlled by the preconscious route to action. The preconscious visual appraisal widens the fingers in anticipation of the actual width of the object to be grasped. Aglioti and his colleagues affixed two red light emitting diodes, one each, to the thumb and forefinger so they could precisely measure the distance between them as the subject reached for the disk. The question they were interested in answering was how wide would the subjects locate their thumbs and forefinger? Would it be the consciously perceived width or would it be the actual width?

What they found was that subjects were influenced by the visual illusion throughout the study. Subjects either perceived differently sized discs as equal or equal sized disks as unequal depending on which array of circles they were shown. However, the subjects accurately opened their fingers to the actual size of the discs. They concluded: "It would seem that the automatic and metrically accurate calibrations required for skilled actions are mediated by visual processes that are separate from those mediating our conscious experiential perception. Earlier studies on patients with neurological deficits suggest that these two types of processing may depend on quite separate, but interacting, visual pathways in the cerebral cortex" (Aglioti, DeSouza, and Goodale. 1995, 679). This study illustrates that although we live in the experience of conscious awareness, for many of our actions we are reliant on the preconscious systems of perception, appraisal, and control of action. More important, we are better for for that because in this instance conscious judgment was incorrect.

This study also suggests that preconscious appraisals are devoted to doing and are not susceptible to visual illusions. On the other hand, conscious visual awareness is devoted to interpreting the subjective world, to understanding. Hence, consciousness is quite amenable to these subtle cues that matters may be out of place.

This extended introduction is to support the following assertions:

- First, a political psychology that does not take into account both pathways of knowledge and action will generate partial accounts. In this case, ignoring the nonconscious route leads to a conclusion of human incompetence, that is, a systematic misjudgment.
- Second, partial accounts are themselves likely to be biased distortions because we will not grasp the factors that actually guide many of our actions.
- Hence, research that presumes that consciousness is the sole pathway to knowing, and that the variants of knowledge contained in semantic accounts are the exclusive resource of what humans know, will be both incomplete and distorted.
- Finally, research that gives no recognition to these two pathways of knowing, acting, and remembering, will miss the dynamic interplay between these two routes, as well as properly understanding the particular abilities and limitations of each.

II. HOW WE MANAGE: DUAL PROCESS MODELS

To understand the role of personality, traits, and the role of contemporaneous factors, state conditions, we must begin with a "dual process" model. The long traditions of political psychology and the inquiry into human nature have focused on the visible, the stream of consciousness because the preconscious was largely unseen. Hence, the continued focus on just one of these processes, the role of consciousness, has missed much of the actual action. Though not always so, action most often begins the unexamined process, the preconscious route. What has to concern political psychology is to integrate how these two processes dynamically modulate their respective roles. These modulations are the result of our dual neural capacities, capacities that rely on the availability of both routes—the preconscious and the conscious. Because the long tradition has largely been blind to the role of the preconscious, the general conclusion of the incompetence of the public to fully engage in governance may rest on a partial and thereby flawed psychology. A fuller psychology might well lead to an array of new understandings and new possibilities. But to explore that possibility we want to have some focus that gives our research a direction to explore.

We have the capacity vested in preconscious processes of perception, appraisal, and control of action for managing the recurring tasks. We have as well the capacity to formulate novel responses by reliance on express deliberative considerations that gives us a far richer adaptive flexibility than if we had but one of these means. That we have both is well-established as a matter of psychology (Evans 2008). What import does it have for political psychology? The normative standard of the autonomous and deliberative citizen, celebrated by most normative theorists, presumes the universal applicability and superiority of deliberative processes in guiding behavior, recurring and novel. But as we have seen the idealization of deliberation ignores its limitations and ignores the benefits of habituation (Baumeister, Masicampo, and Vohs, 2011). Having the dual capacity offers adaptive flexibility. For example, reliance on habituated patterns of action if articulated in familiar conditions are likely to be rewarded for such reliance. But, having the capacity for thoughtful consideration adds to our adaptive flexibility if we turn to deliberation not as a universal solution, but as a solution best used for circumstances not within the capacity of habituated action to ably resolve. Having both capacities also requires that there exist a neural mechanism to identify when to shift from one capacity to the other and then back.

The second tension is also an issue of choice, but here the issue is not orientation to time but rather our orientation to others: Should we work in harmony or should we strive to be self-guided and self-judging individuals? Clearly the normative standard of the autonomous citizen implies we should think, consider, and act primarily as citizens beholden to no other than to our own moral compass. But democracy requires collective action for absent collective action, we would be unable to form coalitions of like-minded actors energized to secure collective goals. Here again, we often find two contradictory normative claims.

One the one hand the French psychologist Gustave Le Bon (1986) argued in his very influential book, *The Crowd*—it was first published in 1895 and was swiftly translated and published in English a year later—that the public mind was readily manipulated to action because however strong of mind they might be as individuals, they were a different animal as a collective—weak of mind and easily manipulated. His work gave rise to the psychology of group action and caught the attention of some notorious individuals, reputedly Adolph Hitler and Benito Mussolini. Collective action, then, would inevitably produce the loss of the autonomous moral citizen, a view then enunciated and sustained by much of the great works of social psychology, Sherif (1958, 1966), Asch (1951), Festinger (1957), Milgram (1974), and Zimbardo (2008), to name but just some of the more prominent who sustained this portrait of the public as gullible, compliant, and obedient. Giving the public the reins to govern the nation, or locale, would then predictably generate public complicity in whatever demagogic leadership emerged especially in times of duress (in addition to the aforementioned, Idi Amin in Uganda, Milosevic in Serbia, Karadžić in Bosnia, Huey Long in Louisiana, Franco in Spain).

To that dire view we can add yet another that challenges the aspiration for individual autonomy on other grounds, one offered by French sociologist Emile Durkheim (1951). His great work, *Suicide* (first published in 1897), foretells of the danger of the autonomous citizen when acting alone.[4] When we are most freed from the obligations of devotion to faith, to family, tradition, we lose the clarity of purpose and meaning and become unhinged. We entertain the risk of anomie, a condition of self-alienation, in which we lose ourselves rather than being a self-construction, our élan or spirit is primarily a social construction. Thus, a conservative might react to the modern vision of cosmopolitan freedom by warning of the dangers of collective action, especially collective

---

4. Durkheim's point that we all need social engagement for a normal and healthy life has also been considered by neuroscientists. John Cacioppo (Cacioppo and Patrick, 2008) made a compelling case that social isolation degraded our well-being.

action undertaken "from below" rather than guided by the benign guiding hand of established authority. The attack on democracy begun by Plato (1974) and extended by Hobbes (1968) among others, has its modern expositors and much of academic psychology and sociology anchored in this ancient tradition of celebrating aristocratic rule by denigrating the capacity of the public to act alone or collectively. Nor, as discussed earlier, should the academic research into electorate competence in political science be excused from its role in endorsing the conservative critique of democracy. The received wisdom, with important dissenters in each discipline, holds that modern well-educated publics in rich democratic regimes are ill informed about civic matters, largely disinterested in politics, approach choice decisions with settled and selfish considerations dominant, and when mobilized, too gullible to the current demagogic leadership. In sum, this portrait confirms the detailed critiques of antidemocratic voices extending from Plato through Hobbes and into the modern era. This creates a compelling appetite for new scholarship, a political psychology that engages this specific long-standing debate between the aristocratic dissenters and the democratic entrepreneurs. An, important feature of this ancient but still relevant debate has been its monocratic portrait of "the citizen," "the public," or "the electorate."

The tenor of this debate turns on contending portraits that do not consider the adaptive flexibility that humans have by virtue of the dual process routes to perception, appraisal, and action. Humans do act with unreflective speed in many, indeed most, situations reliant on the habitual processes known as "automaticity." But humans also, on occasion, give thoughtful consideration of the contemporary choices before selecting among them precedent to acting. The brain shifts between these two orientations. That dynamic capacity requires that the normal brain has the capacity to rely on habit and to rely on consideration. Further, it also means that the normal brain has neural mechanisms to shift from one to the other and back. A fuller engagement with the aristocratic critique of democracy ought to ask whether and if humans opt for the better route based on the anticipated efficacy of that route in the specific context.

The second arm of the aristocratic critique, arguing that collective public action displays rabid and thoughtless irrationality, in the main, is similarly critical. Of course, dueling historical narratives, selecting the particular cases, can be used as debating points. But the conventional debate, arguing the the normative standard for citizens is that of autonomous judge or scientist, removed from group pressures, is not well suited to making an argument about the uses and conditions of collective action. Here, the contemporary discussion in political philosophy is misdirected for the proponents of autonomous judgment presume this normative standard should be ubiquitously applied across all situations, the work of Fishkin (1991, 2009), Rawls (1993) and Habermas (1984) are illustrative. Although in a similar way, the proponents of collective partisan solidarity as the proper route for effective political actions, such as Sanders (1997), Young (1990, 2000), and Rosenblum (1999), argue for its general superiority over the deliberative alternative. Thus, a Draconian choice is presented aligned with one or the other normative argument. Here too, as with the dual processes, adaptive flexibility is gained if we can work alone, in some matters, and work collectively in other matters. That flexibility is adaptive if as with the temporal alternatives of reliance on historical repertoire or considered judgment, individual autonomy and collective solidarity are articulated in the apt circumstances.

Table 8.1. Two alternative orientations—Guidance by the past or future and solidarity or autonomy

Solitary–sociality orientation	Temporal orientation	
	Reliance on the past	Contemporaneous determination
Individual autonomy	Citizen conforms to established traditions	Citizen as deliberative autonomous agent
Collective solidarity	Citizens as patriotic defenders of tradition and nation—sometimes expressed in conservative social movements	Citizens as partisan soldiers joined to achieve new goals—sometimes expressed in progressive social movements

These alternatives generate a four-fold taxonomy of orientations that enable humans a variety of mechanisms to address challenges in various ways at different times and in different circumstances. Table 8.1 depicts these two intersecting frames of reference.

I chose to avoid normative language in describing the two dimensions displayed in table 8.1. But there are potent terms depicting each of these orientations as either praiseworthy or reprehensible. Hence, collective solidarity when joined with a reliance on traditions can be considered patriotic (praiseworthy) or "revanchist" or xenophobic (blameworthy).

Dual process models suggest that as a practical matter we each display both of these capabilities. We all have some baseline inclination of each of these two dimensions but we can each shift in response to changes in the environment, sometimes favoring individual autonomy and sometimes favoring working in collective harmony (ignoring for the moment the rare few who get locked into some past or some rare few who follow the hermetic life to their own special Walden Pond). How does the brain enable each of these possibilities? And, how does the brain enable us to shift from a past orientation to a present and future orientation? How does the brain enable us to act alone while also on other occasions acting in harmony or solidarity with others?

Once we answer those general questions, we can then to turn to the questions of individual difference, why some of us have different baseline orientations, some favor tradition while others are far more willing to abandon convention for new possibilities. And, why some are more inclined to the autonomous life of individuality and others more inclined to the collective subordination to some group activity.

For the past and present to be negotiated so we can thrive by relying on the past and by relying on contemporaneous assessments, the brain has to have mechanisms that enable each capacity, and to further have a "shift" mechanism that enables shifting from one mode to another of self-governance. Further, as noted in table 8.1, we sometimes are attuned to self-interested, self-focused action and at other times attuned to working in a collective fashion, subordinating our individual aims to some joint endeavor. And, just as with the shift to and from reliance on past embedded lessons or to and from reliance on present assessments, so to there must be neural mechanisms that not only enable self-reliant action and collective coordinated action, there must be neural mechanisms that provide shifting from one to the other and back.

These are the two shifts that are the focus of this chapter because democratic politics sometimes asks its leaders and citizens to rely on the past for guidance. But democratic politics, as with all regimes, must have the flexibility to reject reliance on old lessons for consideration of new and novel solutions to new possibilities. As we have seen, reliance on habit has long been recognized as a fundamental capability of humans. Some have lauded this ability and taken it as the principle normative mechanism because of its capacity to serve as a stable guide to action (Burke 1973, Oakeshott 1975).

Automaticity has evolved so that humans can deftly and swiftly rely on what has proved successful in the past. This is the case both for autonomous action, actions intended to serve the best interests of the individual in the moment and actions taken on coordination to serve some collective purpose. Equally, we can find those who laud thoughtful and considered judgment freed from the obligations and authority of traditions (Fishkin 1991; Habermas 1984; Rawls 1993). Indeed it would be hard to consider democracy as a regime without a companion presumption: The past, although a useful array of experiences warranting consideration, is often not a suitable guide. Hence, the human array of faculties should contain the ability to give thoughtful consideration of the challenges now being faced and a free and explicit consideration of the alternatives as how best to deal with those challenges. As politcal philosopher Nancy Rosenblum (1999) argued, there are times when citizens must take note of the special nature of current circumstances and reject deference to others and to established norms and instead seek the more just solution. And, those moments required both the ability to act deliberately, both individually but also collectively, for if one person generates a spark and if that spark does not leap to quicken others than it dies with little effect.

Moral Judgment

This duality of action—habituated action and thoughtful considered guidance—is revealed quite well in the domain of judgment. Here I focus on moral judgment, how to deal with the challenge of judging people, individually or collectively, as good or bad, and classifying actions as good or bad. Hence, the capacity to judge is central to collective life as we confront it—especially in mobile, large, diverse, and dynamic societies—a wide array of circumstances both common and uncommon. We are moral animals but where does this moral capacity lie? On the one hand there is considerable research that sustains the view that moral judgments, like many other types of judgments, flow swiftly from the preconscious realm. Jonathan Haidt (2001) made the case that moral judgments were acquired through osmosis, as it were, by mimicry and observation. His latest work examined how the intuitive system evolved to generate moral foundations that facilitated group formation and allegiance (Haidt and Joseph 2007). Neuroscientists have been engaged in seeking to identify the neural processes that subserve, that is sustain, the so called moral emotions (Zahn et al. 2009; Borg, Lieberman, and Kiehl 2008; Moll and de Oliveira-Souza 2007; Monin, Pizarro, and Beer 2007; Tangney, Stuewig, and Mashek 2007; Takahashi et al. 2004).

Kristen Monroe's (1996) work on heroic action found that those who spring to action to save others did so without reflection, their actions as much a surprise to them as it was to those who asked for help. But, it is also clear that we can be troubled and reflect over what our moral obligations require of us. And, recent work in neuroscience has offered some insight into the how our dual moral capabilities is served by our brains. Neuroscientists have found that each capacity, instant unreflected judgment implemented by preconscious affective appraisals and thoughtful explicit consideration, have their neural substrates (Greene et al. 2004; Greene et al. 2001; Greene and Haidt 2002). This work is nicely arrayed against the microscopic detailed examination of social interactions provided by that superb observer Erving Goffman (1959, 1963, 1971, 1981, 1982, 1986a, 1986b). His large corpus of work is worth careful reading as it goes along way to show that social interactions are largely fluidly enacted with swift application of learned "rules" that largely are acquired, as Haidt argued, outside of conscious awareness let alone conscious control. We can of course observe our interactions, reflect on them, and formulate both legal doctrines as well as philosophical principles to make some of these practices visible and then subject to explicit consideration. And, as sometimes happens, make them subject to modifications much as the American norms of "Jim Crow" racial subordination through a long struggle was overthrown. This change relied on actions from "below," as when Rosa Parks refused to accept the continued practice of going to the back of the bus, as well as from "above" as in the US Supreme Court's 1994 *Brown v. Board of Education* ruling racial segregation of public schools unconstitutional.

Thus, the psychology of moral judgment, presented by Haidt (2001)—as a reliant on a swift intuitive system with a thoughtful reasoning system largely to serve as a our lawyer, defending our prior preconsciously derived moral intuitions—if accurate, would seem to preclude moral judgments as other than mysteriously arising without moral reflection or introspection. Yet, democracy presumes that our intuitions are often likely to be wrong, or at least arcane and inappropriate in a modern and every changing world that present new issues and new circumstances. If our early socializing moral impulses would serve us well throughout our lives then why have the recurring mechanisms for public discussion, political conflict, as well as political judgment that are impelled by the constitutional requirement for frequent, often regular, election so as to require the public and elites to battle over the future course of society? Hence, our moral capacities must have some neural basis for inhibiting our moral intuitions for, instead, a reflective and public reasoning over what the current circumstances require. Here again, our neural processes have processes for activation and for inhibition. Consider the process of attention. Something captures our attention. This process of activation must also have a process of inhibition. Something captures our attention but then, our curiosity satiated; attention must be inhibited, detaching us from that which just before engaged us. Otherwise, what captures our attention, would as it did Narcissus, keep us entrapped in perpetual fascination.

Swift action to expel the poison from being ingested, the disgust impulse that almost instantly expels tainted food, certainly favors the first route (Rozin, Haidt, and McCauley 2000). Reflecting on why a poisonous but attractive fruit or uncertain

---

BOX 8.3   The furies

In ancient Greek mythology the furies were three goddesses of vengeance. Tisiphone was the avenger of murder; Megaera was the goddess of jealousy; and Alecto was the goddess of constant anger. Together they would pursue all offenders striking them down with madness. Aeschylus has Athena, protective goddess of the city of Athens, reducing their role to protectors of the family, the private region beyond the reach of the state. These goddess remain with us still for we, perhaps too often, describe ourselves as *furious* or *infuriated*.

mushroom is making us feel ill is hardly an adaptive strategy likely to yield a positive outcome.

This disgust mechanism appears to have been extended to apply not just to ingestion of bad food but also to the complex, numerous, and diverse social interactions that characterize contemporary life. Having a fast swift rejection mechanism for social punishing circumstances has its shortfalls. Most notably a defended and habituated disgust response will serve to limit learning when new situations arise. The flexibility that openness to learning provides requires an alternative strategy, that of public and considered reflection affords. The former route is well served by vengeance based systems of justice, you injure me and I have the compelling furies driving me to take equal measure to restore the balance (Hutcherson and Gross 2011). Disrespect is a potent motivator, for damages to our status in a society, even if intimate and not widely observed are experienced as wounds and wounds often cry out for redress (D. T. Miller 2001). Direct action by those who experience injustice might have served stable and homogenous societies passably well, though read the famous Icelandic tale, Njál's *Saga*, as well as Aeschylus (1975), *The Oresteia Trilogy*, for clear insight into the limits of such systems (W. I. Miller 1990).

Vengeance clearly ill serves the complex social dynamics of heterogeneous societies. The modern systems of justice of based on law, courts, and trials before citizen juries give some institutional mechanisms for making the many issues of moral judgment public and deliberative rather than private and driven by the hidden furies. Apart from the valued addition of institutions, including in addition to those already mentioned, constitutional guarantees such as the right to a jury trial, provision of legal counsel, the writ of habeas corpus, rejection of the legislative practice of passing bills of attainder (i.e., legislative punishments directed at individuals so as to preclude judicial jurisdiction over matters of crime and punishment), the dual process model view of human psychology provides an account of the neural basis of both vengeance and explicit contemplation as a prerequisite to moral judgment. That we can do either recommends an active research program to better understand the inclinations that move some of us to rely on the embedded habits of moral judgment and others to the more contemplative approach to moral judgment. And, no less important, that the external and internal triggers that move us from one to the other.

Free Will

It is an unfortunate aspect of the history of ideas in the West that the notion of free will was defined in a quite particular fashion. In both secular and Christian thought, the body has long been understood in mechanical fashion. A highly complex machine to be sure, but a machine, and like a watch (and oft used metaphor after accurate watches were developed), once put into motion, that motion obeyed the "laws of nature." Hence, to the extent that we are physical creatures we must also obey those same laws. Hence, it follows, that we cannot be free creatures, unless we have some noncorporeal component, some disembodied spirit, or soul, where because it is outside of the body, something immaterial and apart, freedom can be located. Having a soul then distinguishes us from all other species, who soulless must follow the path that the laws of nature dictate. This spirit body duality has played a large role both in religious doctrines but also in animating a spirited divide between science, which holds to a material explanation of all things and other systems of knowledge, some of which holds to nonmaterial or spiritual as a vital part of human nature. I will not develop that juxtaposition any further here. Rather, the neuroscience account of dual process neural abilities in our and other species suggests that freedom, free will, differently understood has a biological basis.

Although we do not yet have a definitive understanding of how the brain generates consciousness, we can go farther than Haidt (2001) did in celebrating its sometime executive capacities. For Haidt, reasoning served solely as a "lawyer" to defend the prior intuitive judgments that were generated by preconscious appraisals. The fast preconscious affective appraisals always have precedent and hence causal priority over slowly derived reasoning conclusions. Our reasons serve, at most and largely, to articulate the intuitions that always drive moral judgment (Mercier and Sperber 2011). We are chained to these intuitions and reason can do little but to defend them. In this view, Haidt clearly aligned himself with the view of David Hume (1984, 460–62), the Scot enlightenment philosopher who said:

> I shall endeavour to prove first, that reason alone can never be a motive to any action of the will; and secondly, that it can never oppose passion in the direction of the will.

And, more widely known,

> Reason is, and ought only to be the slave of the passions, and can never pretend to any other office than to serve and obey them.

This view leaves consciousness with little to do but to give voice to inarticulate "gut" responses. Before I turn to another understanding of the role and capacities of consciousness, Haidt (2001) presented an excellent summary of the features of preconscious appraisal and its capacities, what he called the intuition system, and the features of consciousness, what he called, the reasoning system. Table 8.2 is a reproduction of this summary depiction, from table 1 of Haidt's principal article. Here he drew on a

Table 8.2. General features of the two judgment systems

The intuitive system	The reasoning system
• Fast and effortless	• Slow and effortful
• Process is unintentional and runs automatically	• Process is intentional and controllable
• Process is inaccessible: Only results enter awareness	• Process is consciously accessible and viewable
• Does not demand attentional resources	• Demands attentional resources, which are limited
• Parallel distributed processing	• Serial processing
• Pattern matching: Thought is metaphorical, holistic	• Symbol manipulation: Thought is truth preserving, analytical
• Common to all mammals	• Unique to humans over the of age two and perhaps some language-trained apes
• Context dependent	• Context independent
• Platform dependent (depends on the brain and body that houses it)	• Platform independent (the process can he transported to any rule following organism or machine)

Note: Reproduced from Haidt (2001)

wide range of psychologists and their work, this is a consensus view of the principal features and capabilities of each, the preconscious and conscious, neural systems.

Some of Haidt's comparisons are incomplete and in important respects not precise. For example, we do not yet know how the reasoning system works in sufficient detail to develop a "platform" that could duplicate it but that may be the result of a lack of imagination and knowledge rather than something inherent in the reasoning system. Further, the intuitive system has access to a richer array of sensory inputs than does the reasoning system not just faster access. And, further still, the reasoning system has generally weak linkages to the somatosensory inputs thus limiting its capacity for enacting and controlling behavior. Nonetheless, the comparison does make some useful points. The reasoning system is a slow system that consumes a considerable amount of energy, which then raises the question of why would so much effort go into the evolution of consciousness for such a limited function, the development of semantic rationales of already decided decisions?

Consciousness then must have some capacity to formulate understandings and then initiate action. Consciousness, in this view, should be able to construct its own understanding by:

1. Constructing a representation of what's going on.
2. Being able to generate one or more plausible accounts of what has gone wrong.
3. Formulating and considering what response options might successfully deal with this novel circumstance.
4. Then, expressly evaluating these alternatives.
5. Finally, choosing among the choices and initiating that choice into action.

However, for the conscious to be aware of these capacities depends on the existence of neural mechanisms to preconsciously recognize—indeed as early as possible—that in this instance to rely on fast habituated routines is likely to founder. There must also be neural mechanisms that can then act to inhibit, to stop, give reliance on these "intuitive" or preconscious processes. And finally, these neural mechanisms must be able to initiate a shift such that conscious attention is directed toward the novelty and initiates reliance on conscious processes for understanding and for action. In sum, although consciousness often acts as a lawyer, or more apt, press agent, articulating the rationale for an already generated course of action, sometimes it can act as the thoughtful and deliberating agent expressly formulating alternative courses of action, choosing among them, and then initiating the chosen course of action. In dual process models, then, we have a different and biological conception of free will. But it is a will made freed by and reliant on our biology.

III. THE SPECIAL CHALLENGE OF MANIPULATION

With the invention of democratic rule in ancient Athens, aristocrats who lost authority found help from those who would cast doubt on the competence of the demos to rule. That long tradition from Socrates, then to his student Plato (1974), and on through Hobbes (1968), Marx (Marx and Engels 2002), Lippmann (1922), and so on, advances a number of claims that all lead to the same result. The public is not suited to rule. One of the more potent claims was that of the supposed gullibility of the public (Herzog 1998; Garsten 2006).

Table 8.3. The various forms of gullibility

Type	Author	Criterion
Inability to think scientifically	Hobbes	The credulity of the public in accepting religious fantasies
False consciousness	Marx	The lack of class solidarity by misconstruing the self as autonomous
Foolishness	One variant of liberal orthodoxy for example, Adam Smith, the self acts rationally but selfishly, while the "hidden hand" solves the collective problem	The failure to be informed and act in self-interest
Selfishness	Madison	Corruption rather than action that serves justice or the common good (the aggregate and collective interest of the community); note the contrast with economic orthodoxy

As I have shown, scientific research in psychology has, in the main, confirmed that the public is largely defenseless because of its credulity. As noted in earlier chapters, Thomas Hobbes (1968) argued for the Leviathan in part because only a few, notably himself, could act as a scientist, carefully and objectively discerning cause and effect. The broad public would, in his view, act and observe not as scientists, but gullibly and passionately. The modern era has examined this claim and found, as with Hobbes, the most people exhibit a number of biases in dealing with the challenge of explaining events whether initiated by themselves or observed in others (Nisbett and Ross 1982).

With respect to politics, the issue of persuasion has of late been fruitfully explored by "framing." Because the number of perspectives and considerations available are quite numerous, which ones we have in mind will likely influence our reactions to politicians. Which is foremost, the state of the economy, war and peace, or some other consideration, can alter our judgments. Our reactions to issues or events will similarly be shaped by the frames of reference (for examples, see Berinsky and Kinder 2006; De Martino et al. 2006; J. N. Druckman and McDermott 2008; J. Druckman 2001). Prospect theory (Levy 1992; Quattrone and Tversky 1988) suggests a general shift from risk aversion to risk seeking and back based on the threat-rewarding condition of the immediate context (Kahneman, Slovic, and Tversky 1982). Finally, even when people have been moved to change their view on some salient position they will deny that they ever held any position other than that they currently assert (Goethals and Reckman 1973).

This then suggests a quite contradictory view of human nature from another pillar of psychology, "motivated reasoning" (Kunda 1990). In this view people are intensely committed to defending their established beliefs. So, there must be a more comprehensive account that can explain when and why people with great facility adopt the views of others, leaders, individuals in authority, or their fellows. And, that comprehensive account must also explain when and why people abandon the defense of even their most entrenched dispositions.

I advanced the argument that dual process insights from neuroscience give us the theoretical foundation to see how the same individual could, at one juncture act to strenuously work to defend prior beliefs yet at another time, as executive functions shifts from preconscious automaticity to deliberative executive conscious control, openly consider the full array of available options, including abandoning the prior convictions that seems to have been so well serving that they warranted defense.

Sometimes we act alone and eschew collective involvement. Indeed, given the array of possible collective ventures all seeking support of many kinds, if we were not guarded, we would soon have to abandon not only our private interests but sort out how to divide the limited hours available to apportion our time between the various competing seductive appeals. But, sometimes we do abandon the personal and private for collective action. We do act together in some perhaps unexpected spasm of collective energy and solidarity, sometimes to good effect and sometimes to bad (de Hooge, Zeelenberg, and Breugelmans 2007; de Quervain et al. 2004; Sullivan et al. 2007).

Finally, it is important to distinguish between the scientific enterprise, the empirical description of how, when, and why people shift from autonomy to solidarity and back, and how, when, and why, people shift from uncritical, thoughtless, but efficient reliance on habits of mind and action and when people abandon habits far from the normative. The normative task is to consider the merit of each of these two routes to judgment, the "should" question. We can all judge the normative by reliance on outcome data. "Could 'a," "should 'a," "would 'a," reflects the ease with which we can make such assessment in retrospect. And, no doubt reflection and scientific examination of outcomes is well worth our time and considered judgment. Indeed, such a consideration would be most helpful if it trumped to tired clichés espousing one route as always preferable to the other.

In the West, while the dominant cliché argues for reliance on deliberative reason, Edmund Burke (1973) and others were dubious, to say the least, of the supposed benefits of scientific planning, reliant on reason. Burke was especially dubious of the conscious reason's ability to discern the substantial from the irrelevant and the true causes of affairs from the spurious. Political scientist James C. Scott (1998) had a variant of that claim. State planning, he argued, often degrades what it seeks to improve. A normative consideration that ignores the flexible adaptability that humans can express by virtue of preconscious automaticity, resting on all the array of neural mechanisms that secures stability of judgment that meshes with continuity in the world, and by virtue of executive conscious consideration, reliant on the neural mechanisms that decouple us from continuity, will be a normative consideration that ill serves us.

IV. RETHINKING CORE CONCEPTIONS

The old debate, nature versus nurture, has been a major impediment to our understanding of the role in biology and politics. So has the western diversion into a mind–body dualism, a conception that presumes the mind to be a "free" element not bound by the biological processes that animate life. The first presumes a simple division between genes and environment. The second assumes that our status as free, our ability to make elective choices, is violated rather than enabled by biology.

The first has since been replaced with models that understand the complex interplay of genetic influences, developmental sequences, and contextual effects, all of which interplay with each other and with individual differences, the latter we group under the heading of personality. These complex interactions are only beginning to be mapped. A considerable agenda remains to be addressed. And, biological and neuroscience will be at the center of those efforts. To advance that agenda, a rich array of readings, the basics and then more advanced, will introduce you to the core foundations of work to date.

The second, the notion that minds are independent of biology also has been detrimental for it leads us away from ourselves, the Socratic invitation to "know thyself" and instead imagine some fantasy of life that is not life. Here also the biological and neuroscientific have much to offer and by beginning to map the preconscious processes that give life and also serve to generate the need for the limited contributions of consciousness enlarges our understanding of the role of the brain in managing the demands and opportunities of life.

I have been relentless in encouraging you to consider the normative framework that shapes every scientific endeavor. Notions of progress and notions of normality are often tied together with implicit understandings of where we have been and where we are going. Or to be more precise, what we understand as the pathological and advisable about our past experiences, and how these medicinal understandings direct our research agendas. Politics is affected by the utopian and dystopian beliefs that provide the foundation of our beliefs. If democracy is to survive, to thrive, it must have a psychology, economics, and sociology, that gives us both understanding and direction. The fields that contribute to political psychology, to this effort to understand how human nature impacts on the wide variety of politics, within nations, states, communities, and neighborhoods and between nations, states, communities and neighborhoods, has greatly expanded. The fulsome and exploding work in biology and neuroscience engages us in the biology of nerves, hormones, genes, neurotransmitters, and neural functions. The way we are is, in part, driven by how we have evolved, and in part, how we craft the institutions and cultural practices that also shape our social environments. What we aspire to be maybe attractive and within reach, but it may also be a distraction from other alternatives that, would we but consider them, give us greater purchase.

The role of preconscious and conscious neural processes makes our consideration of how we live, how we find common purpose, how we engage and resolve matters that divide, creates a great challenge. Most of the focus on citizenship, what are the requisite skills and how are they acquired, has been undertaken with no awareness that many of these skills are not based on beliefs, values, and attitudes as conventionally understood. Rather many citizenship skills are learned, mastered, and deployed through preconscious neural processes. There has been very little research to date that explores which democratic skills rely on preconscious processes beyond that undertaken on the important, but limited, questions of attention, learning, and engagement (MacKuen et al. 2010; Marcus and MacKuen 1993). And, although these are important they are not the full consideration of democratic citizenship competencies that must await new research.

The simpler understandings that preceded the discovery of the extraordinary complexity our neural fabric requires us to move from the older one-to-one causal accounts. The prototypic statistical models of the social sciences have been ordinary least squares, either in linear regression or in analysis of variance. Models that do not consider the dominant role of interactions cannot account for the complexity of life solitary and life social, life as tradition and life as consciously purposive. Interactive statistical models are a challenge as they require a rich and robust theory to identify which interactions warrant attention. Simply considering all possible interactions cannot work as even a simple model, for example with a few independent variables, generates too many interactions (three independent variables will generate one three-way interaction and three two-way interactions; add more independent variables and the number of interactions multiplies explosively). But social science cannot consider any and all possible interactions, nor should it. Theory directs us here and, at the same time away from there. Understanding how genes, neural structures, personality, habits, and feelings, and deliberative capabilities interact with the social and political contexts is a challenge.

EXERCISES

Devise different affirmative and derogatory normative terms for each of the other four cells in table 8.1. See if you can identify contemporary or historical examples that fit each instance.

Devise a list of citizenship characteristics that would exemplify criteria of excellence for judging for when they were reliant on the intuitive system and on the reasoning system. How would you conduct a study to see if people meet these criteria?

REFERENCES

Aeschylus. 1975. *The Oresteia*. New York: Viking Press.

Aglioti, Salvatore, Joseph F. X. DeSouza, and Melvyn A. Goodale. 1995. "Size-Contrast Illusions Deceive the Eye but Not the Hand." *Current Biology* 5:679–85.

Asch, Solomon E. 1951. "Effects of Group Pressure upon the Modification and Distortion of Judgment." In *Groups, Leadership and Men: Research in Human Relations*, edited by Harold Guetzkow, 177–90. Pittsburgh, PA: Carnegie.

Barber, Benjamin. 1984. *Strong Democracy: Participatory Politics for a New Age*. Berkeley: University of California Press.

Baumeister, Roy F., E. J. Masicampo, and Kathleen D. Vohs. 2011. "Do Conscious Thoughts Cause Behavior?". *Annual Review of Psychology* 62:331–61.

Berinsky, Adam J., and Donald R. Kinder. 2006. "Making Sense of Issues Through Media Frames: Understanding the Kosovo Crisis." *The Journal of Politics* 68:640–56.

Borg, Jana Schaich, Debra Lieberman, and Kent A. Kiehl. 2008. "Infection, Incest, and Iniquity: Investigating the Neural Correlates of Disgust and Morality." *Journal of Cognitive Neuroscience* 20:367–79.

Burke, Edmund. 1973. *Reflections on the Revolution in France*. Garden City, NY: Anchor.

Cacioppo, John T., and William Patrick. 2008. *Loneliness: Human Nature and the Need for Social Connection*. New York: Norton.

Campbell, Angus, Philip E. Converse, Warren E. Miller, and Donald E. Stokes. 1960. *The American Voter*. New York: Wiley.

Caplan, Bryan Douglas. 2007. *The Myth of the Rational Voter: Why Democracies Choose Bad Policies*. Princeton, NJ: Princeton University Press.

Converse, Philip E. 1964. "The Nature of Belief Systems in Mass Publics." In *Ideology and Discontent*, edited by David Apter, 202–61. New York: Free Press.

———. 2006. "Democratic Theory and Electoral Reality." *Critical Review* 18:297–329.

de Hooge, Ilona E., Marcel Zeelenberg, and Seger M. Breugelmans. 2007. "Moral Sentiments and Cooperation: Differential Influences of Shame and Guilt." *Cognition and Emotion* 21:1025–42.

De Martino, Benedetto, Dharshan Kumaran, Ben Seymour, and Raymond J. Dolan. 2006. "Frames, Biases, and Rational Decision-Making in the Human Brain." *Science* 313:684–87.

de Quervain, Dominique J.-F., Urs Fischbacher, Valerie Treyer, Melanie Schellhammer, Ulrich Schnyder, Alfred Buck, and Ernst Fehr. 2004. "The Neural Basis of Altruistic Punishment." *Science* 305:1254–58.

Delli Carpini, Michael X., and Scott Keeter. 1996. *What Americans Know About Politics and Why it Matters*. New Haven, CT: Yale University Press.

Doppelt, Jack C., and Ellen Shearer. 1999. *Nonvoters: America's No-Shows*. Thousand Oaks, CA: Sage.

Druckman, James N., and Rose McDermott. 2008. "Emotion and the Framing of Risky Choice." *Political Behavior* 30:297–321.

Druckman, Jamie. 2001. "Evaluating Framing Effects." *Journal of Economic Psychology* 22:91–101.

Durkheim, Emile. 1951. *Suicide: A Study in Sociology*. Glencoe, IL: Free Press.

Engell, Andrew D., James V. Haxby, and Alexander Todorov. 2007. "Implicit Trustworthiness Decisions: Automatic Coding of Face Properties in the Human Amygdala." *Journal of Cognitive Neuroscience* 19:1508–19.

Erikson, Robert S. 2007. "Does Public Ignorance Matter?" *Critical Review* 19:23–34.

Evans, Jonathan St. B. T. 2008. "Dual-Processing Accounts of Reasoning, Judgment, and Social Cognition." *Annual Review of Psychology* 59:255–78.

Festinger, Leon. 1956. *When Prophecy Fails*. Minneapolis: University of Minnesota Press.

Fishkin, James. 1991. *Democracy and Deliberation*. New Haven, CT: Yale University Press.

———. 2009. *When the People Speak: Deliberative Democracy and Public Consultation*. Oxford: Oxford University Press.

Frank, Thomas. 2004. *What's the Matter with Kansas?: How Conservatives Won the Heart of America*. New York: Metropolitan/Holt.

Gamson, William A. 1992. *Talking Politics*. Cambridge: Cambridge University Press.

Garsten, Bryan. 2006. *Saving Persuasion: A Defense of Rhetoric and Judgment*. Cambridge, MA: Harvard University Press.

Goethals, George R., and Richard F. Reckman. 1973. "The Perception of Consistency in Attitudes." *Journal of Experimental Social Psychology* 9:491–501.

Goffman, Erving. 1959. *The Presentation of Self in Everyday Life*. Garden City, NY: Doubleday.

———. 1963. *Behavior in Public Places; Notes on the Social Organization of Gatherings*. New York: Free Press.

———. 1971. *Relations in Public*. New York: Basic Books.

———. 1981. *Forms of Talk*. Philadelphia: University of Pennsylvania Press.

———. 1982. *Interaction Ritual: Essays on Face-to-Face Behavior*. New York: Pantheon.

———. 1986a. *Frame Analysis: An Essay on the Organization of Experience*. Boston: Northeastern University Press.

———. 1986b. *Stigma: Notes on the Management of Spoiled Identity*. New York: Simon & Schuster.

Greene, Joshua D., and Jonathan Haidt. 2002. "How (and Where) Does Moral Judgment Work?" *Trends in Cognitive Sciences* 6:517–23.

Greene, Joshua D., Leigh E. Nystrom, Andrew D. Engell, John M. Darley, and Jonathan D. Cohen. 2004. "The Neural Bases of Cognitive Conflict and Control in Moral Judgment." *Neuron* 44:389–400.

Greene, Joshua D., R. Brian Sommerville, Leigh E. Nystrom, John M. Darley, and Jonathan D. Cohen. 2001. "An fMRI Investigation of Emotional Engagement in Moral Judgment." *Science* 293:2105–8.

Habermas, Jürgen. 1984. *The Theory of Communicative Action*. Boston: Beacon.

Haidt, Jonathan. 2001. "The Emotional Dog and Its Rational Tail: A Social Intuitionist Approach to Moral Judgment." *Psychological Review* 108:814–34.

Haidt, Jonathan, and Craig M. Joseph. 2007. "The Moral Mind: How Five Sets of Innate Intuitions Guide the Development of Many Culture-Specific Virtues, and Perhaps Even Modules." In *The Innate Mind*, edited by Peter Carruthers, Stephen Laurence, and Stephen Stich, 367–92. Oxford: Oxford University Press.

Herzog, Don. 1998. *Poisoning the Minds of the Lower Orders*. Princeton, NJ: Princeton University Press.

Hibbing, John R., and Elizabeth Theiss-Morse. 2002. *Stealth Democracy: Americans' Beliefs About How Government Should Work*. Cambridge: Cambridge University Press.

Hobbes, Thomas. 1968. *Leviathan*. London: Penguin.

Hume, David. 1984. *A Treatise of Human Nature*. London: Penguin.

Hutcherson, Cendri, and James J. Gross. 2011. "The Moral Emotions: A Social–Functionalist Account of Anger, Disgust, and Contempt." *Journal of Personality and Social Psychology* 100:719–37.

Kahneman, Daniel, Paul Slovic, and Amos Tversky. 1982. *Judgment under Uncertainty: Heuristics and Biases*. Cambridge: Cambridge University Press.

Key, V. O., Jr., and M. C. Cummings. 1966. *The Responsible Electorate: Rationality in Presidential Voting 1936–1960*. New York: Vintage.

Kim, Jeansok J., and Mark G. Baxter. 2001. "Multiple Brain-Memory Systems: The Whole Does Not Equal the Sum of Its Parts." *Trends in Neurosciences* 24:324–30.

Kunda, Ziva. 1990. "The Case for Motivated Reason." *Psychological Bulletin* 108:480–98.

Ladd, Everett C. 1978. *Where Have All the Voters Gone?* New York: Norton.

Le Bon, Gustave. 1986. *The Crowd: A Study of the Popular Mind*. London: Unwin.

LeDoux, Joseph E. 1996. *The Emotional Brain: The Mysterious Underpinnings of Emotional Life*. New York: Simon & Schuster.

———. 2000. "Emotion Circuits in the Brain." In *Annual Reviews Neuroscience*, edited by W. Maxwell Cowan, Eric M. Shooter, Charles F. Stevens, and Richard F. Thompson, 155–95. Palo Alto, CA: Annual Reviews.

Levy, Jack S. 1992. "An Introduction to Prospect Theory." *Political Psychology* 13:171–86.

Lippmann, Walter. 1922. *Public Opinion*. New York: Macmillan.

MacKuen, Michael, Jennifer Wolak, Luke Keele, and George E. Marcus. 2010. "Civic Engagements: Resolute Partisanship or Reflective Deliberation." *American Journal of Political Science* 54:440–58.

Mansbridge, Jane J. 1980. *Beyond Adversary Democracy*. New York: Basic Books.

Marcus, George E., and Michael MacKuen. 1993. "Anxiety, Enthusiasm and the Vote: The Emotional Underpinnings of Learning and Involvement during Presidential Campaigns." *American Political Science Review* 87:688–701.

Marx, Karl, and Friedrich Engels. 2002. *The Communist Manifesto (Penguin Classics)*. New York: Penguin Classics.

Mercier, Hugo, and Dan Sperber. 2011. "Why Do Humans Reason? Arguments for an Argumentative Theory." *Behavioral and Brain Sciences* 34:57–111.

Milgram, Stanley. 1974. *Obedience to Authority*. New York: Harper and Row.

Miller, Dale T. 2001. "Disrespect and the Experience of Injustice." *Annual Review of Psychology* 52:527–53.

Miller, William Ian. 1990. *Bloodtaking and Peacemaking: Feud, Law, and Society in Saga Iceland*. Chicago: University of Chicago Press.

Moll, Jorge, and Ricardo de Oliveira-Souza. 2007. "Moral Judgments, Emotions and the Utilitarian Brain." *Trends in Cognitive Sciences* 11:319–21.

Monin, Benoît, David A. Pizarro, and Jennifer S. Beer. 2007. "Deciding Versus Reacting: Conceptions of Moral Judgment and the Reason-Affect Debate." *Review of General Psychology* 11:99–111.

Monroe, Kristen Renwick. 1996. *The Heart of Altruism: Perceptions of a Common Humanity.* Princeton, NJ: Princeton University Press.

Nisbett, Richard, and Lee Ross. 1982. *Human Inference: Strategies and Shortcomings of Social Judgment.* Englewood Cliffs, NJ: Prentice-Hall.

Njál's Saga. 1960. Translated by Pálsson Hermann. Baltimore: Penguin.

Oakeshott, Michael. 1975. *On Human Conduct.* Oxford: Oxford University Press.

Pateman, Carol. 1970. *Participation and Democratic Theory.* Cambridge: Cambridge University Press.

Plato. 1974. *The Republic.* New York: Penguin.

Popkin, Samuel L. 1991. *The Reasoning Voter: Communication and Persuasion in Presidential Campaigns.* Chicago: University of Chicago Press.

Quattrone, George A., and Amos Tversky. 1988. "Contrasting Rational and Psychological Analyses of Political Choice." *American Political Science Review* 82:719–36.

Rawls, John. 1993. *Political Liberalism.* New York: Columbia University Press.

Rosenblum, Nancy L. 1999. "Navigating Pluralism: The Democracy of Everyday Life (and Where It Is Learned)." In *Citizen Competence and Democratic Institutions*, edited by Stanley L. Elkin and Karol Edward Soltan, 67–88. University Park: Pennsylvania University Press.

Rozin, Paul, Jonathan Haidt, and Clark R. McCauley. 2000. "Disgust." In *Handbook of Emotions*, edited by Marc D. Lewis and M. Haviland-Jones, 637–53. New York: Guildford.

Sanders, Lynn M. 1997. "Against Deliberation." *Political Theory* 25:347–77.

Schattschneider, E. E. 1960. *The Semi-Sovereign People.* New York: Holt, Rinehart and Winston.

Scott, James C. 1998. *Seeing Like a State: How Certain Schemes to Improve the Human Condition Have Failed.* New Haven, CT: Yale University Press.

Segall, M. H., D. T. Campbell, and M. J. Herskovits. 1966. *The Influence of Culture on Visual Perception.* Indianapolis, IN: Bobbs-Merrill.

Sherif, Muzafer. 1958. "Group Influences upon the Formation of Norms and Attitudes." In *Readings in Social Psychology*, edited by Eleanor Maccoby, T. M. Newcomb, and E. L. Hartley, 219–32. New York: Holt.

———. 1966. *Group Conflict and Competition.* London: Routledge & Kegan Paul.

Sherry, David F., and Daniel L. Schacter. 1987. "The Evolution of Multiple Memory Systems." *Psychological Review* 94:439–54.

Squire, Larry R., and Eric R. Kandel. 1999. *Memory: From Mind to Molecules.* New York: Scientific American Library. Distributed by Freeman.

Stanton, Mark E. 2000. "Multiple Memory Systems, Development and Conditioning." *Behavioral Brain Research* 110:25–37.

Sullivan, Brandon A., Mark Snyder, and John L. Sullivan. 2007. *Cooperation: The Political Psychology of Effective Human Interaction.* New York: Wiley-Blackwell.

Takahashi, Hidehiko, Noriaki Yahata, Michihiko Koeda, Tetsuya Matsuda, Kunihiko Asai, and Yoshiro Okubo. 2004. "Brain Activation Associated With Evaluative Processes of Guilt and Embarrassment: An fMRI Study." *NeuroImage* 23:967–74.

Tangney, June Price, Jeff Stuewig, and Debra J. Mashek. 2007. "Moral Emotions and Moral Behavior." *Annual Review of Psychology* 58:345–72.

Thompson, Dennis. 1970. *The Democratic Citizen: Social Science and Democratic Theory in the Twentieth Century*. New York: Cambridge University Press.

Todorov, Alexander, and John A. Bargh. 2002. "Automatic Sources of Aggression." *Aggression and Violent Behavior* 7:53–68.

Willis, Janine, and Alexander Todorov. 2006. "First Impressions: Making Up Your Mind after a 100-ms Exposure to a Face." *Psychological Science* 17:592–98.

Young, Iris Marion. 1990. *Justice and the Politics of Difference*. Princeton, NJ: Princeton University Press.

———. 2000. *Inclusion and Democracy*. Oxford ; New York: Oxford University Press.

Zahn, Roland, Jorge Moll, Mirella Paiva, Griselda Garrido, Frank Krueger, Edward D. Huey, and Jordan Grafman. 2009. "The Neural Basis of Human Social Values: Evidence from Functional MRI." *Cerebral Cortex* 19:176–283.

Zimbardo, Philip G. 2008. *The Lucifer Effect: Understanding How Good People Turn Evil*. New York: Random House Trade Paperbacks.

Appendix

WRITTEN WITH PETER HATEMI

The variety of work and the explosive growth of literature on the biology of human nature are far greater than I can cover in this chapter or book. But, with Professor Peter Hatemi, in this appendix I provide a selection of the essential literature, both classical and current.

CRITICAL BOOKS AND ARTICLES EXPLORING BIOLOGICAL SOURCES OF VARIATION IN PERSONALITY

Carey, Gregory. 2003. *Human Genetics for the Social Sciences*. Thousand Oaks, CA: Sage. (book is also on his website in pdf form). Alternative for undergraduates: Plomin, Robert. 2008. *Behavioral Genetics*. New York: Worth.

Bouchard, T., D. Lykken, M. McGue, N. Segal, A. Tellegen. 1990. "Sources of Human Psychological Differences, the Minnesota Study of Twins Reared Apart." *Science* 250:223–28.

Eaves, L. J. 1977. "Inferring the Causes of Human Variation." *Journal of the Royal Statistical Society* 140: 324–55.

Eaves, L. J., H. J. Eysenck, and N. G. Martin. 1989. *Genes, Culture, and Personality: An Empirical Approach*. London: Academic.

Fisher, R. A. 1918. "The Correlation between Relatives on the Supposition of Mendelian Inheritance." *Transactions of the Royal Society of Edinburgh* 52: 399–433.

Jinks, J. L., and D. W. Fulker. 1970. A Comparison of the Biometrical Genetical, Classical and MAVA Approaches to the Analysis of Human Behavior. *Psychological Bulletin* 73:311–49.

Koten, Jan Willem, Jr., Guilherme Wood, Peter Hagoort, Rainer Goebel, Peter Propping, Klaus Willmes, and Dorret I. Boomsma. 2009. "Genetic Contribution to Variation in Cognitive Function: An fMRI Study in Twins." *Science* 323:1737–40.

Oliver, Bonamy R., and Robert Plomin. 2007. "Twins' Early Development Study (TEDS): A Multivariate, Longitudinal Genetic Investigation of Language, Cognition and Behavior Problems from Childhood through Adolescence." *Twin Research and Human Genetics* 10:96–105.

Plomin, Robert. 2003. *Behavioral Genetics in the Postgenomic Era*. Washington, DC: American Psychological Association.

GENE ENVIRONMENT INTERACTIONS

Caspi, Avshalom, and Terrie E. Moffitt. 2006. "Gene-Environment Interaction Research, Joining Forces with Neuroscience." *Nature Reviews Neuroscience* 7:583–90.

Champagne, Frances A., and James P. Curley. 2005. "How Social Experiences Influence the Brain." *Current Opinion in Neurobiology* 15:704–9.

Colvis, Christine M., Jonathan D. Pollock, Richard H. Goodman, Soren Impey, John Dunn, Gail Mandel, Frances A. Champagne et al. 2007. "Epigenetic Mechanisms and Gene Networks in the Nervous System." *The Journal of Neuroscience* 25:10379–89.

Fox, N. A., Nichols, K. E., Henderson, H. A., Rubin, K., Schmidt, L., Hamer, D., Ernst, M., & Pine, D. S. 2005. Evidence for a gene–environment interaction in predicting behavioral inhibition in middle childhood. *Psychological Science* 16:921–26.

Fox, Nathan A., Amie A. Hane, Daniel S. Pine. 2007. Plasticity for Affective Neurocircuitry: How the Environment Affects Gene Expression. *Current Directions in Psychological Science* 16:1–5.

Moffitt, Terrie E., Avshalom Caspi, and Michael Rutter. 2005. "A Research Strategy for Investigating Interactions between Measured Genes and Measured Environments." *Archives of General Psychiatry* 62:473–81.

Rutter, Michael, Terrie E. Moffitt, and Avshalom Caspi. 2006. "Gene-Environment Interplay and Psychopathology: Multiple Varieties but Real Effects." *Journal of Child Psychology and Psychiatry* 47:226–61.

MOTOR ACTION (BEHAVIOR)

Castiello, U., Y. Paulignan, and M. Jeannerod. 1991. "Temporal Dissociation of Motor Responses and Subjective Awareness." *Brain* 114:2639–55.

Jeannerod, Marc. 2006. *Motor Cognition: What Actions Tell the Self.* Oxford: Oxford University Press.

Ramachandran, V. S. 1992. "Filling in the Blind Spot." *Nature* 356:115.

Ramachandran, V. S., D. Rogers-Ramachandran, and S. Cobb. 1995. "Touching the Phantom Limb." *Nature* 377:489–90.

Yang, Tony T., Gallen B. Schwartz, F. E. Bloom, V. S. Ramachandran, and S. Cobb. 1994. "Sensory Maps in the Human Brain." *Nature* 368:592–93.

VISION

Milner, A. D., and Melvyn A. Goodale. 1995. *The Visual Brain in Action.* Oxford: Oxford University Press.

Ramachandran, V. S., and R. L. Gregory. 1991. "Perceptual Filling In of Artificially Induced Scotomas in Human Vision." *Nature* 350:699–702.

MEMORY

Levine, Linda, and Robin Edelstein. 2009. "Emotion and Memory Narrowing: A Review and Goal-Relevance Approach." *Cognition and Emotion* 23:833–75.

Libet, Benjamin. 2004. *Mind Time: The Temporal Factor in Consciousness.* Cambridge, MA: Harvard University Press.

Kim, Jeansok J., and Mark G. Baxter. 2001. "Multiple Brain-Memory Systems: The Whole Does Not Equal the Sum of Its Parts." *Trends in Neurosciences* 24:324–30.

Rolls, Edmund T. 2000. "Memory Systems in the Brain." *Annual Review of Psychology* 51:599–630.

Squire, Larry R., and Eric R. Kandel. 1999. *Memory: From Mind to Molecules*. New York: Scientific American Library. Distributed by Freeman.

SEMINAL PIECES REGARDING GENES AND POLITICAL ATTITUDES

Eaves, L. J., and H. J. Eysenck. 1974. "Genetics and the Development of Social Attitudes. *Nature* 249:288–89.

Martin, N. G., L. J. Eaves, A. C. Heath, R. Jardine, L. Feingold, and H. J. Eysenck. 1986. "The Transmission of Social Attitudes." *Proceedings of the National Academy of Sciences* 83:4364–68.

APPLICATIONS TO POLITICAL PSYCHOLOGY—
SELECTED EXAMPLES

Amodio, David M., John T. Jost, Sarah L. Master, and Cindy M. Yee. 2007. "Neurocognitive Correlates of Liberalism and Conservatism." *Nature Neuroscience* 10:1246–47.

Cacioppo, John T., and Penny S. Visser. 2003. "Political Psychology and Social Neuroscience: Strange Bedfellows or Comrades in Arms?" *Political Psychology* 24:647–56.

Fowler, James H., and Darren Schreiber. 2008. "Biology, Politics, and the Emerging Science of Human Nature." *Science* 322:912–14.

Hatemi, Peter K., Carolyn Funk, Hermine Maes, Judy Silberg, Sarah Medland, Nicholas Martin, and Lindon Eaves. 2009. "Genetic Influences on Social Attitudes over the Life Course." *Journal of Politics* 71: 1141–56.

Hatemi, Peter K., John R. Hibbing, Sarah E. Medland, Matthew C. Keller, John R. Alford, Kevin B. Smith, Nicholas G. Martin, and Lindon J. Eaves. 2009. "Not by Twins Alone: Using the Extended Family Design to Investigate Genetic Influence on Political Beliefs." *American Journal of Political Science* 54:798–814.

Kato, Junko, Hiroko Ide, Ikuo Kabashima, Hiroshi Kadota, Kouji Takano, and Kenji Kansaku. 2009. "Neural Correlates of Attitude Change Following Positive and Negative Advertisements." *Frontiers in Behavioral Neuroscience* 3:1–13.

Knutson, Kristine M., Jacqueline N. Wood, Maria V. Spampinato, and Jordan Grafman. 2006. "Politics on the Brain: An fMRI Investigation." *Social Neuroscience* 1:25–40.

Lieberman, Matthew D., Darren Schreiber, and Kevin Ochsner. 2003. "Is Political Cognition Like Riding a Bicycle? How Cognitive Neuroscience Can Inform Research on Political Thinking." *Political Psychology* 24:681–704.

Marcus, George E. 2002. *The Sentimental Citizen: Emotion in Democratic Politics*. University Park: Pennsylvania State University Press.

Marcus, George E., W. Russell Neuman, and Michael B. MacKuen. 2000. *Affective Intelligence and Political Judgment*. Chicago: University of Chicago Press.

MacKuen, Michael, Jennifer Wolak, Luke Keele, and George E. Marcus. 2010. "Civic Engagements: Resolute Partisanship or Reflective Deliberation." *American Journal of Political Science*. 54:440–58.

Neuman, W. Russell, George E. Marcus, Ann Crigler, and Michael B. MacKuen, eds. 2007. *The Affect Effect: Dynamics of Emotion in Thinking and Behavior*. Chicago: University of Chicago Press.

Oxley, Douglas R., Kevin B. Smith, John R. Alford, Matthew V. Hibbing, Jennifer L. Miller, Mario Scalora, Peter K. Hatemi, and John R. Hibbing. 2008. "Political Attitudes Vary With Physiological Traits." *Science* 321:1667–70.

Spezio, Michael L., Antonio Rangel, Ramon Michael Alvarez, John P. O'Doherty, Kyle Mattes, Alexander Todorov, Hackjin Kim, and Ralph Adolphs. 2008. "A Neural Basis for the Effect of Candidate Appearance on Election Outcomes." *Social and Cognitive Affective Neuroscience* 3:344–52.

Todorov, Alexander, Anesu N. Mandisodza, Amir Goren, and Crystal C. Hall. 2005. "Inferences of Competence From Faces Predict Election Outcomes." *Science* 308:1623–26.

Veen, Vincent van, Marie K. Krug, Jonathan W. Schooler, and Cameron S. Carter. 2009. "Neural Activity Predicts Attitude Change in Cognitive Dissonance." *Nature Neuroscience* 12:1469–74.

Verhulst, Brad, Peter K Hatemi, and Nicholas G. Martin. 2010. "The Nature of the Relationship between Personality Traits and Political Attitudes." *Personality and Individual Differences* 49:306–16.

Westen, Drew, Pavel S. Blagov, Keith Harenski, Clint Kilts, and Stephan Hamann. 2006. "Neural Bases of Motivated Reasoning: An fMRI Study of Emotional Constraints on Partisan Political Judgment in the 2004 U.S. Presidential Election." *Journal of Cognitive Neuroscience* 18:1947–58.

DEVELOPMENTAL PSYCHOLOGY

Dixon, W. E. (2003). *Twenty Studies That Revolutionized Child Psychology*. Upper Saddle River, NJ: Prentice Hall.

Hess, Robert D, and Judith Torney-Purta. 2006. *The Development of Political Attitudes in Children*. New Brunswick, NJ: Aldine.

EARLY SEMINAL WORK ON PERSONALITY

Eysenck, H. J. 1954. *The Psychology of Politics*. London: Routledge and K. Paul.

Gray, Jeffrey A. 1987. *The Psychology of Fear and Stress*. Cambridge: Cambridge University Press.

Wilson, Glenn D. 1973. *The Psychology of Conservatism*. London: Academic.

SOME PRIMERS: EVOLUTIONARY ACCOUNTS AND PROBABILISTIC EPIGENESIS

Darwin, Charles. 1998. *The Expression of the Emotions in Man and Animals*. New York: Oxford University Press.

Davidson, R. J. 2001. Toward a Biology of Personality and Emotion. *Annals of the N.Y. Academy of Science* 935:191–207.

Gottlieb, G. 2007. "Probabilistic Epigenesis." *Developmental Science* 10:1–11.

AFFECTIVE NEUROSCIENCE

Early Basics

James, William. 1883. "What is Emotion?" *Mind* 9:188–204.

———. 1894. "The Physical Basis of Emotion." *Psychological Review* 1:516–29.

Lazarus, Richard. 1984. "On the Primacy of Cognition." *American Psychologist* 39:124–29.

Ochsner, Kevin N., Rebecca R. Ray, Brent Hughes, Kateri McRae, Jeffrey C. Cooper, Jochen Weber, John D. E. Gabrieli, and James J. Gross. 2009. "Bottom-Up and Top-Down Processes in Emotion Generation: Common and Distinct Neural Mechanism." *Psychological Science* 20:1322–31.

Zajonc, Robert B. 1980. "Feeling and Thinking: Preferences Need No Inferences." *American Psychologist* 35:151–75.
This last is a recent article that revisits Zajonc and Lazarus after twenty-five plus years (note that the title implies a spatial relationship, "bottom-up" and "top-down," reflecting how difficult is to give up dated conceptions of the relationship between the intuitive and reasoning systems, to use Haidt's terms, for newer understandings temporality).

Recent Basics

Berkowitz, Leonard. 2000. *Causes and Consequences of Feelings.* Cambridge: Cambridge University Press.

Bradley, Margaret M. 2000. "Motivation and Emotion." In *Handbook of Psychophysiology*, edited by John T. Cacioppo, L. G. Tassinary, and G. G. Berntson, 602–42. New York: Cambridge University Press.

Cacioppo, John T., and Wendi L. Gardner. 1999. "Emotion." *Annual Review of Psychology* 50:191–214.

Cacioppo, John T., David J. Klein, Gary G. Berntson, and Elaine Hatfield. 1993. "The Psychophysiology of Emotion." In *The Handbook of Emotion*, edited by R. Lewis and J. M. Haviland, 602–42. New York: Guilford.

Cacioppo, John T., Jeff T. Larsen, N. Kyle Smith, and Gary G. Berntson. 2004. "The Affect System: What Lurks Below the Surface of Feelings?" In *Feelings and Emotions: The Amsterdam Conference*, edited by Antony S. R. Manstead, Nico H. Frijda, and A. H. Fischer, 223–42. New York: Cambridge University Press.

Cacioppo, John T., Catherine J. Norris, Jean Decety, George Monteleone, and Howard Nusbaum. 2008. "In the Eye of the Beholder: Individual Differences in Perceived Social Isolation Predict Regional Brain Activation to Social Stimuli." *Journal of Cognitive Neuroscience* 21:83–92.

Davidson, Richard J. 1993. "The Neuropsychology of Emotion and Affective Style." In *Handbook of Emotions*, edited by Michael Lewis and Jeannette E. Haviland, 143–54. New York: Guildford.

Davidson, Richard J., and Kenneth Hugdahl. 1995. *Brain Asymmetry.* Cambridge, MA: MIT Press.

Davidson, Richard J., Daren C. Jackson, and Ned H. Kalin. 2000. "Emotion, Plasticity, Context, and Regulation: Perspectives from Affective Neuroscience." *Psychological Bulletin* 126:890–909.

Forgas, Joseph P. 1995. "Mood and Judgment: The Affect Infusion Model (Aim)." *Psychological Bulletin* 117:39–66.

Frijda, Nico H. 1993. "Moods, Emotion Episodes, and Emotions." In *Handbook of Emotions*, edited by Michael Lewis, and Jeannette E. Haviland, 381–403. New York: Guildford.

Frijda, Nico H., Peter Kuipers, and Elisabeth ter Schure. 1989. "Relations among Emotion, Appraisal, and Emotional Action Readiness." *Journal of Personality and Social Psychology* 57:212–28.

Izard, Carroll E. 2009. "Emotion Theory and Research: Highlights, Unanswered Questions, and Emerging Issues." *Annual Review of Psychology* 60:1–25.

Lane, Richard D., Lynn Nadel, and Geoffrey Ahern. 2000. *Cognitive Neuroscience of Emotion.* New York: Oxford University Press.

LeDoux, Joseph E. 1994. "Emotion, Memory and the Brain." *Scientific American* 270:32–39.

———. 2000. "Emotion Circuits in the Brain." In *Annual Reviews Neuroscience*, edited by W. Maxwell Cowan, Eric M. Shooter, Charles F. Stevens, and Richard F. Thompson, 155–84. Palo Alto, CA: Annual Reviews.

Lewis, Michael, Jeannette M. Haviland-Jones, and Lisa Feldman Barrett. 2008. *Handbook of Emotions*. New York: Guilford.

Ortony, Andrew, Gerald L. Clore, and Allan Collins. 1989. *The Cognitive Structure of Emotions*. New York: Cambridge University Press.

Panksepp, Jaak. 1998. *Affective Neuroscience: The Foundations of Human and Animal Emotions*. New York: Oxford University Press.

Phelps, Elizabeth A. 2006. "Emotion and Cognition: Insights from Studies of the Human Amygdala." *Annual Review of Psychology* 57:27–53.

Rolls, Edmund T. 1999. *The Brain and Emotion*. Oxford: Oxford University Press.

———. 2000. "Memory Systems in the Brain." *Annual Review of Psychology* 51:599–630.

———. 2005. *Emotion Explained*. Oxford: Oxford University Press.

Rozin, Paul, Jonathan Haidt, and Clark R. McCauley. 2000. "Disgust." In Handbook of Emotions, edited by Marc D. Lewis and M. Haviland-Jones, 637–53. New York: Guildford.

Scherer, Klaus R., Angela Schorr, and Tom Johnstone. 2001. Appraisal Processes in Emotion: Theory, Methods, Research. Oxford: Oxford University Press.

Consciousness and Preconsciousness

Engell, Andrew D., James V. Haxby, and Alexander Todorov. 2007. "Implicit Trustworthiness Decisions: Automatic Coding of Face Properties in the Human Amygdala." *Journal of Cognitive Neuroscience* 19:1508–19.

Gazzaniga, Michael. 1985. *The Social Brain: Discovering the Networks of the Mind*. New York: Basic Books.

———. 1992. *Nature's Mind: The Biological Roots of Thinking, Emotions, Sexuality, Language, and Intelligence*. New York: Basic Books.

———. 2008. *Human: The Science Behind What Makes Us Unique*. New York: Ecco.

Koch, Christof, and Naotsugu Tsuchiya. "Attention and Consciousness: Two Distinct Brain Processes." *Trends in Cognitive Sciences* 11:16–22.

Libet, Benjamin. 1985. "Unconscious Cerebral Initiative and the Role of Conscious Will in Voluntary Action." *The Behavioral and Brain Sciences* 8:529–66.

Libet, Benjamin, Curtis A. Gleason, Elwood W. Wright, and Dennis K. Pearl. 1983. "Time of Conscious Intention to Act in Relation to Onset of Cerebral Activity (Readiness-Potential)." *Brain* 106:623–42.

Libet, Benjamin, Jr., Elwood W. Wright, Bertram Feinstein, and Dennis K. Pearl. 1979. "Subjective Referral of the Timing for a Conscious Sensory Experience." *Brain* 102:1597–1600.

Öhman, Arne, Ulf Dimberg, and F. Esteves. 1989. "Preattentive Activation of Aversive Emotions." In *Aversion, Avoidance, and Anxiety: Perspectives on Aversively Motivated Behavior*, edited by T. Archer and L. G. Nilsson, 169–93. Hillsdale, NJ: Erlbaum.

Öhman, Arne, and Susan Mineka. 2001. "Fears, Phobias, and Preparedness: Towards an Evolved Module of Fear and Fear Learning." *Psychological Review* 108:483–522.

Öhman, Arne, and Joaquim J. F. Soares. 1993. "On the Automatic Nature of Phobic Fear: Conditioned Electrodermal Responses to Masked Fear-Relevant Stimuli." *Journal of Abnormal Psychology* 102:121–32.

Todorov, Alexander, and John A. Bargh. 2002. "Automatic Sources of Aggression." *Aggression and Violent Behavior* 7:53–68.

Tsuchiya, Naotsugu, and Ralph Adolphs. 2007. "Emotion and Consciousness." *Trends in Cognitive Sciences* 11:158–67.

Wegner, Daniel M. 2002. *The Illusion of Conscious Will*. Cambridge, MA: MIT Press.

Weiskrantz, Lawrence. 1986. *Blindsight: A Case Study and Implications*. Oxford: Oxford University Press.

Willis, Janine, and Alexander Todorov. 2006. "First Impressions: Making Up Your Mind after a 100-ms Exposure to a Face." *Psychological Science* 17:592–98.

AMYGDALA—A BIT OF NEUROBIOLOGY TO GET YOU STARTED

The amygdala (we actually have two) is a small region of the brain that has important roles to play. The selected readings cover many of the early and more recent work on its many functions.

Adolphs, Ralph. 2008. "Fear, Faces, and the Human Amygdala." *Current Opinion in Neurobiology* 18:166–72.

Costafreda, Sergi G., Michael J. Brammer, Anthony S. David, and Cynthia H. Y. Fu. 2008. "Predictors of Amygdala Activation During the Processing of Emotional Stimuli: A Meta-Analysis of 385 Pet and fMRI Studies." *Brain Research Review* 58:57–70.

LeDoux, Joseph E. 2007. "Primer: The Amygdala." *Current Biology* 17:R868–74.

Murray, Elisabeth A. 2007. "The Amygdala, Reward and Emotion." *Trends in Cognitive Sciences* 11:489–97.

Murray, Elisabeth A., and Alicia Izquierdo. 2007. "Orbitofrontal Cortex and Amygdala Contributions to Affect and Action in Primates." *Annals of the New York Academy of Science* 1121:273–96.

Said, Christopher P., Sean G. Baron, and Alexander Todorov. 2008. "Nonlinear Amygdala Response to Face Trustworthiness: Contributions of High and Low Spatial Frequency Information." *Journal of Cognitive Neuroscience* 21:519–28.

Schaefer, Alexandre, and Jeremy R. Gray. 2007. "A Role for the Human Amygdala in Higher Cognition." *Reviews in the Neurosciences* 18:355–63.

Sergerie, Karine, Caroline Chochol, and Jorge L. Armony. 2008. "The Role of the Amygdala in Emotional Processing: A Quantitative Meta-Analysis of Functional Neuroimaging Studies." *Neuroscience and Biobehavioral Reviews* 32:811–30.

Seymour, Ben, and Ray Dolan. 2008. "Emotion, Decision Making, and the Amygdala." *Neuron* 58:662–71.

SOCIAL NEUROSCIENCE

Adolphs, Ralph. 2003. "The Neurobiology of Social Cognition." *Current Opinion in Neurobiology* 11:231–39.

———. 2009. "The Social Brain: Neural Basis of Social Knowledge." *Annual Review of Psychology* 60:693–716.

Adolphs, Ralph, Daniel Tranel, and Antonoio R. Damasio. 1998. "The Human Amygdala in Social Judgment." *Nature* 393:470–74.

Cacioppo, John T. 2002. *Foundations in Social Neuroscience*. Cambridge, MA: MIT Press.

Cacioppo, John T., and Gary G. Berntson. 2004. *Essays in Social Neuroscience*. Cambridge, MA: MIT Press.

———. 2004. *Social Neuroscience: Key Readings*. New York: Ohio State University Psychology Press.

BEHAVIORAL DEVELOPMENT

Jackson, Philip L., and Jean Decety. 2005. "Motor Cognition: A New Paradigm to Study Self-Other Interactions." *Current Opinion in Neurobiology* 14:259–63.

Karmiloff-Smith, A. 1994. "Precis of Beyond Modularity: A Developmental Perspective on Cognitive Science." *Behavioral and Brain Sciences* 17:693–745.

Smith, Linda B., and Esther Thelen. 2003. "Development as a Dynamic System." *Trends in Cognitive Sciences* 7:343–48.

NEURAL DEVELOPMENT

Davidson, Richard J., Daren C. Jackson, and Ned H. Kalin. 2000. "Emotion, Plasticity, Context, and Regulation: Perspectives from Affective Neuroscience." *Psychological Bulletin* 126:890–909.

Rizzolatti, Giacomo, and Corrado Sinigaglia. 2008. Mirrors in the Brain: How Our Minds Share Actions and Emotions. Oxford: Oxford University Press.

Sanes, Dan Harvey, Thomas A. Reh, and William A. Harris. 2006. *Development of the Nervous System.* Amsterdam: Elsevier.

DECISION NEUROSCIENCE

Bechara, Antoine, Hanna Damasio, Daniel Tranel, and Antonio R. Damasio. 1997. "Deciding Advantageously Before Knowing the Advantageous Strategy." *Science* 175:1293–95.

Coricelli, Giorgio, Hugo D. Critchley, Mateus Joffily, John P. O'Doherty, Angela Sirigu, and Raymond J. Dolan. 2005. "Regret and Its Avoidance: A Neuroimaging Study of Choice Behavior." *Nature Neuroscience* 8:1255–62.

Frank, Michael J., and Eric D. Claus. 2006. "Anatomy of a Decision: Striato-Orbitofrontal Interactions in Reinforcement Learning, Decision Making, and Reversal." *Psychological Review* 113:300–26.

Glimcher, Paul W., and Aldo Rustichini. 2004. "Neuroeconomics: The Consilience of Brain and Decision." *Science* 306:447–52.

Grabenhorst, Fabian, and Edmund T. Rolls. 2009. "Different Representations of Relative and Absolute Subjective Value in the Human Brain." *NeuroImage* 48:258–68.

Greene, Joshua D., and Jonathan Haidt. 2002. "How (and Where) Does Moral Judgment Work?" *Trends in Cognitive Sciences* 6:517–23.

Greene, Joshua D., Leigh E. Nystrom, Andrew D. Engell, John M. Darley, and Jonathan D. Cohen. 2004. "The Neural Bases of Cognitive Conflict and Control in Moral Judgment." *Neuron* 44:389–400.

Greene, Joshua D., R. Brian Sommerville, Leigh E. Nystrom, John M. Darley, and Jonathan D. Cohen. 2001. "An fMRI Investigation of Emotional Engagement in Moral Judgment." *Science* 293:2105–8.

Hampton, Alan N., Ralph Adolphs, J. Michael Tyszka, and John P. O'Doherty. 2007. "Contributions of the Amygdala to Reward Expectancy and Choice Signals in Human Prefrontal Cortex." *Neuron* 55:545–55.

Hsu, Ming, Meghana Bhatt, Ralph Adolphs, Daniel Tranel, and Colin F. Camerer. 2005. "Neural Systems Responding to Degrees of Uncertainty in Human Decision-Making." *Science* 310:1680–83.

Kato, Junko, Hiroko Ide, Ikuo Kabashima, Hiroshi Kadota, Kouji Takano, and Kenji Kansaku. 2009. "Neural Correlates of Attitude Change Following Positive and Negative Advertisements." *Frontiers in Behavioral Neuroscience* 3:1–13.

Padoa-Schioppa. 2007. "Orbitofrontal Cortex and the Computation of Economic Value." *Annals of the New York Academy of Science* 1121:232–53.

Sanfey, Alan G., James K. Rilling, Jessica A. Aronson, Leigh E. Nystrom, and Jonathan D. Cohen. 2003. "The Neural Basis of Economic Decision-Making in the Ultimatum Game." *Science* 300:1755–58.

Walton, Mark E., Joseph T. Devlin, and Matthew F. S. Rushworth. 2004. "Interactions between Decision Making and Performance Monitoring Within Prefrontal Cortex." *Nature Neuroscience* 7:1259–63.

Weber, Elke U., and Eric A. Johnson. 2009. "Mindful Judgment and Decision Making." *Annual Review of Psychology* 60:53–85.

SECTION
III

Political Social Psychology

CHAPTER 9

Using the Past and Present to Live in the Future

A Brief Reprise

Humans began as a species living in small hunter-gatherer groups. Unlike most but not all social species, humans have the ability to make choices, individual decisions, to guide us in what to do. In the hunter-gather period, decisions revolved around the individual and collective effort to secure food, shelter, and the effort to protect the group against sundry threats, including other groups of humans. Once humans developed agriculture they gained the ability to store large quantities of food. And, having a stable yield enabled some to be freed from food generation tasks so they could fully engage in nonfood related activities.

More complex social organizations soon developed in which some would become princes and kings, priests, bankers, tradesmen, scribes, leather makers, soldiers, weavers, sculptors, musicians, and more. Thus, specialized expertise associated with each of these activities became a defining feature of human affairs.

BOX 9.1 **Sexual reproduction, imagination, and nature**

A stable, unchanging world needs a best solution. A changing world, especially one that experiences novel changes, needs a species that can generate new responses to new challenges.

Sexual reproduction introduces variety as a normal outcome of the regeneration of the species. This mode of reproduction seems well matched to the demands of changing environments, whether change arise independent of human endeavor or as a consequence thereof. Variety, aligned with the faculty of imagination, generates a richer pool or possible responses to the variety of challenges that await.

And, with that development came systematic training in these tasks as some became acolytes, apprentices, and students attending various schools (among the more influential being military and religious).

As humans created ways of living in settled and ever larger communities the organization of civilized experience became richer, more extensive, and varied. The expectation that the development of civilization is a progressive one, however different people understand the possible trajectories of improvement, remains foundational in the enlightenment project. Humans have throughout the millennia of our time on earth made decisions that changed the landscape, social and physical. How we go about making those decisions is a core focus of political psychology.

The decisions we make construct, in part, the future we thereby shape and enter. Humans have many abilities that aid us in making decisions. We make use of imagination to depict the world we hope to experience. We can recall past experience. We can rely on authorities to make decisions for us. We can gather and discuss our options. However, we lack one specific capacity: omniscience. Humans, no matter how intelligent, observant, and intuitive we might be, do not *know* the future. We cannot see it, smell it, touch it, hear it, or taste it. Lacking the ability to know the future leaves us with a major challenge.

Consider: Should I approach my next social interaction with the expectation that it will be helpful or dangerous? I will not know, no matter how familiar my anticipated partner(s), until *after* I actually experience the event. Of course, that lack of omniscience puts me at risk. I might miss what would turn out to be a very mutually advantageous interaction by being standoffish or suspicious. On the other hand, if I engage with positive expectations, I might face another risk. I might become victimized by a duplicitous glad handing "con man."

In a similar way, as a community, we might decide to launch a new adventure, perhaps to sign a trade agreement with another community, we might decide to settle a long-standing conflict, or instead commence a war against our neighbors. In each instance, the future we enter will, at the moment of decision, be unknown. But, no matter our confidence and certainty, every beginning faces the prospect of unknown results.

History offers a rich array of various means humans have used to deal with the mystery of the unseen and unknown future. We have guessed. We have read tea leaves, thrown the bones, and relied on yet other oracular devices such as "reading" the entrails of sacrificed animals. We have relied on past experience to make a prediction. Science is an activity that evaluates past and present observable patterns with as much objectivity as possible to identify recurring patterns. And, having mapped these recurring relationships, we can and have used them to generate predictions. Of course that

---

BOX 9.2 Con man

The term is a contraction of "confidence man," meaning someone who preys on gullible individuals making the victims feel confident during their common endeavor, not knowing how imprudent that confidence will soon prove to be. All "cons" work by manipulating the victim's expectations.

premise rests on the validity of the expectation that what has been shown to be reliable in the past will prove to so in the future. This applies to decisions meant to manipulate the physical, such as building bridges, and to modify human activity, such as building economies or seeking to enhance social harmony and diminish violent conflict. What happened last time something similar occurred predicts, we hope, what will happen yet again. Perhaps the past will replicate itself.

However we can also reject past patterns and rely on solely contemporary considerations, using our best current grasp of affairs, of our newly conceived options, and our expectation as to likely outcomes associated with each option.

If we began without the presumption of continuity and relied solely on today's signs, what might we conclude about the future of this prospective endeavor? No matter which or both means we use, and setting aside overweening confidence and bluster, we have, at best, fallible *opinions* about the future.

For those who put their trust in science and its ability to domesticate experience, I remind myself (for I am in that camp) and you, that we too often find that science fails. Wars that begin in great confidence of swift and certain victory, guided by military science, often lead to disaster and great cost. Economic growth, guided by economic science often and repeatedly, collapse in financial crisis as the latest bubble bursts. Regulators installed to prevent exploitation, reliant on administrative science, become corrupted. The list of technical expectations derived from established research, political, social, economic, and technological that have failed is lengthy. The most recent financial crisis wiped out trillions of dollars of capital worldwide but, like many other such "unpredictable" events, it has taken a nip out of the economics discipline; though, not to worry, as we can be confident that the ranks of economists will soon repair their confidence in the rightness of their convictions; failings are often just temporary in their impact on human beliefs (Festinger 1956).

I. EXPLAINING HUMAN DECISION MAKING: CONTEXT

To this point I have examined the conventional array of factors that explain how people opt to make decisions. Decisions can be formed by relying on past experience, attending to our abilities in the moment, or combine elements of each. In psychology, this distinction has relied on the language of "trait," the long standing orientations previously secured either from genetic or experience, or "state," the contemporaneous effects of the moment. Table 9.1 provides a simple (and simplistic) listing of representatives of each class. Within each category, we find a large variety of competing taxonomies. The "big five" is currently the most widely agreed on description of personality in psychology and it is proving useful in examining political behavior. But, we have seen that other "traits" have been very usefully applied in political psychology. For example,

---

BOX 9.3   Explicit reason as the source for solutions

While emphasizing that explicit consideration is the primary craft that enables humans to govern themselves, I also remind you that reason has long been tied to tyranny because imaginative reason breaches reliance on previously trusted authorities (Saxonhouse 1988).

Table 9.1. State and trait factors used by political psychologists to explain political judgment

Trait: Past factors	State: Present factors
Genes	Contemporary perceptions
Personality (e.g., the "big five" but also other traits, such as SDO, RWA, etc.)	Contemporary judgments (explicit, deliberative)
Beliefs, values, heuristics, and the like (e.g., ideology, group identifications, etc.)	Contemporary "implicit" assessments (preconscious affective appraisals)
Previously learned affective routines and predisposition and the like	Contemporary behavioral actions and reactions and the like

among traits that have been used are: authoritarianism either as right-wing authoritarianism (RWA), or social conformity (SCS); social dominance (SDO); need for cognition (NFC); ideology; partisan identifications with political parties, group identification (i.e., social identities, including patriotism as but one variant), and more.

Table 9.1 looks quite comprehensive. It identifies factors that have been shown to influence how humans make decisions. It identifies among them, the influence of experience, the past, and the influence of the present, contemporary considerations, including those unavailable to conscious awareness. Humans are also influenced by third aspect of human experience, context. Table 9.1 has a missing column.

The term "context" does not, as yet, have certain scientific meaning. Context's commonsense meaning is clear. Context describes the contemporaneous setting, the circumstances we find ourselves in. For example, I might be walking down a street, and ask myself the question, how safe do I feel? My answer will likely depend on such features as my personality, my physical strength, and as my sense of confidence. But, my decision to walk down that street would also likely depend on the circumstances, the context. Perhaps the street is dark, or not, on a well lit street, or a very busy venue with lots of people around, or perhaps I am alone, with friends, or alone on a street that is unknown to me in a part of a city that I have never visited before. Perhaps it is winter, or a warm summer day. Perhaps it is raining, perhaps it is hailing. These among many other factors, might all shape how safe I feel as I saunter, meander, or hurry, down that street.

Context is a very useful every day, common, word we use to identify different circumstances; all well and good. But, in political psychology, we now have a problem. This problem will not bother us either as citizens or people going about our business. The problem lies in science because science requires that descriptions of the world be uniform and comprehensive (applicable across differences in time and place). And, to that we can add a further scientific goal; the taxonomy should be parsimonious. While in our daily affairs we can readily handle many different situations by adjusting our actions, the goal of science is to collapse the complexities of the world into as few categories as possible.

How many contemporary circumstances, how many contexts are there? If we take the ancient Greek philosopher Heraclitus's point of view the answer is innumerable. Or, as he put it more eloquently: "You could not step twice into the same river; for other waters are ever flowing on to you" (as quoted by Plato in *Cratylus*). But that assertion,

BOX 9.4   Nights and nights

Recall from chapter 2 that by convention we use lower case, here dark night, to refer to a specific observable instance, here a specific dark night on a specific date and precise place. We use capitalized labels to identify a class, here Dark Night refers to all possible exemplars, past, present, and future.

that each moment, each circumstance, is truly unique, precludes the development of any science, not just political psychology.

To have a science we must adopt the view that circumstances can be compared with some grouped as alike and others seen as different. A scientific response to Heraclitus is water is that which has the composition of H_2O (two molecules of hydrogen bonded to one molecule of oxygen). Understanding water as science does would lead to the opposite conclusion from Heraclitus that stepping in river twice is the same because water is water.

A dark night, defined as a moment in time that is absent of sunlight, is a dark night no matter where or when it occurs.

We can, of course, find that our definition of a class—here a context—is not quite right. We often rectify our definitions in light of further research. But, notwithstanding that caution, to form scientific hypotheses, we have to group "like" with "like" to form a class. And, to do that we need to have definitions. What makes one circumstance like another? Answer that question and we can begin to establish how many circumstances there are.

For science to proceed, as science, to understand how context impacts judgment, we have to generate a plausible (and revisable) taxonomy of context. But, as we shall see, that task has yet to be successfully realized. Let's begin by seeing how context has been used by scholars in various disciplines.

Context in Political Philosophy

Let us begin with an example from political philosophy. One example should suffice. Here, I return to the basic argument of Thomas Hobbes (1968) in his signature work the *Leviathan*:

> Man in the state of nature, the world that existed before social order was installed, impelled humans to make decisions in a world of one against all. But, if we give to a monarch full sovereign authority, we would find ourselves living in a world more tranquil, settled, and beneficent. Having a sovereign sustained by public endorsement will make a difference not only in how we relate to our ruler, the Leviathan, but also in how we interact with each other.
>
> If we had been born in the state of nature, no matter our various individual qualities, this brutal world would impose its cruel discipline on us. But, if we could be transported into a society governed by a beneficent ruler, then we would, nothing else changed, make different decisions, decisions based on this new, for us, more settled, predictable, and secure social environment.
>
> While inhabiting the state of nature we would be selfish, crafty or, perhaps, act with bluster. We would use whatever our talents afford to protect ourselves

against others with whatever strength and guile we could muster. Or, if we judged our talents too weak, we would seek protection by servile submission to someone stronger. The war of strong against strong and predation against the weak would dominate and thereby define social patterns. Yet, when living in the liberal monarchy ruled by the Leviathan we would act more congenial, inclined to engage in mutual accommodations for mutual benefit, secure that our arrangements would be protected by the rule of law.

Here context matters and, if Hobbes had it right, it matters a lot. Civil society is quite different from the state of nature, as Hobbes imagined it. And, how humans act to each other depends on which context we inhabit.

Other philosophers have generated their own variations of such comparisons. Depending on their point of view, they argued we can gain purchase on our future prospects by comparing some past historical period or by considering an imagined future. Engaging in comparison allows us to see alternatives that otherwise might not be visible (Burke and Hyman 1964). For the scholars of the enlightenment an imagined but beneficent world of trade and democratic rule lay available before us if we made the right choices. If we welcomed progress, moved to reason, and abandoned faith and tradition, then a cosmopolitan world, beneficent, fecund, and peaceful, would emerge. This narrative did in fact help move us from a context of fixed and murderous conflicts over faith and glory to a commonwealth more cosmopolitan and generous, marked by ever-expanding possibilities, cultural and material. Although it should be said again that the historical trajectory brought along with it surprises, many far from beneficial. However, comparing historical periods, real or imagined, is but one means of considering context.

Hobbes's (1968) argument can be restated in the following way: You may think that human nature, our character, habits, and actions, is driven by our own habits, goals, and motives: but you would be wrong. Rather than finding the true causes in a fully psychological account, you need to consider the character of the regime under which people live: context matters. Exclude context and we misconstrue what explains our behavior, misattributing to psychological causes because, we ignore the role that the political structure plays in shaping human affairs. As different regimes encourage some and discourage other forms of human feeling, thought, and action, a fuller theory would encompass the following:

1. specify how regimes differ (requires a taxonomy of regimes);
2. specify the patterns of thought, feeling, and behavior they encourage and discourage (requires a taxonomy of alternative modes of feeling and thought as they impact on alternatives modes of choice making);
3. and specify how humans make the switch if they move from one regime to another (i.e., what psychological mechanisms are involved in recognizing different contexts and then, thereafter, activating and inhibiting different affective, cognitive, and behavioral routines).

Consider how we can use Hobbes's example of the role of regime and context to reconsider Milgram's (1974) influential work on obedience. Milgram, along with many other scholars in the same tradition, Sherif (1958, 1966), Asch (1951), Festinger (1956), and Zimbardo (2008), held that humans were generally too ready to accept orders given to them, to believe what they were told, and to execute orders given, no matter how troubling those orders. He, and they, drew the clear conclusion that their subjects complied with the demands of those in authority and that this was and is a general insight into human nature. They held that humans do not sufficiently act with autonomous self-regard for the moral issues before them. Because Milgram believed that if they were able and willing to use their capacity for moral judgment and action, they would have refused such contemptible orders. And, in this conclusion they mirrored the aristocratic critique of democracy (Herzog 1998; Le Bon 1986). So, much rides on the validity of that conclusion.

However, Hobbes reminded us that much depended on the context in which we find ourselves. If their subjects had been placed in an equalitarian context, one in which their autonomous authority was clear and self-evident then it is likely that they would not have be so willing to execute the orders given to them by others. Rather than suggesting that humans are too willing to engage in evil actions, these types of studies suggest that humans are too willing to reside within hierarchical systems and suffer the moral restrictions and limitations that are induced (Tyler 1990, 1997). This point should not be construed to suggest that this body of research is not important, it is. But, by not considering the role of context they may be misunderstand how human nature adapts to different contexts, contexts that, in this instance are themselves human constructions.

Broadly comparing time periods, as Hobbes and other political philosophers did, is one way to identify different contexts, there are other comparison strategies. One way is to examine different times and places within local situations that humans occupy. This strategy helps by limiting the range of experience and joining to it clear empirically observable behavior.

Context in Psychology

Some psychologists interested in accounting for how humans act turned to personality as a vital explanation. The initial expectation was that, once the proper traits were identified, these traits would then explain how people thought, felt, and behaved. People who score high on agreeableness—one of the big five traits—would feel and act agreeably in social interactions. Or, those high on conscientiousness—another of the big five—would be very diligent in their work. And, in a similar, those low in either of these two traits would be thought to have the opposite effect. The expectation was that research would reveal a strong relationship between the trait score and the behavior displayed. In the above example, it was expected that agreeable people would be generally agreeable and conscientious people would apply themselves with diligence in any task they undertook.

Psychologist Walter Mischel was the first to call attention to the general failure of research to confirm this seemingly self-evident expectation. He made note of two consistent findings in research on the relationship between personality, choice, and action (Mischel and Peake 1982; Wright and Mischel 1982; Mischel 1984). First, measures of personality showed considerable robust stability over the life time of subjects (Conley 1984). Second, the ability of personality traits to account for how humans act in social situations was far less clear. This is a puzzle because if personality traits are dispositions, inclinations to act in certain ways, then it follows we should find that, for example, extraverts act more extroverted and introverts act more introverted.

The failure to find those robust relationships between trait and behavior led Mischel and his colleagues (Wright and Mischel 1987; Shoda, Mischel, and Wright 1989; Mischel and Shoda 1995) to develop a local explanation. They theorized that dispositions were not generally enacted across all situations, but rather, were used within specific circumstances: context matters. Mischel and Shoda (1995, 254) developed the CAPS theory (cognitive affective personality system):

> When certain configurations of situation features are experienced by an individual, a characteristic subset of cognitions and affects becomes activated through this distinctive network of connections in the encoding process. Th[is] indicates that within any individual a rich system of relationships among the cognitive and affective units guides and constrains further activation of other units throughout the network, ultimately activating plans, strategies, and potential behaviors in the behavior generation process.

It is only within specific situations that we can expect to find robust relationships between traits and behavior. In situations calling for active defense, such as aggression, that some traits might then matter. But as Mischel (Mischel and Shoda 1998, 229) noted, the effort to connect "contextually sensitive processing dynamics to stable dispositions facilitates the reconciliation within a unitary framework of dispositional (trait) and processing (social cognitive–affective–dynamic) [but this leaves] the realization of this promise [as yet] to be seen."

In proposing a context solution to the personality–behavior relationship, Mischel offered an important advance; the relationship between personality and contemporary thought, feeling and action is conditioned by context. However, left unresolved was the problem of taxonomy. Suggesting that circumstances can be grouped into sets, contexts, that have common features requires some means, theoretical and methodological, for reducing the extraordinary heterogeneity of conditions into some small(er) set of defined contexts. What makes some situations similar to other situations? What are the defining features that make different places and times similar to one another? What makes different circumstances similar and hence members of a class?

Before we turn to exploring that various proposals for defining context, there is one feature of social experience we should keep in mind. Central to politics but also to other domains of social interactions is the role of authority in its various guises. And authority is one feature of life that calls for a suitable taxonomy of context.

The Role of Authority in Defining Context

Social existence is replete with sundry differences. Humans organize by using authority to regularize who directs the flow of action. Many social interactions take place in circumstances that are hierarchical. Among these are family, intimate and extended, religious practices (most but not all), military and police circumstances, economic activity, and many but not all, political circumstances. In these environments, some will expect deference (superordination; as in parents expectations of the acceptance by their children of their parental authority or those in command situations in police, military, economic, and bureaucratic positions over those lower in the hierarchy) while others will be deferent (subordination as when we defer to our parents in particular, or to elders, in general, or to our teachers).

Still other social circumstances are "flat" in that we we expect equality, you nod your head, signaling hello and I nod mine in reply, or when as citizens we each claim the right to our own opinions as of equal weight ("one person one vote"). When under the sway of equalitarian authority we expect each to have equal standing no matter what status differences may exist.

And, still further, some of these flat relationships may be hostile, as in the circumstances of "us" versus "them." Systems of authority hold over specific, if sometimes unclear, boundaries. And these boundaries might be physical, as in borders, or status, as in the existence of slavery in ancient Athens, the first democracy that limited the status of citizenship excluding not only slaves but also women. Thus, even flat systems have limits as to whom the expectation of equality applied. Systems of hierarchy retain authority in the hands of small number (no matter how they gain that their positions) whereas systems of equality share authority widely (if not universally). Hence, we can expect that the nature of authority should loom large in the definition of contexts pertinent to the science of political psychology. Psychologist Tom Tyler's (1990, 1997) research shows how authority functions. But psychologists rarely consider authority as one of the defining features that shape contexts, not surprising in that politics is, in general, peripheral to the primary goals of the psychology discipline. There have been important examinations of authority in sociology; one I particularly recommend is Duncan's *Communication and the Social Order* (1962). Sociologists have given considerable attention to the central role of authority (Coser 1956; Gould, 2003) and their work, especially that of Erving Goffman (1959, 1971, 1982, 1986) is well worth integrating into political psychology.

Prison Experiments: Producing Autocracy or Collective Action

Perhaps the most influential version of the context matters argument is the Stanford prison experiment. Here, as the story goes, when people enter a context—a prison—the roles that define that context overwhelm the influence of personal judgment. The dominant message that Philip Zimbardo has: People have little to no control over themselves. They willingly do what they have been told to do; this is similar to the work of scholars Solomon Asch (1951), Muzafer Sherif (1958, 1966), Stanley Milgram (1974), Robert J. Lifton (1986), and also Erich Fromm (1965), and historian Christopher Browning (1992). Humans are too compliant. Hence, giving people the authority over self- and collective rule is likely to lead to all the horrors that the critiques of democratic regimes have advanced.

The best and most influential demonstration of this view is the demonstration project, mislabeled as an experiment, Stanford psychologist Philip Zimbardo's "Stanford prison experiment." The tale has been widely told, though the underlying data, to this day, remains unpublished. Stanford undergraduates, having been screened to have normal personalities, were recruited to participate in this project. Some were randomly assigned to be prisoners, some guards. Thereafter a reign of terror soon emerged in which, so the story goes, guards acted tyrannically and prisoners docilely adopted the subordinate role into which they were cast. So overwhelming was the power of situation and role that the experiment was aborted for fear of lasting damage to the participants.

The website developed by Professor Zimbardo (1999) has his version of what happened and why, as does one refereed journal publication (Haney, Banks, and Zimbardo 1983), and a recent book reflecting on that study and its broader meaning (Zimbardo 2008). The website http://www.prisonexp.org/ is well worth exploring in some detail.

However, there are challenges to this tale. And, they also come from social psychology. Psychologists Alex Haslam and Steve Reicher were approached by the BBC (which produces a science show) and were invited to propose a project that could be the produced on the show, which led to the BBC prison study. The BBC project was not an exact replication of the Stanford project—among other differences this study had an oversight panel of experts to ensure that no harm was done, they used male adults rather than undergraduates, and they did not interject the principal investigator and his graduate assistant into the head guard positions among other differences. Haslam and Reicher (2008) developed a website where information about the BBC show and related materials can be found: http://www.bbcprisonstudy.org/.

There are some parallels with the Stanford project. As was its progenitor, the BBC experiment was stopped a couple of days short of its expected two week run. But unlike it progenitor, in this study prisoners and guards did not easily adopted the fixed roles of prisoner and guard. Indeed over the twelve days a number of different regimes evolve. Much of this is readily apparent in the BBC show which is available for replaying. The publications so far available report on the theoretical and evidentiary perspectives that illuminate these dynamics as the participants go from tranquility to rebellion, then to organized resistance, then to a system collapse, then to a commune, and finally, a likely attempt to impose a tyrannical regime by a group of the former prisoners and a guard (Haslam and Reicher 2006, 2007; Reicher and Haslam 2006).

It is well worth dedicating a thorough considered comparison of these two studies. The case of Zimbardo's Stanford prison experiment, a powerful and simple account: People do what they are told to do. Hence, to prevent evil one must have some institutional protections that puts benign leaders in charge as the public does not have the foundation for resistance when pressed to engage in evil.

On the other hand, in the case of the Reicher and Haslam's BBC prison experiment, people make sense of their surroundings: They do consider the options and choose whichever route seems most appealing and promising. And, whether and to what end they collectively marshal themselves depends on the ability of leadership to emerge. And, for that to happen, someone must be able to articulate an understanding, to formulate a course of action, to guide the development of a consensus, and to gain the trust of the group.

Failures, as well as successes, of leadership as well as failures of followers, all readily observable as the days of the BBC experiment unfolds, reveals the complexity of individual and collective action.

Applying the theoretical views of Henri Tajfel (Tajfel and Turner 1979; Turner 1987), Reicher and Haslam offered a fuller and richer understanding of how, when, and why, individuals sometimes act alone, sometimes retire in passive acceptance, but also sometimes group together to achieve common aims. Thus, the BBC prison study reveals—rather than a world of constants, tyrannical guards, docile prisoners—a world of variables. It is our task to identify the variables, specify the relationships, direct, indirect, and interactive, that account for the flow of actions over the course of the study.

BOX 9.5   **External validity**

A big question for these types of studies, indeed for the Milgram, Asch, Sherif, and Festinger studies, among many others, is whether the results specific to these experiments can be generalized to the "real world."

With respect to these two "prison" experiments, there is a very important limitation. In the real world, states have a license to kill. And, in both of these studies, violence of that sort was expressly precluded.

After human societies discovered how to grow enough food to generate a surplus, some were freed to do something other than engage in hunting or agriculture. This led to the development of political regimes which then and now recruited young men to work for the state as guards, police, and soldiers and for other agencies of state authority. And obedient killing at the direction of those who held authoritative positions was an essential task above all others.

In these experiments violence was expressly prohibited. In the real world, it is often the case that political regimes fall when they cannot kill. Thus, when Hungarian border guards began to refuse to shoot as Hungarians fled to Austria, their example was followed by East German guards who refused to shoot as East and West Germans gathered at the Berlin Wall to tear it down, it was not long after that these regimes collapsed. Regimes, particularly those not popular, are especially prone to treat their enforcers well and trained to kill if necessary protect their privileges and to identify with the rulers they serve.

A Preliminary Consideration of Authority and Context in Politics

Strict hierarchies, such as theocratic rule, or the rule of a single party whether its claims are proclaimed to be scientific (Marxist systems such as those in North Korea, Cuba, or China) or just the rule of the powerful who wish to secure their claims over others by whatever means available (e.g., Burma or Iran), raise the issue for those not in power: accept the authority in place or resist facing prison, torture, or other forms of punishment. Sometimes resistance succeeds (as when solidarity in Poland, with the help of others, brings to an end the supposedly scientific leadership of the Polish—and USSR—communist party; or when Ayatollah Ruhollah Khomeini led others to overthrow the Shah Mohammad Reza Pahlavi's secular authoritarian rule), and many more times resistance fails. But even when strict authoritarian rule seems to be stable such states commit considerable resources to intelligence and suppression suggesting that hierarchical systems are often unstable absent the threat and use of force.

And in representative and democratic societies, conflict between both legal and that which is illegal (e.g., assassination, acts of terror, and civil war) is also ever present. Thus Hobbes suggested, absent general consent, conflict is endemic to human life (unlike many, but not all, other social species). Those conflicts might be over the enforcement of traditional practices, and if so which ones, the choice among new prospects, and over leadership, at the level of regime, or the regular reconsideration of which leaders and parties in democratic regimes. Our genetic makeup manufactures many differences, and hence, conflict in perspective, belief, value, habit, and reasoning is a normal condition of human affairs.[1] Our destiny is one of uncertainty about the future and the challenge of selecting from among many possibilities.

---

1. Unless a regime seeks to prevent the emanations of difference by imposing doctrines of faith and obedience, either founded on secular or religious grounds.

Hence, in constructing a taxonomy of contexts suggests the following core considerations:

1. What is nature of the regime (hierarchical or equalitarian)?
2. Is the political authority legitimate (and if not, contested by whom)?
3. Is the context within which action is to take place defined within existing boundaries (within members of a common neighborhood, community, class, race, gender, religion, nationality, etc.) or across salient memberships?
4. Are the expectations of those engaging: mutually harmonious, mutually antagonistic, or conflicted (i.e., some expecting harmony of interaction whereas others hold agonistic expectations)?
5. Within the broad terrain of a regime, are there "spaces," contexts, where different authorities' contexts hold local sway (and these include "nonpolitical" authorities, such as social, economic, and religious organizations, whether voluntary or enforced)?
6. And, how often do opposing individuals, or opposing groups, come into contact because of mobility across time and space are as much a part of social life as stable enduring conditions.

These necessary considerations take us beyond psychology to the interaction between psychology and social organization. Before we return to this interface we need to take up a more pressing task. That task is to explore the ways in which human psychology takes context into account. Circumstances differ in innumerable ways, which of the differences are material?

II. A PROVISIONAL PSYCHOLOGICAL TAXONOMY OF CONTEXT

Thirty years ago, Daniel Kahneman and Amos Tversky (Kahneman, Slovic, and Tversky 1982; Kahneman and Tversky 1982, 1984) published an important and highly influential series of publications. They reported that people take one of two approaches to decision making when choosing between policy alternatives: People express either a risk aversion approach or a risk seeking approach depending on the apparent context. Their work has come to be called prospect theory, and it also has been very influential across all the social sciences (Levy 1992; Quattrone and Tversky 1988). Before I turn to the consideration of context and the import of their finding has had, let's begin with a close reading of the actual finding.

We begin with their definitions of the key terms (Kahneman and Tversky 1984, 341).

> ...consider the choice between a prospect that offers an 85% chance to win $1000 (with a 15% chance to win nothing) and the alternative of receiving $800 for sure. A large majority of people prefer the sure thing over the gamble, although the gamble has higher (mathematical) expectation. The expectation of a monetary gamble is a weighted average, where each possible outcome is weighted by its probability of occurrence. The expectation of the gamble in this example is $.85 \times \$1000 + .15 \times \$0 = \$850$, which exceeds the expectation of $800 associated with the sure thing. The preference for the sure gain is an instance of risk aversion. In general, a preference for a sure outcome over a gamble that has higher or equal expectation is called

BOX 9.6 Point estimation

You are walking through a western national park in the United States that is home to grizzly bears. Do you wander over to the next valley to further explore, to see the sights? What is the risk of confronting a mother grizzly and her young cub? One could make a single choice or one could, if a gambling expert walk to one-hundred or one-thousand valleys at different times of the day or night and generate a table of results. That would generate the precise estimates you need to calculate the risk. If you survived to complete the task.

risk averse, and the rejection of a sure thing in favor of a gamble of lower or equal expectation is called risk seeking.

People confront two policy options: One policy offers certainty whereas the other offers risk along with the prospect of a higher gain if the gamble pays. It is worth noting that the outcome of the gamble is calculated by presuming that one plays the gamble many times and so that one can assess the overall performance of repeated trials. Bear in mind that such an approach presumes that one's safety is not, itself, at risk during the time required to execute and observe the repeated trials. For, if one is going to toss a dice, say one thousand times, to see if it is a true, that is, not a loaded (weighted) dice designed to produce a specific result more than by chance, then one has to be around to perform, observe, and assess the repeated throws. And, with computers and mathematical tools one can replay, in the abstract form, many of these sorts of gambles to see very quickly how they should play out in real-world experience.

However, our evolutionary status does not guarantee the condition of safety, we have evolved by making decisions weighted to preserve rather than to assess gambles. Hence, our brains are designed to engage in point estimation (what is going to happen next) rather than to to assess how repeated trials might turn out.

So, how do people choose which strategy to rely on? To find out, they then conducted the following study, again, I quote Kahneman and Tversky (1984, 341).

> ...the possible outcomes of a gamble can be framed either as gains and losses relative to the status quo or as asset positions that incorporate initial wealth. Invariance requires that such changes in the description of outcomes should not alter the preference order. The following pair of problems illustrates a violation of this requirement. The total number of respondents in each problem is denoted by N, and the percentage who chose each option is indicated in parentheses.
>
> Problem 1 (N = 152): Imagine that the U.S. is preparing for the outbreak of an unusual Asian disease, which is expected to kill 600 people. Two alternative programs to combat the disease have been proposed. Assume that the exact scientific estimates of the consequences of the programs are as follows:
>
> If Program A is adopted, 200 people will be saved. (72%)
>
> If Program B is adopted, there is a one-third probability that 600 people will be saved and a two-thirds probability that no people will be saved. (28%)
>
> Which of the two programs would you favor?
>
> The formulation of Problem 1 implicitly adopts as a reference point a state of affairs in which the disease is allowed to take its toll of 600 lives. The outcomes of

the programs include the reference state and two possible gains, measured by the number of lives saved. As expected, preferences are risk averse: A clear majority of respondents prefer saving 200 lives for sure over a gamble that offers a one-third chance of saving 600 lives. Now consider another problem in which the same cover story is followed by a different description of the prospects associated with the two programs:

Problem 2 (N = 155): If Program C is adopted, 400 people will die.(22%)

If Program D is adopted, there is a one-third probability that nobody will die and a two-thirds probability that 600 people will die. (78%)

It is easy to verify that options C and D in Problem 2 are undistinguishable in real terms from options A and B in Problem 1, respectively. The second version, however, assumes a reference state in which no one dies of the disease. The best outcome is the maintenance of this state and the alternatives are losses measured by the number of people that will die of the disease. People who evaluate options in these terms are expected to show a risk seeking preference for the gamble (option D) over the sure loss of 400 lives. Indeed, there is more risk seeking in the second version of the problem than there is risk aversion in the first.

People pay attention to these two contexts and make different decisions depending on which is apparent.

Assessing the Empirical Story

Before we turn to a discussion of the substantive results, it is important to emphasize the very first contribution of Kahneman and Tversky. Most importantly, they offer a comprehensive taxonomy of context. In their formulation although humans confront a very rich variety of social experiences we can ignore all of that rich variety as we seek to explain how people make policy choices. And, that is because all the many variations of conditions can be reduced to just two contexts.

On the one hand, we have contexts in which we expect to flourish, domains of gain. On the other, hand we have contexts in which we expect to be diminished, domains of loss. This is a very major advancement over Mischel's work because we have moved from a recognition that some circumstances differ from other circumstances to a formal taxonomy of context.

There is a further, influential point they drew from their finding, confirmed many times in other studies (Levy 1992). They had a theory about how people decided when they were within each of these contexts. People are risk aversive when confronting a likely loss but they are risk seeking when confronting a likely gain. Taken together this theory suggests a new version of table 9.1, with an added column, context.

Into this column go just two rows: the domain of gain (when people are risk seeking) and the domain of loss (when people are risk averse). Table 9.2 displays this extended taxonomy of explanatory factors as well as using prospect theory of offer an initial "cut" at the psychology of context.

That people formulate choices by considering context raises a number of empirical questions. Among these is how does context enter into political judgment. Is the influence of context shaped through explicit consideration? The research guided by mortality salience theory, which argues that people move to risk aversion on their awareness

Table 9.2. Revised and extended factors used by political psychologists to explain political judgment

Past trait factors	Present state factors	Prospect theory's taxonomy of context
Genes	Contemporary perceptions	Domains of perceived gains—risk seeking "bias"
Personality	Contemporary judgments (explicit, deliberative)	
Beliefs, values, heuristics, and the like	Contemporary implicit assessments (preconscious affective appraisals)	Domains of perceived loss—risk aversion "bias"
Previously learned affective routines and predisposition and the like	Contemporary behavioral actions and reactions and the like	

of the explicit prospect of death, suggests that route (Landau et al. 2004). Or, is the influence of context via implicit consideration "outside" of awareness? Much of recent work in political psychology has emphasized the role of the nonaware influences on human judgment (Gilens 1999; Valentino 1999; Devine 1989; Devine et al. 1991). Or, yet another likelihood is that context might come into play via either implicit and/or explicit consideration. Failing to take into account the ways in which, and the extent to which, context influences political judgment will leave us with unspecified theories and empirical findings. It is likely that explanations that properly belong to influence of context will, if we do not identify its role, be misattributed to past, trait, or present, state, factors.

The Normative Story

However a second consideration also is clear. As they make quite clear, this robust finding violates the norm of rationality as given by the definition of rational choice. That is to say, rational people should give equal weight to gains and losses and choose the policy option that maximizes the first and minimizes the second. Using context as an auxiliary consideration is, in their view, irrational. Again, in the words of Kahneman and Tversky (1984, 344):

> ...the susceptibility to framing and the S-shaped value function produce a violation of dominance in a set of concurrent decisions. The moral of these results is disturbing: Invariance is normatively essential, intuitively compelling, and psychologically unfeasible.

When people expect to be in a context of recurring gains they opt to take risks to gain larger, if less certain gains, yet, when they expect to be facing grim circumstances they opt to avoid risks and take certain, if smaller, gains. But as gains are gains and losses, then this seems irrational. And, demonstrating this "irrationality" undermines the central premise of the enlightenment: Reducing reliance on faith and established hierarchical authority enables individuals to make autonomous choices for themselves, and collectively, for all of us. The enlightenment projected the decline in hierarchical authority and the rise of equalitarian choice systems, either in the realm of economic choices through market mechanisms (I spend on what I want rather than having allocations made on my behalf by my betters), or through representative or direct referendum in the realm of politics (one person one vote).

That empirical prognostication is warranted becomes a normatively justifiable expectation because the underlying premise is that people, freed to act autonomously would thereby choose rationally. And, here the central normative conclusion of prospect theory is that people act irrationally. Moreover, Kahneman and Tvesky demonstrated this irrationality not only on private judgments; judgments, the consequences of which fell solely on the individuals who made them, but in the realm of collective choice.

We should be leery of adopting Kahneman and Tversky's normative assessment. First, survival is the end result of many factors. And, survival is influenced both by the choices we make and the character of the changing context in which we experience the consequences of those choices. In the end, it is the end that matters. The unstated premise of prospect theory is that rational choice, as a process of decision making, is the best route to optimal results. That premise would be warranted if two conditions are met. First, that we have "full" information that would require a full and accurate delineation of all costs and all benefits for otherwise an assessment of "costs" and "benefits" if incomplete or incorrect would lead to incorrect conclusions. But humans do not have full information, if by full information we mean full awareness of all the costs and all the benefits. Here's what we do *not* know:

1. Information that is not representable in consciousness (for millennia humans could not see the various viruses and bacteria that influenced us, often to the good, but often to cause the death of many). We have technologies that make many of these previously invisible aspects of nature visible (telescopes, microscopes, and the more recent work on "subatomic" particles, among many other devices). Even with the advantage of science and technology there remains more relevant "information" not available to even the most observant individuals.
2. Knowledge of the future (e.g., the location and magnitude of hurricanes, earthquakes, new disease outbreaks, economic bubbles yet to be born, new technologies not yet invented and their effects, etc.).
3. Second, for good or ill there are nonconscious choice mechanisms and these do not lend themselves to the process requirements of rational choice (i.e., explicit representation of information in consciousness for deliberate consideration). Excluding these is implausible, except under specific (i.e., not general) choice circumstances.

The principal finding of Kahneman and Tversky is that we have a facility for taking into account context, a "bias" for considering the immediate landscape as part of the choice process. Another way of putting their faith in the claim that "Invariance is normatively essential" (1984, 344) is to argue that taking into account the changing character of the world world should not be entered into the choice equation.

Finding that people apply differential "weights" into the choice equation, as prospect theory research demonstrates, suggests that humans violating the conventional understanding of rational choice as process might nonetheless be relying on a decision process that yields better outcomes. If we attribute the apparently ubiquitous role to its evolutionary value, a dangerous assumption to be sure, then perhaps the normative thrust of prospect theory needs reconsideration.

III. AFFECT AND CONTEXT

However, there is a further empirical issue to discuss before adopting table 9.2 as the best overview. Prospect theory was developed in a period before the role of preconscious appraisals was understood. In that period, it was plausible to view judgment as an activity essentially taking place within consciousness. Here, I want to call attention not to space (where judgment lies, *within* consciousness or *outside* in the "gut" or "heart") but to time. Because consciousness generates a sense of instantaneous access to the world (what we see, here, and so on), and links our thinking to that representation; it was a reasonable, though false, presumption that judgment was a singular process unfolding as we participated in the reasoning process. But, neuroscience has shown that much of neural processing that supports human judgment takes place *before* consciousness. As I showed in earlier chapters the conventional view of rationality—a process of explicit formal deliberation of the relative explicit costs and benefits—is not the sole mechanism for achieving optimal outcomes. And, the before brings us back to the preconscious affective processes discussed in chapters 5 and 6.

When prospect theory was developed in the 1980s and 1990s affect was generally understood as a summary preference storage mechanism. The term "affect tag" conveys that meaning quite clearly. As such, affect served a very limited role in understanding the process of human choice. Affect was the summary result of prior reasoning. Affect tags stored *conclusions*—our likes and dislikes—our preferences. Moreover, preferences so conceived could safely be characterized as a valence dimension running from "like a lot" to "dislike a lot." That formulation led to the development of preference measurements such as "feeling thermometers." These feeling thermometers asked respondents to rate someone, some group or policy, along a spectrum running from 100 (really like this a lot—this is really "hot") to 0 (I really feel cold about that!). In one number then, we learned people's preferences to politicians, groups (e.g., labor unions or corporations), policies ("cutting taxes"), and more. It was thought that humans may forget the reasoning or rationale how they arrived at a summery conclusion. Why are we "pro" or "con" to this or that political party? Although we may forget the how, we would retain and rely on that stored preference, the "affect tag" that attached to any attitude object. In sum, affect was thought to be the mechanism by which humans solved the "approach–avoidance" task, should we be friends or enemies.

If taking context into account is a positive adaptation then doing so must add some survival value. If that premise is warranted then it also follows that it should be considered as a primary consideration. If context matters, then identifying the context must be a first-order task. Moreover, identifying the context requires not only a fast identification but also benefits by doing so at the outset of the judgment process. If it matters what the context is, then getting a depiction of that context has to be a swift and early task. Further, analysis of the context, defining the context, among the possible set, or taxonomy, of contexts, also has to be executed quickly. Finally, the judgment process has to be adjusted to suit the contextual demands. If different domains, different

contexts, should promote, or inhibit, different decision processes then the identification and assessment of context is best located at the beginning of the judgment process,
not an end of the judgment process.

Bear in mind that conscious awareness is not well suited to meet these requirements.
As covered in earlier chapters, the features of consciousness are now better understood
than in the past and considerable ongoing research is deepening our understanding of
the capacities and limitations (Dehaene 2001). To recapitulate as relevant here, I restate
the following.

- First, consciousness takes a significant amount of time to generate (on the order
  of five-hundred milliseconds).
- Second, consciousness, although giving the impression of veridical comprehen-
  siveness, an exact, instantaneous, and comprehensive portrait of the external
  world, it is not. That is to say: It is not instantaneous. It is not exact (having various impositions as best calculated by the brain to meet the momentary demands
  of the moment). It is not comprehensive (it gives much cruder representations of
  internal and external affairs than other neural representations).
- Third, consciousness has very limited access to the precise neural maps that
  guide action routines in the brain (i.e., our consciousness knows we can run, lift
  things, smile, and so on, but consciousness does not have access to the neural
  maps that execute and modulate these actions in their various manifestations).

On the other hand, affective processes do have the features that make it well suited to
enable humans to take context into account.

- First, the affective representations are developed and accessible far faster than
  consciousness. Remember that consciousness represents its understanding of
  the external world in some five-hundred milliseconds whereas affective appraisals arise approximately five times faster.
- Second, affective processes operate over a very wide range of sensory inputs, our
  affective awareness of external affairs is far richer than the simplified representation of awareness. That is to say, we are more emotionally aware of our surroundings than the representation that arises in in conscious awareness.
- Third, affective representations are also more detailed, deft, and swifter, with
  respect to the initiation and control of action than the slow and crude mechanisms available in consciousness. If context matters, then, we better be able to
  use that understanding in action, and here again, preconscious appraisals can
  make deft use of the fast routes to the initiation and control of action that are not
  available to consciousness.
- Fourth, and most critical, these early appraisals inform which of two judgment
  processes to rely on for dealing with imminent choice. The rich literature on dual
  process in the human brain rectifies the simplistic view of human judgment that
  characterizes judgment as purely and solely an explicit process located in consciousness (Chaiken and Trope 1999; Evans 2008).

In sum, if taking current circumstances into account matters then it makes good
sense that the appraisal of current circumstances primarily rests in preconscious
appraisals especially as the availability of two different choice/judgment mechanisms

depends on the completion of such as assessment because the choice process selection has to be completed before a judgment process is initiated.

This suggests that we develop another provisional taxonomy for context. This taxonomy follows from what we now understand about the structure and functionality of preconscious appraisals. That understanding, suggested by the neuroscience of emotion, as translated into political psychology, is known as the theory of affective intelligence. This theory implies not a twofold taxonomy of context, a domain of gains and a domain of losses, but rather a threefold taxonomy. The combined effects of the surveillance and disposition systems locate us into one of three contexts: (1) the domain of novelty and hence, uncertainty; (2) the domain of certain familiar rewards; (3) the domain of certain familiar punishment. These three domains require somewhat different judgment processes.

The first, the domain of novelty places us in a context in which the past is not an apt guide to the future we seek. Moreover, rather than relying on the fast automatic processes that swiftly and deftly convert goals, current assessments, and past learned habits of thought, feeling, and action, into routines that succeed, these are set aside. Instead, knowing that the present is unusual, the slow reflective and explicit consideration enables alternatives to be constructed in consciousness and their respective usefulness deliberated, both introspectively but also with others. A critical element not considered in prospect theory is the sequence of considerations. The idealization of rationality as a process presumes that it is both safe and wise to gain full information, at least all that is practical and accessible to obtain, with the hope that the information on costs and benefits is unbiased. Hopefully, that once assembled a calculation of plausible outcomes can be generated with the most optimal rising to the top.

The role of preconscious appraisals is to give us the earliest warning possible well before we have "full information," in the sense that economists use that term. We do not wait until we have everything; our brains take action at earliest possible moment of relevant consideration. We ingest something spoiled and our brain tells us to disgorge immediately. Something is tossed at us, we duck. Each of these examples happens before consciousness has a clue as to what is going on.

Hence, the identification of uncertainty, a critical strategic consideration, is given temporal precedence (as shown in table 9.3). If we entered a context, reliance on the fast and swift operation of habituated routines would be inefficient and likely dangerous: That is because the presumption of reliance on habituated routines is that past practices achieves, if relied on here and now, the same results as previously experienced. But, if the past is not quite like the past, even without knowing why, we cannot expect such a continuity of result. Hence, the first task of contemporary appraisal is to determine whether this moment is familiar. If familiar, fine, let's continue with swift habituated processing and thereby achieve prior results. If not familiar, wait, stop what you are doing, and shift to deliberate.

The second and third domains, the domains of familiarity, either of reward or punishment, do find us in the world that promises familiar outcomes, and hence enables us to make efficient and rational use of what we have already learned.

First, we have practiced routines for recurring rewarding tasks. And, here we arrive at a different normative conclusion than that of Kahneman and Tversky. If the domain is both familiar and one in which positive rewards are likely then, a risk taking adjustment makes good sense. Shall we work with others to achieve common goals or is that risky? That, in part, depends on the assessment of others: are they friendly or antagonistic? If our preconscious appraisal is a positive one, then our brain's preconscious has generated a signal that foretells the likely positive, fallible, assessment of a possible gain. Enthusiasm, confidence is an assessment of the past, what have similar experiences generated in results, and a predictor of future results. Although a risk and a gamble, a gamble based on preconscious appraisals that suggest past experience is relevant and contemporary preconscious appraisals confirm we are in a familiar context is a gamble worth taking.

Second, we have each learned practiced routines for dealing with recurring punishing circumstances. Here also, the past is a useful guide, especially if we can swiftly identifying a current circumstance as presenting what we have found aversive in the past. When we confront a similar current circumstance, we can draw on previously proven methods. And, in such contexts, acting with a risk aversive bias, seems prudent.

If we located the role of consciousness as having the central priority that the prospect theory gives it, we would locate it not just as the highest, that is to say, better than any other judgment process, but also recommended to be used *first*. The normative claim of Kahneman and Tversky was that a rational person *should* use rationality first generally because it gave a rational outcome. But our brains have evolved to locate the rational process in a "work space" (i.e., consciousness) to manage a limited and hopefully, infrequent set of situations. Those are circumstances that are too novel and uncertain to make reliance on proven and mastered routines prudent. The primary weakness of reliance on past proven methods is that they presume that the present is similar to the past. Determining whether is it is safe to make that presumption is an analytic task that is executed before consciousness for two principal reasons. First, making the determination of whether the current circumstance is novel or familiar should precede any other determination because that determination guides the judgment process that is best suited for the just identified context. Second, consciousness does not have access to full information as it has a biased and reduced sensory representation compared to that available to preconscious appraisals.

The neuroscience of judgment is complex and has multiple routes and context enters into each of these multiple routes in different ways (see table 9.3). The integration of preconscious appraisals to the consideration of context offers a number of important routes for further work. First, a central distinction raised earlier is that between risk, a condition of novelty and uncertainty, and threat, a condition of known punishment, that is, threat. These are different in more than just the contexts they each define. They are different as to the antecedents that activate each, uncertainty and familiar punishment, respectively. They are different in how we experience these contexts, anxiety in the case of uncertainty–novelty; and aversion, for example, rage, disgust, contempt, hatred, and synonyms, in the case of familiar punishment, threat.

Moreover, table 9.3 suggests that though a "negative" experience, the domain of familiar punishment is more like the domain of familiar reward than it is the other "negative" context, uncertainty. Both familiar domains rely on past routines to resolve choice. Both familiar domains seek to protect the value of previous learned, habituated actions and thoughts. That is both exemplify "motivated reasoning" rather than deliberative processes.

Table 9.3. Provisional context taxonomy for consideration by political psychologists seeking to explain political judgment

	A provisional taxonomy of context	
Contexts	Domains of uncertainty—Identify unexpected and novel circumstances; assess how salient, and as salience increases, inhibit automaticity (reliance on extant learned habituated routines) and activate deliberative processes (formal processes of explicit consideration); as anxiety moderates, as uncertainty is resolved, as the domain of uncertainty is left, returns choice mechanisms to automaticity	Domains of familiar rewards (i.e., gains)—Continuity of habitual reward seeking actions; actions in a favorable context warrants risk seeking "bias"
		Domains of familiar punishment (i.e., Loss)—Continuity of habitual punishment management actions; actions in a harsh environment warrants risk aversion "bias"
Judgment mode	Deliberative: Explicit consideration within consciousness	Heuristic guidance (automaticity): Regulation by preconscious control mechanisms

Rationality as a process is held by Kahneman and Tversky as the always normatively superior mode of judgment. They are not alone in their view.

Anything else that introduces biases will lead to fewer, degraded judgments. However, we have two routes to judgment, not just the one. What should we make of that duality?

Rather than normatively endorse just one single judgment process as universally applicable and universally superior, dual process models outline a more complex design. We have two routes for judgment because it would seem, each is best suited for a particular context and each would be inappropriate if applied to another context. And presumably, each of these judgment processes has both adaptive benefits and liabilities. Each is a master of its domain but each is highly unsuitable to the other.

Acting pleasantly in the domain of threat on the off chance that kindness will be reciprocated may well be a generally bad idea. Acting on the basis of prior convictions in the domain of novelty would seem to be similarly a bad idea. Acting threatening in the domain of familiarity, when kindness is offered might prove to be yet another poor choice.

It should also be recognized that preconscious identification of the immediate context may prove to be mistaken. The preconscious affective appraisals are not errorless. They are fallible. Nonetheless, they offer more and earlier relevant information than what is available later and in reduced form in consciousness. And, people do seem to moderate the judgment process they rely on based on the preconscious identification of context (MacKuen et al. 2010).

BOX 9.7 Faith and reason

Of course, the old and persistent rivalry between the exponents of reason (proclaiming its gifts of autonomy and progress) and the advocates of faith (proclaiming the gifts of solidarity with god, nation, or other collective ideals sustained by inculcated sensibilities) lives on. Nonetheless few today, apart from those seeking to secure religious authority, argue that reason properly deployed is other than generally if not ubiquitously useful route.

IV. A TAXONOMY OF CONTEXT OR A TAXONOMY OF CONTEXTS

One of the major misrepresentations in consciousness is the sense that everything out there is available before us in a single coherent integrated representation. That is a great accomplishment but it misrepresents how the brain actually understands the world in which we live. You see a word on a page, hear a spoken word, or see a picture on a wall. Each of these is heard or seen as a complete entity: the word or the picture. But the brain only arrives at this integrated coherent completeness by a sequential analysis of electrical signals (apart from smell, the one sense that is direct the brain touching an object). And, the sequential analysis is multimodal. For example, the brain has different areas of the cortex devoted to early analysis of the optic electrical signals, some modules are devoted to object definition (using straight edges for example to mark a boundary) with a special module to identify faces, other modules are devoted to movement (and here movement toward is distinct and separately treated than movement from side to side), color, and other qualities. While these are finally assembled in a region at the back of our brains (in the region of the brain called V1), the brain makes use of these intermediate assessments, which makes good strategic sense. Why wait to duck, flinch, or raise a guarding hand, when an object is rapidly approaching your head because, as yet, the brain has not figured out the color of the object? The brain does not wait.

One of the fundamental processes executed by the human brain is its ability to execute sequential and parallel analyses of many different external and internal signals that arrive by various sensory and somatosensory routes. And, more important, the brain has the ability to make appropriate adjustments on basis of these intermediate and ongoing analyses, leading to the capacity to make swift and ongoing adjusts to the appropriate response. All of that, seeing choice and behavior as an ongoing and continuous adjustments, suggests a further refinement in the integration of context in political psychology. Rather than treating the identification of context as a one time consideration, it is likely that we will find that sequential contextual considerations, of different sorts, are part of a normal unfolding process of considerations. Some of these are likely to be influential very early in the period of preconscious appraisals but others will be continuing appraisals, some extending into conscious awareness.

I offered some plausible expectations. No doubt other scholars will generate a different array of predictions. Which of these expectations will prove the most useful awaits considerable research. The challenge awaits imaginative and ambitious scholars.

Political psychologist Stanley Feldman's formulation of the relationship between social conformity and its manifestation under conditions of threat is one of the first of what I expect will be a wave of work exploring the context specific relationship between personality and traits (Feldman 2003; Feldman and Stenner 1997). More recent work is exploring precisely this route and I expect yet more in the future (Gerber et al. 2010; Mondak et al. 2010).

EXERCISES

Select some of the major philosophers and generate the taxonomy of contexts that they use. Among those you might use are: Aristotle, Plato, John Locke, Karl Marx, John Stuart Mills, and John Rawls. How many contexts do they identify (be specific as to which pages and paragraphs they identify the contexts they have in mind)? What are

Table 9.1E. Philosophers and context

Philosopher	Contexts				
Karl Marx	Primitive communism	Feudal society	Capitalist society	Socialist society	Communist society
Context	Equality of condition	Strict class structure	Strict class structure	State owner-ship of means of production	Equality—from each according to ability, to each according to need
Authority relationships	Equalitarian	Hierarchical	Hierarchical	Quasi-equalitarian	Equalitarian
Which utopic?	√				√
Which dystopic?		√	√		

the critical features of each context? Which contexts are utopic and which are dystopic? Table 9.1E gives an example of a partial workup for Karl Marx.

For follow up, are the contexts spatial (different places) or temporal (a historical cycle or a progressive sequence from one period to another)?

If context defines when and how our stable of skills acquired and our dispositions are useful then we can theorize about when and under what circumstances traits and context interact.

Use table 9.2E to select one trait (either one listed or another, such as social dominance orientation), read the literature on that trait, and then theorize what relationships you expect for each of the three domains. Discuss and search the literature for research findings.

Read James Madison's Federalist Paper No 10 and identify which contexts he identifies as relevant to politics.

Table 9.2E. Theorizing the likely relevance of traits in provisional taxonomy of contexts

Traits	Contexts of automaticity	Context of deliberation
Extraversion	Reward:	
	Punishing:	
Neuroticism	Reward:	
	Punishing:	
Openness to experience	Reward:	
	Punishing:	
Agreeableness	Reward:	
	Punishing:	
Conscientiousness	Reward:	
	Punishing:	
Need for cognition	Reward:	
	Punishing:	
Social conformity	Reward:	
	Punishing:	

4. After viewing the BBC prison experiment, return and map the various "regimes" as they unfold. There is the opening phase, when prisoners who chose to do so could apply to change their status to guards. There is the final stage, when the experimenters stopped the experiment just as a small group began to implement their plan to install a new and harsh regime, returning to the fixed authority of guards over prisoners. How many other regimes unfolded over the time of the BBC experiment? Who emerged as leaders among the prisoners and why? Why did the leadership change? When leadership failed to emerge, as with the guards, why do you think this happened?

5. Select a society that imposes some restrictions on the free expressions of their people. Determine the rationale given by those in society. Typically, the argument will be some variant of "we do so for their own good." Then, what sort of research might one plan to ascertain whether that claim is sustained by empirical evidence?

REFERENCES

Asch, Solomon E. 1951. "Effects of Group Pressure upon the Modification and Distortion of Judgment." In *Groups, Leadership and Men: Research in Human Relations*, edited by Harold Guetzkow, 177–90. Pittsburgh, PA: Carnegie.

Browning, Christopher R. 1992. *Ordinary Men: Reserve Police Battalion 101 and the Final Solution in Poland*. New York: HarperCollins.

Burke, Kenneth, and Stanley Edgar Hyman. 1964. *Perspectives by Incongruity*. Bloomington: Indiana University Press.

Chaiken, Shelly, and Yaacov Trope, eds. 1999. *Dual Process Models in Social Psychology*. New York: Guilford.

Conley, James J. 1984. "Longitudinal Consistency of Adult Personality: Self-Reported Psychological Characteristics across 45 Years." *Journal of Personality and Social Psychology* 47:1325–33.

Coser, Lewis A. 1956. *The Functions of Social Conflict*. Glencoe, IL: Free Press.

Dehaene, Stanislas. 2001. *The Cognitive Neuroscience of Consciousness*. Cambridge, MA: MIT Press.

Devine, Patricia G. 1989. "Stereotypes and Prejudice: Their Automatic and Controlled Components." *Journal of Personality and Social Psychology* 56:5–18.

Devine, Patricia G., Margo J. Monteith, Julia R. Zuwerink, and Andrew J. Elliot. 1991. "Prejudice With and Without Compunction." *Journal of Personality and Social Psychology* 60:817–30.

Duncan, Hugh Dalziel. 1962. *Communication and Social Order*. New York: Bedminster.

Evans, Jonathan St. B. T. 2008. "Dual-Processing Accounts of Reasoning, Judgment, and Social Cognition". *Annual Review of Psychology* 59:255–78.

Feldman, Stanley. 2003. "Enforcing Social Conformity: A Theory of Authoritarianism." *Political Psychology* 24:41–74.

Feldman, Stanley, and Karen Stenner. 1997. "Perceived Threat and Authoritarianism." *Political Psychology* 18:741–70.

Festinger, Leon. 1956. *When Prophecy Fails*. Minneapolis: University of Minnesota Press.

Fromm, Erich. 1965. *Escape From Freedom*. New York: Avon.

Gerber, Alan S., Gregrory A. Huber, David Doherty, Conor M. Dowling, and Shang E. Ha. 2010. "Personality and Political Attitudes: Relationships across Issue Domains and Political Contexts." *American Political Science Review* 104:111–33.

Gilens, Martin. 1999. *Why Americans Hate Welfare: Race, Media, and the Politics of Antipoverty Policy.* Chicago: University of Chicago Press.

Goffman, Erving. 1959. *The Presentation of Self in Everyday Life.* Garden City, NY: Doubleday.

———. 1971. *Relations in Public.* New York: Basic Books.

———. 1982. *Interaction Ritual: Essays on Face-to-Face Behavior.* New York: Pantheon.

———. 1986. *Stigma: Notes on the Management of Spoiled Identity.* New York: Simon & Schuster.

Gould, Roger V. 2003. *Collision of Wills: How Ambiguity About Social Rank Breeds Conflict.* Chicago: University of Chicago Press.

Haney, Craig, Curtis Banks, and Philip Zimbardo. 1983. "Interpersonal Dynamics in a Simulated Prison." *International Journal of Criminology and Penology* 1:69–97.

Haslam, S. Alexander, and Stephen Reicher. 2006. "Debating the Psychology of Tyrrany: Fundamental Issues of Theory, Perspective, and Science." *British Journal of Social Psychology* 45:55–63.

Haslam, S. Alexander, and Stephen Reicher. 2007. "Beyond the Banality of Evil: Three Dynamics of an Interactionist Social Psychology of Tyranny." *Personality and Social Psychology Bulletin* 33:615–22.

———. 2008. "The BBC Prison Study," accessed November 23, 2011, www.bbcprisonstudy.org/.

Herzog, Don. 1998. *Poisoning the Minds of the Lower Orders.* Princeton, NJ: Princeton University Press.

Hobbes, Thomas. 1968. *Leviathan.* London: Penguin.

Kahneman, Daniel, Paul Slovic, and Amos Tversky. 1982. *Judgment under Uncertainty: Heuristics and Biases.* Cambridge: Cambridge University Press.

Kahneman, Daniel, and Amos Tversky. 1982. "The Psychology of Preferences." *Scientific American* 246:136–42.

———. 1984. "Choices, Values, and Frames." *American Psychologist* 39:341–50.

Landau, Mark J., Sheldon Solomon, Jeff Greenberg, Florette Cohen, Tom Pyszczynski, Jamie Arndt, Dale T. Miller, Daniel M. Ogilvie, and Alison Cook. 2004. "Deliver Us from Evil: The Effects of Mortality Salience and Reminders of 9/11 on Support for President George W. Bush." *Personality And Social Psychology Bulletin* 30:1136–50.

Le Bon, Gustave. 1986. *The Crowd: A Study of the Popular Mind.* London: Unwin.

Levy, Jack S. 1992. "An Introduction to Prospect Theory." *Political Psychology* 13:171–86.

Lifton, Robert Jay. 1986. *The Nazi Doctors: Medical Killing and the Psychology of Genocide.* New York: Basic Books.

MacKuen, Michael, Jennifer Wolak, Luke Keele, and George E. Marcus. 2010. "Civic Engagements: Resolute Partisanship or Reflective Deliberation." *American Journal of Political Science* 54:440–58.

Milgram, Stanley. 1974. *Obedience to Authority.* New York: Harper and Row.

Mischel, Walter. 1984. "Convergences and Challenges in the Search for Personality." *American Psychologist* 39:351–64.

Mischel, Walter, and Philip K. Peake. 1982. "Beyond Déjà Vu in the Search for Cross-Situational Consistency." *Psychological Review* 89:730–55.

Mischel, Walter, and Yuichi Shoda. 1995. "A Cognitive-Affective System Theory of Personality: Reconceptualizing Situations, Dispositions, Dynamics, and Invariance in Personality Structure." *Psychological Review* 102:246–68.

———. 1998. "Reconciling Processing Dynamics and Personality Dispositions." *Annual Review of Psychology* 49:229–58.

Mondak, Jeffery J., Matthew V. Hibbing, Damarys Canache, Mitchell A. Seligson, and Mary R. Anderson. 2010. "Personality and Civic Engagement: An Integrative Framework for the Study of Trait Effects on Political Behavior." *American Political Science Review* 104:85–110.

Quattrone, George A., and Amos Tversky. 1988. "Contrasting Rational and Psychological Analyses of Political Choice." *American Political Science Review* 82:719–36.

Reicher, Stephen, and S. Alexander Haslam. 2006. "Rethinking the Psychology of Tyranny: The BBC Prison Study." *British Journal of Social Psychology* 45:1–40.

Saxonhouse, Arlene W. 1988. "The Tyranny of Reason in the World of the Polis." *American Political Science Review* 82:1261–75.

Sherif, Muzafer. 1958. "Group Influences upon the Formation of Norms and Attitudes." In *Readings in Social Psychology*, edited by Eleanor Maccoby, T. M. Newcomb, and E. L. Hartley, 219–32. New York: Holt.

———. 1966. *Group Conflict and Competition*. London: Routledge & Kegan Paul.

Shoda, Yuichi, Walteri Mischel, and Jack C. Wright. 1989. "Intuitive Interactionism in Person Perception: Effects of Situation-Behavior Relations on Dispositional Judgments." *Journal of Personality and Social Psychology* 56:41–53.

Tajfel, Henri, and John C. Turner. 1979. "An Integrative Theory of Intergroup Conflict." In *The Social Psychology of Intergroup Relations*, edited by W. G. Austin and S. Worchel, 33–47. Monterey, CA: Brooks/Cole.

Turner, John C. 1987. *Rediscovering the Social Group: Self-Categorization Theory*. Oxford: Blackwell.

Tyler, Tom R. 1990. *Why People Obey the Law*. New Haven, CT: Yale University Press.

———. 1997. "The Psychology of Legitimacy: A Relational Perspective on Voluntary Deference to Authorities." *Personality and Social Psychology Review* 1:323–45.

Valentino, Nicholas A. 1999. "Crime News and the Priming of Racial Attitudes During Evaluations of the President." *Public Opinion Quarterly* 63:293–320.

Wright, Jack C., and Walter Mischel. 1982. "Influence of Affect on Cognitive Social Learning Person Variables." *Journal of Personality and Social Psychology* 43:901–14.

———. 1987. "A Conditional Approach to Dispositional Constructs: The Local Predictability of Social Behavior." *Journal of Personality and Social Psychology* 53:1159–77.

Zimbardo, Philip G. 1999. "Stanford Prison Experiment website," accessed November 23, 2011, www.prisonexp.org/.

———. 2008. *The Lucifer Effect: Understanding How Good People Turn Evil*. New York: Random House Trade Paperbacks.

CHAPTER 10

Conclusion

Political Psychology and Politics

I. INTRODUCTION

For recent history, the period that begins with the twentieth century and extends into the present, the unfolding of time's trajectory has been filled with turbulent and unexpected events. There is little evidence that the transition from faith, tradition, provincial, and hierarchical authority to reason, scientific doubt, cosmopolitan, and democratic authority has been universally popular and productive of greater freedom.

I want to be precise here about what I mean by that phrase "greater freedom." The philosopher Isaiah Berlin (1969), in an important essay argued that freedom, or liberty, took two forms. The first, he called "negative" liberty, is the liberty that resulted when external authority withdraws and does not force our compliance with law, doctrine, or policy. The second, he called "positive" liberty, is the ability to enact ourselves to achieve whatever inspires us. So, in the case of an athlete, the combination of talent and years of training with competent trainers, allows for an athlete to run faster and longer and to leap higher. In the case of a writer, positive liberty is be the craft that enable the writer to generate a narrative of whatever fashion that gave life to his or her imagination. In the case of a citizen, negative liberty is the ability to organize without fear of retaliation by established political authority. And for a citizen positive liberty is the ability to freely formulate a cause joined with the learned and practiced the skills of oratory and administration that gives life to political movement. The spread of freedom that I referred to earlier is the same as that referred to by de Tocqueville (2000), the fostering of creating ideas leads to empowerment. In that sense, our species has gained more positive freedom over its long history, though at any given time it must be clear that not everyone has the same portion. Communication is cheaper, more widely available, and faster than in the past. A range of technological developments have added to the longevity and vigor of life spans but here again, not equitably, lengthier lives attend to those who have access to clean water, sewage systems, vaccinations, clean air, and the modern medical apparatus built on the disease model of medicine. In the category of negative freedom, the historical pattern is less clear. Autocratic regimes have fallen and but others have risen and still others have proven to date quite resilient. So, also have democratic regimes. And, democratic regimes have a mixed record on the dual standards of justice and liberty.

And, more troubling, for many, freedom in both its guises is experienced by many as a burden. Indeed, political scientist Robert E. Lane (2000) generated a compelling analysis that further experience with the combination of democracy and market economies will generate a sustained decline in the overall happiness of the public. And, Lane is hardly alone in finding lacking the simplistic formulation that spreading democracy and market economies is by itself sufficient to produce the expected flourishing of economic, political, and social well-being.

Hence, for citizens and political psychologists there is much work yet to be done. As citizens we face challenges. Principal among these is the predictable clash between the confident and comfortable reliance on convictions, of whatever source, as they confront an intractable world. Even the most casual observers of the modern condition will conclude that continued reliance on the cliché of the "march of progress" or belief in the inevitable victory of freedom and democracy spreading, everywhere overturning autocratic regimes, is largely utopian. We confront the continued appeals of tradition and autocracy each displayed in numerous variants around the world. As citizens and scholars we need better understandings and better evidence to sustain those understandings than are now available. Perhaps in each role a steadfast critical stance of "oh yeah? Prove it" might be our best approach to the many decisions we will face.

However, another defense is reliant on political psychology. Political psychology has always been multidisciplinary. As such it has the benefit of drawing on political science, psychology, economics, philosophy, sociology, and anthropology. Now, with the development of neuroscience we have a new purchase to re-examine old and stagnant questions. Moreover, as a multidisciplinary endeavor, those of us who partake of it are less likely to become wedded to the grip of certainty. As a discipline that draws on many disciplines, political psychology invites challenges from many sources, from the many disciplines but also from the many locales that host scholars in universities and colleges located there. And, as with any discipline we benefit from contributions from the young no less than from the old.

Notwithstanding these benefits political psychology does have limitations. I take up these limitations in the next section. Thereafter, I discuss an agenda for political psychology; feel free to generate your own. Thereafter I continue with suggestions for the young scholar in political psychology; and, conclude with the uses of political psychology for us in our role as citizens.

II. The Limitations of Political Psychology

The discipline of political psychology has analytic tools to approach any of the following topics. Hence, another title for this section would be "great opportunities."

I would place the first limitation as a good example of the lacunae of work that often results from and reflects the greater appeal of other topics. Consider that few examples of research on the political psychology of institutions exist. Apart from the BBC prison experiment, previously described, some of the most influential experiments take place in institutional settings yet the focus is elsewhere. Milgram (1974) was not interested in experiments as institutional settings of authority. Zimbardo (2008) was and remains interested in human judgment, not in the ways in which institutional settings function. The same can be said for Muzafer Sherif's (1958, 1966) focus. Even Lifton's (1986) exploration of the role of Nazi doctors in the extermination camps is not on the institutional but on the psychological mechanisms that enabled doctors to commit their heinous crimes. The most serious and sustained example of the political psychology of institutions is the Federalist Papers (Hamilton, Jay, and Madison 2001). An extensive literature on that exists (Epstein 1984; Scanlan 1959; White 1987; Wills 1981): but it stands apart from the contemporary focus on individual level and group level analysis. It would do all of us good to revisit that exemplar for encouragement as well as guidance.

Premodern time, time as recurring cycles, and modern time, a progressive linear trajectory, remain to dominate our thinking about time. We have business cycles, election cycles, weather cycles, and so on. We have progressive expectations that co-exist with the inescapable presumption of repetitive "wheels of fortune." We easily shift from one to the other and back as circumstances warrant. Time has rarely been formalized as a variable in political psychology (the use of panel studies and "growth curves," that is to say, diffusion studies, not withstanding). It would do us well to think through time as a formal scientific variable, allowing for different formulations, so that time could be given an explicit role in our theoretical and empirical work.

A third lacunae is generated by the focus on pathological factors that are presumed to be arresting or otherwise inhibiting the "natural" movement of the enlightenment trajectory toward cosmopolitan economic well-being social accommodation and democratic authority. To take one example, as noted in earlier chapters, prejudice (Allport 1954) is simultaneously a favoring of one's group and its traditions and a disfavoring of other groups and their traditions. Moreover, it is a disposition toward the automatic, along with a disinclination to engage in thoughtful and explicit consideration, as the favored route to judgment. This has lead to a fulsome effort to pin down the who, when, and why of prejudice (Adorno et al. 1950; Pettigrew and Tropp 2006; Altemeyer 1996; Duckitt 1989; Ekhardt 1991; Geddes and Zaller 1989; Martin 2001; Oesterreich 1995; Rickert 1998; Sanford 1973; Saucier 2000). This is hardly of marginal importance given the often dire violence that can result in periods of great distress (Staub 1989).

This focus has two limitations that bedevil political psychology. First, it may well be that the impetus to group solidarity and distrust of others—individuals, groups, practices, and traditions—is not some ancient residue now made irrational by progress. This is to suggest that rationality, in the sense of explicit reliance of formal conscious consideration of alternative courses of action, has its uses but also its fallibilities. Focusing on the supposed pathologies of reliance on habits or on those that result from reliance on reason leaves us blind to each's often essential but limited usefulness.

Second, are there causal factors that impel against prejudice? The research literature is tightly focused on authoritarianism and more recently, social dominance orientation (Pratto et al. 1994; Sidanius and Pratto 2004) as two foundations of prejudice. Fine, but are there counterbalancing factors? There has been a long established interest in empathy as a critical route toward the enlightened personality (Batson et al. 1991; Brothers 1989; Chlopan et al. 1985; Davis 1985; Greif and Hogan 1973; Johnson, Cheek, and Smither 1985; Lanzetta and Englis 1989; Levenson and Ruef 1992; Miller and

Eisenberg 1988; Tangney, Stuewig, and Mashek 2007). But, in the main that research literature is as Balkanized into its own self-reflective focus as the prejudice literature. It has taken over fifty years for both incentives and disincentives to prejudice to be explored. In a recent article, political psychologist Sam McFarland (2010) showed that the two established factors, authoritarianism and social dominance orientation, do animate prejudice. He also explored two other personality dispositions that animated against prejudice, empathy and principled moral judgment.[1]

The topic of moral judgment is yet a further area that political psychology has dealt with from a perspective that both illuminates but also blinds. The presumption is that evil arises, granting the role of many other factors, from the moral failings of the many (though the role of evil leaders, malevolent leaders has not passed unnoticed; Gilbert 1950; Post and George 2004; Winter 2002). The precepts of the enlightenment assigned to individual autonomy the core platform for moral judgment. Strong group allegiances are commonly seen as antithetical to individual autonomy and hence the capacity for moral judgment as conventionally understood.[2] If Haidt (2001), Monroe (1996), and Devine (1989), among others, are correct, this perspective on both normative and empirical grounds needs to be re-imagined. If moral judgments arise more so from preconscious processes than a call for explicit moral judgment is going to be misdirected. The interplay between "automatic" and explicit judgments needs to be confronted. And, further, largely unexamined has been the process of "object identification." Although this may seem "obvious" when is a moral task is before us? What makes a decision moral? That some tasks, behaviors, or decisions have moral dimensions is clear but what is not clear is how the brain goes about the task of identifying which of those behaviors and decisions are morally dense and which have little or no moral content, whatever other factors of importance they may have. The neural processes are only beginning to be identified (Borg, Lieberman, and Kiehl 2008; Singer, Critchley, and Preuschoff 2009; Koenigs et al. 2007; Greene et al. 2004; Harenski et al. 2010; Borg et al. 2008; Moll and de Oliveira-Souza 2007; Moll et al. 2007; Schnall, Benton, and Harvey 2008; Takahashi et al. 2004; Tangney et al. 1996; Tangney et al. 2007; Zahn et al. 2009). Much more work remains to be done.

III. An Agenda for Political Psychology (Redux)

It has not been just liberals who find the end of politics plausible (Bell 1960; Fukuyama 1992). Whether placing the demise of politics in some future when all major conflicts have been resolved (Kant 1970b, 1970a; Marx and Engels 2002) or by a return to some authoritarian certainty rested on elite wisdom or religious doctrine (Plato 1974; Popper 1963), it would seem that many hope politics will quietly disappear.

---

1. Principled moral judgment is the highest stage in Lawrence Kohlberg's (1984) stage theory of moral judgment. It rests above conventional moral thinking and selfishness stages as the basis for adjudicating morally ambiguous circumstances. In Kohlberg's framework, as a stage theory, one rises from a lower to a higher stage and that then becomes one's stable platform for moral decisions. But this work was developed before the dual process investigations or the neural investigation of moral judgment by Greene et al. (2004) and Greene et al. (2001), both suggested that we have dual routes to moral judgment, just as we do for all judgment. Hence, moral practices are likely to be an admixture of both stable dispositions and state adaptations to changing circumstances.

2. Though as political philosopher Nancy Rosenblum (2008, 1999) properly noted, solidarity is often the route by which claims of justice arise and are dealt with.

Why then politics? Although we have always attached great certainty to our convictions, human knowledge whether it is preconscious or conscious (affective or cognitive) is not omniscient either with respect to the present (space) or future (time). That combined with the variations among us derived from our various talents and limitations, our different experiences within a cultural domain and the different cultural domains present within and across different political settings, we will confront both shared and conflicted beliefs, values, sentimental dispositions, and practices. We can seek certainty by cementing a set of traditions and practices that endorse an authoritarian solution. Or, we can embrace the complex intertwining of shared and conflictual practices and aspirations: If the latter then we have politics. And only democratic politics seek to entertain the widest array of contributions from all parties and asserts the formal equality for all impacted individuals participating in the resolution among considered choices and conflicts.

Politics also are impelled because the brain has multiple ways of knowing, each with different biases, strengths, and liabilities. One of these ways of knowing lurks largely hidden outside of conscious consideration but the other is best suited to considering what can be done when we confront the unknown. This latter means of knowing is well suited to democracy at the collective level. When *we* have to figure out what to do and how best to do it and that collective consideration requires the explicit representation and semantic articulation of considerations, reason, and expectations it is best that we do so when we are in a thoughtful, reasoning, frame of mind, a condition most likely in the contested realm of politics when uncertainty generates the anxiety that is bellwether of deliberation.

The challenge of knowing is further complicated by our different histories, our different proclivities, and our different talents. Hence, politics is the mechanism that must be used to resolve the diversity of views that commonly arise. Though human societies try to eliminate risk and domesticate threat (two different conditions), they often fail (e.g., Katrina or the economic collapse of 2008, the latest of bubbles, both "known" but largely ignored risks). Given the unavoidable plethora of divergent ideals and divergent dispositions (genetic and augmented by experience) rare will be circumstance when consensus can exist, and when it does, we should view such occasions with great suspicion. Hence, politics becomes the venue for deciding what to do. Hence, we return to where we began, with a first-order choice of regime. Who shall rule? The chosen one, the wise elites, or the many? Politics is a collective activity even when entrusted to a single authority or to one established doctrine for all to bear the consequences of collective decisions.

Research on the following topics would add considerably to our understanding of how humans can better organize and confront the challenges that wait.

Sociability: Humans are social but not always. We often bond to various groups, familiar, community, and national (among other types and forms of group attachments). But humans also have some capacity for individual autonomy of thought and action. These capabilities arise as dispositions (some of us rest more comfortably in the realm of the social; others rest more comfortably in autonomous self-regard). But these capabilities are also available to each, in some measure, as we navigate from circumstance to circumstance. Each of these capabilities plays out in politics in various ways, among them:

- Engaging in civil conflict: Who engages and whether as leaders or followers. Solidarity to achieve some new justice or rectify an old injustice is often, appropriately, celebrated. But solidarity is often the vehicle by which groups oppress and cause injury. In a similar way the capacity for individuals to stand apart and assert their self-reliance is often, appropriately, celebrated. But, as Sophocles argued in his play *Philoctetes* (Grene and Lattimore 1960), isolation for its own sake can destroy both the isolated individual and wound the community from which the isolate has withdrawn. The challenges of engagement and withdrawal remain not well understood. A further aspect of the issue of engagement is the sustenance of a civil order that provides for the arena for sustained and enduring vigorous contestation over policy and over leadership. Sustaining political tolerance and indeed generating a tradition of tolerance remains a core task for the modern world.

- The success of installing regimes consistent with the vision of Adam Smith, market based democracies, also has generated some unexpected results. The first is the apparent antipathy to politics (Hibbing and Theiss-Morse 2002, 1995). Second, rather than creating a vigorous joyful and vibrant society, we too often seem to find xenophobic hostility (Kinder and Kam 2010). And, third, rather than the expansive cosmopolitan world of peace, for at least some, there seems to be an enduring submission to distrust and paranoia (Hofstadter 1965, 1966).

- Hence, we could do well to learn when do individuals adopt group norms, as against rejecting them, accept group authority and accept the leadership of others to determine their behavior. Here, especially, there are multiple dynamics (and hence motivational) forces at play: not only personality and dispositions, but also historical background (e.g., the end of World War I and its impact on the interim developments in France, Britain, Germany, Poland, etc.), as well as the contemporary circumstance and its interpretation.

Individual autonomy

- A long-standing claim, going back to Plato, is the propensity, or so he, and others since, have claimed, of the public, the many, being easily seduced by even the most ludicrous of claims. In a word: gullibility. Though often this charge is leveled at the many, one could with perhaps greater force, level the charge against the experts, leaders. Wars begun based on leaders' delusional beliefs of the likely outcome have been launched causing the deaths of millions. World War I, to take but one from hundreds examples, is an exemplar of elite folly (Tuchman 1962; Taylor and Mayer 1974). The recent Bush administration (2000–2008) is replete with examples as administration that mastered self-delusion in support of endeavors domestic and foreign, though to be sure they are merely the latest (Halberstam 1972). The circumstances that give rise to elite gullibility have been plumbed by political scientist Irving Janis (1982) and others (Tetlock et al. 1992) but given the importance, a more exhaustive exploration is warranted. Elite competency is no less a critical consideration than that of electorate competence. We have seen the discipline devote considerable energy to the latter topic, more needs to be devoted to the former.

IV. POLITICAL PSYCHOLOGY FOR THE YOUNG SCHOLAR

As a social science discipline, political psychology has a number of institutional forces that undermine its goals as a discipline. The practices of rewarding scholarship based on publication and prominence invites us to take these sanctions, positive and negative, into account as we engage research. We can observe in all the social sciences the overall consequence of these pressures. First and foremost is the pressure to "Balkanize," to seek some narrow domain that one can "franchise." Second is the pressure to be mindful of the level of external interest in the questions that engage you. These two pressures have pernicious consequences, however well they may serve our self-serving careerist ambitions.

The pressure to publish has over the past fifty or so years spawned an increase in journal pages. The number of peer review journals has proliferated over the decades, bedeviling librarians and the acquisition budgets of even the richest institutions. On the other hand, technology provides us with tools to quickly scan for relevant research and to deliver the products as digital files to our computers. As a result we benefit from a greater expanse of outlets for research and the tools to manage that increase. However, another less attractive trend has been the search for some narrow domain that a scholar can exploit to secure some niche as his or her private pond in which to play. That leaves us with lots of experts but each with often a very narrow and restricted perspective. "Big" issues are left unexamined. Inviting younger scholars still vulnerable to the demands of "publish or perish" to take up the big issues is dangerous advice. Moreover, asking younger scholars, when finally settled in more secure institutional settings, to then turn to the "big" issues, setting aside the narrow and safe niches that have yielded their security, is hardly an effective alternative. Asking young scholars to solve these institutional level problems is not going to be effective (or just). That leaves the challenge of make big issues more inviting and rewarding to senior scholars, whether as from positions of power or as mentors, to take the lead.

The second challenge, the seductive temptation of selecting research vectors based on their contemporary relevance and interest, is somewhat easier to address. There are risks therein. Interests quickly rise and fall. Linking topics of the moment carries risks of having interests disappearing. The interest in how authoritarian governments use their security apparatus to manage their populations had a decline after the end of the Soviet Union and its various clients. How democratic governments use their security apparatus is now a more timely issue, especially in Great Britain and in the United States, but for how long it is hard to say. My own interest in what neuroscience has to say about emotion arose in 1983, at a time when emotion was not in the forefront of the research agendas in political science or political psychology. It would be some years before the neuroscience of emotion became 'respectable,' then shortly thereafter "cutting edge," then mainstream. Given the hoped for expectations that intellectual creativity will continue, there may well come a time, perhaps not too far into the future, when this interest in emotion and neuroscience will become passé (Kuhn 1982).

The behavioral revolution in American political science began in the 1950s with the advent of survey research, and the cognitive focus in academic psychology began in much the same time period. Whether you opt to affiliate or oppose the current enthusiasms, each tactical focus has its risks and prospects for gain; you should learn how to "read" the state of intellectual play (as well as identifying the major players).

The time to master a field and the time that contemporary interest in a field sustains are two different time processes. They may be sufficiently in harmony to suit but they may not. In my example, emotion and neuroscience, my interest and the later evolving interest in the discipline, after some rather solitary work, came together. But that will often not be the case. My advice is to focus on your interest and its largest significance.

V. CHOOSING RESEARCH TOPICS

The long tradition does not determine what you will choose as the focus of your research. As you consider the topics to engage, and how you might begin a program of research, you should ponder some important pragmatic considerations. I emphasized that political psychology is directed at creating and testing explanations. The scope of topics in political psychology is very wide, as an examination of any of the handbooks of political psychology makes clear. That leaves you with an abundance of choices. Among those topics, which topics are worth your time and effort? I have suggested that the concern with governance, which regime is best, is central but that is an argument that you and others need not find persuasive. You may argue, correctly, that the topics you pursue are well worth pursuing, that the topic has importance to the field. Few indeed are the scholars who pursue a topic that is not important to them or holds little interest to others. The array of topics is vast and each topic has its proponents. Indeed one of the challenges that those who put together handbooks of political psychology, or volumes that combine "classic" or "essential" readings, is how to get to a manageable number of chapters and readings.

You should apply the following considerations when choosing research topics:

First, how interesting is the topic to you? After all, it is your energy and engagement that will sustain you. Second, you will find yourself comfortable and competent in some, but probably not all, of the research methodologies that are used by political psychologists. It makes sense to fit the research skills you have mastered to the topics that you engage. For example, if you find statistical analysis a challenge then it does not make a great deal of sense for you to engage research topics that are generally undertaken with experimental or survey methodologies. If you have not learned a methodology that seems to be important in the topic that has engaged you, then you should continue your education whether as an undergraduate, graduate student, a postdoctoral fellow, or at any point in your career.

So, after some perusal, you discover a topic that interests you, perhaps among those discussed in these chapters or in one of the readings assigned to complement this book. Then what should you consider? First, begin by finding as many of the published, and recent unpublished, articles, papers, chapters, and books on the topic that engage you. You will then confront a pile of articles, papers, some chapters, and books on the topic.

Begin your examination by arraying that pile from oldest to most recent. A variety of answers can emerge from that pile. The number of publications is a crude but often revealing indicator of how important this topic is to scholars. And, if you chart the publications by year, you can discover whether interest is rising, more publications among the more recently published, or fading as recent publications are fewer in number. Whether the apparent level of interest is declining or increasing should not be determinative of whether you should pursue research on that topic, but it is useful to know whether others share your interest or whether they have found the vein all played out. You should ask yourself why interest is rising or failing. If so, for what reasons, theoretical, methodological, whatever, for those reasons may offer you opportunities for your research. Try to understand why the interest is rising or falling. Is it a problem of imagination? Perhaps a general consensus has emerged that "we know all we need to know here." Or, perhaps the scholarship has not produced anything of note in the more recent period thus leading to stagnation.

My colleague Tim Cook (1985) wrote an important article some years ago. The title will give you an example of what I have in mind: "The Bear Market in Political Socialization and the Costs of Misunderstood Psychological Theories." While research was ongoing at that time on political socialization, principally lead by M. Kent Jennings and Richard Niemi (1981), Tim's assessment was that much more could and should be done. He went on to say in the abstract for the article on page 1079:

> Not so long ago, political scientists were enthusiastically proclaiming that political socialization was a growth stock. But interest in the subfield has slackened, and the bull market has turned bearish. This article argues that a central cause of this recent scholarly neglect is a lack of theoretical confidence. Political socialization has been branded as less worthy of study largely because it is difficult to study in the absence of an explicit psychological model of learning. A strong theoretical rationale must be developed to return the subfield to its deserved place of priority.

Tim made this cogent point: Having a rich theory to generate novel hypotheses is a prerequisite for obtaining a productive social science.

As you further review your pile of literature, the pile that you have found by using various research strategies I covered earlier, you should expressly consider the following:

- Identify the prevailing theories, research methodologies, and findings.
- Is there a consensus on the best theory?
- If so, then perhaps you can discover a theoretical focus that has been ignored, providing you a way to reinvigorate that field by showing new analytic prospects, much as Tim did in his article.
- Is there a consensus on the findings, and if not, is that related to the specific research methods used?
- If so, then perhaps you can see if the findings, whether there is a consensus, can be explored by a research method not widely used in this topic domain.
- If there is contention among the scholars, if there is an existing argument about which of the extant theories is better, perhaps you can devise a study

---

BOX 10.1 Comment

If political psychology relied on theories that produced explanations that mirrored those we find around us, we would then have no real need for the discipline beyond its ability to add rigor so we could discern those clichés of everyday life that have merit from those that do not.

BOX 10.2 Abstract of Quattrone and Tversky (1988, 719)

"We contrast the rational theory of choice in the form of expected utility theory with descriptive psychological analysis in the form of prospect theory, using problems involving the choice between political candidates and public referendum issues. The results showed that the assumptions underlying the classical theory of risky choice are systematically violated in the manner predicted by prospect theory. In particular, our respondents exhibited risk aversion in the domain of gains, risk seeing in the domain of losses, and a greater sensitivity to losses than to gains. This is consistent with the advantage of the incumbent under normal conditions and the potential advantage of the challenger in bad times. The results further show how a shift in the reference point could lead to reversals of preferences in the evaluation of political and economic options, contrary to the assumption of invariance. Finally, we contrast the normative and descriptive analyses of uncertainty in choice and address the rationality of voting."

that pits the opposing theoretical claims against each other and produces an empirical test; a good example is Quattrone and Tversky (1988). Another good example is that executed by Michael Neblo (2009). Professor Neblo reexamined an ongoing controversy between scholars modern or symbolic racism. Some scholars argued that white people's opinions about race policy are driven by group conflict between white and black interests. Others argued that white people's opinions were driven by negative animus against blacks. Still a third position was argued: That racial animus has receded to be replaced by ideology such that conservative principles argue against government help for any needy group. Neblo then executed a study that suggested that rather than one of these accounts proving to be the better empirical explanation, with the other two proven wrong, each of the three are right! Neblo argued that his data show that a specific portion of the white public is driven by group conflict, while another portion is driven racial animus, and yet another portion by ideological conviction. Hence, he contributed a taxonomy that segmented a previously thought homogeneous population, the white population into distinct segments.

Many years ago, Thomas Kuhn (1982) noted that theories come into fashion and then after a period of dominance are challenged and then replaced. His analysis suggests a normal cycle. When new theories are proposed they are most often resisted by those who have accepted the dominant theory. If you have an immediate need to demonstrate publishing success, bear in mind that some topics, those at the cutting edge, those topics not in favor, or theories that challenge widely accepted explanations, will face greater tests before being accepted by refereed journals. These types of topics are more likely to confront reviewers who are suspicious of challenges to received wisdom than find the few reviewers open to new possibilities.

Mentors and advisers to young scholars often suggest that they pick topics that are likely to produce statistically significant results. There are a number of relatively safe strategies to achieve that goal, publications in refereed journals. Among these, augmenting is the most useful. An augmenting strategy has a number of variants.

Perhaps in a domain, some independent variables have been shown to impact a specific dependent variable. One way to augment is to add one or more variables that have not yet been examined, though this has its risks. The new variables you choose may have been already shown not to be useful in explaining that dependent variable. But, because negative results are generally not published, you may not know that such an investigation has already been discovered to be fruitless. Here conference papers may be very useful as they often report on false leads.

Another way to augment is to look for limiting conditions. A general finding has been shown, that factor A causes factor B. It is useful to theorize that the relationship may be weaker, or stronger, here than there. For example, in the hypothesis that good weather encourages voting while bad weather impedes, this relationship may not be as strong among the rich as it might be among the poor.

Here is yet another way to augment. If the scholarship has been heavily reliant on a specific method, say survey methods, then can you formulate it as a topic for experimentation (or vice versa)?

Finally, if the scholarship has been largely confined to a specific nation or region, you could design a study for other nations, or other cultures, thus turning culture and other factors into variables if cross polity difference emerges. John Sullivan (Sullivan et al. 1985) and Jim Gibson (Gibson and Gouws 2003; Gibson and Duch 1993) followed this last strategy to see if an earlier published model that explained political tolerance in the United States applied when examined in other nations.

Following these strategies will be safer than jumping into the void by selecting a topic that either has not been explored by scholars or has been rejected as not promising because of some supposed problem, perhaps that a requisite theoretical foundation has not been discovered. Of course there is great promise for making a new discovery or sustaining a new theoretical insight so playing it safe may not, in the end be the best strategy. For an excellent insight into how scholars come up with their ideas, I highly recommend a book, *The Research Process in Political Science* edited by W. Philip Shively (1984). The book consists of an array of important studies with narrative accounts provided by the principals of how their project came into being.

VI. POLITICAL PSYCHOLOGY FOR THE CITIZEN

The ancient Greek aphorism, "know thyself" offers little in the way of explanation of how one might go about doing so. Hopefully, we gain some insight from experience, though often hard won. But, as we have seen, neuroscience reveals that much of our mental life is not available to us from introspection either solitary or in therapeutic environments. Awareness gives us access to some of ourselves inner workings.

BOX 10.3 Model

The term model is often used to describe a theory that has multiple independent variables and each of the relationships between the variables precisely specified. Empirical data and statistical analyses provide the statistical estimates of the theoretical parameters.

Political psychology, particularly with the aid of neuroscience, gives us a vantage to understand ourselves. We can now observe ourselves as we engage in "motivated reasoning" if we try. We can observe the rarer—than we might wish to acknowledge—circumstances when we set aside convictions for the harder work of thoughtful reconsideration. Seeing these two patterns arise in our own actions, in situ, is hard work. Observing certainty and conviction play out in others is quite easy. Harder is to stand "outside" oneself and observe the force with which our convictions bind and blind ourselves is a far greater challenge. Observing the pull and tug of the claims of individual autonomy against the pull and tug of collective solidarity is hard when one is in the midst of that struggle. Knowing that we have these dual capabilities gives us some perspective on our own mind and how it works. Political psychology offers a vantage on which you can stand to observe not only others but yourself.

When Milton Rokeach (1964) inquired of his three christs what they made of each other we can observe our own certainties at play no less blissfully covering up contradictions. When we observe many, though not all, of the subjects in Stanley Milgram's (1974) experiments we can ask ourselves how we would have behaved in a similar circumstance. When research shows political learning primarily is spurred by anxiety (Marcus and MacKuen 1993) we can investigate our own patterns of attentiveness to political news. Do we depart from our desultory habits? And, if so when? When we observe groups in violent conflict we can turn to the literature of group dynamics to gain some purchase on how best to assess various policy options.

As citizens we are often bombarded by the claims of competing pundits and by political parties, political actors, and interests. These efforts, however solicitous their clothing, are often proclaimed at the service of some interest, sometime apparent, sometime not. Political psychology can arm us as we engage in the world. As we decide where, when, and on whose behalf to be effective citizens, it is better to have analytic tools that empower us to assess who is doing what and why and how we can achieve what is just and self-serving so that we are not beholden to our convictions without reflection nor driven by the ambitions of others. And, this is what political psychology offers.

REFERENCES

Adorno, Theodor, Else Frenkel-Brunswick, Daniel Levinson, and R. Nevitt Sanford. 1950. *The Authoritarian Personality*. New York: Harper and Row.
Allport, Gordon, W. 1954. *The Nature of Prejudice*. Cambridge, MA: Addison-Wesley.
Altemeyer, Bob. 1996. *The Authoritarian Specter*. Cambridge, MA: Harvard University Press.
Batson, C. Daniel, Judy G. Batson, Jacqueline K. Slingsby, Kevin L. Harrell, Heli M. Peekna, and R. Matthew Todd. 1991. "Empathic Joy and the Empathy-Altruism Hypothesis." *Journal of Personality and Social Psychology* 61:413–26.
Bell, Daniel. 1960. *The End of Ideology: On the Exhaustion of Political Ideas in the Fifties*. Glencoe, IL: Free Press.
Berlin, Isaiah. 1969. "Two Concepts of Liberty." In *Four Essays on Liberty*, 118–72. London: Oxford University Press.
Borg, Jana Schaich, Debra Lieberman, and Kent A. Kiehl. 2008. "Infection, Incest, and Iniquity: Investigating the Neural Correlates of Disgust and Morality." *Journal of Cognitive Neuroscience* 20:367–79.

Brothers, Leslie. 1989. "A Biological Perspective on Empathy." *American Journal of Psychiatry* 146:10–19.

Chlopan, Bruce E., Marianne L. McCain, Joyce L. Carbonell, and Richard L. Hagen. 1985. "Empathy: A Review of Available Measures." *Journal of Personality and Social Psychology* 48:635–53.

Cook, Timothy E. 1985. "The Bear Market in Political Socialization and the Costs of Misunderstood Psychological Theories." *American Political Science Review* 79:1079–93.

Davis, Mark H. 1980. "A Multidimensional Approach to Individual Differences in Empathy." *JSAS Catalog of Selected Documents in Psychology* 10:85

de Tocqueville, Alexis. 2000. *Democracy in America*. Translated, Edited, and With an Introduction by Harvey C. Mansfield and Delba Winthrop. Chicago: University of Chicago Press.

Devine, Patricia G. 1989. "Stereotypes and Prejudice: Their Automatic and Controlled Components." *Journal of Personality and Social Psychology* 56:5–18.

Duckitt, John. 1989. "Authoritarianism and Group Identification: A New View of an Old Construct." *Political Psychology* 10:63–84.

Ekhardt, William. 1991. "Authoritarianism." *Political Psychology* 12:97–124.

Epstein, David F. 1984. *The Political Theory of the Federalist*. Chicago: University of Chicago Press.

Fukuyama, Francis. 1992. *The End of History and the Last Man*. New York: Free Press.

Geddes, Barbara, and John Zaller. 1989. "Sources of Popular Support for Authoritarian Regimes." *American Journal of Political Science* 33:319–47.

Gibson, James L., and Raymond M. Duch. 1993. "Political Intolerance in the USSR: The Distribution and Etiology of Mass Opinion." *Comparative Political Studies* 26:286–329.

Gibson, James L., and Amanda Gouws. 2003. *Overcoming Intolerance in South Africa: Experiments in Democratic Persuasion*. Cambridge: Cambridge University Press.

Gilbert, Gustave M. 1950. *The Psychology of Dictatorship*. New York: Ronald Press.

Greene, Joshua D., Leigh E. Nystrom, Andrew D. Engell, John M. Darley, and Jonathan D. Cohen. 2004. "The Neural Bases of Cognitive Conflict and Control in Moral Judgment." *Neuron* 44:389–400.

Greene, Joshua D., R. Brian Sommerville, Leigh E. Nystrom, John M. Darley, and Jonathan D. Cohen. 2001. "An fMRI Investigation of Emotional Engagement in Moral Judgment." *Science* 293:2105–8.

Greif, Esther B., and Robert Hogan. 1973. "The Theory and Measurement of Empathy." *Journal of Counseling Psychology* 20:280–84.

Grene, David, and Richmond Alexander Lattimore. 1960. *The Complete Greek Tragedies*. New York: Modern Library.

Haidt, Jonathan. 2001. "The Emotional Dog and Its Rational Tail: A Social Instuitionist Approach to Moral Judgment." *Psychological Review* 108:814–34.

Halberstam, David. 1972. *The Best and the Brightest*. New York: Random House.

Hamilton, Alexander, John Jay, and James Madison. 2001. *The Federalist: A Collection*. Indianapolis, IN: Liberty Fund.

Harenski, Carla L., Olga Antonenko, Matthew S. Shane, and Kent A. Kiehl. 2010. "A Functional Imaging Investigation of Moral Deliberation and Moral Intuition." *NeuroImage* 49:2707–16.

Hibbing, John R., and Elizabeth Theiss-Morse. 1995. *Congress as Public Enemy: Public Attitudes toward American Political Institutions*. New York: Cambridge University Press.

———. 2002. *Stealth Democracy: Americans' Beliefs about How Government Should Work*. Cambridge: Cambridge University Press.

Hofstadter, Richard. 1965. *The Paranoid Style in American Politics, and Other Essays*. New York: Knopf.

———. 1966. *Anti-Intellectualism in American Life*. New York: Vintage.

Janis, Irving L. 1982. *Groupthink*. Boston: Houghton Mifflin.

Jennings, M. Kent, and Richard G. Niemi. 1981. *Generations and Politics: A Panel Study of Young Adults and Their Parents*. Princeton, NJ: Princeton University Press.

Johnson, John A., Jonathan M. Cheek, and Robert Smither. 1985. "The Structure of Empathy." *Journal of Personality and Social Psychology* 45:1299–312.

Kant, Immanuel. 1970a. "An Answer to the Question: 'What is Enlightenment?'" In *Kant's Political Writings*, edited by Hans Reiss, 54–60. Cambridge: Cambridge University Press.

———. 1970b. "Idea for a Universal History with a Cosmopolitan Purpose." In *Kant's Political Writings*, edited by Hans Reiss, 41–53. Cambridge: Cambridge University Press.

Kinder, Donald R, and Cindy D Kam. 2010. *Us Against Them: Ethnocentric Foundations of American Opinion*. Chicago: University of Chicago Press.

Koenigs, Michael, Liane Young, Ralph Adolphs, Daniel Tranel, Fiery Cushman, Marc Hauser, and Antonio Damasio. 2007. "Damage to the Prefrontal Cortex Increases Utilitarian Moral Judgements." Nature 446:908–911.

Kohlberg, Lawrence. 1984. *The Psychology of Moral Development: The Nature and Validity of Moral Stages*. San Francisco: Harper & Row.

Kuhn, Thomas. 1982. *The Structure of Scientific Revolutions*. Chicago: University of Chicago Press.

Lane, Robert Edwards. 2000. *The Loss of Happiness in Market Democracies*. New Haven, CT: Yale University Press.

Lanzetta, John T., and Basil G. Englis. 1989. "Expectations of Cooperation and Competition and Their Effects on Observers' Vicarious Emotional Responses." *Journal of Personality and Social Psychology* 56:543–54.

Levenson, Robert W., and Anna M. Ruef. 1992. "Empathy: A Physiological Substrate." *Journal of Personality and Social Psychology* 63:234–46.

Lifton, Robert Jay. 1986. *The Nazi Doctors: Medical Killing and the Psychology of Genocide*. New York: Basic Books.

Marcus, George E., and Michael MacKuen. 1993. "Anxiety, Enthusiasm and the Vote: The Emotional Underpinnings of Learning and Involvement during Presidential Campaigns." *American Political Science Review* 87:688–701.

Martin, John Levi. 2001. "The Authoritarian Personality, 50 Years Later: What Lessons Are There for Political Psychology?" *Political Psychology* 22:1–26.

Marx, Karl, and Friedrich Engels. 2002. *The Communist Manifesto*. New York: Penguin Classics.

McFarland, Sam. 2010. "Authoritarianism, Social Dominance, and Other Roots of Generalized Prejudice." *Political Psychology* 31:453–77.

Milgram, Stanley. 1974. *Obedience to Authority*. New York: Harper and Row.

Miller, Paul A., and Nancy Eisenberg. 1988. "The Relation of Empathy to Aggressive and Externalizing/Antisocial Behavior." *Psychological Bulletin* 103:324–44.

Moll, Jorge, and Ricardo de Oliveira-Souza. 2007. "Moral Judgments, Emotions and the Utilitarian Brain." *Trends in Cognitive Sciences* 11:319–21.

Moll, Jorge, Ricardo de Oliveira-Souza, Griselda Garrido, Ivanei E. Bramati, Egas M. A. Caparelli-Daquer, Mirella L Paiva, M. F., Roland Zahn, and Jordan Grafman. 2007. "The

Self as a Moral Agent: Linking the Neural Bases of Social Agency and Moral Sensitivity." *Social Neuroscience* 2:336–52.

Monroe, Kristen Renwick. 1996. *The Heart of Altruism: Perceptions of a Common Humanity.* Princeton, NJ: Princeton University Press.

Neblo, Michael A. 2009. "Three-Fifths a Racist: A Typology for Analyzing Public Opinion About Race." *Political Behavior* 31:31–51.

Oesterreich, Detlef. "A Psychological Measure of Authoritarianism: Evidence from Three Empirical Studies." Paper presented at the *International Society of Political Psychology Annual Scientific Meetings,* Washington, DC, July 1995.

Pettigrew, Thomas F., and Linda R. Tropp. 2006. "A Meta-Analytic Test of Intergroup Contact Theory." *Journal of Personality and Social Psychology* 90:751–83.

Plato. 1974. *The Republic.* New York: Penguin.

Popper, Karl Raimund. 1963. *The Open Society and Its Enemies.* Princeton, NJ: Princeton University Press.

Post, Jerrold M, and Alexander L George. 2004. *Leaders and Their Followers in a Dangerous World: The Psychology of Political Behavior.* Ithaca: Cornell University Press.

Pratto, Felicia, Jim Sidanius, Lisa M. Stallworth, and Bertram F. Malle. 1994. "Social Dominance Orientation: A Personality Variable Predicting Social and Political Attitudes." *Journal of Personality and Social Psychology* 67:741–63.

Quattrone, George A., and Amos Tversky. 1988. "Contrasting Rational and Psychological Analyses of Political Choice." *American Political Science Review* 82:719–36.

Rickert, Edward J. 1998. "Authoritarianism and Economic Threat: Implications for Political Behavior." *Political Psychology* 19:707–20.

Rokeach, Milton. 1964. *The Three Christs of Ypsilanti: A Psychological Study.* New York: Knopf.

Rosenblum, Nancy L. 1999. "Navigating Pluralism: The Democracy of Everyday Life (and Where It Is Learned)." In *Citizen Competence and Democratic Institutions*, edited by Stanley L. Elkin and Karol Edward Soltan, 67–88. University Park: Pennsylvania University Press.

———. 2008. *On the Side of the Angels: An Appreciation of Parties and Partisanship.* Princeton, NJ: Princeton University Press.

Sanford, Nevitt. 1973. "Authoritarian Personality in Contemporary Perspective." In *Handbook of Political Psychology*, edited by Jeanne Knutson, 139–70. San Francisco: Jossey-Bass.

Saucier, Gerard. 2000. "Isms and the Structure of Social Attitudes." *Journal of Personality and Social Psychology* 78:366–85.

Scanlan, James P. 1959. "The Federalist and Human Nature." *Review of Politics* 21:657–77.

Schnall, Simone, Jennifer Benton, and Sophie Harvey. 2008. "With a Clean Conscience: Cleanliness Reduces the Severity of Moral Judgments." *Psychological Science* 19:1219–22.

Sherif, Muzafer. 1958. "Group Influences upon the Formation of Norms and Attitudes." In *Readings in Social Psychology*, edited by Eleanor Maccoby, T. M. Newcomb, and E. L. Hartley, 219–32. New York: Holt.

———. 1966. *Group Conflict and Competition.* London: Routledge & Kegan Paul.

Shively, W. Phillips, ed. 1984. *The Research Process in Political Science* Itasca, IL: Peacock.

Sidanius, Jim, and Felicia Pratto. 2004. "Social Dominance Theory: A New Synthesis." In *Political Psychology: Key Readings*, edited by John T. Jost and Jim Sidanius, 315–32. New York: Psychology Press.

Singer, Tania, Hugo D. Critchley, and Kerstin Preuschoff. 2009. "A Common Role of Insula in Feelings, Empathy and Uncertainty." *Trends in Cognitive Sciences* 13:334–40.

Staub, Ervin. 1989. *The Roots of Evil: The Origins of Genocide and Other Group Violence*. New York: Cambridge University Press.

Sullivan, John L., Michal Shamir, Patrick Walsh, and Nigel S. Roberts. 1985. *Political Tolerance in Context*. Boulder, CO: Westview.

Takahashi, Hidehiko, Noriaki Yahata, Michihiko Koeda, Tetsuya Matsuda, Kunihiko Asai, and Yoshiro Okubo. 2004. "Brain Activation Associated with Evaluative Processes of Guilt and Embarrassment: An fMRI Study." *NeuroImage* 23:967–74.

Tangney, June Price, Rowland S. Miller, Laura Flicker, and Deborah Hill Barlow. 1996. "Are Shame, Guilt, and Embarrassment Distinct Emotions?" *Journal of Personality and Social Psychology* 70:1256–69.

Tangney, June Price, Jeff Stuewig, and Debra J. Mashek. 2007. "Moral Emotions and Moral Behavior." *Annual Review of Psychology* 58:345–72.

Taylor, A. J. P., and S. L. Mayer. 1974. *History of World War I*. London: Octopus.

Tetlock, Philip M., Randall S. Peterson, Charles McGuire, Shi-jie Chang, and Peter Field. 1992. "Assessing Political Group Dynamics: A Test of the Groupthink Model." *Journal of Personality and Social Psychology* 63:403–25.

Tuchman, Barbara Wertheim. 1962. *The Guns of August*. New York: Macmillan.

White, Morton. 1987. *Philosophy, the Federalist, and the Constitution*. New York: Oxford University Press.

Wills, Garry. 1981. *Explaining America: The Federalist*. New York: Doubleday.

Winter, David G. 2002. "Motivation and Political Leadership." In *Political Leadership for the New Century: Personality and Behavior among American Leaders*, edited by Linda O. Valenty and Ofer Feldman, 27–47. New York: Praeger.

Zahn, Roland, Jorge Moll, Mirella Paiva, Griselda Garrido, Frank Krueger, Edward D. Huey, and Jordan Grafman. 2009. "The Neural Basis of Human Social Values: Evidence from Functional MRI." *Cerebral Cortex* 19:176–283.

Zimbardo, Philip G. 2008. *The Lucifer Effect: Understanding How Good People Turn Evil*. New York: Random House Trade Paperbacks.

INDEX

Note: Page numbers followed by *b, t* and *f* refer to boxes, tables and figures, respectively. Page numbers followed by "n" indicate footnotes.